WARREN-ADAMS LETTERS

VOL. I

1743-1777

AMS PRESS
NEW YORK

James Warren
*From the original painting by Copley
in the possession of Winslow Warren*

WARREN-ADAMS LETTERS

Being chiefly a correspondence among
John Adams, Samuel Adams,
and James Warren

VOL. I

1743-1777

THE MASSACHUSETTS HISTORICAL SOCIETY

1917

Library of Congress Cataloging in Publication Data

Massachusetts Historical Society, Boston.
  Warren-Adams letters.

  Original ed. issued as v. 72-73 of Massachusetts Historical Society. Collections.
    CONTENTS: v. 1. 1743-1777.--v. 2. 1778-1814.
    1. U. S.--History--Revolution--Sources. 2. U. S.--History--Colonial Period--Sources. I. Adams, John, Pres. U. S., 1735-1826. II. Adams, Samuel, 1722-1803. III. Warren, James, 1726-1808. IV. Series: Massachusetts Historical Society, Boston. Collections, v. 72-73.
E203.M37 1972   973.2   79-158225
ISBN 0-404-06854-5

Reprinted from the edition of 1917-1925, Boston
First AMS edition published in 1972
Manufactured in the United States of America

International Standard Book Number:
Complete Set: 0-404-06854-5
Volume I: 0-404-06855-3

AMS PRESS INC.
NEW YORK, N. Y.   10003

Contents

ILLUSTRATIONS xxix

PREFATORY NOTE xxxi

1743

June 17. JAMES OTIS, JR. TO JAMES OTIS, SENR. 1
Expences of commencement. Will share with Russell.

1766

April 11. JAMES OTIS TO MERCY WARREN 1
Death of Rebecca Otis. Engrossed by his occupations. Question of slavery or liberty. A scurrilous article. Court service.

1767

December 5. JOHN DICKINSON TO JAMES OTIS 3
Sends a Farmer's Letter. Opinion of Otis. Question at issue. Moderation urged.

1768

January 25. JOHN DICKINSON TO JAMES OTIS 4
Sends corrected copy of Farmer's Letters. Recommends version in *Pennsylvania Gazette*. A vindication of rights.

April 11. JOHN DICKINSON TO JAMES OTIS 5
Letters to Boston expressing sense of obligation. Why he should be dear to Otis. America is arousing.

July —. JOHN DICKINSON TO JAMES OTIS 6
Sends Maryland's proceedings. Wishes for Boston. Hutchinson's pension.

1769

April 27. CATHARINE MACAULAY TO JAMES OTIS 7
Sends a copy of her *History*. Wishes an account of American affairs.

Contents

1771

March 25. SAMUEL ADAMS TO JAMES WARREN 8
    News from England. Language of despair. Hutchinson and Caesar. Prudence and moderation. Lovell's oration.

1772

April 13. SAMUEL ADAMS TO JAMES WARREN 10
    Motion to remove General Court from Cambridge to Boston. A boy for his service. Condolence and sympathy.

November 4. SAMUEL ADAMS TO JAMES WARREN 11
    A town meeting. Otis on committee of correspondence. Plymouth should follow.

November 27. SAMUEL ADAMS TO JAMES WARREN 12
    Town meeting proceedings. Plymouth petitions and Tory lies. Roxbury prospects. Heath and Gerry. Exertion necessary.

December 9. SAMUEL ADAMS TO JAMES WARREN 14
    No cause to despair. Reply to the Hingham writer. Position of Lancaster. Town meetings. Plan of the Tories.

1773

January 4. HANNAH WINTHROP TO MERCY WARREN 16
    Her animating letter. Ministerial decree for trial of colonists. Awaiting the meeting of the Assembly.

April 12. HANNAH WINTHROP TO MERCY WARREN 17
    Is gratified by the assembly's action. The capital and its pleasures.

December 5. ABIGAIL ADAMS TO MERCY WARREN 18
    No act will surprise. Tea in Boston. Blood may flow. Awaiting an outbreak. On Molière.

December 28. SAMUEL ADAMS TO JAMES WARREN 19
    Invitation to Plymouth festivity. Approval of town's proceedings. Plymouth's protest. Tea in other colonies. Correspondence re-opened. The assembly. Intelligence.

1774

January 3. JOHN ADAMS TO MERCY WARREN 21
    Bishop Burnet to Lady Russell. The Plymouth anniversary. Public and private business. May shine as a farmer. His intentions sincere.

Contents

January 3. JAMES WARREN TO JOHN ADAMS 23
    A bold stroke necessary. Scarecrows and bugbears. A union of sentiment and spirit. Recantation of protesters.

March 31. SAMUEL ADAMS TO JAMES WARREN 24
    Public attitude towards colony in England. Hutchinson's plans. A colonial post office. Position of the Tories.

May 21. SAMUEL ADAMS TO JAMES WARREN 26
    Avoid blood and tumult. Give other provinces opportunity to think. Violence will mean ruin.

July 14. JAMES WARREN TO JOHN ADAMS 26
    Regret at not having seen him. The grand congress. Great expectations held of it. Danger of timidity and narrow plans. An annual congress. Want of gratitude in mankind.

July 17. JOHN ADAMS TO JAMES WARREN 29
    Public confidence in the Congress. Feels his own insufficiency. How to distress Great Britain. A non-exportation. Nothing to expect from their justice.

July 25. JOHN ADAMS TO JAMES WARREN 31
    Serene retreat at Braintree. Death of Louis XV. Futility of imagining how great men would have acted.

September 27. HANNAH WINTHROP TO MERCY WARREN . . . 32
    Disturbed condition of Boston. News from England. Preparations for a battle. An ingenious satire on love of dress.

December 19. JAMES WARREN TO JOHN ADAMS 34
    Results of the elections. Military honors. The English elections and American grievances. Engrossing civil and military duties.

1775

January 15. JAMES WARREN TO JOHN ADAMS 35
    Votes of Maryland commended. Opinion of Chase. Tories active. The new Congress.

January 30. MERCY WARREN TO JOHN ADAMS 36
    Is grateful for his good opinion. Personal reflections and sarcasm. Proper limits on satire. 'The Group.' Anxiety for the future.

February 11. JOHN ADAMS TO JAMES WARREN 39
    Introducing Buchanan and Tolley. Permission to open letters. Negligence and unkindness.

Contents

February 20. JAMES WARREN TO JOHN ADAMS 40
    Hoped to have seen him in the Provincial Congress. 'Massachusettensis.' Wasted time in the Congress. Authorship of 'The Group.'

March 15. JAMES WARREN TO JOHN ADAMS 41
    Sends an article for use in 'The Group'?

March 15. JOHN ADAMS TO MERCY WARREN 42
    Personal reflections and satire. What is feared from its use. A high compliment.

April 6. JAMES WARREN TO MERCY WARREN 44
    Reasons for not adjourning the Congress. News from England unfavorable. Preparations for war. Inhabitants of Boston moving.

May 7. JAMES WARREN TO JOHN ADAMS 46
    In the Provincial Congress. That body much weakened. Regulation of army and expenses. More experienced direction wanted, and a settled government. Infatuation of Boston inhabitants. Pitiable plight of refugees and Tories. Hutchinson's letters.

May 18. JAMES WARREN TO MERCY WARREN 49
    A daily letter. Congress to be revered. What was done in South Carolina and Halifax. Detestation of Tories. Effect of an advance towards Charlestown.

May 21. JOHN ADAMS TO JAMES WARREN 51
    Congress moving slowly. Multitude of objects before it. Reprinting 'The Group.' Martial spirit in Pennsylvania.

May 26. JOHN ADAMS TO JAMES WARREN 52
    Introducing Messrs. Hall.

June 7. JOHN ADAMS TO JAMES WARREN 52
    Canada and the Indians. Brown and Price as agents. Cruelty of Indians.

June 10. JOHN ADAMS TO JAMES WARREN 53
    Cleanliness and health in the army. Lee on Burgoyne. Militia, powder and pikemen. Casting of cannon.

June 10. SAMUEL ADAMS TO JAMES WARREN 54
    Effect in England of the battle of Lexington. Difficulty of possessing Congress with news. Resolution to aid Boston. Gunpowder.

June 11. JAMES WARREN TO JOHN ADAMS 56
    Anxiety to hear from Congress. Question of assuming civil government. Elation over aid from the Congress. Cushing's discouraging letter.

Contents

June 18. JOHN HANCOCK TO JOSEPH WARREN 57
    Has obtained leave to give some information on acts of Congress. Appointment of Washington as commander-in-chief. Ward and Lee. Riflemen for Boston, and a continental army. A fast day.

June 18. JAMES WARREN TO MERCY WARREN 59
    Battle of Bunker Hill. Death of Warren. Return of Dr. Church with intelligence. Mode of government. Behavior of James Otis.

June 20. JOHN ADAMS TO JAMES WARREN 61
    An army and appointments to command. Struggle over Charles Lee. Review of troops.

June 20. JAMES WARREN TO JOHN ADAMS 62
    Has communicated Lee's opinion of the British generals. Battle of Bunker Hill. Death of Warren. A general needed. Reports of the English dead. Does not approve of form of government.

June 20. SAMUEL ADAMS TO JOSEPH WARREN 64
    Appointment of Continental generals. Is more and more satisfied with that of Lee.

June 21. JOHN ADAMS TO JOSEPH WARREN 65
    The question of generals. A government and Tories. Skene and Tryon. William Tudor. Powder.

June 27. JOHN ADAMS TO JAMES WARREN 66
    Death of Dr. Warren. News of the Bunker Hill fight and powder. Wished to make him a general. North Carolina affairs. The riflemen. Hint on saltpetre.

June 27. JAMES WARREN TO JOHN ADAMS 67
    The army at Cambridge and Roxbury. Satisfaction with generals. Provision for General Thomas. Situation in Boston. Absorbed by army. A pamphlet.

June 28. SAMUEL ADAMS TO JAMES WARREN 69
    Bunker Hill engagement. Warns against suspicions of their generals. Lee and the conditions of his appointment. Loss of Dr. Warren. Sends letters to his care.

July 5. MERCY WARREN TO JOHN ADAMS 71
    Remissness of correspondents. Mr. Warren too busy to write. Sad situation of those in Boston. Piratical acts of the enemy. Corruption and cruelty of Gage. Wishes for Congress. Dr. Eliot said to be confined.

July 6. JOHN ADAMS TO JAMES WARREN 73
    Wishes his correspondence. Error in appointing general officers. Ap-

pointments of Warren and a lesson. Powder and cannon. Introduces Collins and Keays. What may be expected from Great Britain. Effect on proceedings of Congress. Addresses and programme.

July 6. JOHN ADAMS TO JAMES WARREN 75
Riflemen ordered to Massachusetts. A German Hussar. Jealousy in raising troops.

July 7. JAMES WARREN TO JOHN ADAMS 77
Washington and Mifflin. Opinion of General Lee. Size of army and the British force. Losses at Bunker Hill. General officers. Prisoners in Boston. Powder. Proposition for a fleet. Pay of officers. A lying account of battle from Boston.

July 10. JOHN ADAMS TO JAMES WARREN 79
Addresses sent to England. Kirkland and the Indians. General officers. Discretion enjoined.

July 11. JOHN ADAMS TO JAMES WARREN 80
Addresses from Congress. Size of the Continental Army. Paper money. Observance of fast day. Appointment for young Samuel Adams.

July 11. JAMES WARREN TO JOHN ADAMS 81
No letters. Army should be increased. A navy and armed vessels. Looks for action.

July 12. SAMUEL ADAMS TO JAMES WARREN 82
Introduces Hugh Hughes.

July 20. JAMES WARREN TO JOHN ADAMS 82
A visit to Plymouth. Council making. The fast day. Affairs at Long Island and Brown's house. Strength of Roxbury lines. Lighthouse burnt. Navy and riflemen. Smallpox and conciliation. Derby's report on English affairs. Reinforcements and Tories.

July 23. JOHN ADAMS TO JAMES WARREN 85
Thomas receives a commission. Reasons for the other general officers. Example from Connecticut — Spencer and Wooster. Willingness to serve. Staff appointments. Names suggested. Secrecy enjoined. Discouraging features. Defense of trade and free trade.

July 24. JOHN ADAMS TO JAMES WARREN 88
Frank opinion on discussion and his obstructive policy. Powder. Matters to be acted upon. Charles Lee and his dogs.

July 24. SAMUEL ADAMS TO JAMES WARREN 89
Suspicions of generals. Want of information. An adjournment possible. A place for his son.

Contents

July 26. JOHN ADAMS TO JAMES WARREN 90
    Appointment of staff officers. Paymaster. Pigeon and Palmer. Duties of officers. Characters and biographies. Engineers.

July 26. JOHN ADAMS TO JAMES WARREN 92
    Position of Quartermaster General. Care in appointments. Money and powder.

July 27. JOHN ADAMS TO JAMES WARREN 93
    A hospital establishment and Dr. Church. Warren as paymaster general. Powder. Introductions.

July 29. SAMUEL ADAMS TO JAMES WARREN 93
    Changes in House. Paymaster general. Commendation of Lux. Appointment of Church. His own son.

July 30. JOHN ADAMS TO JAMES WARREN 94
    The paymaster generalship. Secretary of the Province.

July 31. JAMES WARREN TO JOHN ADAMS 95
    Gratified by Thomas's appointment. Conduct of Spencer. Embarrassments from narrow views. Open ports to the foreign trade. Military actions. The lighthouse attack. Washington on army appointments. The constitution of government. Trade with the enemy. A treaty with Gage and its observance.

August 6. GEORGE WASHINGTON TO JAMES WARREN 99
    Proposed release of Hichborn. The intercepted letters.

August 9. JAMES WARREN TO JOHN ADAMS 99
    Providential arrival of powder. Riflemen restrained. Machias takes vessels. Other captures. Prisoners held in Boston. Officers by Massachusetts appointment. Hichborn's adventure. Tories in Boston.

August 17. HANNAH WINTHROP TO MERCY WARREN 102
    Washington's character. The people of Boston and Gage. Situation of her brother Mason. Treatment of Charlestown. Warren's appointment as paymaster general.

August 26. JOHN ADAMS TO MERCY WARREN 104
    Rejoiced to be in the country. Effect of rest and family intercourse. No vexations or annoyances. This happy period must end.

August 27. ABIGAIL ADAMS TO MERCY WARREN 105
    Safe arrival at home. Has not heard of alarms. Mr. Adams soon to return to Congress. The intercepted letters.

Contents

September 4. MERCY WARREN TO JOHN ADAMS 106
    Fear an attack at Halifax. Tranquillity at camp. Preparations to bombard Prospect Hill.

September 11. JAMES WARREN TO JOHN ADAMS 107
    Works around Boston. Trouble with the Riflemen. Foreign intelligence. Need of powder and money. Arnold's expedition to Quebec. Some vessels taken. Patrick Henry. Council appointments.

September 17. JOHN ADAMS TO JAMES WARREN 109
    Reply of King to city of London. Marriage of Hancock. Samuel Adams rides a horse.

September 19. JOHN ADAMS TO JAMES WARREN 112
    Return of Peyton Randolph. The Virginia delegation. Wishes a new selection from Massachusetts. Congress feels the spirit of war.

September 19. JAMES WARREN TO JOHN ADAMS 112
    No intelligence to offer. The situation in Boston. Skirmishing. Great need of money. Versifying in Boston.

September 26. JOHN ADAMS TO JAMES WARREN 115
    Influence of the sex. Efforts to get powder and saltpetre. Accounts of the Province against the continent. Urges a change in the delegation. Wishes to retire, and the reasons.

September 26. JOHN ADAMS TO MERCY WARREN 118
    The intercepted letters. Has boasted of his happiness.

September 28. JOHN ADAMS TO JAMES WARREN 118
    The provincial accounts.

September 30. JOHN ADAMS TO JAMES WARREN 119
    A committee of Congress to the camp. The members described.

October 1. JOHN ADAMS TO JAMES WARREN 120
    Draper's newspaper and foreign intelligence. Fears for Mrs. Adams. The committee of Congress.

October 1. JAMES WARREN TO JOHN ADAMS 121
    Detection of Dr. Church's correspondence. Circumstances so far as known. Captures of vessels. Turtle and letters. Intelligence from Canada. Arnold's progress. Money and powder.

October 2. JOHN ADAMS TO JAMES WARREN 124
    Introduces Major Bayard. Secrecy of proceedings. Spirited measures in order. Messages from Lux. Mrs. Adams.

Contents xiii

October 3. SAMUEL ADAMS TO JAMES WARREN 124
    Introduces Bayard. Committee to camp. Folly to petition. Army must not remain inactive.

October 7. JOHN ADAMS TO JAMES WARREN 126
    Secrecy in Congress. Questions on the trade of America. Ambassadors to foreign courts. Offer of sovereignty, alliance and commerce. Protection of trade. Must depend on their own resources. A sea force.

October 7. SAMUEL ADAMS TO JAMES WARREN 129
    Intelligence from Great Britain. Preparation necessary. Hessians to be employed. Colony accounts.

October 8. JOHN ADAMS TO JAMES WARREN 129
    Channels in Boston Harbor. Forts on the islands. Plan of town and harbor. Row gallies. News from the northward. Government for Canada. Court committees.

October 10. JOHN ADAMS TO JAMES WARREN 132
    Recommending Jonathan Mifflin. Canada. Powder and saltpetre. Information desired. Cannon for America.

October 10. SAMUEL ADAMS TO JAMES WARREN 132
    Intelligence from Great Britain. Military preparations. Flat boats for the lakes. Designs near Boston. The northern expedition.

October 12. JOHN ADAMS TO JAMES WARREN 134
    Article on powder from Antigua. Wishes latest and fullest intelligence. Details on powder in West Indies.

October 13. JOHN ADAMS TO JAMES WARREN 136
    Is pleased on reception of a passage in the intercepted letter. Charles Lee and his fondness for dogs. Expressions of sincerity. No timidity in Congress.

October 13. JOHN ADAMS TO JAMES WARREN 139
    Church's misfortune. Has not influenced position of delegates. The northern expedition and successes at sea.

October 13. SAMUEL ADAMS TO JAMES WARREN 140
    No intelligence sent from Massachusetts. Desires an attack upon Boston. Honor in British army. Church's letter.

October 18. JOHN ADAMS TO JAMES WARREN 142
    Church's letter. Opinion in Congress. Dismissed from his office. Dr. Morgan chosen to succeed him. Unfortunate appointments from Massachusetts. Morgan's character. A committee of Congress on hostilities.

October 19. JOHN ADAMS TO JAMES WARREN 143
    Nothing from the committee of correspondence. Urges vouchers for accounts against the continent. A committee on hostilities.

October 19. JOHN ADAMS TO JAMES WARREN 145
    An American fleet and the possibilities. Protection of trade, north and south. A public fleet.

October 19. JOHN ADAMS TO JAMES WARREN 146
    What measures on trade are necessary. Change of habit and prejudice. Prohibition or permission of commerce. Invitation to foreign nations to trade. The West Indies.

October 19. ABIGAIL ADAMS TO MERCY WARREN 147
    Has had few letters. Church and his punishment. Curiosity and women. Little inclination to go into company.

October 19. SAMUEL ADAMS TO JAMES WARREN 148
    Introduces Captain Gist. Critical situation of affairs. Consolation.

October 20. JAMES WARREN TO JOHN ADAMS 149
    Committee from Congress entertained. Justices in the Supreme Court. Candidates and claims. The situation in Boston. Putnam's venture. Threats against sea-board towns. Prizes and accounts. Bills of credit. An offensive movement uncertain. Conference with committee of Congress. Church's affair. Trade and saltpetre. Burning of Falmouth. Hichborn. Row gallies. Government of Canada.

October 20. JOHN ADAMS TO JAMES WARREN 155
    Need for foreign trade. Clothing and materials. Impatience of merchants and laborers.

October 20. JOHN ADAMS TO JAMES WARREN 156
    Introducing John McPherson.

October 21. JOHN ADAMS TO JAMES WARREN 157
    Recommendation of John Folwell and Josiah Hart. Saltpetre. Hancock's conduct.

October 21. JOHN ADAMS TO JAMES WARREN 158
    Necessity of saltpetre. Examples of success. Rock of saltpetre in Virginia.

October 23. JOHN ADAMS TO JAMES WARREN 159
    Grateful for condolence. Accounts and prices. Relation of hostilities.

October 24. JOHN ADAMS TO JAMES WARREN 160
    Searching of hearts by men. Art of a politician. Difficulty of applying it in Congress.

Contents

October 24. JOHN ADAMS TO JAMES WARREN 161
    Death of Peyton Randolph. His character.

October 24. SILAS DEANE, JOHN ADAMS, AND GEORGE WYTHE TO
    JAMES WARREN 162
    Asks for an account of hostilities committed by British.

October 25. JOHN ADAMS TO JAMES WARREN 163
    Method of collecting saltpetre from the air. Sulphur and lead. O'Brian and Carghill.

October 25. JOHN ADAMS TO JAMES WARREN 164
    Morgan to succeed Church. His experience and character.

October 25. JOHN ADAMS TO JAMES WARREN 165
    Appointments for the sons of Governor Ward of Rhode Island.

October 28. JOHN ADAMS TO JAMES WARREN 166
    The Continental association. Should non-exportation be extended? Possible benefit to Tories.

October —. JOHN ADAMS TO JAMES WARREN 167
    A North American monarchy. Quakers and land jobbers.

October 28. JAMES WARREN TO JOHN ADAMS 168
    Opinion of Joseph Reed. *The Group*. Powder and rumored quantity.

November 4. SAMUEL ADAMS TO JAMES WARREN 169
    Powder and captured British colors. Committee from camp. New battalions. Exportation permitted only for powder. Will not violate secrecy of Congress. Internal police of colony. Schools and principles of morality. Character of public men. The secretaryship of Massachusetts. Church.

November 5. JOHN ADAMS TO JAMES WARREN 174
    Committee from camp. Seamen and their numbers. Ships and their construction. Commanders. Government permitted.

November 5. JAMES WARREN TO JOHN ADAMS 175
    Prices and trade. Non-exportation. Purchase of beef and hay. Monopolies charged. Need for wood. Questions on trade. Protection against enemy ships and saltpetre. Militia and appointment of officers. The supreme court. A test act. New delegates and prizes.

November —. ABIGAIL ADAMS TO MERCY WARREN 179
    A missent letter. Punishment of Church. A continental connection and morals.

Contents

November 14. JAMES WARREN TO JOHN ADAMS 181
News from Canada. Enos deserts Arnold. Whalemen and privateering. Shipwrights. Commanders suggested. Government and representatives. The dispute over officers. Military and naval courts. Foreign trade. Many matters.

December 3. JOHN ADAMS TO JAMES WARREN 186
Arrears of army pay. Crafts and Trot recommended.

December 3. JAMES WARREN TO JOHN ADAMS 187
Has not yet seen Dr. Morgan. Success of northern army. Marston's assurance to Howe. Difficulties of the general on army. Prizes and saltpetre. Confidence in Congress. Medical appointments.

December 5. SAMUEL ADAMS TO JAMES WARREN 191
Introducing Jonathan B. Smith. Grant of money to Massachusetts. Dunmore's acts in Virginia. A government recommended. Dispute on militia appointments. Want of public spirit. Need of prudence.

December 11. JAMES WARREN TO JOHN ADAMS 192
Progress in making saltpetre. Powder mills. Prizes and privateers. Militia and their conduct. Prospects of army. Appointments.

December 26. SAMUEL ADAMS TO JAMES WARREN 195
Present form of government, and its improvement. Fear of a free government. Control of legislative bodies. Change of manners.

1776

January 7. SAMUEL ADAMS TO JAMES WARREN 197
Militia establishment. Dangers of a standing army. Should teach art of war and principles of government. Powder and saltpetre. A confederation and the obstacles. Disposition of Captain Horn on burning of Norfolk.

January 8. MARTHA WASHINGTON TO MERCY WARREN 200
Thanking her for offer of shelter in case of removal. The general's wishes.

January 8. JOHN ADAMS TO MERCY WARREN 201
Is charmed by her characters. A monarchy or republic. Effect of the form of government. Public virtue. An engagement. In suspense as to issue.

January 10. SAMUEL ADAMS TO JAMES WARREN 203
Export of produce. Resolutions adopted. Case of James Lovell. Fry and Arnold. *Common Sense.*

Contents

February 7. Mercy Warren to Abigail Adams 205
    Whispers of malice and apprehensions. The intercepted letters. Her correspondence with John Adams.

February 18. John Adams to James Warren 206
    A committee to go to Canada. Description of the members. John Carroll also to go. Lee ordered to Canada. Need of conquering that province.

February 28. James Bowdoin to Mercy Warren 208
    Paine's *Common Sense*.

March 7. James Warren to John Adams 209
    Fears negotiations with Great Britain. Commissioners appointed. Cannot account for hesitancy. Move upon Boston. Prizes. Baron de Woedtke. Bounties for enlistments.

March 8. Samuel Adams to James Warren 211
    Conduct of Cushing. A subscription in support of his character.

March 21. John Adams to James Warren 212
    A mighty question pending. Change in the Pennsylvania representation. Privateers and open trade. End of Quaker interest in Philadelphia.

March 23. James Bowdoin to Mercy Warren 214
    The British commissioners to negotiate. How both sides will conduct the matter. Fear of bribery. A treaty in outline. Question of independence. Opinion of Paine.

March 29. John Adams to James Warren 216
    Fortifying Boston Harbor. Obstructing the channel.

March 30. James Warren to John Adams 217
    Topsy-turvy condition of affairs. Departure of the British fleet and the future. Sending troops from Boston. The paymaster generalship. Resigns. Audit of accounts. Levelling spirit and united sentiment. His resignation. Prizes.

April 2. Martha Washington to Mercy Warren 220
    Cannot accept her invitation to dinner. Good wishes.

April 3. John Adams to James Warren 220
    Howe's intentions. Troops needed for Washington's army.

April 16. John Adams to Mercy Warren 221
    Women great politicians. Forms of government. Spirit of commerce. No faith in the British commissioners.

Contents

April 16. SAMUEL ADAMS TO JAMES WARREN 224
    Evacuation of Boston and independence. The commissioners to treat. Should renounce all treaty with them. Independence.

April 16. JOHN ADAMS TO JAMES WARREN 225
    Defence of Boston Harbor. His letter of resignation. The new judges. Independence and the opposition. Privateering. Alliances.

April 17. MERCY WARREN TO ABIGAIL ADAMS 228
    Describes a visit to Mrs. Washington. The Custis family. Mrs. Morgan.

April 20. JOHN ADAMS TO JAMES WARREN 230
    Opinion on independence in the southern colonies. Origin of his 'Thoughts on Government.'

April 22. JOHN ADAMS TO JAMES WARREN 232
    Requirements of the governing machine. Advance towards desired end. Massachusetts should alter constitution. An instruction for independency. Reluctance to change and independence. Respect for those in authority. The election in May.

April 27. ABIGAIL ADAMS TO MERCY WARREN 234
    Thanks for characters. Letters from John Adams. Her list of female grievances. His retort.

April 30. JAMES WARREN TO JOHN ADAMS 236
    Doings of the General Court. Fortifying town and harbor. A successor to Ward. The pay of troops. Powder supplies. British at George's Island.

May 8. JAMES WARREN TO JOHN ADAMS 239
    Boston to be attacked. Want of defense. Regiments and appointments. Representation in the General Court.

May 12. JOHN ADAMS TO JAMES WARREN 242
    Ill health and anxieties. Braxton's address to the Virginia convention. Judges' salaries. A negative for the governor. Governments in colonies. Influence of Thomas Paine. Resigns from Board.

May 12. SAMUEL ADAMS TO JAMES WARREN 244
    Need of strengthening Boston. Avoidance of disputes. Congress and the Eastern district. To press inlistments. Money for the paymaster.

May 15. JOHN ADAMS TO JAMES WARREN 245
    Preamble to resolution on government. What remains to be done. Battalions for Massachusetts. Appointments of officers. Gates and Mifflin.

Contents

MAY 18. JOHN ADAMS TO JAMES WARREN 247
    Plans of the enemy. The provincial militia. Dismal news from Canada. The phantom of commissioners. Scandalous flight from Quebec. Promotions. Specie for the Canada service. Ripe for independence.

MAY 20. JOHN ADAMS TO JAMES WARREN 249
    Progress of independence. Changes in instructions and delegates. Most decisive measures not very remote. Dickinson's change of heart. Prospect of carnage and devastation.

JUNE 2. JAMES WARREN TO JOHN ADAMS 252
    'Thoughts on Government.' The Council and House. The Salem election. Forming a government. Judges and Bowdoin. Slow inlistments. Manning the ships. His accounts as paymaster. Distress for money. Prize ship.

JUNE 5. JAMES WARREN TO JOHN ADAMS 254
    Arrival of Dr. Church and his treatment. Prizes taken. Covering British property by the West Indians.

JUNE 6. SAMUEL ADAMS TO JAMES WARREN 255
    Better appearance of affairs in Canada. Important motion pending. Contention to be avoided.

JUNE 9. JOHN ADAMS TO JAMES WARREN 256
    In doubt on his office. In ignorance of the election. A treatise on fire ships. Washington and Boston.

JUNE 16. JOHN ADAMS TO JAMES WARREN 257
    Braxton's 'Address.' Henry's opinion. The Virginia constitution forecast. Continental battalions from Massachusetts. Smallpox. Importance of holding ground in Canada. British property.

JULY 10. JAMES WARREN TO JOHN ADAMS 258
    General Court's transactions. Inlistments and bounties. Burden of towns. His own position. Plot in New York. Prizes taken. Alliances and confederation. Young's 'Rural Oeconomy.'

JULY 15. JOHN ADAMS TO JAMES WARREN 260
    Gerry leaves for his health. Expectations from New York.

JULY 17. JAMES WARREN TO JOHN ADAMS 261
    Spread of inoculation. Has received the declaration of independence. Congress and Massachusetts. The Southern colonies. Defenceless state of colony. Howe's treatment of captured vessels. Condition of Boston. Portugal and Great Britain.

July 24. JOHN ADAMS TO JAMES WARREN 263
    Inoculation and use of mercury. The court and confederation. Much depends on militia. Burgoyne wishes to retire.

July 26. JOHN ADAMS TO JAMES WARREN 264
    Must return home. Recommends General Ward, and Dana and others.

July 27. JOHN ADAMS TO JAMES WARREN 264
    Need of fresh delegates. Condition of those in Philadelphia. Has sent in his resignation.

August 7. JAMES WARREN TO JOHN ADAMS 266
    Uneasiness over Adams' health. Unhealthiness of Philadelphia. Smallpox.

August 11. JAMES WARREN TO JOHN ADAMS 267
    Mrs. Temple's application. No important intelligence. Privateering and idle vessels. Filling the battalions. No commander appointed. Currency and inoculation. News from France.

August 17. JOHN ADAMS TO JAMES WARREN 269
    Earnestly desires to retire. Numbering the Massachusetts regiments. Information wanted on navy and privateers. Odd manner of telling a story. Wanted, a horse.

August 21. JOHN ADAMS TO JAMES WARREN 270
    Will aid Mrs. Temple. Privateers and the navy. Men of business wanted. Ward to command in eastern department. Force at New York. Laziness of Massachusetts.

September 4. JOHN ADAMS TO JAMES WARREN 272
    S. Adams and Gerry. Situation at New York. Sullivan's mission. Will remain during the crisis. Introduces Mr. Hare. Suggests a brewery of porter. Resolution on Mrs. Temple's application.

September 19. JAMES WARREN TO JOHN ADAMS 273
    Troops for New York and Rhode Island. Is appointed a major-general. Matters attended to by General Court. Has not seen Mr. Hare. Question of delegates. Sullivan's message and Howe's mission.

September 25. JOHN ADAMS TO JAMES WARREN 275
    New plan of an army. Commissions and inlistments.

November 6. SAMUEL ADAMS TO JAMES WARREN 275
    Pay of militia. Inlisting a new army. Committee of war. Inlistments and bounties. Officers' rank.

November 16. SAMUEL ADAMS TO JAMES WARREN 277
  Carleton's retreat. The British fleet. Philadelphia may be the object. Preparations must be continued.
December 6. SAMUEL ADAMS TO JAMES WARREN 278
  Supplies of clothing for army. Want of intelligence. Accounts from the northward. Destruction of British vessels proposed.
December 12. SAMUEL ADAMS TO JAMES WARREN 279
  Movements of the two armies. Lethargy in Pennsylvania and New Jersey. Dickinson most to blame. Cause will be supported. Need of an army. Adams and Paine leave Congress. Wants news from New England. Caution against neglect.

1777

January 1. SAMUEL ADAMS TO JAMES WARREN 281
  Is satisfied with what has been done. Assurances given by the continental ministers abroad. Success in New Jersey. Washington's powers increased. Mission of Lieut.-Col. Stewart.
January 14. HANNAH WINTHROP TO MERCY WARREN 282
  New Year presents a brighter view. Success in New Jersey. Franklin goes abroad. A prophetical egg. Astronomical matters. Her sister.
January 16. SAMUEL ADAMS TO JAMES WARREN 285
  Money for payment of bounty. Vote of the province in Congress. Needs advice and assistance. Has never had so happy feelings. Introduces John Allan.
February 1. SAMUEL ADAMS TO JAMES WARREN 286
  Proceedings of the New England states on prices. A letter from a delegate. Want of information. Excuses his neglect to write. The board of war and purchases of flour. S. and R. Purviance commended. Sons of Warren and Mercer.
February 3. JOHN ADAMS TO JAMES WARREN 288
  Has reached Baltimore. The recruiting service. British ministry ask for Cossacks. Must destroy British army. New England in high estimation.
February 11. SAMUEL ADAMS TO JAMES WARREN 290
  Account of expenses. Clothes and other charges. Horsehire. Time of service. Arrival of arms.
February 16. SAMUEL ADAMS TO JAMES WARREN 291
  Suppression of Maryland tories. Case of Cheney. Dangers to be apprehended. Should be rooted out. Congress and Lee. Howe and British atrocities.

February 17. JOHN ADAMS TO JAMES WARREN 293
  Change in Congressional representation. Familiar faces remaining. Government of states acquiring vigor. A military engagement. Will return to Philadelphia. The new army.

February 22. JAMES WARREN TO JOHN ADAMS 294
  Anxiety about him. Russians for Great Britain. Wishes to see foreign merchantmen in harbors. Bounties and inlistments. Apprehensions of Schuyler on Ticonderoga. Newport and promotions. The constitution. Freedom of conscience. The navy. Requisitions by Congress.

March 6. JOHN ADAMS TO JAMES WARREN 297
  Dr. Jackson and the lottery. State governments. Loans. Cost of living.

March 15. GEORGE WASHINGTON TO JAMES WARREN 298
  Friendly greetings and acknowledgment. Disapproves method of raising troops. A campaign about to open.

March 21. JOHN ADAMS TO JAMES WARREN 299
  Object of the enemy uncertain. Their reinforcements. Cossacks and Hessians. Cannot hold Philadelphia and their communication through New Jersey. The city a small conquest.

March 21. JAMES WARREN TO MERCY WARREN 301
  Arrival of *Independence* with supplies from France. Reception of Franklin. Recognition by France of American independence. Libel from the Tories. French officers.

March 23. JAMES WARREN TO JOHN ADAMS 303
  Likes old faces, acquaintance and connections. The new army. Levy on towns. Bounties extended to artillery. No move on Rhode Island. Conduct of the Fleet. Local Boards. Recommends captains. The regulating act. A convention on a constitution. Recommends Joseph Ward.

March 24. JOHN ADAMS TO JAMES WARREN 306
  Arrival of arms. An interposition of Providence.

March 26. JOHN ADAMS TO JAMES WARREN 306
  A cannon of bar iron. Advantages on trial.

March 31. JOHN ADAMS TO JAMES WARREN 307
  Encouraging news from France. Arms and powder arriving. Patience and perseverance wanted. Must depend on selves.

April 1. JOHN ADAMS TO JAMES WARREN 308
  Sends important letter. Stocks at Amsterdam. Dutch may be friendly.

April 3. JAMES WARREN TO JOHN ADAMS 309
 Desires war between Great Britain and France. Interest on loans, and the lottery. Articles of confederation. A constitution for Massachusetts. The enemy at Rhode Island. Hancock as treasurer of Harvard College.

April 6. JOHN ADAMS TO JAMES WARREN 310
 Suppresses a letter. Naval matters. Changes in the naval committee and its needs.

April 6. JOHN ADAMS TO JAMES WARREN 312
 Naval administration and boards. Officers should communicate their sentiments freely. Is against an embargo on privateers. Trade enterprise and Massachusetts.

April 16. JOHN ADAMS TO JAMES WARREN 313
 A vessel from France. Intelligence from Europe. Great Britain threatens war with France. Other differences.

April 17. SAMUEL ADAMS TO JAMES WARREN 314
 An invasion by sea. Lee on cultivating Europe. Losses of British merchants. Great warlike preparations. New England the object. Measures against the tories.

April 23. JAMES WARREN TO JOHN ADAMS 316
 War in Europe to be looked for. Supplies from France. Prizes and privateers. Forces for Rhode Island. Low estimate of militia. An important arrival.

April 27. JAMES WARREN TO JOHN ADAMS 318
 Frigates infecting the coasts. An hostile challenge. A committee to confer with the captains, and other measures taken. Is pleased with Conway. Agriculture. Purchasing agents. Livingston and Turnbull. Otis recommended. Feeling against the Portuguese.

May 2. JOHN ADAMS TO JAMES WARREN 321
 Introducing Dr. Brownson.

May 3. JOHN ADAMS TO JAMES WARREN 321
 On European war and trade. Cowardly to pant after a French war. How to secure her aid. The question of revenue. The articles of confederation. The state constitution.

May 5. JAMES WARREN TO JOHN ADAMS 323
 The affair at Danbury. Little dependence on militia. Distribution of forces. Sacrifices and southern appreciation. Has written Washington.

May 6. JOHN ADAMS TO JAMES WARREN 324
  Navy board at Boston. Names considered and the choice made. Salaries and duties.

May 8. JAMES WARREN TO JOHN ADAMS 325
  Military and naval intelligence. Bounties to battalions. Move against the tories.

June 5. JAMES WARREN TO JOHN ADAMS 326
  Completing the state quota. Obliged to become speaker. Ill news from Ticonderoga. The navy board. Equal representation.

June 11. JOHN ADAMS TO JAMES WARREN 328
  Introducing Joseph Hewes. Plans of Howe. His experience in New Jersey. Rhode Island. The constitution.

June 11. JAMES WARREN TO JOHN ADAMS 329
  British men of war on coast. Gates in command of northern army. Rhode Island. War between France and Great Britain. The regulating act and taxation.

June 18. SAMUEL ADAMS TO JAMES WARREN 331
  Introducing Colonel Whipple. General Court matters. Movements of the enemy. Dislikes a Fabian war.

June 19. JOHN ADAMS TO JAMES WARREN 332
  Massachusetts must lead. The navy board and residence. Difference between General Court and town of Boston. The constitution. Numbering of regiments. Embarrassed with foreign officers. Cost of living at Philadelphia.

June 22. JAMES WARREN TO JOHN ADAMS 334
  British may take Philadelphia. Depends upon him for information. The regulating act. The constitution. Question of representation. Bill for freeing negroes. Operations of cruisers and the navy. Navy board.

June 23. SAMUEL ADAMS TO JAMES WARREN 336
  Situation and movements of armies.

June 30. SAMUEL ADAMS TO JAMES WARREN 337
  Uncertainty in post office. The confederation. Votes of each state. A constitution for Massachusetts.

July 7. JOHN ADAMS TO JAMES WARREN 339
  Does not expect Howe in Philadelphia. The Massachusetts regiments not filled. Matter of arms. The constitution. Bill for freeing negroes. Naval commissions. The governorship.

Contents

July 10. JAMES WARREN TO JOHN ADAMS 340
    Forces raised in Massachusetts. Progress on the constitution. No disunion between Boston and the General Court. Foreign officers. Expenses of living. Ticonderoga and Howe's plans. Gerry's ship.

July 11. JAMES WARREN TO JOHN ADAMS 342
    Evacuation of Ticonderoga.

July 22. SAMUEL ADAMS TO JAMES WARREN 343
    Charges on the evacuation of Ticonderoga. Regiments in garrison.

July 31. SAMUEL ADAMS TO JAMES WARREN 344
    Congress to investigate the evacuation of Ticonderoga. Schuyler's appointment and support. St. Clair and public opinion. Wants numbers sent to Ticonderoga. The enemy expected.

August 1. SAMUEL ADAMS TO JAMES WARREN 346
    British fleet at sea. Congress investigates loss of Ticonderoga and Mount Independence. Deliberation and design intimated. May recover and win.

August 10. JAMES WARREN TO JOHN ADAMS 347
    Results of the evacuation of Ticonderoga and New England. New levies and arms. Indignation and distrust. News of northern operations. Question of rank. Resigns his commission. New England convention. Navy board and situation of vessels. The constitution. Distribution of arms.

August 12. SAMUEL ADAMS TO JAMES WARREN 351
    Schuyler's letter to Congress, and his strictures on Massachusetts. Gates gone to take command. The English fleet. Schuyler's letter of August 4.

August 6. JOHN GLOVER TO JAMES WARREN 353
    The northern campaign. Outbreak of Indians and panic. Position and strength of the enemy. The militia leaving the army. Defends commanders. Need of reinforcements.

August 11. JOHN GLOVER TO JAMES WARREN 355
    Affair at Fort Schuyler and Herkimer's death. Effect of recall of Schuyler and St. Clair. Burgoyne and militia.

August 12. JOHN ADAMS TO JAMES WARREN 357
    Schuyler's letters and troops. Inquiry on Ticonderoga. Howe and the Jersies. Washington's army. News from France.

Contents

August 14. ABIGAIL ADAMS TO MERCY WARREN 358
    Memorable anniversary. Should have a history of courts. Cruelty of the enemy. Sends copy of Lee's letter. Loss of Ticonderoga. French cotton and a cloth commission.

August 18. JOHN ADAMS TO JAMES WARREN 359
    Copies of letters from Arthur Lee. The northern department. Massachusetts should exert herself. Finance. Letters of Arthur Lee, January 31 and February 3 and 11. Attempt to colonize the Musquito shore. War preparations. Trade convoys. Letters of marque. American prisoners for India.

September 4. JAMES WARREN TO JOHN ADAMS 363
    Schuyler's letters. Burgoyne's situation. Sullivan's success. Howe and Philadelphia. Prizes. Currency and taxation. Vacant lands as a fund.

September 7. JAMES WARREN TO JOHN ADAMS 365
    The navy board and popular expectation. Dispute between Manley and McNeill. Powers of board and money. Arnold's success. Prizes. News from London. Economy and a clerk. Prices.

September 17. JAMES WARREN TO JOHN ADAMS 367
    No news. Operations against Burgoyne. Machias. The Constitution. Salt and molasses from cornstalks. Extravagance and outbreaks. Agent of clothier general.

September 17. SAMUEL ADAMS TO JAMES WARREN 369
    Fighting near Philadelphia. Washington retires. A battle expected. Jesuits' bark for R. H. Lee. Movements of the enemy. Affairs were never in a better situation.

October 10. JAMES WARREN TO JOHN ADAMS 370
    Howe and Philadelphia. Opposition offered by Washington. Burgoyne and Rhode Island. Removal of Congress.

October 12. JAMES WARREN TO JOHN ADAMS 371
    Who possesses Philadelphia? Situation in the northern department. The Rhode Island expedition not promising. The *Boston*. Wants power over navy officers. Captain McNeill's conduct and an inquiry. News of a northern victory.

October 24. JOHN ADAMS TO JAMES WARREN 373
    Only rumors from the northward. On the confederation. Plan of taxes.

October 26. SAMUEL ADAMS TO JAMES WARREN 374
    Success to the northward and on the Delaware. A day of public thanks-

giving. Letter from Jonathan Mifflin on defence of Red Bank. Howe's handbill on Burgoyne.

October 29. SAMUEL ADAMS TO JAMES WARREN 375
Defence of Red Bank. Articles of confederation and their provisions. Leave of absence. Arts of flattery. Question of a governor. The prisoners from Saratoga. The victory. Currency and taxation.

October 30. SAMUEL ADAMS TO JAMES WARREN 377
Hancock's speech on leaving chair.

November 4. SAMUEL ADAMS TO JAMES WARREN 378
Hancock's speech. Debate on motions.

November 29. ARTHUR LEE TO ——— 379
Mismanagement of commercial affairs in France. Efforts of Lee to secure better methods. Deane's jealousy and neglect of Lee. House at Passy. Extravagance of agents. Suspicious of French court.

Illustrations

JAMES WARREN . . . . *Frontispiece*
    From a portrait by John Singleton Copley in the possession of Winslow Warren.

JAMES OTIS, JR., TO JAMES OTIS, SR., 1743 1
    From the Warren Papers.

CAPTAIN JOHN DERBY 84
    From a silhouette in the possession of Dr. Frederick Cheever Shattuck.

JOHN ADAMS TO JAMES WARREN, 1775 118
    From the Warren Papers.

PLEDGE OF SECRECY BY THE MEMBERS OF THE CONTINENTAL CONGRESS, 1775–1777 126
    From the original in the Library of Congress.

TITLEPAGE OF MERCY WARREN'S *The Group* 168
    From the original in the Massachusetts Historical Society.

MARTHA WASHINGTON TO MERCY WARREN, 1776 200
    From the Warren Papers.

TITLEPAGES OF THE PHILADELPHIA AND BOSTON ISSUES OF JOHN ADAMS' *Thoughts on Government*, 1776 230

JAMES WARREN TO MERCY WARREN, 1774 294
    From the Warren Papers.

SAMUEL ADAMS TO JAMES WARREN, 1777 330
    From the Warren Papers.

ABIGAIL ADAMS TO MERCY WARREN, 1775 358
    From the Warren Papers.

Prefatory Note

THE letters in these volumes are drawn from two sources. Those addressed to James or Mercy Warren are in the possession of Mr. Winslow Warren, a member of this Society; those written by James Warren to John Adams are in the Adams Papers, the trustees[1] of which courteously permitted them to be used.

Material so abundant and historically rich needed no additions from other collections. No other single correspondence of the period offers such a picture of the hopes and fears of the patriot faction, or of the transactions in Continental Congress and in Massachusetts General Court, by leading participants. More than half of the letters were written before the peace of 1783, and for the period of war the subjects treated are those of greatest concern to the "rebellious" colonies and independent states. After 1783 the letters become less consistent but not less intimate and come from a wider circle. The interest is maintained to the end. The series not only presents an exchange of views and a relation of incident in full freedom of almost family intercourse, but it adds much to what has been known of the motives of the conduct of public characters, and the estimation in which they were held. Each writer is strongly individual, keenly alive to what was passing, a good reporter and a strong adherent to the cause of the War for Independence.

Letters which passed between John Adams and Mercy Warren, July–August, 1807, on her *History of the American Revolution*, were printed in 5 *Mass. Hist. Collections*, IV. 315, and are not reprinted in these volumes. The introductory note to those letters, written by Mr. Charles Francis Adams, Sr., may profitably be read in this connection.

WORTHINGTON CHAUNCEY FORD.

BOSTON, *April,* 1917

[1] Messrs. Charles Francis Adams, Henry Adams, Brooks Adams, and Charles Francis Adams, 2d.

Boston June the 17th 1748

Honoured Sir I wrote to you the 11th Currant but omitted some things which I shall now enumerate 15 Shillings for brushing Cheses for three Quarters Shining 24 Shillings for a Sett of Buckles 13 Shillings. And if I make any manner of Entertainment there will be a great many things to buy, tho I shall not put you to much Charge for that not intending to keep much of a commencement and what I do will be with Russell. Pray Sir send me money enough for I beleive I shall not write again before commencement Your most obedient Son James Otis

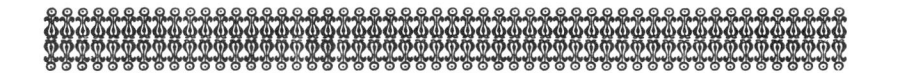

WARREN-ADAMS LETTERS

JAMES OTIS, JR. TO JAMES OTIS, SENR

BOSTON, *June the* 17th, 1743.

HONOURED SIR, — I wrote to you the 11th Currant, but omitted Some Things which I Shall now enumerate viz. 15 Shillings for Printing Theses, for three Quarters shoing 24 shillings, for a Sett of Buckles 15 shillings, and if I make any manner of Entertainment there will be a great many things to buy, tho I shall not put you to much Charge for that, not intending to keep much of a commencement and what I do will be with Russell.[1] Pray Sir send me money Enough for I believe I Shall not write again before commencement. Your most Obedient Son,

JAMES OTIS[2]

JAMES OTIS TO MERCY WARREN

DEAR SISTER, — I received yours informing me of the death of sister Otis.[3] I am heartily grieved for brother and his children. Their loss can never be made up. I am more and more convinced of the vanity of things under the sun. Hope we shall all be prepared for a better state. I can truly say I long to indulge to those feelings of tenderness and humanity that are proper as far as possible at all times, and never more so than in mourning with and comforting our friends and relations under their afflictions. But

---

1 Lothrop Russell, a classmate (1725–1745).
2 Otis (1725–1783) had been prepared for college under the care of the Rev. Jonathan Russell, of West Barnstable, and entered at Cambridge, June, 1739. He took his degree of A.B. in 1743, and that of A.M. three years later.
3 Rebecca Sturgis, wife of Joseph Otis (1726–1810).

alas, hard is my case. Dear sister, for near two years I have not had it in my power to spend any time for myself; it has been taken up for others and some of them perhaps will never thank me. The time however I hope is at hand when I shall be relieved from a task I shall never envy any man who in performing it shall pass the anxious wearisome days and nights which I have seen. This country must soon be at rest, or may be engaged in contests that will require neither the pen nor the tongue of a lawyer.

The enemies of our peace entertain hopes we shall get no relief from home, but I am positive all appearances are against them. If we are to be slaves the living have only to envy the dead, for without liberty I own I desire not to exist here. I think I have written you diverse letters within the period you mention and will write you many more.

This you may depend on, no man ever loved a sister better, and among all my conflicts I never forget that I am endeavoring to serve you and yours.

My love to my dear brother Warren. Tell him to give himself no concern about the scurrilous piece in Tom Fleet's paper;[1] it has served me as much as the song did last year. The Tories are all ashamed of this as they were of that. The author is not yet certainly known, tho' I think I am within a week of detecting him for certain. If I should, shall try to cure him once for all by stringing him up, not bodily, but in such a way as shall gibbet his memory to all generations *in Terrorem*. It lies between Barnard,[2] Waterhouse[3] and Jona. Sewall.[4] The first they say has not wit

[1] This refers to a long communication, without title or signature, printed in the *Boston Evening Post*, March 31, 1766. Under the name of Bluster, Otis is described, and in terms even more scurrilous than was usual at that time. It opens and closes with the words "So! Jemmy — so! so! Jemmy — well — well," etc., which may give the clue to the "song of last year." For in the same paper, May 13, 1765, appeared the "Jemmibullero: a Fragment of an Ode of Orpheus." One of the lines reads "and Jemmy *blusters* all the morn." See Tudor, *Life of James Otis*, 239.

[2] John Barnard (?), a refugee from Boston in 1776.

[3] Samuel Waterhouse, of Boston, an officer of the customs, and described by John Adams as "the most notorious scribbler, satirist, and libeller in the service of the conspirators against the liberties of America." He embarked for Halifax at the evacuation of Boston by the British, and was in London in November, 1776, dining with other Loyalists at the London Coffee House, on Lord Mayor's day. In 1778 he was among those proscribed and banished by Massachusetts, and in 1779 addressed the King in a loyalist petition. Waterhouse was probably the writer of the article.

[4] Jonathan Sewall, the attorney general of Massachusetts.

enough to write anything; the second swears off, and the third must plead guilty or not guilty so soon as I see him. I should have been with you before now but was concerned at the Supr. Court at Charlestown, not knowing but they would go on.

Next week they sit here and must stay, to know what they will do. Besides till matters are settled in England I dare not leave the Town, as men's minds are in such a situation that every nerve is requisite to keep things from running to some irregularity or imprudence, and some are yet wishing for an opportunity to hurting the country. I am your very affectionate Brother,

J. OTIS

April 11, 1766.

JOHN DICKINSON TO JAMES OTIS [1]

DEAR SIR, — The Liberties of our Common Country appear to me to be at this moment exposd to the most imminent Danger; and this Apprehension has engag'd me to lay my Sentiments before the Public in Letters, of which I send you a Copy.[2]

Only one has yet been publish'd and what there Effect may be, cannot yet be known; but whenever the Cause of American Freedom is to be vindicated, I look towards the Province of Massachusetts Bay. She must, as she has hitherto done, first kindle the Sacred Flame, that on such occasions must warm and illuminate the Continent.

Words are wanting to express my sense of the Vigilance, Perseverance, Spirit, Prudence, Resolution, and Firmness, with which your Colony has distinguish'd herself, in our unhappy Times. May God ever grant her noble Labors the same successful Issue, which was obtain'd by the Repeal of the Stamp-Act.

In my Gratitude to your Province in general, I do not forget the Obligations, which all Americans are under to you in particu-

---

[1] This and the three letters following were found among Mrs. Warren's correspondence. Otis and Dickinson had served together in the Stamp Act Congress of October, 1765.

[2] The first of the "Farmer's Letters" appeared in the *Pennsylvania Chronicle*, December 2, 1767, and the series continued to February 15, 1768. The first of the series, with some omissions, appeared in the *Boston Evening Post*, December 21, 1767, and the later letters followed in quick succession. See the "bibliographical note" in Paul L. Ford, *Life and Writings of John Dickinson*, II. 279.

lar, for the indefatigable Zeal and undaunted Courage you have shewn in defending their Rights. My Opinion of your Love for your Country induces me to commit to your hands the inclos'd Letters, to be dispos'd of as you think proper, not intending to give out any other Copy. I have shewn them to three Men of Learning here, who are my Friends. They think, with me, that the most destructive Consequences must follow, if these Colonies do not instantly, vigorously, and unanimously unite themselves, in the same manner they did against the Stamp Act. Perhaps they and I are mistaken. I therefore send the Peice containing the Reasons for this Opinion, to you, who I know can determine its True worth; and if you can discover no other merit in it, permit me at Least to claim the merit of having wrote it, with the most ardent affection for the British Colonies, the purest intentions to promote their Welfare, an honest Desire to assert there Rights, and with a deep sense of their impending Misfortunes.

Our Cause is a cause of the highest Dignity. It is nothing Less, than to maintain the Liberty with which Heav'n itself "hath made us free." I hope it will not be disgrac'd in any Colony, by a single rash Step. We have constitutional methods of seeking Redress; and they are the best Methods.

This Subject Leads me to inform you with Pleasure, because I think it must give you Pleasure, that the Moderation of your Conduct in composing the Minds of your Fellow-Citizens, has done you the highest Credit with us; you may be assured I feel a great satisfaction in hearing your praises; for ev'ry Thing that advances your Reputation or Interest, will always afford sincere Joy, to, Dear Sir, your most affectionate, and most hble Servt

JOHN DICKINSON

PHILADELPHIA, *December* 5th, 1767.

JOHN DICKINSON TO JAMES OTIS

[*January* 25, 1768.] [1]

DEAR SIR, — I have just receiv'd your Favor of the first of this Month, and am extremely happy in finding myself so much

[1] The date is obtained from the endorsement.

esteem'd by you. I very sincerely return you the kind Wishes you make for me; and am particularly oblig'd to you, for the attention you have been pleas'd to bestow on the Papers, I ventur'd to trouble You with.

I have made several alterations in the Copy, from which, that I sent to you, was taken: And the only correct one publish'd here, is printed in the *Pensylvania Gazette* of Hall and Sellers. I find that the "Letters" publish'd to the Eastward, are taken from our *Chronicle*,[1] which being incorrect, I should be glad if you would be so kind as to mention to any of the Printers you may happen to see, that the *Gazette* is much the most exact.

I have great hopes from what I hear, that nothing more is wanting, in order to rouse our Country-men, into a proper vindication of their just Rights, than those Examples of public Spirit, which "the cold Regions of the North" have been us'd to give to the languid Latitudes of the South. . . . [2]

JOHN DICKINSON TO JAMES OTIS

DEAR SIR, — I beg you will pardon the Liberty I take, in desiring you to add to the favors you have already conferrd upon me, by transmitting the inclos'd to your much honor'd Fellow-Citizens.[3] To attempt to express my sense of the Obligations I owe them, would lead me to many words, which after all my Labors would convey but an extremely faint Idea of what I feel. Permit me therefore to wave the Subject, by rendering to you, now deservedly placed at the Head of such excellent Citizens, my most hearty Thanks for the kind offices which I am sure your friendship has lately perform'd towards me. Retain I beseech you a Place for me in your affections, notwithstanding the Distance by which I am so unhappily seperated from you. I desire this the more boldly, because I am certain that I profess two Qualities, that render any man dear to *You*. I mean, an inextinguishable

[1] The *Boston Evening Post* reprinted from the *Chronicle*.
[2] The rest of the letter is missing.
[3] This refers to a letter addressed by Mr. Dickinson on this day to the "very respectable inhabitants of the town of Boston," expressing the "reverential gratitude" with which he had received the "very great honor you have been pleased to confer upon me by your late letter." Dickinson's communication is printed in the *Boston Evening Post*, May 2, 1768.

Love for my Country in General, and a particular affection for the town of Boston. May God almighty grant her all the prosperity a people can know, and that she may always retain that esteem for me, which is the great Ornament of my Life, and the great Delight of my Soul.

With the utmost Satisfaction I can acquaint you, that all America is rousing in Assertion of her Liberty. I am this moment told that the Assembly of Virginia have just publish'd the most spirited Resolves.[1] A second Defeat of Greenvillian Art and Malice, I trust in heaven, will convince Great-Britain, that it is as difficult to cheat as to fright us into Servitude, and that she ought to leave us in the peaceable Enjoyment of that Liberty, which Americans receiv'd with their Birth, and are resolv'd to retain till their Death.

With the Sincerest Wishes for your Happiness, I am Dear Sir, Your most affectionate and most humble Servant

JOHN DICKINSON

PHILADELPHIA, *April* 11th, 1768.

P.S. This is the best made Pensylvania paper I can get.

JOHN DICKINSON TO JAMES OTIS

[*July*, 1768]

MY DEAR SIR, — Hearing of a Vessel sailing for your Port, I inclose To you the Message of Govr. Sharpe to the Assembly of Maryland, with their Answer.[2] I hope they will very quickly come to your Hands and give sincere Pleasure to you and your glorious Fellow-Citizens, by shewing what a wretched Success, the vile attempt of an infamous Administration, to disunite the Colonies, has met with.

I write in a great Hurry. May God almighty prosper all the

[1] Probably the resolutions entered in the *Journals* of the House of Burgesses, April 7, 1768. They provided for an humble and dutiful petition to the King, and a memorial to Parliament, among other things, to "assert with decent Firmness, becoming Freemen, but at the same Time with great Deference to the Wisdom of Parliament, the Rights of the Colonists to be bound by such Laws only, respecting their internal Polity or Taxation, as are consented to by Representatives chosen by themselves; And to represent that we cannot but consider several late Acts of the *British* Legislature, imposing Duties and Taxes to be collected in the Colonies, as an Infringement of those Rights."

[2] *Journals of the Maryland House of Delegates*, June 25, 1768.

Undertakings of Boston, and may her virtue save not only herself, but those miserable deluded people, who are willing to embrace Destruction. I am with inexpressible Affection, Dear Sir, yr humble servt.[1]

Please to inform me, whether it is indisputable, that a Pension has been granted to Govr. Hutchinson, out of the American Revenue. I should be very glad, if it is possible, to have the Words of the Grant.[2]

CATHARINE MACAULAY [3] TO JAMES OTIS

LONDON, *April* 27, 1769.

SIR, — Your patriotic conduct and great Abilities in defence of the rights of your fellow Citizens claim the respect and admiration of every Lover of their Country and Mankind. The principles on which I have written the History of the Stewart Monarchs are I flatter myself in some measure correspondent to those of the great Guardian of American Liberty. To you, Sir, as one of the most distinguished of that Number I offer a Copy of this Work. I beg leave to assure you that every partizan of liberty in this Island simpathizes with their American Brethren: have a strong sense of their Virtues and a tender feeling for their sufferings, and that their is none among us in whom such a disposition is stronger than in myself. I shall be very glad to have the Honour of an ac-

---

[1] The signature has been cut from the original.

[2] It was the intention to defray the salaries of the civil list in America by the proceeds of the Townshend Duties. Thomas Pownall wrote to Hutchinson, from London, September 9, 1767: "However, I may venture to explain to you the first part of his [Duke of Grafton's] letter. It is meant that you shall have a handsome salary fixed as Chief Justice, as soon as the American revenue shall create a fund. I think on that occasion it would be right to solicit a patent from the Crown for that place." A knowledge of the proposed salaries soon reached Massachusetts, and much was made of it in the circular letter of the Legislature to Deberdt in January, 1768. It served a purpose in the hands of the faction when Hutchinson's name came up for re-election to the Governor's Council, as Bernard explained to the Earl of Hillsborough: "In this interval, the two chief heads of the faction (Otis and Adams) told the House that the Lieutenant Governor was a pensioner of Great Britain, and averred that he had a warrant from the Lords of the Treasury for two hundred pounds a year out of the new duties which they were then opposing. This being urged in a manner which left no opportunity or time for refutation or explanation, gave a turn against him, so that, upon the second polling, he had ten votes less than before."

[3] Catharine (Sawbridge) Macaulay, known after her second marriage as Catharine Macaulay Graham (1731–1791). Four volumes of her *History of England from the Accession of James I* had appeared before the date of this letter.

count from your own hand of the present state of American affairs and am, Sir, with high admiration for your Virtues, Your Most Obedient Humble Servant

CATHARINE MACAULAY

When you favour me with an answer if you please to send it to Messieurs Dilly,[1] Bookseller in the Poultry, London, the proprietors of my History of England.

SAMUEL ADAMS TO JAMES WARREN

BOSTON, *March* 25, 1771.

MY DEAR SIR, — I am affraid you have before this time suspected that I have not that warm Affection for you, which I have professed; ungrateful as I may appear to have been, in neglecting to acknowledge the Letter I received from you of the 9 Jan'y. last, I think it is a sufficient apology to say that it was not in my Power to write anything that could please or profit you. I have been waiting for news from England worth informing you of, but in vain till yesterday when a Letter from Dr. Franklin to the Speaker assured us that our Enemies there have at length laid aside the thoughts of vacating our Charter in form;[2] but this can afford no sort of Consolation to us if the people should be disposed to compliment away the *essential* Rights of it as often as a ministerial Minion shall take it in his head to require it.

Your Letter expresses a noble Spirit of Resentment which I cannot but admire; but when you *once* spoke the Language of Despair, allow me to tell you, it gave me offence. Can you think that this Country is to be finally subdued by a man[3] who never possessed real Greatness, etc. and with all his Art could never counterfeit it?

You compare him to Julius Caesar, that publick Executioner of his Countrys Rights: He has, it is true, Caesars Ambition and Lust of Power; but who ever yet suspected that he had Caesars

---

[1] Edward Dilly (1732–1779), said to have been an admirer of the person as well as of the politics of Mrs. Macaulay. He had as a partner in the publishing business, his brother, Charles Dilly (1739–1807).

[2] See *Franklin to Thomas Cushing*, February 5, 1771, in *Writings of Franklin* (Smyth), v. 292.

[3] Thomas Hutchinson.

courage? Recollect the time when he was oblig'd to abandon his Troops, by which he had hoped to awe the People: It was then, if Fancy deceived me not, I observ'd his Knees to tremble. I thought I saw his face grow pale (and I enjoyd the Sight) at the Appearance of the determined Citizens peremptorily demanding the Redress of Grievances. Did he then discover such an intrepid mind, as a man must be possessed of who can reduce a free People to slavery? I confess, we have, as Wolfe expressd it, a Choice of Difficulties; but they rather make one fretful than desperate. If the People are at present hushd into Silence, is it not a sort of sullen Silence, which is far from indicating your Conclusion, that the glorious Spirit of Liberty is vanquishd and left without hope but in miracles. It is the Effect of a *mistaken* Prudence, which springs from Indolence or Cowardice or Hypocricy or I know not what, in those who should point out to them the constitutional Methods of Opposition to arbitrary Power. Too many are affraid to appear for the publick Liberty, and would fain flatter themselves that their Pusilanimity is true Prudence. For the sake of their own Ease or their own Safety, they preach the People into paltry Ideas of Moderation: But in perilous times like these, I cannot conceive of Prudence without Fortitude; and the Man who is not resolvd to encounter and overcome Difficulties when the Liberty of his Country is threatend, no more deserves the Character of a Patriot, than another does that of a Soldier who flies from his Standard.

I expect that many who to gain the popular applause have bore the name of Whigs, will adore the rising Sun: They will fawn and flatter and even lick the Dust of their Masters feet: But you and I acknowledge no *Master;* and I trust there are more than seven Thousand who will scorn to bow the Knee of Servility.

I joyn with you in resolving to persevere with all the little Strength we have and preserve a good Conscience: It is no Dishonor to be in a minority in the Cause of Liberty and Virtue: When the Multitude desert that Cause, we will look down upon them with all that Contempt, which our Caesar has been wont to cast upon them when they were virtuous and free. *Magna est Veritas et praevalebit.* Our Sons, if they deserve it, will enjoy the happy Fruits of their Fathers Struggles.

The horrid Massacre of the 5th of March, 1770, is to be commemorated on Tuesday the 2 of April next, by an Oration to be deliverd at Faneuil Hall by Mr. James Lovel.[1]

Mrs. Adams joyns in Compliment to Mrs. Warren. I am sincerely Your Friend,

SAM ADAMS

SAMUEL ADAMS TO JAMES WARREN

BOSTON, *April* 13, 1772

MY DEAR SIR, — I had the pleasure of receiving your Letter of the 4th Instant.

The Session began with a motion made by a friend of mine, that a Message go up to the Govr to pray him that in Consideration of the many *Inconveniences* that attend the sitting of the Court at Cambridge, he would be pleasd to remove it to its *ancient usual* and only *convenient* Seat, the Court house in Boston. This we opposd with firmness as tacitly giving up our own main principles. There were 57 members and we obtain a Majority against the Question of Nine Members including myself who acted as Moderator, Mr. Speaker Cushing being absent.[2] The other particulars together with the Speech and Answer you will see in the inclosd paper. The Tories I believe are greatly disconcerted, as I hope they always will be.

I am much obligd for your Care in procurng for me a Boy. I shall be ready to receive him about the middle of next month and shall take the best care of him that shall be in my Power till he is 14 years old, perfecting him in his reading and teaching him to write and cypher if capable of it under my own Tuition for I cannot spare him the time to attend School. Will strictly regard his Morals and at the End of the time I will if his parents shall desire it, seek a good place for him to learn such a Trade as he and they shall chuse.

[1] Then Usher of the Grammar-School. This oration, the first of a series of commemoration addresses, was printed in a quarto, with appropriate mourning borders, by order of the Town of Boston.

[2] The motion is printed in the *Journals*, April 8, 1772, but the name of the mover is not given.

My dear Mrs Adams [1] joyns with me in expressing the sincerest thanks to Mrs Warren for her kind Letter of Condolence. To mingle Sorrows is the part of a friend *only*. Those who are not possessd of the inextinguishable Principle of *real* friendship are Strangers to the pleasure of sharing in Affliction. What is Life without Friendship! To partake in the Joys of the rude World is often dangerous but seldom satisfactory. The Tears of sincere friendship are refreshing like gentle Showers after a scorching Drought and always produce the harvest of solid Comfort.[2]

I write in great haste. Hope to see you soon your affectionate friend,

SAMUEL ADAMS

SAMUEL ADAMS TO JAMES WARREN

BOSTON, *November* 4, 1772

MY DEAR SIR, — I have not at present time or Inclination to take up your thots in complaining of Tyrants and Tyranny. It is more than Time that this Country was rid of both. Your Colleague and the Newspapers will inform you of the Transactions of this Town at a late Meeting,[3] and your opinion of Hutchinson, if it is necessary, may be confirmd. The Town thought it proper to take, what the Tories apprehend to be *leading Steps*. We have long had it thrown in our faces, that the Country in general is under no such fears of Slavery, but are well pleasd with the measures of Administration, that the Independency of the Governor and Judges is a mighty harmless and even a desireable Manoeuvre. In order to ascertain the Sense of the People of the province a Committee is appointed, of which our Patriot Otis is Chairman,[4] to open a free

---

[1] Elizabeth Wells (1736–1806).

[2] Hannah Winthrop wrote to Mercy Warren, June 22, 1772, "I think it surprising that Candidates for another state and even those dignified with high stations and vested with power can be willing to be so blinded by ambition and love of domination as to give up the heartfelt satisfaction of making happy, and losing the esteem of their fellow men. The General Court is indeed carried to Boston but done with so ill a grace as entirely destroys all the Merit of it."

[3] The meeting was held October 28, and the proceedings are given in the *Boston Gazette*, November 2, 1772.

[4] The committee consisted of twenty-one persons. A notice was issued as a handbill of a town meeting to be held November 20.

Communication with every town. A State of Rights with the violation of them is to be reported by this Committee, and transmitted to each Town. I wish our Mother Plymouth would see her way clear to have a Meeting and second Boston by appointing a Committee of Communication and Correspondence. The sooner this is done, I think, the better.[1] I have receivd Letters from Marblehead, Newburyport, etc. fraught with manly Resentment. Whenever the friends of the Country shall be assured of each others *Sentiments*, that Spirit which is necessary will not be wanting. I have scribbled in great haste and am without Ceremony. Your friend,

SAML ADAMS

Pray write me by the first opportunity.

SAMUEL ADAMS TO JAMES WARREN

BOSTON, *Nov.* 27, 1772

MY DEAR SIR, — I herewith inclose you a printed Copy, as far as it is workd off, of the Proceedings of this Town. The Selectmen of Plymouth will have it sent to them as soon as the Printers can finish it. The Tories are taking all imaginable Pains, to disparage it in the Minds of the other Towns. I am under no apprehensions with Regard to Plymouth. The Copy of your Petition was very acceptable to me; I have publishd it in three of our Papers, and the Friends of Liberty are highly pleasd with the Spirit of it. I am very desirous of knowing the consequent Proceedings of the Town though I doubt not but you have acted your part well. There is a Peice in Drapers paper under the Signature I. H.[2] said to be wrote

---

[1] A petition for a meeting, signed by a hundred of the reputable inhabitants of Plymouth, was presented to the selectmen on November 13, 1772. The meeting was not held until November 24, when a standing committee of communication, with James Warren as chairman, was named. The petition will be found in the *Boston Evening Post*, November 23, 1772.

[2] Printed in the *Massachusetts Gazette*, November 26, 1772. It is dated H-ng-m, Nov. 24, 1772, and contains the following reference to Plymouth: "I expect some of your writers will say that a doting old Fellow has published what he supposes to be the Mind of one Tory Town only, and that the country in general and his neighbouring Town of Plymouth in particular is of another mind. But it is a mistake, Mr. Draper, for as for the Town of Plymouth, I know many of the best Men in Plymouth who never would sign their Petition for a Town-Meeting; and if I was to speak my Mind I should say it was handed to them from a Town forty Miles off by a certain Creed-maker, who I hear drew up the circular Let-

in Hingham; If I could believe this, I should think it was the genuine Production of Deacon H—y's Genius, it is much like the Rant which you and I have heard. I rather think however it was *"fabricated"* in the Cabal. You are particularly interested, in behalf of your Town, to take Notice of it. The same paper impudently "reports" that there were not twenty men at the Town meeting besides the Selectmen and some of the Committee when the Letter was passed, which you may rely upon to be false, as hundreds who were present can testify.[1] You know the Tories have a "scurvy trick of lying" to serve the Purposes of Despotism. The Town of Roxbury have appointed a Committee of Nine to take into Consideration the proceedings of this Town, five of this Committee are said to be Whigs, on the other side are Isaac Winslow[2] and the Mr. Mayo,[3] who was foreman of the Grand Jury who cleard the Soldiers, and afterwards was advanced to the Rank of Major of the Regiment, though our Friend Heath (who is of this Committee) thought himself, and in the Opinion of Major Genl. Brattle[4] was, degraded thereby. Cap. Heath[5] bids me expect that matters will go right at the adjournment of their Meeting. On his Zeal and Integrity as well as good Sense you know we may rely. I hear that Marblehead is to have a Meeting next Week.[6] I have received favorable accounts from our worthy friend Mr. Gerry,[7] and hope for good Tidings from thence.

ter that is to be sent from the Metropolis to all the Towns in the Province. And I am well informed that nothing is like to be acted in any of the Towns below Plymouth relative to those Matters." A reply from Plymouth was printed in the *Boston Gazette*, December 21, 1772.

1 "It is reported with some Confidence, that when the Vote passed for sending the Letter of Correspondence, which was about ten o'clock Friday Evening, there was not twenty Men present, beside the Gentlemen Selectmen and some of the Committee, and that not Ten Persons voted for it. The country ought to be satisfied whether the Report be true or false." In the *Gazette* of December 7 is a reply signed by six Selectmen asserting that "there was a very respectable number of the inhabitants, who attended the meeting through the day; and when the letter, which had been twice read and amended in the meeting, was accepted and voted to be sent, it appeared to us, and we are well satisfied, that there were not less than three hundred inhabitants present, and in the opinion of others the number was much larger." See also "Candidus" in the *Gazette* of December 14, 1772.

2 (1709–).   3 Joseph Mayo, of Roxbury.
4 William Brattle (1706–).
5 William Heath, afterwards Major-General. He was now the representative of Roxbury in the General Assembly.
6 The meeting was held on December 8, and the resolutions are printed in the *Boston Gazette*, December 14, 1772.
7 Elbridge Gerry.

My dear Sir, we must exert ourselves to awaken our Country men to a Sense of the danger they are in of immediate and perhaps irrecoverable Ruin. Every kind of Opiate is administerd daily which our Enemies can invent. If the Old Colony fails, I shall be apprehensive indeed; but I will not entertain the Thought while Coll. Warren and others, tho' few, remain in it. I have wrote in great Haste and must now conclude. Yours,

SAML ADAMS

Pray write by the first Opportunity.

SAMUEL ADAMS TO JAMES WARREN

BOSTON, *Decr* 9, 1772

MY DEAR SIR, — I had the pleasure of receiving your Letter of yesterday date, this Morning, by the Hands of our Friend, Mr. Lothrop. Am much obligd to you for the pains you took in distributing the Letters sent to your Care. I am very sorry to find in your Letter anything that discovers in you the least approach towards Despair. *Nil desperandum.* That is a Motto for you and me. All are not dead; and where there is a Spark of patriotick fire, *we* will enkindle it. Say you, that the Tories spare no pains to disparage our Measures? I knew they would, and should have greatly doubted of the Importance of the Measures if they had not been much nettled.

The Sachem of Chesemuttock is a Bastard, and has none of the Blood of his ancient Predecessors running in his Veins, he is pitifull, contemptible. I am glad your promising young Genius has undertaken to chastize the Hingham Writer,[1] though I could wish he had a fitter Subject to employ his pen. Who knows but he may rise to be one day, under God, the Savior of his Country. You "wish that our Measures would take a general Run." So do I; and I believe they will. Could you think that Lancaster would fall in with them? If they should, what Prospects would you not entertain of other Towns? I have a verbal Message from a sensible Whig there, that he expected they would act with Spirit, and that even the Tories there exclaim against the Independency of the Judges.

[1] He signed "From a Lover of Truth and his Country."

The Selectmen of Medford have unanimously agreed to call a Meeting of their Town. Charlestown have met, and appointed a Committee to consider the Independency, and report *three Weeks* hence.[1] Our Pamphlet was read and upon the Motion of your *Cousin*, the Consideration of it was referrd till March Meeting! I expect every Moment to hear from Marblehead; they had their Meeting the day before yesterday; it is reported that they have appointed a Committee to write to ours, after the good Example of Plymouth, and that Coll. Orne [2] and Mr. Gerry are of the Committee, two Gentlemen whose good Sense and Integrity as well as firmness I think may be much relyed upon. Roxbury I have Reason to hope will terminate Matters well at their Adjournment next Monday. There has been no Dissension among the friends of the Cause here. *None* between my Brother Otis and myself. It is likely this is one of the Tory Lies at Plymouth. It may arise from some of the Whigs refusing when nominated to be of our Committee; but I believe most of them were then unaware of the evil Tendency of their Conduct. Mr. Cushing has frequently met with the Committee, and appears to be hearty in forwarding the Measure. I am informd that your *own* Minister refused, when desired, to read the Letter of this Town; You will excuse me if I whisper in your Ear, that in my opinion it would have done as much Good as one of *his* Sermons, the Benefit of which however you would not have been deprived of.

The Tories are determined to play a poor hand to the best Advantage; they are therefore for instructing the Representatives to prevent the Independency of the Judges taking place; but it must be done by enlarging their Salaries, which would be a tacit acknowledgment of a Right in the Crown and making a mean Bargain. This Manoeuvre in my Opinion is most to be apprehended. I rest with Esteem Yours affectionately

S. ADAMS

1 See Frothingham, *History of Charlestown*, 286.   2 Azor Orne.

HANNAH WINTHROP[1] TO MERCY WARREN

Jany 4, 1773

DEAR MRS. WARREN, — Your kind Favor of Novr 13 was truly animating. That noble patriotic spirit which sparkles thro your agreeable Letter must certainly warm the heart that has the least Sensibilities, especially must it invigorate a mind Possest of a like Fellow feeling for this once happy Country. But as my mind is too often apt to harbor gloomy Ideas I very much Fear whether the last Noble exertion of those truly Patriotic Spirits who have formed a newly established Correspondence will meet with the desird Success. What a spirit of contradiction and Toryism do we see prevailing! how often do we see people blind to their own interests Precipitately madding on to their own destruction.

I think one of the most extraordinary Political Maneuvers this Century has produced is the Ministerial Mandate to the Newportians for transporting them a thousand Leagues for Trial. O America you have reason to tremble and arouse if we of this side of the Atlantic are not able to say to this Royal Vengeance, hitherto shalt thou go and no further, here shall thy proud Waves be stayd. I should rejoice to see the Plymothean Spirit prevail which discovers such a Noble disinterested Virtue and such a sacred regard to rights purchasd at the expence of every thing Valuable by those persevering Self denying Patriarchs who if permitted to be Spectators of these Terrestrial Scenes must view those of their Sons who set so little Value upon the dear bought purchases with displeasure. Many are waiting impatiently the meeting of our Assembly earnestly wishing they may be endued with that Spirit of True Liberty and independance which they have discoverd on former Occasions. I hope Coll. Warren wont fail of favoring his Country with his presence at that important Crisis where every eye will be upon our Political Fathers. . . .

---

[1] Hannah Fayerweather, widow of Farr Tolman of Boston. She was Prof. John Winthrop's second wife.

HANNAH WINTHROP TO MERCY WARREN

CAMBRIDGE, *April* 12, 1773

. . . .
I must now give you joy on the diffusion of that noble Spirit of Liberty we have Lately seen exhibited. Our house of Commons deserve immortal Praise. What a disinterested Largeness of Soul have they Shown. How happy the heart that has never opened itself to the Flattering allurements of Ambition! that heart must feel the Divine pleasure of communicating happiness to Posterity. Free from the ignoble Satisfaction of aggrandising its little self such heavenly Beneficence which extends its Views must be the true Source of Felicity. I heartily wish a Perseverance in the Blissful path and may every Avaritious Despot who aims at grasping all the good things with which heaven meant to Bless Mankind be made sensible he is not the only Figure of importance in the Creation.

I have not been to the Capital for more than three months. I suppose when I make my appearance I shall look not unlike one of the last Century, at least like one unacquainted with Polite Life, the encreasing dissipation the round of Elegant amusements which are become the work of every Evening have not those Attractive Charms for you and myself. Neither are we calld to support under the intolerable dissapointment of not shining at a Concert or a Ball by reason of the rude Season nor the mortifying loss of a Morgan Lecture on Buffoonery. What a different circle do we tread? immured in the Country and yet happy perhaps in contemplating the Lives of those who walkd the stage before us or perhaps improving our Ideas by the rational Conversation of our Dear Preceptors. Mine joyns me in the highest Esteem and best Compliments to you and yours and hope to have the pleasure of a Visit from you before long. As the Assembly were deprivd of Coll Warren's presence and assistance the last Session I hope at the important election he will be able to give his Personal Attendance. After my kind love to the little boys you will give me Leave to subscribe Yours Affectionately

HANNAH WINTHROP

ABIGAIL ADAMS TO MERCY WARREN

BOSTON *December* 5 1773

MY DEAR MRS WARREN, —

. . . .

You, Madam, are so sincere a Lover of your Country, and so Hearty a Mourner in all her Misfortunes that it will greatly aggravate your anxiety to hear how much she is now oppressed and insulted. To you who have so thoroughly looked thro the Deeds of Men, and Develloped the Dark designs of a Rapatio [1] Soul.

No action however base or sordid, no measure however Cruel and Villanous will be matter of any Surprize.

The Tea that bainfull weed is arrived. Great and I hope effectual opposition has been made to the landing of it. To the publick papers I must refer you for particulars. You will there find that the proceedings of our Citizens have been united spirited and firm. The flame is kindled and like lightning it catches from Soul to Soul. Great will be the devastation if not timely quenched or allayed by some more Lenient Measures.

Altho the mind is Shocked at the thought of Sheding Humane Blood, more especially the Blood of our Countrymen and a civil war is of all wars the most dreadfull, Such is the present spirit that prevails, that if once they are made desperate Many, very Many of our Heroes will Spend their lives in the cause with the Speach of Cato in their Mouths "what a pitty it is, that we can dye but once to save our Country."

"Tender plants must bend but when a Government is grown to strength like some old oak rough with its armed bark it yealds not to the tug but only Nods and turns to Sullen State."

Such is the present Situation of affairs that I tremble when I think what may be the direfull consequences. And in this Town must the Scene of action lay, my Heart beats at every Whistle I hear and I dare not openly express half my fears. Eternal Reproach and Ignominy be the portion of all those who have been instrumental in bringing these fears upon me. There has a Report pre-

---

[1] Rapatio is the name given by Mrs. Warren to Hutchinson in her play of "The Adulateur," printed at Boston in 1773.

vaild that tomorrow there will be an attempt to land this weed of Slavery. I will then write further till then my worthy friend adieu.

December 11

Since I wrote the above a whole week has elapsed and nothing new occurred concerning the tea. Having met with no opportunity of sending this I shall trespass further upon your patience. I send with this the 1 volm of Molière and should be glad of your oppinion of them. I cannot be brought to like them. It seems to me to be a general want of Spirit, at the close of every one I have felt disappointed. There are no characters but what appear unfinished and he seems to have ridiculed vice without engageing us to Virtue; and tho he sometimes makes us laugh, yet tis a Smile of indignation. There is one Negative Virtue of which he is possess'd, I mean that of Decency. His Cit, turnd Gentleman, among many other has met with approbation. Tho I can readily acknowledge that the cit by acting so contrary to his real character has displayed a stupid vanity justly deserving ridicule, yet the fine Gentleman who defrauds and tricks him is as much the baser character as his advantages are superior to the others. Molière is said to have been an Honest Man, but Sure he has not coppied from his own Heart. Tho he has drawn many pictures of real life, yet all pictures of life are not fit to be exibited upon the Stage. I fear I shall incur the charge of vanity by thus criticising upon an author who has met with so much applause. You, Madam, I hope will forgive me. I should not have done it if we had not conversd about it before. Your judgment will have great weight with your Sincere Friend [1]

ABIGAIL ADAMS

SAMUEL ADAMS TO JAMES WARREN

BOSTON, *Decr* 28, 1773

MY DEAR SIR, — I had the pleasure of receiving your Letter of the 16th Instant, but not till Eleven Days after it was written. The pressing Invitation you have repeatedly given me, to your

[1] Letters from John Adams to James Warren, December 17 and 22, 1773, in this collection, are printed in *Life and Works of John Adams*, IX. 333, 334.

annual Festivity, is very obliging. My Heart was much set upon it; and I had prepared to go, with one of my Neighbors, a very worthy Man, but was the Evening before prevented, not to say forbid, by some of our Common Friends. You are sensible that I am the Servant of all.

It is a great Consolation to find, that our Friends in the Country approve of the Conduct of this and the Neighboring Towns at the late Meetings. We are assured of this by the Letters we almost daily receive. I think we have put our Enemies in the wrong; and they must in the Judgment of rational Men, be answerable for the Destruction of the Tea, which their own Obstinacy had rendered necessary. Notwithstanding what your Tories have given out, the People here are universally pleas'd, excepting the disconcerted Hutchinson and his few, very few Adherents.

The Plymouth Letter and Resolves are highly applauded by all the Friends of Liberty.[1] The Protest,[2] as you will of Course easily perceive, is the subject of Contempt. One of the Signers has already cryed, peccavi! and publishd his Recantation; and between you and me, if the others whom they have pressd, or rather coaxd into their Service, have no more to say for themselves than it seems he has, the Party have Nothing to boast of.

We had yesterday the Return of Mr Revere who at the Request of the Committee of Correspondence carried the important News of the Fate of the Tea to New York. By him we are informed, that a Tea Ship with 270 Chests had arrived at Charlestown, South Carolina. The Inhabitants were determined she should return with her detested Cargo. Before the Arrival of this and the News from Boston, the Citizens of New York had got to be divided; many of them being for storing the Tea. But immediately they became united and determined that it should not be landed; and Governor Tryon made a Virtue of Necessity and promisd that it should be sent (when it arrivd) directly back to London. This will operate much against Hutchinson; who, I think, in every part of his Conduct, discovers the Want of those Abilities, which his too liberal Countrymen have supposd him to have. The Ministry

---

[1] See *Massachusetts Gazette*, December 20, 1773.
[2] *Ib.*, December 27. It was presented by Edward Winslow.

could not have devisd a more effectual Measure to unite the Colonies. Our Committee have on this Occasion, opend a Correspondence with the three New England Colonies, besides New York and Philadelphia. Old Jealousies are removed, and perfect Harmony subsists between them. The Committee of the House seems to be the only inactive Body. I am sorry to say it, tho to you only.

The General Assembly, I am informd will meet on the 26th of next month. There is much to be done by the House and much will be done, if Timidity does not prevent it. You must not fail, with Mr. Lothrop[1] to attend. The Cause will suffer by your Absence. The House will forfeit their Honor and the Confidence of the virtuous Part of their Constituents, if they do not conduct the Affair of the Judges in particular, with *Dignity*.

I must recommend your retracting Townsman to your Favor. I dare say you can furnish us with some Anecdotes, respecting the Protest. I hear that many Towns in the Country are calling Meetings. The Instituting Committees of Correspondence will as you predicted be attended with great and good Consequences. I conclude in haste, with due Regards to Mr. Lothrop and other honest Men. Your assured friend,

S. ADAMS

We are concernd that we hear nothing of the Tea at Cape Cod. It is thought by some of our friends in London, that our Petition against the great Delinquents will not be brot to a Hearing unless they desire it, but that they will be removed, that Lord Dartmouth will resign and Weymouth succeed him.

JOHN ADAMS TO MERCY WARREN

BRAINTREE *Jan* 3 1774

MADAM, — I remember that Bishop Burnet in a letter he once wrote to Lady Rachell Russell, the virtuous Daughter of the great Southampton, and unfortunate wife of Lord Russell who died a Martyr to English Liberties, says, "Madam I never attempt to write to you but my Pen conscious of its Inferiority falls out of my Hand." The polite Prelate did not write to that excellent Lady in

1 Isaac Lothrop.

so bold a figure with half the Sincerity that I could apply it to myself when writing to Mrs. Warren.

I will however strive to grasp my Pen hard enough to write one Line in answer to her kind Billet [of] December 30.

Mr. Adams assures Mrs. Warren, that nothing would have given him greater Pleasure than a Visit to Plymouth at the late Anniversary, but it was out of his Power. He thanks Mr. and Mrs. Warren however most heartily for their very kind and repeated Invitations. He shall think himself happy if he can find an opportunity, before the Month of May to make a Visit to his Friends at Plymouth, but it has been his Misfortune to have been so often and so long absent from home for these twelve months past, that he really thinks his Duty to his family oblige him to leave it as little as possible.

Mrs. Warren is pleased to mention Mr. Adams's "needfull application to public, and his close Attention to private Business." His private Business, Madam, has been totally annihilated these twelve months past and more by the inauspicious course of public affairs, and he has no kind of Prospect of its ever coming into Existence again. He has therefore, learnt the important Lesson of Resignation to what he cannot alter and should be very happy the remainder of his Days to get his Bread by his Labour and Attention to a Farm. He thinks he could shine as an industrious Farmer, but he is too old to make a Figure in Arms the Profession to which we must for the future perhaps be obliged for our Safety and our Liberty as much as formerly we were to that of the Law. If the Standards should be erected and a Camp formed, however, ten to one but he flies to it, but whether it will be for Shelter or as a Volunteer, Time alone must discover.

He thanks Mrs. Warren most kindly for her friendly Wishes for his Peace, Health, and Prosperity, and especially, when she wishes that he may return Laden with the Applauses of his Country, but most of all when she wishes he may return with a self approving Mind. Of the last he is sure, if plain, direct, simple and sincere Intentions to do what the cause of Truth, Justice Liberty and Humanity according to his Conceptions require of him, at whatever Hazard it may be can insure it, and as long as he shall act upon these Principles he does not doubt of enjoying that sweetest Music to an honest Ear the approbation of his Country, for this is seldom refused to Integrity of Heart, how inconsiderable soever the abilities that direct it. I am, Madam, with more esteem than I have Power or Words to express your Friend and Servt

JOHN ADAMS

JAMES WARREN TO JOHN ADAMS.[1] ADAMS MSS.

PLYMOUTH, *January* the 3d, 1774

DEAR SIR, — I received your last,[2] and am to acknowledge that the Contents of it gave me great pleasure. Have for some time thought it necessary that the People should strike some bold stroke, and try the Issue. They have long enough submitted to Oppressions and Insults following one another in a rapid Succession without finding any Advantage. They have now indeed passed the River, and left no Retreat, and must therefore abide the Consequences. What those will be seems to be the great matter of Speculation, and as People are determined by Reason, or by the frightful List of Scarecrows and Bug bears (mentioned in your last, and which are employed on this Occasion) their speculations will differ. As your Judgment will be regulated by the first I should be glad to hear it. I think the Ministry have one way at least to avoid the necessity of advancing or retreating at this time, and that is by laying the Blame of the whole on their own, and East India Company's Officers, which have drove the People to this desperate step, and this Justice and Truth (Company they have not been used to) will countenance them in. In what proportion this Blame is to be laid to each may be adjusted among them, and if they quarrel in the settlement of that matter, we may avail ourselves of the old Proverb. I admire Doane's reasoning, and if he was not assisted by the Author of the Letter in the Methodical Arraignment of his Propositions I think he reasoned better on this, than any other Occasion. I made good use of your Letter without mentioning the Author's Name, to encounter the Tory Bugbears

[1] At Boston. "Per favour of Mr. Crosswell."
[2] Letter of December 17, 1773. Printed in *Life and Works of John Adams*, IX. 333.

and allay the frightful Apprehensions they had raised in some minds, otherwise firm. I congratulate you on the Union of Sentiment and Spirit prevailing through the Continent, which makes even our Tory Protestors hang their Ears, and may in Time affect the obdurate Heart and inveterate Resolution of H[utchinso]n himself, especially when he finds himself forsaken by a Tryon. The recantation made in Boston by one of our Protestors has sickned some others. Divers of them intending to Boston last week are still at home. I am inclined to think many or several others here will follow his Example, tho' great Pains are taken to prevent it. . . .[1]

Samuel Adams to James Warren

BOSTON, *March* 31, 1774

MY DEAR SIR, — I have for some time past been waiting for the arrival of a Ship from London, that I might have some thing of Importance to communicate to you. No Ship has yet arrivd. I cannot however omit writing to you by our worthy Friend Mr. Watson, by whom I receivd your obliging Letter of the 27 Instant. Although we have had no Arrival from London directly to this Place, we have heard from thence by the Way of Philadelphia as you have doubtless observd in the Newspapers. The account they first received of our Opposition to the East India Act as it is called, particularly the Transactions at Liberty Tree, they treated with Sneer and Ridicule, but when they heard of the Resolves of the Body of the People at the Old South Meeting house the Place from whence the Orders issued for the Removal of the Troops from this Town in 1770, they put on grave Countenances. No Notice is taken of America in the King's Speech. Our Tories, as you observe, tell us to expect Regiments to be quartered among us. What Measures an injudicious Ministry, (to say the least of them) will take cannot easily at present be foreseen, it will be wise for us to be ready *for all Events*, that we may make the *best Improvement* of them. It is probable that Mr. Hutchinson will make the Death of

---

[1] A letter from Samuel Adams to James Warren, January 10, 1774, in this collection, is printed in 1 *Mass. Hist. Soc. Proceedings*, XIII. 205.

his Brother Oliver[1] a plea for postponing a Voyage to London, and if troops should arrive *it may be best that he should be* [absent]. I never suffer my Mind to be overmuch [*cut*] prospects. Sufficient for the Day is the Evil thereof. It is our Duty at all Hazards to preserve the Publick Liberty. Righteous Heaven will graciously smile on every manly and rational Attempt to secure that best of all his Gifts to Man from the ravishing hand of lawless and brutal Power.

Mr. Watson will inform you what Steps our Committee of Correspondence have taken with Regard to the Establishment of a Post Office upon constitutional Principles. Mr. Goddard[2] who brought us Letters from New York, Newport and Providence relating to that Subject, is gone with Letters from us on the same Subject to the principal trading Towns as far as Portsmouth. I will acquaint you with the state of the Affair when he returns, and our Committee will, I doubt not, then write to yours. The Colonies must unite to carry through such a Project, and when the End is effected it will be a pretty grand Acquisition.

I refer you also to Mr. Watson, who can inform you respecting one of your Protesters who has been in Town. The Tryumph of your Tories as well as ours I hope is short. We must not however boast as he that putteth off the Harness. H[utchinso]n is politically sick and I fancy despairs of returning Health. The "lack-learning" Judge[3] I am told is in the Horrors, and the late Lieutenant[1] (joynt Author of a late Pamphlet intitled *Letters* etc.[4]) a few Weeks ago "died and was buried." Excuse me from enlarging at Present. I intend to convince you that I am "certainly a Man of my Word." In the Mean time with assurance of unfeigned Friendship for Mrs. Warren and your agreeable Family in which Mrs. Adams joyns me, I remain Yours Affectionately

S. ADAMS

1 Andrew Oliver, lieutenant governor, died March 3, 1774.
2 William Goddard (1740–1817), who made a petition on the subject to the Continental Congress, October 5, 1774.
3 Peter Oliver (1713–1791), a brother of Andrew.
4 His letters, with those of Hutchinson and others, had been sent over from London by Franklin, and published in Boston.

SAMUEL ADAMS TO JAMES WARREN

MY DEAR SIR, — I beseech you to implore every Friend in Boston by every thing dear and sacred to Men of Sense and Virtue to avoid Blood and Tumult. They will have time enough to dye. Let them *give the other Provinces opportunity to think and resolve.* Rash Spirits that would by their Impetuosity involve us in unsurmountable Difficulties will be left to perish by themselves despisd by their Enemies, and almost detested by their Friends.

Nothing can ruin us but our Violence. Reason teaches this. I have indubitable Intelligence, *dreadful*, as to the *Designs* against us; *consolatory*, if we are but *prudent*.

These are the Sentiments of a man, who, you know, my dear Sir, loves the People of Boston and that Government, with the Tenderness of a Brother. I am your affectionate Friend.

[*No signature.*]

PHILADA, *May* 21, 1774.

JAMES WARREN TO JOHN ADAMS.   ADAMS MSS.

PLYMOUTH, *July* the 14th, 1774

DEAR SIR, — Yours of the 25th of last month [1] never reached me till yesterday. It would have given me great pleasure to have seen you when I returned from Salem,[2] and I was really greatly disappointed to find you and Family gone, and more especially as I was apprehensive I should have no other Opportunity of seeing you, till the Time called for your Attendance at the Grand Council of America,[3] an Assembly in my Opinion of as great Dignity and Importance as any, either ancient or modern, that ever met. However, as I am deprived of the pleasure of seeing you, I shall sincerely wish and pray, that your satisfaction and pleasure on this Journey may fully equal the Honour of being a Member of so august a Body. Which is in Effect wishing that you may conduct Matters in a way the most Honorable to yourselves, and advan-

---

1 Printed in *Life and Works of John Adams*, IX. 338.
2 Where the General Court had assembled, June 7.
3 The first Continental Congress.

tageous to the publick. Great are our Expectations, and great will be the Expectations in Europe; and therefore great and difficult is the Task assigned you. With these Sentiments my Friendship to you had no Interest in your Appointment further than to promote your Honour. My Friendship to my Country engaged me to it, and when I knew it was at the Expence of your Ease, and so well satisfied am I with the Major Part of our Committee,[1] and such Expectations have I from the Zeal and firmness of the other Colonies in this measure, that I have not given myself the Trouble to think much about the measures they will take. I presume the greater part of you will be Masters, learned in politicks and the true Interest of your Country, not Scholars yet to learn them. Prophets replete with the true Spirit of Prophecy, and Statesmen both wise and upright. From you therefore we shall look for streams that shall gladden all the Cities and Towns in North America, and confound the barbarous Politicks of Britain. With these Sentiments of your Body, it certainly would be presumtion in me, to advise to measures, or conduct. However to a Friend I will venture to say, I apprehend much greater danger from the Timidity and narrow Plans of some of your Body, than I do from the Spirit and enlarged views of the rest of you. My Opinion is, that the Confidence of the People in the Congress is such that they will support whatever Plan you adopt, however spirited, and be in danger of resting satisfied with the Terms you may be contented with, however inadequate to their rights and Interests. And besides Administration be from the first more encouraged to go on with their System than provoked by the last. That we have nothing to expect from their Justice, but every thing to hope from their fears, is a maxim as true, and perhaps as wise as any of Solomon! Therefore if I was enquired of, what I thought should be done with the Claim of Exemption from Parliamentary Legislation, as well as Taxation, and some other Grand Questions that have been agitated here, I should answer that it was proper, practicable, expedient, wise, just, good, and necessary, that they should be held up in

[1] The Delegation to the Congress from Massachusetts consisted of Thomas Cushing, Samuel Adams, John Adams and Robert Treat Paine. Bowdoin was named, but declined to serve. The credentials speak of them as "a committee."

their full extent in the Congress at Philadelphia, and that means should be devised to support them.

To determine on an annual Congress I think very important, both for the purpose of depressing the Scheems of our Enemies and raising the Spirits and promoting the Interest of our Friends.[1] A Rotation I am very fond of in most Cases, but in this at present should be for confining it only to a new election annually. A scarcity of men fit to govern such mighty Interests clashing in the present Contests, is a sufficient Objection to a further Limitation, and that reason will likewise prevail to alter your determination not to engage in politicks on any other System. The want of Gratitude in Mankind, their little Attention to their true Interest, and the consequent Fate of many of their friends, are really disagreeable reflections. But if Brutus and Cassius, Hampden, Sydney, Harrington, etc. had lived in inglorious Ease, they might have died in a few months after, in languishing and painful Sickness, without Fame, without the Applause of the vertuous of all ages. I have strong faith that the now rough and perilous paths of politicks will soon be smoothed, and that our sons may walk in them without danger, especially if we submit the Instruction of them to our two Friends[2] you mention, who will certainly form them to Vertue, and establish that Integrity that will secure them at least good Consciences. The Cause of Liberty, Truth and Vertue, must be supported, and in the present degenerate Situation of Mankind, that must be done by the few, even under the mortifying Circumstances of seeing the many who reap the Benefit attentive to private matters, and enriching themselves and families, even at the Expence of their Friends. And I presume you will never fail to be among the few, at a time when your Character, Circumstances, and Education, etc conspire to call you out. . . .

[Mrs. Warren adds:]

Though Mr. Adams has condescended to ask my sentiments in conjunction with those of a person qualified (by his integrity and attachment to the interest of his Country) to advise if it were

[1] "I am for making it annual, and for sending an entire new set every year, that all the principal geniuses may go to the university in rotation, that we may have politicians in plenty." *John Adams to Warren*, June 25, 1774.

[2] Mrs. Adams and Mrs. Warren.

needful at this important Crisis, I shall not be so presumtuous as to offer anything but my fervent Wishes that the Enemies of America may hereafter forever tremble at the Wisdom, the firmness, the prudence and the justice of the Delegates, departed from our Cities, as much as ever the Phocians or any other petty State did at the power of the Amphytiones. . . .

JOHN ADAMS TO JAMES WARREN

BRAINTREE, *July* 17, 1774

DEAR SIR, — Among many other agreeable Things which occurr'd to me on my Return from my eastern Circuit, I found your Letter of the fourteenth Instant. Your sentiments always inspire and animate me; but never more upon any Occasion, than on this. I believe with you that the Confidence of the People in the Congress, is so great, that they will Support its Decisions, as far as possible. And indeed, It may well be expected, that many Men of Sound Judgment, will be of that Assembly. But, what avails, Prudence, Wisdom, Policy, Fortitude, Integrity, without Power, without Legions? When Demosthenes, (God forgive the Vanity of recollecting his Example) went Ambassador from Athens to the other States of Greece, to excite a Confederacy against Phillip, he did not go to propose a Non-Importation or Non-Consumption Agreement ! ! !

You "presume the greater Part of the Number will be Masters in Politicks" "Prophets replete with the true Spirit of Prophecy." I hope it will be so. But I must say I am not one of those Masters. I must be a scholar. I feel my own insufficiency for this important Business. I confess myself ignorant of the Characters which compose the Court of Great Britain as well as of the People who compose the Nation; at least I have not that minute and accurate knowledge of either which an American Senator ought to have of both. I have not that Knowledge of the Commerce of the several Colonies, nor even of my own Province which may be necessary.

In short, as comprehensive Knowledge of Arts and Sciences, especially of Law and History, of Geography, Commerce, War and of Life, is necessary for an American Statesman at this Time as was ever necessary for a British or a Roman Senator, or a British or Roman General.

Our New England Educations are quite unequal to the Production of such great Characters.

There is one Point in which most Men seem to be agreed viz — that it is in our Power so to distress the Commercial and Manufacturing Interests in G. Britain, as to make them rise up and become importunate Petitioners for us, to the King, Parliament and Ministry. But others deny this. Some of the higher Tories say that all we can do of this Kind will be despised — ridiculed — and that they can live longer without us than We can without them. That the distresses We can occasion would be of but a few Individuals, and the Clamours or Miseries of these will be disregarded as Trifling Considerations in Comparison of the Loss of the Obedience of the Colonies, etc., etc., etc.

That nothing Short of such Distresses as should produce Convulsions would effect any Thing at all.

However I have no Faith in these Doctrines. The National Debts and Taxes are so excessive, that it seems to me impossible, the People should bear the Loss of so great a Part of their Trade.

But what do you think of a non-Exportation to Great Britain? Is it expedient to advise to a general Non-Exportation? Will not Such a Measure hurt ourselves? What will be the Consequence? Must not Fish, Rice, Wheat, Tobacco, etc. etc. etc. perish on our Hands, or must not Thousands of Families perish who once lived by raising and producing those Commodities in America?

Your Maxim, that We have nothing to expect from their Justice but everything to hope from their fears I have ever thought is just as "any of Solomon"; But I confess I have grown more Scrupulous of late than ever — more disposed to discuss, examine and minutely weigh every political Position, than usual. I have employed the best Force of my Understanding, in considering this Apophthegm; and the Result is that We have indeed nothing to expect from their Justice. The Ministry, the beggarly prostituted Voters, high and low, have no principles of public Virtue on which we can depend, and they are interested to plunder us. But I am not so clear that we have everything to hope from their Fears. They are a gallant brave high Spirited People Still; and if any Means can be found to make the Chastisement of the Colonies popular, a Minister, who means nothing by serving in a public Station but to make a Fortune in Wealth and Titles, may push a Measure to dreadful Extremities. Yours

JOHN ADAMS

JOHN ADAMS TO JAMES WARREN

BRAINTREE, July 25, 1774

DR SIR, — There never was I believe, a greater Contrast, than I perceive, between the Noise and Hurry of Queen Street, and the Serene Retreat, which I enjoy here. No Clients disturb me, no Politicians interrupt me, no Tories vex me, no Tyrants govern me, I had almost said No Devils tempt or torment me.

The chaste Pleasures of Agriculture engage me as much [as] Cards, or Assemblies ever did a fair Lady. You can Sympathize with me, in all this. You live in a Land of Rain this Year, as well as I, and it is our infinite Consolation to us both, to see the Wisdom and Benevolence of Heaven, counteracting the Folly, the Malice and Madness of our Tyrants.

It would do your Heart good to see me, mowing, raking, carting and frolicking with my Workmen, as unconcernd as if No Port Bill or regulating Bill or Murder Bill, had ever existed.

I catch myself however, now and then, among the Hay Cocks bestowing most hearty Execrations, on a few Villains who have dignified themselves by Superlative Mischief to their native Country the British Empire and the World.

The Demise of the French Crown,[1] is a great Event in the Political System of Europe, and of Consequence, must be a mighty Link in the Chain of Causes in American Politicks. I am not enough acquainted with the State of the French, Spanish and German Courts to predict with any Confidence, what Revolutions will Succeed the death of Lewis 15th. But if two young Fellows at the Head of the German Empire, and the French Monarchy, both warm and active dont make Mischief in Europe it will be a Wonder.

1 Louis XV died of smallpox, May 10, 1774.

I remember when I was young and sometimes amused myself with Poetry and Criticism I used to see it frequently prescribed as a Rule to consider how Homer or Virgill or Horace or Ovid would have imagined or expressed a Thing. But I believe it required almost as much Genius and Skill to Say how they would imagine or express a Thing, as they had themselves. I can't help, applying this Rule sometimes to Politicks, and enquiring what Plans would be adopted at the Congress, if a Sully, a Cecil, a Pitt or a Ximenes, a Demosthenes or a Cicero were there — or all of them together. I am at no Loss, at all, to guess. [torn] pretend to Skill and Capacity like [torn] G—d knoweth — I dont compa [torn] an atom to the Globe. But is it easy to believe they would propose Non Importation? Non Exportation? Non Consumption? If I mistake not, Somewhat a little more Sublime and Mettlesome, would come from Such Kind of Spirits. However Patience, Prudence, Resignation [torn] Candour and all that, must [torn] [Amer]ican Plans. We must fast a[nd pray, learn to] bear and forbear. We must [have that charity which] suffereth long and is kind, which be[areth all things and] hopeth all things.[1] ...

HANNAH WINTHROP TO MERCY WARREN

CAMBRIDGE, *Sept.* 27, 1774

MY DEAR FRIEND, —

. . . .

The frequent Manuvers of an arbitrary G[enera]l with his disciplined Troops which spread alarms thro the Country and Occasion great Commotion among a poor, oppressd, devoted, tho I hope determined People, often fill a Female heart with Tears. The preparations on Boston neck, the Assembled multitude lately at Cambridge [2] with many other Circumstances give me a painful

---

[1] These sentences have been filled in from 1 Corinthians XIII, 4-7.

[2] Rowe, *Diary*, 285, notes on September 7, "The General has Doubled the Guards at the Neck and I believe designs to Fortify it"; on September 10, "The 59th Regiment came from Salem and encamped on the West Side of Boston Neck." On Sunday, the 14th, some officers of the navy spiked the guns of the North Battery. The assemblage at Waltham, Watertown and Cambridge was caused by the conduct of General Brattle, who made a "flimsy Recantation" and the people dispersed on the following day. This and the insults to Hallowell, a commissioner of customs, led Gage to reinforce the troops on the Neck.

Idea of the Horrors of Civil War, and with you I cant help anticipating the distresses Consequent thereon; but that Centre of all Consolation to which you point me—That grand Superintendant of the Universe is the only firm Foundation for us to Build our hopes upon, our Cause is righteous. Let us Posses our Souls in Patience.

By Capt. Scot who has Lately arrivd we are told by the representations of Mr. H[utchinso]n the people of England are made to believe we are perfectly acquiescent under the new model of Government and other Cruel Acts. How can this Insulted People any longer forbear bursting forth with rage and desperation! Must not that heart be truly Infernal that Could Meditate such Acts of barbarity and even persuade people to believe they are Acts of Mercy and goodness! after this what is not the heart of Man Capable of? The Merchants of London are pouring in Loads of English goods. If the united Virtue of American Delegates is not exerted for our help, we are we must be ruind. The dissolution of all Government gives a dreadful Prospect, the fortifying Boston Neck, the huge Canon now mounted there, the busy preparations, the agility of the Troops, give an Horrid prospect of an intended Battle. Kind Heaven avert the Storm! I hope Coll. Warren intends to meet the General Assembly. I hear the Constitutional Council Intend to Resume their Seats. . . .

I have Lately receivd great pleasure from an ingenious Satire on that Female Foible Love of dress in the Royal American Magazine.[1] I have heard the Author guessd to be Miss Mercy Scollay, and the Gentleman who requested it Dr. Warren. I am not enough acquainted with that Lady's Poetic Talents to judge whether they are equal to that elegant production. Mr. Winthrop joyns in the Sincerest regards to Coll. Warren and you. I subscribe your Affectionate

HANNAH WINTHROP

[1] Printed in the June number, p. 233.

JAMES WARREN TO JOHN ADAMS.[1] ADAMS MSS.

PLYMOUTH, *December* 19, 1774

DEAR SIR, — It always give me pleasure to hear of the Existence and Health of my Friend and his Family, and more especially to have it from his own hand.

The partiality discovered in yours of the 13th Instant is a strong Evidence of Friendship. I am sorry it should give you any Uneasiness, if the Elections you refer to are not just such as you and I should approve. I am inclined to think they would not have been mended in the way you now think of. The drudgery of Application with some little Experience may qualifie a man to make a tolerable, or at least not a disagreeable figure in any small Circle, but nothing can supply the want of those Abilities, and that perticular Genius that alone must support his Character in the other Station, and perhaps be necessary to preserve even his Memory from Contempt if not Infamy. I have therefore no uneasiness myself, but what arises from pride, which in an Officer may assume the Title of military Honour, and may reduce me to the Dilemma of either forfeiting my Character by not doing my duty, or lessening it by doing it under certain Circumstances. I am pleased to find your Town makes such a Figure in the military way. The Spirit is catching, and spreads into every Corner, and bids fair to cherish the seeds, and support the Stock of a rising Empire.

The last Vessel from England arrived here last Fryday, left Bristol 8th. November. I am told the Master says, that near two-thirds of the Members chosen are new ones,[2] that the general Expectation was that the American Grievances would be redressed. He dined in Company with Mr. Burke two or three days before he came away, who was in high Expectation of a Committee from your Congress, which was looked for every day, and that Doctor Franklin had postponed his Voyage to America on the same Account. However they may be disappointed in this, I presume before now they have seen your demands. Extending so far beyond the repeal of the Acts of the last Session, that it will be hard work

[1] At Braintree.
[2] See "The General Election of 1774" in Trevelyan, *The American Revolution*, Pt. I. 210.

to Cure the wounds, without leaving a Splinter behind, and I hope if there be one left, it will rankle till extracted. Will the Continent be satisfied short of their demands? I hope not, but sometimes hope with fear and trembling.

I have been extreamly engaged since my return, as a Citizen and Soldier. Civil and military matters engage my whole Attention, and engross all my Time. To execute the Resolves of the Congress, to settle my military matters, and prevent the feuds and dissentions that generally arise from the Folly of some, and the Ambition of others, is my whole Business, and has superceded the delightful Study of Agriculture, and scarce left a Trace in my mind of *Tull's* fine Phylosophical System of Vegetation. If those matters continue, I may as well beat my plow shares into Swords, and pruning Hooks into Spears.

I am sorry to find you half resolved not to attend our Anniversary. Your Company would give me the greatest pleasure, and add much to the festivity of the day. . . .

JAMES WARREN TO JOHN ADAMS.   ADAMS MSS.

PLYMOUTH, *January* 15, 1775

MY DEAR SIR, — I admire the Votes and Resolves of the Maryland Convention.[1] They breath a Spirit of Liberty and Union which does Honour to them, and indeed the whole Continent. I am greatly puzzled to determine what Consequences the united force of all these things will produce in Britain. They must be infatuated to a degree I can hardly conceive of, if these things make no Impression, and yet in general I think, or rather fear, they will not. I am upon the whole much of the Opinion of your friend Chase,[2] that we have but little room to hope for a favourable Event, and that now is the Time, the exact Crisis, to determine the point, and the sooner the better, before the Tories here can compleat their efforts to disunite and embarrass. They are more assiduous than Satan was with our first Parents, and equal him in deceit and Falsehood, and with many find Success. No Stone is left un-

[1] See *Adams to Warren*, January 3, 1775, in *Life and Works of John Adams*, IX. 352.
[2] Samuel Chase (1741–1811).

turned to effect their purposes. By that means we are continually perplexed, which added to the Contemplation (from one time to another) of a War at last, is (as you say) a state as bad as can be.

The time for the setting of our Congress draws nigh. I am impatient to hear that you are a member, and shall be unhappy if you are not. What reason can be given that the question for assuming and exercising Government has not been stated and agitated in the publick Papers. Has any particular policy prevented? It seems to me it would have had good effects on the other Colonies. They may hardly believe it so necessary as we know it to be, while so little is said about it.

The Tories it is observed hold up their heads lately whether from Encouragement taken from the late publications, or a Spirit of delusion diffused among them by the infernal Junto at Boston, I know not.

Inclosed are for your Amusement two acts of a dramatic performance. Composed at my particular desire they go to you as they came out of the hand of the Copier, without pointing or marking. If you think it worth while to make any other use of them, than a reading, you will prepare them in that way, and give them such other Corrections and Amendments as your good Judgment shall suggest. . . .[1]

JAS. WARREN

Is it consistent with prudence that we should hold our Sessions at Cambridge? I am not more subject to fear than others; but if we mean to do anything important, I think it is too near the whole strength of our Enemies. If not, I shall repent leaving my own fire side at this severe Season. I shall be glad to hear from you before you leave Home.

MERCY WARREN TO JOHN ADAMS.   ADAMS MSS.

PLIMOUTH, *January* 30, 1775

SIR, — The very polite introduction to yours of Jan. 3d. I consider not only as a Compliment far beyond any merit I can presume to claim, but as resulting in some Measure from that partial Byas

[1] *The Group, a Farce.* These two acts were printed in the *Boston Gazette*, January 23, 1775.

which ever leads us to view through the most favourable Medium whatever regards those we consider in the Light of Friendship.

But when assured that I think myself both honoured and obliged whenever Mr. Adams takes up the Pen to favour me with a Line, I hope he will again attempt to grasp it hard enough to gratify me further in the same way. More especially as I am about to submit a casuistical query to his Decision, in whose judgment I place great Confidence, both from the Ability and Rectitude of Mind which guide its Determinations.

Personal Reflections and sarcastic Reproaches have generally been decryed by the wise and the worthy, both in their Conversation and Writings. And though a Man may be greatly criminal in his Conduct towards the Society in which he lives. How far, sir, do you think it justifiable for any individual to hold him up the Object of public Derision.

And is it consistent with the Benevolent System of Christianity to vilify the Delinquent, when we only wish to ward of the fatal Consequences of his Crimes.

But though from the particular Circumstances of our unhappy time, a little personal Acrimony might be justifiable in your Sex, must not the female Character suffer. (And will she not be suspected as deficient in the most amiable part thereof, that Candour and Charity which ensures her both Affection and Esteem,) if she indulges her pen to paint in the darkest shades, even those whose Vice and Venality have rendered contemptible.

Your undisguised Sentiments on these points will greatly oblige a person who is sometimes doubtful whether the solicitations of a beloved Friend may not lead her to indulge a satirical propensity that ought to be reined in with the utmost Care and Attention. But such are the multiplied injuries the Community receives, from a set of unfeeling, unprincipled Hirelings; such the Discord sown by their wicked Machinations, and such the Animosity of parties, that may we not all with some Reason apply to ourselves, what a noble Author has put into the Mouth of the celebrated Pope when meeting the admired Boileau in the Elysian Shades, that neither of them could boast that either their Censure or their praise was always free from partiallity; and that their pens were often drawn against those with whom it was more shameful to contend, than honourable to vanquish.

I know not what may be your opinion of a late Composition, but as it was so readily ushered into Light, and by a Gentleman of your Discernment offered to the publick Eye, you cannot wonder if I presume you thought it might in some small degree be beneficial to society. If so the Author must be highly gratified, and will be even better pleased with picking some useful Flower from the Foot of Parnassus, than if she were able to ascend the utmost Heights, and gather the Laurel or the garland from its summit, when the glowing Beauties have no tendency either to correct the Manners of others, or to improve the Virtue of her own Heart. Your Criticism, or Countenance, your Approbation or censure, may in some particulars serve to regulate my future Conduct.

In your last to Mr. Warren you seem to be quite weary of a state of suspence. It is painful, it is vexatious. How many years have the hopes of the contending parties been alternately rising or sinking with the Weight of a Feather, and yet little prospect of a period to their Employment.

How much longer, sir, do you think the political scale can hang in Equilibrium. Will not Justice and Freedom soon preponderate till the partizans of Corruption and Venality, even backed with the Weight of ministerial power, shall be made to kick the Beam.

You will not think it strange that the timidity and tenderness of a Woman should lead her to be anxious for the Consequences of every important step, and very solicitous for the termination of those Disputes which interrupt almost every social Enjoyment and threaten to spread Ruin and Desolation over the fairest possessions.

But if you, sir, will candidly excuse this interruption, I will no longer call off your Attention from more momentous affairs. Yet let me add my fervent Wishes that you and the other Gentlemen of the ensuing Congress may be endowed with Wisdom and Resolution equal to the Difficulties of the Day, and if you attempt to repair the shattered Constitution, or to erect a new one, may it be constructed with such symmetry of Features, such Vigour of Nerves, and such strength of sinew, that it may never be in the power of Ambition or Tyranny to shake the durable Fabrick.

In the mean time I hope all necessary Attention will be payed to the personal safety of the worthy Guardians of our Freedom and Happiness. Which leads my trembling Heart to wish my Friends were at a further Remove than Cambridge, from the Headquarters of vindictive Enemies. I am, sir, with great Esteem your real Friend and humble Servant

M. WARREN

JOHN ADAMS TO JAMES WARREN

PHILADELPHIA, *Feb.* 11, 1775

DR SIR, — Mr. Archibald Buchannan and Mr. Walter Tolley, both of Maryland and hearty Friends of America, introduced to me by my Friend, Mr. Chase, are bound to the Camp and Mr. Chase requested a Letter from me.

Chase is a Man of common Sense.

I recd your Packett. I am obliged to you for opening the Letter from our Friend Mr. Adams, and if you had opened all the others, you should have been equally welcome, Altho I would not give a similar Permission to more than two or three other Persons in the World. I have no Correspondences for private Amusement, or Personal Interest, and therefore most Letters to me might be seen by any public Man of public Virtue, good Understanding and Common Decency without Danger, Inconvenience, or offence. But as so many Persons who have not all those Qualities become in the Course of Things public Persons, We cannot be too cautious, I find, what We write, whom we write to, and how it is conveyed.

I have seen the Copy of a Letter. Let the Writer's Passions fume away unnoticed. Peepers often Spy disagreeable Objects. Let them pay for their Peeping. I have Reason to complain of Negligence in one Gentn and, I fear, of Unkindness in another upon this Occasion, but I will not complain.

They shall take all Advantages against me that they can get. They cannot hurt me nor you. The only Advantage they have got upon this Occasion is to torment themselves, and gratify others. The Gentn promised me to deliver those Letters into the Hand of Mr. S. A. but he did not.

I have only this Moment to write. Yours, sincerely.

[No signature.]

JAMES WARREN TO JOHN ADAMS.[1]   ADAMS MSS.

PLYMOUTH, February 20, 1775

MY DEAR SIR, — I need not tell you that I was greatly disappointed and chagrined at not seeing you at Cambridge a member of our Congress.[2] If it was the Choice of your Town, I know not how they can excuse, or even extenuate the fault. Surely a small Degree of Patriotism would have dictated a very different Conduct. My disappointment was increased by not having the pleasure of seeing you on my way there, or return here. As matters are, I am to content myself for the present with my share in those valuable publications I have the pleasure of reading every week in the Papers,[3] and no small pleasure it is to me to consider my particular Friend advancing (*passibus aequis*) his Country's Interest and his own honour, by exposing to publick view (with a nervous Eloquence) the Arts and Wickedness of our Enemies, and asserting by derisive Arguments the rights of his Country. May the Applauses of the present and the Blessings of future Generations (a much better reward to a Virtuous mind than pensions and Salaries),

---

1 At Braintree.

2 Convened February 1. Colonel Joseph Palmer represented Braintree. Adams had been a member of the Provincial Congress of October, 1774. "As to my being of the Congress, I think our town did right in not choosing me, as they left out [Ebenezer] Thayer, and as Mr. Palmer is as good a hand as they can employ, and having been for some time in the center of all their business in the County, Town and Province, is the best man they have. Indeed, I was not at the Meeting, and never had been at any Meeting in this Town, for eight years. To say the Truth, I was much averse to being chosen and shall continue so; for I am determined, if things are settled, to avoid public Life. I have neither Fortune, Leisure, Health nor Genius for it, being a man of desperate Fortune, and a Bankrupt in Business. I cannot help putting my Hand to the Pump, now the Ship is in a Storm, and the Hold full of Water; but as soon as she gets into a Calm and a Place of Safety, I must leave her. At such a Time as this, there are many dangerous things to be done, which nobody else will do, and therefore I cannot help attempting them; but in peaceful Times, there are always hands enough." *John Adams to James Warren*, March 15, 1775. *Works of John Adams*, ix. 354.

3 His replies to "Massachusettensis." They are included in *Works of John Adams*, III. 8.

united with the Goodness of his own heart, still animate into Exertion those great Abilities which God in his Mercy has bestowed for the Advantage of this Country.

I supposed our Congress would have adjourned the day I left them, but it seems they found means to prolong the Sessions a few days without having in view any apparent Advantage that I could conceive of. However I hope some good will come of it. I was concerned before I came away that we had then spent ten days about what might have been effected in four, and perhaps as well. They appeared to me to be dwindling into a School for debate and Criticism rather than to appear as a great Assembly to resolve and act. A certain Lady of your Acquaintance is much concerned at hearing it is reported that she wrote the *Group*. Parson Howe[1] told a large Company at Table that she was the Author of it. If this was true how came he by his Information. Would a certain friend of ours have so little discretion as to communicate such a matter to his Parson, if he knew, and much less if he only conjectured it. Do speak to him about it. If he has set his parson a prating, he ought to stop him. We have no arrivals, no news. Our military Gentry remain *in statu quo*, at the Councillors Mansion House at Marshfield. No body but the Tories there and here take any notice of them....

JAS. WARREN

JAMES WARREN TO JOHN ADAMS. ADAMS MSS.

PLYMOUTH, *March* 15, 1775

DEAR SIR, — With some difficulty I have obtained the inclosed.[2] Some scruples which you have not resolved, and some fears and apprehensions from Rumors abroad have occasioned the delay and reluctance. The Copy I got last night. Have had no time to read it over. You will please to examine and correct, etc, and do with it as you think proper, having as I dare say you will a proper regard to prudence under present Circumstances. It is a long while since

[1] Rev. Joseph Howe (1747–1775), pastor of the New South Church. See Dexter, *Yale Biographies*, III. 127.
[2] Probably the manuscript of *The Group*, the publication of which was announced in the *Boston Gazette*, April 3, 1775.

I had a line from you. Perhaps some may have miscarried. The bearer waits and I can only add my regards to Mrs. Adams, and that I am your Friend etc.

J. WARREN

JOHN ADAMS TO MERCY WARREN

BRAINTREE, *March* 15, 1775

MADAM, — I thought myself greatly honoured by your most polite and agreable Letter of January the thirtieth; and I ought to have answered it, immediately: but a Variety of Cares and Avocations, at this troublesome Time, which I confess are not a Justification of my Negligence, as they were the real Cause of it, will with your goodness of Disposition be allowed as an Excuse.

In requesting my opinion, Madam, concerning a Point of Casuistry, you have done me great Honour, and I should think myself very happy if I could remove a Scruple from a Mind, which is so amiable that it ought not to have one upon it. Personal Reflections, when they are artfully resorted to, in order to divert the Attention from Truth, or from Arguments, which cannot be answered, are mean and unjustifiable: but We must give up the Distinction between Virtue and Vice, before we can pronounce personal Reflections, always unlawfull. Will it be said that We must not pronounce Cataline a Conspirator, and Borgia a Rascall, least we should be guilty of casting personal Reflections? The faithfull Historian delineates Characters truly, let the Censure fall where it will. The public is so interested in public Characters, that they have a Right to know them, and it becomes the Duty of every good Citizen who happens to be acquainted with them to communicate his Knowledge. There is no other way of preventing the Mischief which may be done by ill Men; no other Method of administering the Antidote to the Poison.

Christianity Madam, is so far, from discountenancing the severest Discrimination, between the good and the bad, that it assures us of the most public and solemn one conceivable, before Angells and Men; and the Practice and Example of Prophetts, and Apostles, is sufficient to sanctify Satyr of the sharpest Kind.

The Truth is, Madam, that the best Gifts are liable to the worst uses and abuses, a Talent at Satyr, is commonly mixed with the choicest Powers of Genius and it has such irresistable Charms, in the Eyes of the World, that the extravagant Praise, it never fails to extort, is apt to produce extravagant Vanity in the Satirist, and an exuberant Fondness for more Praise, until he looses that cool Judgment, which alone can justify him.

But the lawfulness of the Exercise of this brilliant Talent, may be argued from its being a natural one. Nature, which does nothing in vain, bestows no mental Faculties which are not designed to be cultivated and improved. It may also be inferred from its admirable Utility and Effects. If we look into human Nature, and run through the various Classes of Life, We shall find it is really a dread of Satyr that restrains our Species from Exorbitances, more than Laws, human, moral or divine, indeed the Efficacy of civil Punishments is derived chiefly from the Same Source. It is not the Pain, the Fire etc. that is dreaded so much as the Infamy and disgrace. So that really the civil Magistrate may be said in a good Sense to keep the World in order, by Means of Satyr, for Gaols, Stocks, Whipping Posts and Gallows's are but different Kinds of it. But classical Satyr, such as flows so naturally and easily from the Pen of my excellent Friend has all the Efficacy, and more, in Support of Virtue and in Discountenancing of Vice, without any of the Coarseness and Indelicacy of those other Species of Satyr, the civil and political ones.

If you examine the Life and Actions of your poorest, lowest and most despised Neighbour, the meanest Servant you know, you will find, that there is some one or more Persons, of whose Esteem and good opinion he is ambitious, and whose Scorn and Derision he dreads perhaps more than any other Evil. And this Desire of Esteem and dread of Scorn is the principle that governs his Life and Actions. Now the Business of Satyr is to expose Vice and vicious Men as such to this Scorn and to enrobe Virtue in all the Charms which fancy can paint, and by this Means to procure her Lovers and Admirers.

Of all the Genius's which have yet arisen in America, there has been none, Superiour, to one, which now shines, in this happy, this exquisite Faculty. Indeed, altho there are many which have received more industrious Cultivation I know of none, ancient or modern, which has reached the tender the pathetic, the keen and severe, and at the same time, the Soft, the Sweet, the amiable and the pure in greater Perfection. I am, madam, with great Respect, your Friend

JOHN ADAMS

JAMES WARREN TO MERCY WARREN

CONCORD, *April* 6, 1775

MY DEAR MERCY,— Four days ago I had full Confidence that I should have had the pleasure of being with you this day, we were then near closeing the Session. Last Saturday we came near to an Adjournment, were almost equally divided on that question, the principle argument that seemd to preponderate, and turn in favour of sitting into this week was the prospect of News and News we have.[1] Last week things wore rather a favourable aspect, but alas how uncertain are our prospects. Sunday Evening brought us accounts of a Vessel at Marblehead from Falmouth, and the English Papers etc by her. I have no need to recite perticulars. you will have the whole in the Papers, and wont wonder at my forgoeing the pleasure of being with you. I dare say you would not desire to see me till I could tell you that I had done all in my power to secure and defend us and our Country. We are no longer at a loss what is Intended us by our dear Mother. We have Ask'd for Bread and she gives us a Stone, and a serpent for a Fish. However my Spirits are by no means depressd, you well know my Sentiments of the Force of both Countrys, you know my opinion of the Justness of our Cause, you know my Confidence in a Righteous Providence. I seem to want nothing to keep up my Spirits and to Inspire me with a proper resolution to Act my part well in this difficult time but seeing you in Spirits, and knowing that they flow from the heart. How shall I support myself if you suffer these Misfortunes to prey on your tender frame and Add to my difficulties an affliction too great to bear of itself. The

[1] The Congress adjourned April 15.

Vertuous should be happy under all Circumstances. This state of things will last but a little while. I believe we shall have many chearful rides together yet. We proposed last week a short adjournment and I had in a manner Engaged a Chamber here for my Beloved and pleased myself with the health and pleasure the Journey was to give her; but I believe it must be postponed till some Event takes place and changes the face of things. All things wear a warlike appearance here. This Town is full of Cannon, ammunition, stores, etc., and the Army long for them and they want nothing but strength to Induce an attempt on them. The people are ready and determine to defend this Country Inch by Inch. The Inhabitants of Boston begin to move. The Selectmen and Committee of Correspondence are to be with us, I mean our Committee, this day. The Snow Storm yesterday and Business prevented them then. From this Conference some vigorous resolutions may grow. But to dismiss publick matters, let me ask how you do and how do my little Boys, especially my little Henry, who was Complaining. I long to see you. I long to sit with you under our Vines etc and have none to make us afraid. Do you know that I have not heard from you since I left you, and that is a long while. It seems a month at least. I can't believe it less. I intend to fly Home I mean as soon as Prudence Duty and Honour will permitt. I am with regards to all Friends and the greatest Expressions of Love and regard to you, your very affect. Husband,

JAS. WARREN

Love to my Boys. I feel disposed to add to this long letter but neither time nor place will permit it. *April* 7th. I am up this morning to add. Mr. Lothrop is the bearer of this and can give you an Acct. of us. The Inhabitants of Boston are on the move. H[ancock] and A[dams] go no more into that Garrison, the female Connections of the first come out early this morning and measures are taken relative to those of the last. The moving of the Inhabitants of Boston if effected will be one grand Move. I hope one thing will follow another till America shall appear Grand to all the world. I begin to think of the Trunks which may be ready against I come home, we perhaps may be forced to move: if we are let us strive to submit to the dispensations of Providence with Christian resignation and phylosophick Dignity. God has given you great abilities; you have improved them in great Acquirements. You are possessd of eminent Virtues and distinguished Piety. For all these I esteem I love you in a degree that I can't express. They are all now to be called into action for the good of Mankind, for the good of your friends, for the promotion of Virtue and Patriotism. Don't let the fluttering of your Heart interrupt your Health or disturb your repose. Believe me I am continually Anxious about you. Ride when the weather is good and don't work or read too much at other times. I must bid you adieu. God Almighty bless you. No letter yet. What can it mean? Is she not well? She can't forget me or have any Objections to writing.

JAMES WARREN TO JOHN ADAMS.   ADAMS MSS.

WATERTOWN, *May* 7, 1775.

MY DEAR SIR,—After I had executed my Commission at Providence, I returned home, set Mrs. Warren down in her own Habitation, made the best provision I could for the security of our Family, and some of our Effects, which we considered to be not very safe at Plymouth, and immediately hastened to this place, to contribute my Mite to the publick Service in this Exigence of Affairs. Here I have been near a week, every day resolving to write to you, without beginning to execute such a resolution till now. And indeed every thing seems to be in such Confusion, that I hardly know where to begin, and perhaps shall be at as great a Loss to know where to end. I find our own Body extreamly weakened by the several detachments (to use the stile of the Times) made from it. When I see the Seats of many of my Friends on whom I used to place my principal dependance empty, and feel the want of them as I do, at a Time when they are more wanted than ever, I am almost discouraged. However as I was born to struggle with difficulties, [I] shall endeavour to answer the End of my Creation as well as I can. The Congress since I have been here has generally been full, unanimous and spirited, ready and willing to do every thing in their power, and frequently animated by the most agreeable News from the other Colonies. The principal Objects of our Attention have been the regulation and officering of the Army, and arming the men, and devising ways and means to support the enormous Expence incurred under our present Situation; and those I dare say you can easily conceive to be attended with many difficulties, under the present Circumstances of our Government, in which recommendations are to supply the place of Laws, and destitute of coercive power, exposed to the Caprice of the People, and depending entirely on their virtue for Success. We have voted to issue Notes for 100.000£ and to request your aid in giving them a Currency.[1] The Committee of Ways and Means to sit again. We are embarrassed in officering our Army by the Establishment of Minute Men.[2] I wish it had never taken place, and the necessity of having our Field Officers appointed is every day seen, and indeed in my Opinion that should have been the first thing done. As to the Army, it is in such a shifting, fluctuating state as not to be capable of a perfect regulation. They are continually going and coming. However, they seem to me to want a more experienced direction. I could for myself wish to see your Friends Washington and L[ee][3] at the Head of it, and yet dare not propose it, tho' I have it in Contemplation. I hope that matter will be considered with more propriety in your Body than ours. If you establish a Continental Army, of which this will be only a part, you will place the direction as you please. It is difficult to say what Numbers our Army consists of. If a return could be had one day, it would by no means answer for the next. They have been so reduced at some times that I have trembled at the Consequences

[1] *Journals of the Provincial Congress* (Mass.), 189.
[2] The term is believed to be derived from a motion made by Col. William Henshaw in a meeting of local Committees of Correspondence at Worcester, September 21, 1774, recommending that one-third of the men of the respective towns, between sixteen and sixty years of age be inlisted, "to be ready to act at a minute's warning." 1 *Proceedings*, xv. 69. The Provincial Congress on October 26, provided for such a force which should hold itself in readiness to march "on the shortest notice" from the Committee of Safety. *Journals*, 33.
[3] In the light of subsequent events it seems strange that so much credit was given to Charles Lee at this time. He made himself active in the cause of the Colonies and his *Strictures* on Dr. Myles Cooper's *Friendly Address to all Reasonable Americans*, first issued at Philadelphia, in 1774, ran through six editions in a few months, two of the issues coming from Boston printers. His connections were Southern, rather than New England, and the first pressure for his appointment to high command in the army probably came from Virginia and Maryland. At this time he was in Philadelphia, training raw troops and cultivating influence in the Continental Congress, which convened May 10.

that might take place. Our new Levies are coming in, and by that means I hope they will be in a more permanent state. I believe there are about 6,000 in Camp at present. They are employed at Cambridge, in heaving up Intrenchments, somewhere about Phips Farm. I have not seen them. The extream want of the Exercise of a fixt settled Government is sufficiently felt here at this time, and has produced the Assignment of a Time to take that matter under Consideration. Next Tuesday is the time.[1] What will be done I know not. I am inclined to think they will vote to assume a Government. But who is to form this Constitution, who is to rigg the ship, I can't tell. It appears to me a Business of such a nature, so important, and in which an Error once committed, will probably be as lasting as the Constitution itself, that I am afraid to meddle. It is sufficient for such a genius as mine to know the places and use of the several ropes after the ship is rigg'd. However, we have a Chance. Success is the Criterion that generally determines the Judgment. If we should either by accident or by the force of our great Abilities build up a Grand Constitution with the same ease we could a Bird Cage, we shall be equally clever fellows. If I don't tire your patience now, you shall hear more of this in my next.

The Infatuation of the Inhabitants of Boston has reduced us and themselves to the precise state I have expected it would do. We have been obliged for their sakes to pass some votes, that we did not well relish. We have admitted the refugees to send out for their Effects, tho' I don't expect any advantage from it.[2] In short I voted for it more to gratifie my friend Warren, than from any other motive. There is no Guard against the General's Treachery. He will find some pretences for the base Arts practiced to abuse that People, and will finally keep a large number of them there. When he lets them out at all it is very slowly. When the Tories and Tory Effects are in, and his Reinforcement arrives, I presume no more of them will come out. They are to be pitied, tho' this

---

[1] The question was postponed to Friday, May 12. When it was agreed to make an application to the Continental Congress, "for obtaining their recommendation for this colony to take up and exercise civil government, as soon as may be." *Journals of the Provincial Congress* (Mass.), 219.

[2] *Journals of the Provincial Congress* (Mass.), 184, 195.

is the Effect of their own folly. The misery they are already reduced to in the Town is great, and may be seen described in the Joy of the Countenances of those who get out. By the way I have just heard that Edes [1] has stole out. I wish his partner was with him. . . .

I think they go on charmingly and swimmingly at [New] York.

Inclosed are a Letter from Mrs. Adams, and an Extract of a Letter from Hutchinson, found among a curious Collection of Letters now in the hands of our Friends.[2] I am well assured of the Authenticity of it, and send this particular Extract more because it seems to be especially calculated to be used where you are than because it shews a greater degree of Wickedness than many others.

JAMES WARREN TO MERCY WARREN

WATERTOWN, *May* 18, 1775

MY DEAR MERCY, — What a Letter every day! Was ever a Woman doom'd to such drudgery before to be obliged to read half a Sheet, and some times a whole one, full of Impertinence before dinner, is enough at least to take away one's Appetite; but you see I presume my wife will not complain or scold in this way, her Love for reading, or affection for her Husband will secure a welcome to his Scribbles. I had not your Letter when I wrote yesterday. You must not look for me too soon. If I do not get home on Thursday, hope I shall on Saturday or Sunday — depend on it as soon as I can. In the mean Time you will digest a System of politics, for I find you in that strain. But remember to revere our Congress, for if we have lost many good Members we have many left; and, if we

---

1 Benjamin Edes (1732-1803), printer of the *Boston Gazette*. His partner was John Gill (-1785). They had issued a paper on April 17, and their partnership was then dissolved. Edes again started it at Watertown, June 5, returned to Boston in October, 1776, and continued to print it until December, 1780. Matthews, in *Collections* of the Col. Soc. of Mass., IX. 444.

2 "We hear that the Letters lately wrote by Governor Hutchinson are providentially in the Hands of the People; and, when published, will astonish every one, who has not before been thoroughly sensible of the evil Designs of that Man against the Liberties of this Country." *Essex Gazette*, May 2, 1775. Letters of Hutchinson are in the *New England Chronicle*, June 8, 1775, and subsequent issues. See *Familiar Letters of John Adams and his Wife*, 52.

have not all the Sense and property of the province among us, we have as good a Share as commonly is in such an Assembly, it will no longer therefore do to delay a question that should have been determined 6 months ago. Nevertheless we have gone no further than an application to the Grand Congress. There is a degree of Timidity and slowness in our movements which my Soul abominates. As soon as South Carolina got the rumour of the action here, and an uncertain one too, they took Immediate possession of all the Arms and Stores belonging to the King there, drove the Men on Board the Ships and sware they shall no more set foot on shore there. At Hallifax they burnt all the Hay which Genl. Gage depended on, and had sent Transports for, and made several Attempts to Burn the Magazines and dock Yards. They are resolved that no Tory shall come in and reside in that Province. poor Dogs, where will they go and what will they do, there is no Country where a Sentiment worthy of a Man is Entertained but detests them. Turkey or Algiers may do, but their principles and Conduct are not Calculated for any part of America. The first part of your Letter shew you as cool as a Philosopher or a politician but the last as Agitated as a Modern Soldier. Oh, the horrors of a reinforcement! Let me tell you a Story. Last Saturday[1] our Troops at Cambridge took into their heads to March to Charlestown. Accordingly about 4000 marched down in very good order, with a Genl.[2] at their head. This movement produced a Terror in Boston hardly to be described. You may have an Idea of it if I tell you that the Genl. once gave orders to have the Guns at the Castle spiked up, but on a little recollection and some remonstrances from one of his Colonels recoverd himself and revoked his Orders. Let your Colonel's remonstrances etc. have a Similar Effect. My cold is almost well, be not Concerned for me, take care of yourself and I hope we shall both do well. The Blessing of heaven rest on you is the daily Prayer of your Affect Husband,

JAS. WARREN

1 May 13. See Frothingham, *Siege of Boston*, 107.   2 Putnam.

JOHN ADAMS TO JAMES WARREN

PHYLADELPHIA, *May* 21, 1775

MY DEAR FRIEND,—I am vastly obliged to you for your Letter. It was like cold Water to a thirsty Soul. We suffer, greatly for Want of News from you and Boston.

I am very unfortunate in my Eyes and my Health. I came from Home Sick and have been so ever Since. My Eyes are so weak and dim that I can neither read, write, or see without great Pain.

Our unwieldy Body moves very slow. We shall do something in Time, but must have our own Way. We are all secret. But I can guess that an army will be posted in New York, and another in Massachusetts, at the Continental Expence.

Such a vast Multitude of Objects, civil, political, commercial and military, press and crowd upon us so fast, that We know not what to do first. The State of fifteen or sixteen Colonies, to be considered, Time must be taken.

Pray write me by every opportunity and intreat all my Friends to do the same — every Line from you, any of you does good.

One half the *Group* [1] is printed here, from a Copy printed in Jamaica. Pray send me a printed Copy of the whole and it will be greedily reprinted here. My friendship to the Author of it.

The Martial Spirit throughout this Province is astonishing, it arose all of a Sudden, Since the News of the Battle of Lexington. Quakers and all are carried away with it. Every day in the Week Sundays not excepted they exercise, in great Numbers. The Farmer [2] is a Coll. and Jo. Reed another. Their officers, are made of the People of the first Fortune in the Place.

Uniforms and Regimentals are as thick as Bees. America will soon be in a Condition to defend itself by Land against all Mankind.

[No signature.]

[1] Printed by James Humphreys, Jr. An edition was printed in New York by John Anderson, omitting the second and third scenes of Act II.
[2] John Dickinson. Reed was lieutenant-colonel, and Mifflin, major.

JOHN ADAMS TO JAMES WARREN

PHYLADELPHIA, *May* 26, 1775

DR. SIR, — The Bearers of this are two young Gentlemen from Maryland, of one of the best and first Families in that Province, one of them is a Lawyer, the other a Physician; both have independent Fortunes. Such is their Zeal in the Cause of America and Such their fellow Feeling for the People of our Province, that they are determined to Spend the Summer in our Camp in order to gain Experience and perfect themselves in the Art military. They are Soldiers already. Their Name is Hall.[1] It will be of great Importance that these Gentn should be treated with the utmost Delicacy and Politeness; their Letters to their Friends will have a great Influence on the Southern Colonies.

I should take it as a favour if you would introduce these Gentlemen to all our best Friends and to the Knowledge of every Thing that can Serve the Cause.

I can not inform you of any Thing passing here that is worth knowing. I hope We shall give Satisfaction. But it must be a work of Time. I am your Friend,

JOHN ADAMS

JOHN ADAMS TO JAMES WARREN

PHYLADELPHIA, *June* 7, 1775

DEAR SIR, — We have been puzzled to discover what we ought to do with the Canadians and Indians. Several Persons have been before Congress who have lately been in the Province of Canada, particularly Mr. Brown[2] and Mr. Price,[3] who have informed us

---

[1] Heitman gives Edward and Elihu Hall, of Maryland, as holding continental commissions.

[2] John Brown, who had brought intelligence of the capture of Ticonderoga. His testimony on the disposition of the Canadians is in the *Pennsylvania Packet*, May 22, 1775.

[3] The *Journals of the Continental Congress*, II. 66, record May 27: "Information being given that there is a gentleman in town who can give the Congress a full and just account of the state of Affairs in Canada; *Ordered*, that he be introduced, and he was accordingly introduced." A letter "To the oppressed Inhabitants of Canada" was prepared and sent to Canada "by the gentleman just introduced." *Ib.*, 67, 68. It was translated into French and 1000 printed by Fleury Mesplet, at Philadelphia. The Congress printed it also in English. On James Price see Codman, *Arnold's Expedition to Quebec*, 8.

that the French are not unfriendly to us. And by all that we can learn of the Indians they intend to be neutral.

But whether We should march into Canada with an Army Sufficient to break the Power of Governor Carlton, to overawe the Indians, and to protect the French, has been a great Question.[1] It seems to be the general Conclusion that it is best to go, if We can be assured that the Canadians will be pleased with it and join. The Nations of Indians inhabiting the Frontiers of the Colonies are numerous and warlike. They seem disposed to Neutrality. None have as yet taken up the Hatchet against us; and We have not obtained any certain Evidence that either Carlton or Johnson have directly attempted to persuade them to take up the Hatchet. Some Suspicious Circumstances there are.

The Indians are known to conduct their Wars so entirely without Faith and Humanity, that it will bring eternal Infamy on the Ministry throughout all Europe if they should excite these Savages to War. The French disgraced themselves last War by employing them. To let loose these blood Hounds to scalp Men and to butcher Women and Children is horrid. Still it [is] Such kind of Humanity and Policy as we have experienced from the Ministry.

JOHN ADAMS TO JAMES WARREN

PHYLADELPHIA, *June* 10, 1775

DR. SIR,— I have written a few lines to Dr. Warren to whom I refer you.

It is of vast Importance that the officers of our Army should be impressed with the absolute Necessity of Cleanliness, to preserve the Health of their Men. Cleanness is one of the three Cardinal Virtues of a Soldier, as Activity and Sobriety are the other two. They should be encouraged to go into Water frequently, to keep their Linen washed and their Beds clean, and should be continually exercised in the manual and Maneuvres.

General Lee, has an Opinion of Burgoine, Clinton and How.

---

[1] On June 1 the Continental Congress resolved, "that no expedition or incursion ought to be undertaken or made, by any colony, or body of colonists, against or into Canada." *Journals of the Continental Congress*, II. 75.

Burgoine he says is very active and enterprizing, fond of Surprizes and Night Attacks and Alarms. He entreats me to inculcate a most unremitted Vigilance, to guard against Surprizes, specially in the Night.

We have a most miraculous Militia in this City, brought into Existence out of Nothing since the Battle of Lexington. Measures are taken here and at New York to procure Powder. But we must be Sparing of that Article. The Supineness of the Colonies hitherto concerning it, amazes me. Genl. Lee and Major Gates are very fond of a Project of procuring Pikes and Pike men.[1] I hope we shall send you some Rifle Men; they shoot with great Exactness, at amazing Distances.

They are casting Pateraras [2] and making Amuzettes [3] in this City, and preparing for War, with an alacrity which does them Honor.

[*No signature.*]

Samuel Adams to James Warren

PHILADELPHIA, *June* 10, 1775

DEAR COLL. WARREN, — I have been impatiently waiting for the Fulfillment of your Promise to write to me, but I can easily excuse you knowing that your hands as well as mine must be full at this important glorious Crisis. The Battle of Lexington will be famed in the History of this Country. Four Accounts of it have doubtless by this time reached England. Our insulting Enemies there must be convinced that Americans are not such dastardly Cowards as a Coll. Grant [4] and others have represented them to be, and our Friends have received a sure pledge that we will not desert them by deserting ourselves, and leave them to the Contempt of those most contemptible Wretches the King's Ministers. Whether the People of England will hereby be brought to reflect on their own Danger, or whether their pride will be touchd at this

---

[1] March 20, 1776, Congress directed Colonel Magaw to have a pike or spear made, and on the following day he submitted two samples. *Journals of the Continental Congress*, IV. 218, 224.

[2] A corrupt form of *pedrero*, a piece of ordnance originally for discharging stones.

[3] A light field-cannon, invented by Marshal Saxe.   [4] James Grant (1720–1806).

unexpected and signal Defeat of British Troops is to me uncertain. If their Resentment should run high against us, our Friends will have a political Game to play, to turn the whole Force of that Resentment upon the Authors of these Disturbances, viz. Hutchinson and the Ministry. It is however the Duty of America to be still upon its Guard, for there is no Dependence to be had on the People of England, and I am convinced most abundantly that it is the Determination of the K. and his Ministers to establish arbitrary Government in the Colonies by Acts of Parliament and to enforce those Acts by the Sword. Could the publick Sentiment be otherwise it would be a Delusion leading directly to Destruction. The Spirit of Patriotism prevails among the Members of this Congress but from the Necessity of things Business must go on slower than one could wish. It is difficult to possess upwards of Sixty Gentlemen, at once with the same Feelings upon Questions of Importance that are continually arising. All mean the Defence and Support of American Liberty and Matters are finally well decided; I have endeavored to Act with. that kind of *Prudence* which I dare say, when I shall explain my Conduct to you, *you* will not condemn.

Mr. Fessenden [1] a Courier from your Congress arrived here yesterday. I could not help flattering my Self that your pressing Demand was political, but I was much pleasd to see every Gentleman present anxiously sollicitious to relieve the Necessities of and yield a full Supply to the "American Army before Boston." Our worthy President has Communicated to yours a Resolution for this purpose.[2]

Every Step is taking here for the procuring of Gunpowder from abroad and setting up the Manufacture of it in America and I believe they will be successfull.

Mr. Mifflin [3] assures me that large Quantities are expected in a few Weeks in this place and 200 Barrels every hour.

If our Army behave with Spirit this Summer (as I am confident they will) and their Efforts are succeeded, I trust in God, we shall be superior to all future Difficulty. Be cautious of the enterprising

---

1 Josiah Fessenden.   2 *Journals of the Continental Congress*, II. 83.
3 Thomas Mifflin (1744–1800).

Spirit of Burgoin and Howe. Dr. Church[1] left us this Morning. I disclosd to him as much as I could consistent with the Injunctions I am under. I refer you to him for particulars. Present my affectionate Regards to all the Friends of Liberty, especially the Circle of our Acquaintance. Pray write to me. Adieu my Friend.

S. ADAMS

JAMES WARREN TO JOHN ADAMS.   ADAMS MSS.

WATERTOWN, *June* 11, 1775

MY DEAR SIR, — Since my last I have waited with Impatience to hear from you. I mean individually. The public Expectation to hear from the Congress is great. They don't complain, but they wonder that the Congress should sit a month without their receiving something decisive with regard to us. I presume we shall have it in due time; at least that nothing will be wanting in your power to relieve the distresses of your Country. I intended to have devoted some part of this Day to write to you, but have been diverted by Calls that I could not dispence with. Since I knew of this Opportunity I have not been able to get a minute till now when the Express is just going off. You will collect from the publick Letter by this Express our Sentiments with regard to the necessity of assuming civil Government constantly increasing upon us; what we apprehend to be the strength of our Enemies, and what have been and still are the subjects of some of our Contemplations. I have not time to add any thing more with regard to our proceedings or the state of the Army. I can only say we have difficulties enough to struggle with. I hope we shall do well at last. It is said General Howe gives out that he intends soon to have a frolic with the Yankees. They are ready for him, and wish for nothing more. Their Grenadiers and Light Infantry have been exempted from duty for ten or twelve days. We were greatly elated this morning with an Account that you had voted 70,000 men, and 3,000,000 sterling to be struck off in Bills for their support.[2] Our Joy was

---

[1] Benjamin Church, Jr. He was bearer of a letter from the Provincial Congress of Massachusetts to the Continental Congress. *Ib.*, 76.

[2] One of the rumors of the day. It was not until June 22 that the Congress voted to make its first issue of bills of credit — 2,000,000 dollars — resting on the credit of the twelve confederated colonies. *Journals of the Continental Congress*, II. 103.

damped at 10 o'clock by a Letter from your Brother Cushing. I wish it had miscarried, that I might have enjoyed the pleasure a little longer of contemplating the dignity of your Conduct, as well as the rising Glory of America. His Letter was dated the 1st. Instant; and if he had been in the Clouds for seven years past, I think he would have had as just Ideas of our situation and necessities as he has expressed to his Friend Hawley.[1] He thinks a very inconsiderable reinforcement is to be expected, and when arrived, that Gage will not have more than 5 or 6,000 men, and queries whether we had not better discharge part of our Army, to prevent involving ourselves in an immense Debt; a hint that we are to expect no support from the Continent; but at the same time talks of an Union and the Day is ours, as saith Dr. Franklin. . . .

JOHN HANCOCK TO JOSEPH WARREN [2]

SUNDAY MORNG, 18 *June*, 1775. PHILADA.

MY DEAR SIR, — I intended writing you a long Letter, but am prevented by my Attention to the orders of Congress in Dispatching an Express and writing to Govr. Trumbull on matters of infinite Importance. In short from my Scituation in Congress I have great Duty to Do, but I will persevere even to the Destruction of my Constitution. I am under a strict Injunction not to Communicate the Doings of Congress, but two or three Circumstances having Taken place in Congress which affected our Army, inducd me to ask Leave to mention them, which I obtain'd with this positive Direction that at present they be not mentiond in the Newspapers which you will please to observe.

The Congress have appointed George Washington, Esqr., General and Commander in Chief of the Continental Army. His Commission is made out and I shall Sign it to morrow. He is a Gentleman you will all like. I submit to you the propriety of providing a suitable place for his Residence and the mode of his Reception. Pray tell Genl. Ward of this with my Respects, and that we all Expect to hear that the Military Movements of the

[1] Joseph Hawley.
[2] This letter was received by James Warren as the successor of Joseph Warren as presiding officer over the Provincial Congress.

Day of his Arrival will be such as to do him and the Commander in Chief great honour.

General Ward is appointed Second in Command and am sure you will Approve this. General Lee is Appointed third in Command, but have not his Answer, As to the last Appointment. I hope it will Turn out well. I say no more on that head. Genl. Washington will set out in a few Days. Would it not be proper to have a Troop at the Entrance of our Province to escort him down; and then the Fort ready to Receive him. Pray do him every honour.[1] By all means have his Commission read at the head of the whole Forces. I can't write Genl. Ward; do mention to him my hurry and lay your plans well.

The Congress have also order'd Ten Companies of Rifle Men from this Province, Maryland and Virginia of 68 Men each properly officerd, to proceed immediately to join the Army near Boston. This is a good Step and will be an excellent additional Strength to our Army. These are the finest Marksmen in the world. They do Execution with their Rifle Guns at an Amazing Distance. The Congress have also Determined upon 15,000 Men as a Continental Army. The Committee of the whole Congress have agreed to Report that Two Million of Dollars be emitted in Bills for the Use of the Continent to pay Troops, etc. This is all I am allowed to mention.

I have sent you the Orders for a Fast thro' the Continent which please to make publick.[2]

The Inclos'd Letters please to Deliver. Remember me to Genl. Ward, Heath, Dr. Cooper and all Frends, particularly to my good Friend J. Pitts.[3] I have supplied Fessenden with Twenty pounds Lawf. Money wch I could ill spare, you will order it Returnd me here, inclos'd is his Rect. Do Write me. We know nothing of our Friends in Boston. How is Gill.

Adieu, I am in great haste, yours without Reserve.

JOHN HANCOCK

I send you a copy of a Letter from London — what Rascalls they are there. We will do for them.

[1] *Journals of the Provincial Congress* (Mass.), 391, 398.   [2] For July 20.
[3] John Pitts (1737–1815). See *Memorial . . . of James Pitts.* 1882.

JAMES WARREN TO MERCY WARREN [1]

WATERTOWN, *June* 18, 1775

MY DEAR MERCY,— The Extraordinary Nature of the Events which have taken place in the last 48 Hours has Interrupted that steady and only Intercourse which the situation of publick affairs allows me. the Night before last our Troops possessd themselves of a Hill in Charlestown and had time only to heave up an Imperfect Breastwork. The regular Troops from the Batterys in Boston and two Men of War in the Ferryway began early next Morning a Heavy Fire on them which was Continued till about Noon, when they Landed a large Number of Troops and after a Stout resistance and great Loss on their side dispossessed our Men, who with the Accumulated disadvantages of being Exposed to the fire of their Cannon and the want of Ammunition and not being supported by fresh Troops were obliged to abandon the Town and retire to our Lines towards Cambridge, to which they made a very handsome Addition last Night. With a Savage Barbarity never practised among Civilized Nations, they fired and have Utterly destroyed the Town of Charlestown. We have had this day at Dinner another Alarm that they were Advancing on our Lines, after having reinforced their Troops with their Horse, etc., and that they were out at Roxbury. We expected this would have been an Important day. They are reinforced but have not Advanced. So things remain at present as they were. We have killed them many Men and have killed and wounded about an hundred by the best Accounts I can get, among the first of which to our inexpressible Grief is my Friend Doctor Warren who was killd it is supposed in the Lines on the Hill at Charlestown in a Manner more Glorious to himself than the fate of Wolfe on the plains of Abraham. Many other officers are wounded and some killd. It is Impossible to describe the Confusion in this place, Women and Children flying into the Country, armed Men Going to the field, and wounded Men returning from there fill the Streets. I shant Attempt a description. Your Brother [2] borrowed a Gun, etc., and

[1] Printed in part in 1 *Mass. Hist. Soc. Proceedings*, XII. 68.
[2] Joseph Otis (1726-1810).

went among the flying Bullets at Charlestown returned last Evening 10 o'clock. the Librarian [1] got a slight wound with a musket Ball in his hand. Howland has this minute come in with your Letter. The Continental Congress have done and are doing every thing we can wish. Dr. Church retd. last Evening and Brot. resolutions for assuming Govt. and for supplying provisions and powder, and he tells us tho under the rose that they are contemplating and have perhaps finished the Establishment of the Army and an Emission of money to pay and support them, and he thinks the operations of yesterday will be more than sufficient to Induce them to recommend the Assumption of new forms of Govt. to all the Colonies. I wish I could be more perticular. I am now in a Committee of Importance and only steal time to add Sentences seperately. I feel for my Dear Wife, least her Apprehensions should hurt her health, be not concerned about me, take care of your Self. you can secure a retreat and have proper Notice in Season, and if you are safe and the Boys I shall be happy fall what will to my Interest. I cant be willing you should come into this part of the Country at present. I will see you as soon as possible; can't say when. The mode of Govt prescribd is according to the last Charter. Some are quite satisfied with it, you know I wishd for a more perfect one, it is now Monday Morning. I hear nothing yet but the roaring of Cannon below, but no Body regards them. I need not say that I long to see you, perhaps never more in my life. I shall try hard for it this week. I hope your Strawberries are well taken care of and that you have fine feasting on them. Your Brother is waiting for Freeman,[2] who with all his patriotism has left us for 10 days. I have Letters from both Mr Adams and Cushing. I can't Inclose them, because I must answer them when I can get Oppy. I am calld on and must Conclude with my wishes and prayers for your Happiness and with Love to my Boys and regards to Friends. Your aff Husband,

JAS. WARREN

S. Adams is very unwell — the Jaundice to a great degree and his Spirits somewhat depressd. Church hopes he will recover. I hope some of us will survive this Contest. Church has put into my

[1] James Winthrop, librarian of Harvard College.   [2] Samuel Freeman, of Falmouth?

hands a Curious Letter full of Interesting Intelligence. I wish I could give it to you you may remember to ask me about it and the author. I have shown it to Coll. Otis. If he goes before me enquire of him. Your Brother Jem dined with us yesterday, behaved well till dinner, was almost done and then in the old way got up went off where I know not; has been about at Cambridge and Roxbury several days. Adieu.

JOHN ADAMS TO JAMES WARREN

PHYLADELPHIA, *June* 20, 1775

MY FRIEND,—This Letter will go by the Sage, brave and amiable General Washington, to whom I have taken the Liberty of mentioning your Name.

The Congress has at last voted near twenty thousand Men in Massachusetts and New York, and an Emission of a Continental Currency to maintain them.

You will have Lee, as third in Command, Ward being the Second, Schuyler of New York the fourth, and Putnam the fifth. Ten Companies of Rifle Men, too, are ordered from Pennsylvania, Maryland and Virginia.

Nothing has given me more Torment, than the Scuffle We have had in appointing the General Officers. We could not obtain a Vote upon our seat for L[ee]. Sam and John fought for him, however, through all the Weapons. Dismal Bugbears were raised. There were Prejudices enough among the weak and fears enough among the timid, as well as other obstacles from the Cunning: but the great Necessity for officers of skill and Experience, prevailed. I have never formed any Friendship or particular Connection with Lee, but upon the most mature Deliberation I judged him the best qualified for the Service and the most likely to connect the Colonies, and therefore gave him my Vote, and am willing to abide the Consequences.

I am much obliged to you for yours of June 11. Pray write me a State of the Army, their Numbers, and a List of the officers and the Condition of the poor People of Boston. My Heart bleeds for them.

We have a great Show this Morning here. Our great Generals Washington and Lee review the three battalions of this City. I believe there never was two thousand Soldiers created out of nothing so suddenly, as in this City. you would be surprized to behold them, all in Uniforms, and very expert both in the Manual and Maneuvres. They go through the wheelings and Firings in subdivisions, grand Divisions, and Platoons, with great Exactness, our Accounts from all Parts of the Continent are very pleasing. the Spirit of the People is such as you would wish.

I hope to be nearer to you at least, very soon. How does your Government go on? If We have more bad News from England the other Colonies will follow your Example.

My Love to all Friends. Yours,

JOHN ADAMS

JAMES WARREN TO JOHN ADAMS. ADAMS MSS.

WATERTOWN, *June* 20, 1775

MY DEAR SIR,— Since my last I have the pleasure of several of yours. I am extreamly obliged to you, and to continue your attention to me in this way can assure you I don't fail to make use of any thing I think will serve the publick from your Letters. I communicated to both our Generals that paragraph of your Letter containing General Lee's opinion of the Generals and character particularly of Burgoine. Yours per Mr. Hall I never received till the day before yesterday. I have never seen those Gentlemen; shall observe your recommendation when I do. You will doubtless hear before this reaches you of another Action here on Saturday last, which terminated with less success on our side than any one that has taken place before. However, they have nothing to boast of but the possession of the Ground. You will say that is enough. It is enough to mark with Infamy those who suffered it; but they have paid very dearly for it, in the loss of many men. They landed about 2000. I can't learn who commanded them. Were more than repulsed by the Bravery of our men in the imperfect Lines hove up the Night before, who, had they been supplied with Ammunition, and a small reinforcement of fresh men, would, tho' under every disadvantage have in all probability cut them to pieces. Here fell our worthy and much lamented Friend Doctor Warren, with as much Glory as Wolf on the Plains of Abraham, after performing many feats of Bravery and exhibiting a Coolness and Conduct which did Honour to the Judgment of his Country in appointing him a few days before one of their Major Generals. At once admired and lamented in such a manner as to make it difficult to determine whether regret or envy predominated. Had our brave men, posted on Ground injudiciously at first taken, had a Lee or a Washington instead of a General destitute of all military Ability [1] and Spirit to command them, it is my Opinion the day would have terminated with as much Glory to America as the 19th of April. This is our great Misfortune, and is remediless from any other quarter than yours. We dare not superceed him here; it will come well from you, and really merits your attention. That and a necessary article which makes me tremble to name or think of is all we want. Our men were harrassed all the morning by Cannon from 2 Batteries, 2 Ships, and a Bomb Battery, and at the Attack by a great number of armed Boats, and nevertheless made a stout resistance. Some fatality always attends my Attempts to write you. I am called away and fear I shan't be able to add another paragraph.

    I must beg you would make my Acknowledgments to Mr. Cushing and my good Friend Mr. Adams for their kind favours. I fully designed to have wrote them, but this Express goes off so suddenly as not to give me an Opportunity. Shall embrace the next as well as to enlarge to you. The Hurry of our Affairs can hardly be described. We have just received an Account by a Man who is said to have swam out of Boston, that we killed and wounded 1000 of them, among the first of which is a General, Majors Sherrif and Pitcairn and 60 other officers. 70 officers wounded. The whole of the Troops landed at Charlestown were 5000. This Account is not improbable to me, but I cannot warrant the Authenticity of it. I am your Friend. Adieu.

J. WARREN

    Mrs. Adams and family were well when I last heard from them. I have had great pleasure in conversing with Doctor Church who

[1] Artemas Ward.

gives me a good account of your Spirit, Unanimity, etc. I am well pleased with most of your resolves. I can't however say that I admire the form of Government prescribed. But we are all Submission and are sending out our Letters for calling an Assembly. I hope we shall have as good an opportunity for a good Government in some future time.

SAMUEL ADAMS TO JOSEPH WARREN [1]

PHILADA., *June* [20], 1775

DEAR SIR, — I have but one Moment to inform you that this Congress, having as I before wrote you appointed General Washington to the Command of all the American Forces, and Majors General Ward and Lee, they yesterday proceeded to the appointment of two more Majors General, viz. Schuyler and Putnam. General Lee has accepted of his appointment and will I suppose tomorrow set off with General Washington for Cambridge. The Congress seems determined to support their Army before Boston. They are fully sensible of the Importance of it and have recommended to the Colonies of Connecticutt, R. Island and N. Hampshire to send the Troops they have agreed to raise without Delay to Cambridge, there to remain till further Orders (excepting such as were destined to the several Posts in the Colony of N. York.) [2]

You have doubtless been informed by Mr. H[ancock] that you may soon expect ten Companies of Rifle men to joyn the Army.

I am more and more satisfied in the Appointment of General Lee. He is certainly an able officer and I think deeply embarked in the American Cause. The Congress have agreed to indemnify him from any loss of Property he may sustain by acting as an officer in the Army, but this I mention only to you at present and the small Circle. If any should be disaffected to his Appointment, pray use your utmost Endeavor to reconcile them to it. I am in great Haste, Your assured friend,

S. ADAMS

[1] Received by James Warren after the death of Dr. Warren.
[2] *Journals of the Continental Congress*, II. 99.

JOHN ADAMS TO JOSEPH WARREN [1]

PHYLADELPHIA, *June* 21, 1775

DR. SIR, — This Letter I presume will be delivered into your own Hand by the General. He proposes to set out, tomorrow, for your Camp. God speed him. Lee is Second Major General, Schuyler who is to command at N. York is the third and Putnam the fourth. How many Brigadiers general we shall have, whether five, seven or eight, is not determined, nor who they shall be. One from N. Hampshire, one from R. Island, two from Connecticutt one from N. York, and three from Massachusetts, perhaps.

I am almost impatient to be at Cambridge. We shall maintain a good Army for you. I expect to hear of Grumbletonians, some from parsimonious and others from Superstitious Prejudices. But we do the best we can, and leave the Event.

How do you like your Government? Does it make or remove Difficulties? I wish We were nearer to you.

The Tories lie very low both here and at New York. The latter will very soon be as deep as any Colony.

We have Major Skeene [2] a Prisoner, enlarged a little on his Parol, a very great Tool. I hope Govr. Tryon [3] will be taken care of. But We find a great many Bundles of weak Nerves. We are obliged to be as delicate and soft and modest and humble as possible.

Pray stir up every Man, who has a Quill to write me. We want to know the Number of your Army, a List of your officers, a State of your Government, the Distresses of Boston, the Condition of the Enemy, etc. I am, Dr Sir, your Friend,

JOHN ADAMS

We have all recommended Billy Tudor [4] for a Secretary to the General. Will he make a good one?

This moment informed of Powder arrived here, 500 Blls they say. We must send it along to you.

1 The letter is endorsed "Received by General James Warren after the death of General Joseph Warren."
2 Philip Skene (1725–1810). See Adams, *Familiar Letters*, 61.
3 William Tryon (1725–1788).
4 William Tudor (1750–1819). He was appointed Judge Advocate of the army, July 29, 1775.

JOHN ADAMS TO JAMES WARREN

PHYLADELPHIA, *June* 27, 1775

MY DEAR FRIEND, — I am extremely obliged to you for your Favour of the 20th of June. The last Fall I had a great many Friends who kept me continually well informed of every Event as it occurred: But this Time I have lost all my Friends, excepting Coll. Warren of Plymouth, and Coll. Palmer of Braintree, and my Wife.

Our dear Warren has fallen, with Laurells on his Brows as fresh and blooming as ever graced an Hero.

I have suffered infinitely this Time, from ill Health and blind Eyes at a Time when a vast Variety of great Objects were crowding upon my Mind, and when my dear Country was suffering all the Calamities of *Famine*, *Pestilence*, *Fire*, and *Sword* at once.

At this Congress we do as well as we can. I must leave it to some future opportunity, which I have a charming Confidence will certainly come to inform you fully of the History of our Debates and Resolutions.

Last Saturday night at Eleven o'clock an Express arrived from the worthy Govr Trumbull informing of the Battle of Charlestown. An hundred Gentlemen flocked to our Lodgings to hear the News. At one o' Clock Mr H[ancock] Mr A[dams] and myself went out to enquire after the Committee of this City, in order to beg some Powder. We found Some of them, and these with great Politeness and Sympathy for their brave Brethren in the Mass. agreed to go that night and send forward about Ninety Quarter Casks and before Morning it was in Motion. Between two and three o'Clock I got to bed.

We are contriving every Way we can think of to get you Powder. We have a Number of Plans for making Salt Petre and Gentlemen here are very confident that we shall be able to furnish Salt Petre and Powder of our own Manufacture, and that very Soon. A Method of making it will be published very soon by one of our Committees.[1]

[1] Printed by Bradford at Philadelphia, and reprinted, with additions by William Whiting, by Benjamin Edes.

Before this reaches you, Gen. Washington, Lee, etc., will arrive among you. I wish to God, you had been appointed a General Officer in the Room of some others. Adams and Adams strove to get it done. But, Notions, narrow Notions prevented it — not dislike to you, but fear of disobliging Pomroy,[1] and his Friends.

Your Govt. was the best We could obtain for you. We have passed some Resolutions concerning North Carolina which will do a great deal of good.[2] We have allowed them to raise 1000 Men, and to take Care of Traytors, if necessary. This must be kept secret.

We are sending you Ten Companies of Rifle Men. These, if the Gentlemen of the Southern Colonies are not very partial and much mistaken, are very fine fellows. They are the most accurate Marksmen in the World; they kill with great Exactness at 200 yards Distance; they have Sworn certain death to the ministerial officers. May they perform their oath.

You will soon find that the Continental Congress are in, deep enough. The Commissions to the officers of the Army; the Vote for your Government; the Votes about North Carolina; and a Multitude of other Votes which you will soon hear of will convince you.

I have inclosed you a hint about salt Petre. Germans and others here have an opinion that every stable, Dove house, Cellar, Vault, etc., is a Mine of salt Petre. The inclosed Proclamation, coincides with this opinion. The Mould under stables, etc., may be boiled soon into salt Petre it is said. Numbers are about it here.

[*No signature.*]

JAMES WARREN TO JOHN ADAMS. ADAMS MSS.

WATERTOWN, *June* 27, 1775

MY DEAR SIR, — I feel great reluctance in suffering any opportunity to pass without writing to you. I can easily suppose your anxiety as well as curiosity make you sollicitous to hear every thing that passes here.

Since my last nothing material has taken place. The military operations have consisted in a few movements, and a few shot exchanged with very little effect, sometimes on the side of Roxbury,

[1] Seth Pomroy (1706–1777).   [2] *Journals of the Continental Congress*, III. 107.

and sometimes on the side of Charlestown. Our army have taken every precaution in their power for their defence, and future operations. They are heaving up lines from Charles to Mystick River and have them in great forwardness. They are carried across Temple's farm, and his beautiful groves of locusts have fallen a sacrifice to the necessity of the times. At Roxbury they have fortified themselves in a manner almost as impregnable as Gage has done in Boston. We want but one article to enable us to act offensively, and make a vigorous campaign. Men in fine spirits, well provided with every thing but the one I mention. The Generals appointed give us great satisfaction, especially the first and the third, whose characters have for a great while been such as to fix our esteem and confidence. Your attention must be fixed on the article of powder, or — I will say no more. I can't but hope you will make some suitable provision for our General Thomas.[1] His merits in the military way have surprised us all. I can't describe to you the odds between the two camps. While one has been spiritless, sluggish, confused and dirty, I mean where General Putnam and our Friend Warren's influence have not had their effects; the other has been spirited, active, regular and clean. He has appeared with the dignity and abilities of a General.

We have no intercourse with Boston, get no intelligence from there but by those who steal out. From them we have certain accounts of the amazing slaughter made in the last action. Their men die of the slightest wounds, owing to the manner of living they are reduced to, so there will in the end be but little odds between being killed or wounded, and we may return perhaps 14 or 1500 killed. I am told General Howe says the army shall not return to Boston but by the way of Roxbury. A very pretty march. It is with confidence said that Burgoine has not been seen since the action, and it is given out that he is gone home. We are not without our hopes that we shall have little trouble from his enterprising genius. With regard to us, we are as busy as you ever saw pismires on a mole hill. Our attention is principally fixed on the

---

[1] John Thomas (1725-1776), who had just (May 25) accepted the appointment of lieutenant general of the Massachusetts army. *Journals of the Provincial Congress* (Mass.), 258.

army, to equip, regulate, quiet and inspirit them, and enough it is at times for us. Generals Washington and Lee I dare say will relieve us. . . .

JAS. WARREN

I have not been able to obtain the pamphlet you mentioned, and indeed after seeing it advertised in a [New] York paper have been less sollicitous, supposing you would have it from there.

SAMUEL ADAMS TO JAMES WARREN

PHILADELPHIA, June 28, 1775

MY DEAR SIR, — I have received your Letter of the 21 Instant and am beyond Measure rejoycd at the tryed Bravery of the American Troops in Charlestown. I hope speedily to receive a particular and exact Account of the killed and wounded on both sides. If the List on the side of the ministerial Army comes near to 1000, as seems to be the general opinion it may cool the Courage of the three Generals lately arrivd;[1] of the Courage of Gage I have been taught to entertain no Opinion.

I find by the Letters from our Friends that a Suspicion prevails of the Courage, Activity, or military Knowledge of some of our Generals. But, my dear Sir, take Care lest Suspicions be carried to a dangerous Length. Our Army have behavd valiantly. There may have been an Error; but that Error may have proceeded not from a Want of Spirit but a Want of Judgment. We have appointed the Generals you ask for. Preserve that Union upon which every thing we wish for depends. The Experience of Washington and Lee may make good all Deficiencies. Why should any of our Friends hesitate about the propriety of giving a Command to Genl. Lee?[2] He was not born an American, but he has heartily

[1] Howe, Burgoyne and Clinton.
[2] "I feel very, very happy in being able to give you assurances that will relieve an anxiety that I discover in your letter. You may rely on it, no suspicions, no uneasiness prevails at all with regard to our old generals, and everybody seems to be perfectly satisfied with the appointment of the new ones. I mean Washington and Lee. I have not heard a single objection to the last of them. . . . I know not what to say of your friend Lee. I believe he is a soldier, and a very industrious, active one; he came in just before dinner, drank some punch, said he wanted no dinner, took no notice of the company, mounted his horse, and went off again to the lines. I admire the soldier, but think civility, or even politeness not incompatible with his character. But this *inter nos.* I shall take care to speak highly of him on all occasions." *James Warren to Samuel Adams*, July 9, 1775. In Wells, *Life of Samuel*

espoused the Cause of America and abhors the oppressive Measures of the British Government against America. Prince Eugene, if I mistake not was a Frenchman[1] but he was a Scourge to France, and Marshall Saxe would have been equally, perhaps more so, if Great Britain had not foolishly slighted his offered Service. Admitting his Integrity, of which I cannot doubt, I think the sound Policy of appointing General Lee is evident, other English officers may from hence be assured that if they will afford a sufficient Pledge of their Merit they may have the Opportunity of distinguishing their Valor in the Cause of Liberty in America. So desirous was the Congress, that this Country should avail itself of the Abilities of Lee that they have voted to indemnify him for the Loss of property he may incur by engaging in this Service to the amount of £11,000 sterling, being the Estimate of his Estate in England, as soon as it shall be made to appear that such loss or any part of it hath happend.

This I think interests him strongly, and I mention it by no means that it should be made publick, for I think that would be imprudent, but to induce our Circle of Friends with the greater Cheerfulness to reconcile his Appointment to any, if such there be, who have any Scruples about it.

I sincerely lament the Loss of our truly amiable and worthy Friend Dr. Warren. There has scarcely if ever been a Cause so evidently just as that in which he fell so gloriously.

Pray write to me by every Opportunity. I have not time to enlarge or even to correct what I have written. Adieu my Friend.

S. ADAMS

The two inclos'd Letters to Mrs. Hooper[2] and Mrs. Inman[3] are from Wm Hooper, Esqr.,[4] one of the Delegates from N. Carolina who desires me to recommend them to your Care.[5]

Adams, II. 315. Lee did not make a wholly pleasing impression on Mrs. Warren. Lossing, *Field Book* (1853), II. 224 *n*. See the "address" of the Massachusetts Provincial Congress and Lee's reply in N.Y. Hist. Soc. *Collections*, 1871, 186.

1 François Eugène, of Savoy (1663–1736), was born in Paris, son of the Count of Soissons and the niece of Cardinal Mazarin.
2 Annie Clark.
3 Elizabeth Murray (Campbell) Inman, wife of Ralph Inman, of Cambridge.
4 William Hooper (1742–1790).
5 A letter from Samuel Adams to James Warren, July 2, 1775, is in Wells, *Life of Samuel Adams*, II. 317.

MERCY WARREN TO JOHN ADAMS.   ADAMS MSS.

WATERTOWN, *July* 5, 1775

DEAR SIR, — I have had the pleasure of seeing several of your letters in which you complain that your friends are rather remiss with regard to writing you, which I think inexcusable at a time when the liberties of all America and the fate of the British Empire depends in a great measure on the result of your deliberations. For if that respectable body of which you are a member fails, either from want of early intelligence or from any other cause at this important crisis, to pursue the wisest measures, what but inevitable destruction to this country must follow.

Could I have hoped it was in my power to give you either pleasure or intelligence, I should long ere this have taken up my pen, and added one more to the triumvirate of your friends. For be assured there are very few who can with more sincerity subscribe their names to the list. But as I write in compliance with Mr. Warren's request, I must tell you his application to public affairs leaves him little time to attend to the demands of private friendship. And could you look into a certain Assembly you would not wonder that his time is wholly engrossed, or that we ardently wish you may soon be here to assist in the public counsels of your own distressed Province.

I shall not attempt to give you a description of the ten fold difficulties that surround us. You have doubtless had it from better hands. Yet I cannot forbear to drop a tear over the inhabitants of our capital, most of them sent naked from the city to seek a retreat in the villages, and to cast themselves on the charity of the first hospitable hand that will receive them. Those who are left behind are exposed to the daily insults of a foe lost to that sense of honour, freedom and valour, once the characteristic of Britons, and even of the generosity and humanity which has long been the boast of all civilized nations. And while the plagues of famine, pestilence and tyranny reign within the walls, the sword is lifted without, and the artillery of war continually thundering in our ears.

The sea coasts are kept in constant apprehensions of being made miserable by the depredations of the once formidable navy of Britain, now degraded to a level with the corsairs of Barbary.

At the same time they are piratically plundering the Isles, and pilfering the borders to feed the swarms of veteran slaves shut up in the town. They will not suffer a poor fisherman to cast his hook in the ocean to bring a little relief to the hungry inhabitants without the pitiful bribe of a dollar each to the use of Admiral Greaves.

The venal system of administration appears to the astonishment of every good man in the corruption, duplicity and meanness, which run through every department, and while the faithless Gage will be marked with infamy for breach of promise, by the impartial historian, will not the unhappy Bostonians be reproached with want of spirit in putting it out of their own power to resent repeated injuries by giving these arms into the hand, which would have been better placed in the heart of a tyrant.

And now they are forbidden even to look out from their own house tops when he sends out his ruffians[1] to butcher their brethren, and wrap in flames the neighbouring towns. But I think this advertisement was as great a mark of timidity as the transaction was of a savage ferocity.[2] The laws of gratitude surely demanded that they should spare that town at least whose inhabitants from a principle of humanity saved the routed troops of *George the Third* from total destruction after the battle of Lexington.

But nothing that has taken place is more regretted than the death of your friend, the brave, the humane, the good Dr. Warren.

And though he fell covered with laurels and the wing of fame is spread over his monument, we are almost led to enquire why the useful, the virtuous patriot is cut off ere he reaches the meridian of his days, while the grey headed delinquent totters under the weight of accumulated guilt, and counting up his scores, is still adding crime to crime, till all mankind detest the hoary wretch, yet suffer him to live, to trifle with the rights of society, and to sport with the miseries of man.

The people here are universally pleased with the appointment of Generals Washington and Lee. I hope the delegates of the united Colonies will continue to act with dignity to themselves, and in a

---

[1] This may be Russians.   [2] See Adams, *Familiar Letters*, 74.

manner which will promote the glory, virtue and happiness of America. Let not the indiscreet nor the sanguinary conduct of any individual damp the ardor of such as are ready to fly to our assistance and generously to sacrifice the enjoyments of domestic life in support of freedom, and the inherent rights of their fellow men.

Your friend Dr. Cooper has just informed me that Dr. Eliot is confined on board a man of war,[1] and several of the inhabitants of Boston imprisoned. The crime of the first was the praying for Congresses, Continental and Provincial, and that of others was wishing success to American army.

Sad reflections on the times into which we are fallen crowd fast upon my mind; but I will no longer call off your attention from most important matters by expressing them....

M. WARREN

JOHN ADAMS TO JAMES WARREN

PHYLADELPHIA, *June* [*July*] 6th, 1775

DEAR SIR, — Every Line I receive from you gives me great Pleasure and is of vast Use to me in the public Cause. Your Letters were very usefull to me last Fall. Your Character became then known and much esteemed. The few Letters I have recd from you this Time, have increased the Desire of more, and some other Gentlemen who happened to know you, particularly Governor Hopkins[2] and Ward[3] of Rhode Island, have confirmed every good opinion which had been formed. I must intreat you to omit no Opportunity of Writing and to be as particular as possible.

Want of frequent Communication and particular Intelligence led us into the unfortunate Arrangement of General Officers which is likely to do so much Hurt. We never recd the most distant Intimation of any Design to new model your Army; and indeed Some of us were obliged to give up our own Judgments merely from Respect to what We took to be the Arrangement of our provincial Congress. I have made it my Business ever since I heard of this Error to wait upon Gentn. of the Congress at their Lodgings and

---

[1] Andrew Eliot (1718-1778), pastor of the New North Church in Boston. He was not thus confined.
[2] Stephen Hopkins (1707-1785).   [3] Samuel Ward (1725-1776).

elsewhere to let them into the Secret and contrive a Way to get out of the Difficulty, which I hope we shall effect.

I rejoice to hear of the great military Virtues and Abilities of General Thomas.

Alas poor Warren! *Dulce et decorum est pro Patria mori.* Yet I regret his Appointment to such a Command. For God's Sake my Friend let us be upon our Guard, against too much Admiration of our greatest Friends. President of the Congress, Chairman of the Committee of Safety, Major General and Chief Surgeon of the Army, was too much for Mortal, and This Accumulation of Admiration upon one Gentleman, which among the Hebrews was called Idolatry, has deprived us forever of the Services of one of our best and ablest Men. We have not a sufficient Number of such Men left to be prodigal of their Lives in future.

Every Brain is at Work to get Powder and salt-Petre, I hope We shall succeed, but We must be very Oeconomical of that Article. We must not use large Cannon if We can possibly avoid it.

This Letter will go by two fighting Quakers. Mr. Stephen Collins[1] and Mr. John Kaighn [Keays]. The first is the most hospitable benevolent Man alive. He is a Native of Lynn, a brother of Ezra Collins[2] of Boston and is rich, and usefull here. The last has been the Instrument of raising a Quaker Company in this City, who behave well and look beautifully in their Uniforms. My Love, Duty, Respects etc. where due. Adieu.

JOHN ADAMS

Secret and Confidential, as the Saying is.

The Congress is not yet so much alarmed as it ought to be. There are still hopes, that Ministry and Parliament, will immediately receed as soon as they hear of the Battle of Lexington, the Spirit of New York and Phyladelphia, the Permanency of the Union of the Colonies etc.: I think they are much deceived and that we shall have nothing but Deceit and Hostility, Fire, Famine, Pestilence and Sword from Administration and Parliament. Yet the Colonies like all Bodies of Men must and will have their Way and their Humour, and even their Whims.

These opinions of Some Colonies which are founded I think

---

[1] (1733-1794), son of Zaccheus and Elizabeth Collins.   [2] (1729-1807).

in their Wishes and passions, their Hopes and Fears, rather than in Reason and Evidence will give a whimsical Cast to the Proceedings of this Congress. You will see a strange Oscillation between love and hatred, between War and Peace — Preparations for War and Negociations for Peace. We must have a Petition to the King[1] and a delicate Proposal of Negociation, etc. This Negociation I dread like Death: But it must be proposed. We cant avoid it. Discord and total Disunion would be the certain Effect of a resolute Refusal to petition and negociate. My Hopes are that Ministry will be afraid of Negociation as well as We and therefore refuse it. If they agree to it, We shall have Occasion for all our Wit Vigilance and Virtue to avoid being deceived, wheedled threatened or bribed out of our Freedom. If we Strenuously insist upon our Liberties, as I hope and am pretty sure We shall however, a Negotiation, if agreed to, will terminate in Nothing. it will effect nothing. We may possibly gain Time and Powder and Arms.

You will see an Address to the People of G. Britain,[2] another to those of Ireland,[3] and another to Jamaica.[4]

You will also see a Spirited Manifesto.[5] We ought immediately to dissolve all Ministerial Tyrannies, and Custom houses, set up Governments of our own, like that of Connecticutt in all the Colonies, confederate together like an indissoluble Band, for mutual defence, and open our Ports to all Nations immediately. This is the system that your Friend has arrived at promoting from first to last: But the Colonies are not yet ripe for it — a Bill of Attainder, etc., may soon ripen them.

JOHN ADAMS TO JAMES WARREN

PHYLADELPHIA, *June* [*July*] 6th, 1775

DR SIR, — I have this Moment Sealed a Letter to you which is to go by my hospitable honest benevolent Friend Stephen Collins.

---

[1] *Journals of the Continental Congress*, II. 158.   [2] *Ib.*, 162.   [3] *Ib.*, 212.
[4] *Ib.*, 204. This was in recognition of an humble petition and memorial of the Assembly of Jamaica to the King, dated December 28, 1774, and printed in *Massachusetts Gazette* March 2, 1775.
[5] On taking arms. *Ib.*, 128.

But I have several Particulars to mention to you which are omitted in that Letter. Ten Companies of expert Riflemen have been ordered already from the 3 Colonies of P[ennsylvania], M[aryland], and V[irginia][1] some of them have marched under excellent officers. We are told by Gentlemen here that these Riflemen are Men of Property and Family, some of them of independent Fortunes, who go from the purest Motives of Patriotism and Benevolence into this service. I hope they will have Justice done them and Respect shewn them by our People of every Rank and order. I hope also that our People will learn from them the Use of that excellent Weapon a Rifled barrell'd Gun.

A few Minutes past, a curious Phenomenon appeared at the Door of our Congress — a german Hussar, a veteran in the Wars in Germany, in his Uniform and on Horseback, a forlorn Cap upon his Head, with a Streamer waiving from it half down to his Waist band, with a Deaths Head painted in Front, a beautifull Hussar Cloak ornamented with Lace and Fringe and Cord of Gold, a Scarlet Waist coat under it, with shining yellow metal Buttons, a Light Gun strung over his shoulder, — and a Turkish Sabre much Superior to an high Land broad sword very large and excellently fortifyed by his side — Holsters and Pistols upon his Horse — In Short the most warlike and formidable Figure, I ever saw.[2]

He says he has fifty Such Men ready to inlist under him immediately who have been all used to the service as Hussars in Germany, and desirous to ride to Boston immediately in order to see Burgoigne's light Horse. This would have a fine Effect upon the Germans through the Continent of whom there are Multitudes. What will be done is yet uncertain. I should not myself be fond of raising many Soldiers out of N. England. But the other Colonies are more fond of sending Men than I expected. They have their Reasons, some plausible, Some whimsical. They have a Secret

[1] *Journals of the Continental Congress*, II. 89.
[2] "On motion, *Resolved*, That the delegates from Pennsylvania have liberty to treat with and employ 50 Hussars, who have been in actual service, and send them forward to join the troops before Boston under General Washington." *Journals of the Continental Congress*, II. 173. This action was hasty and ill-advised, and three weeks later Congress directed the discharge of any who had been engaged under this resolution. *Ib.*, 238. In June, 1776, the Congress determined to raise a German battalion in Pennsylvania and Maryland. 2 *Pennsylvania Archives*, XI. 73. Its colonel, Nicholas Haussegger, commissioned in July, 1776, deserted to the British in July, 1778.

Fear, a Jealousy, that New England will soon be full of Veteran Soldiers and at length conceive Designs unfavourable to the other Colonies. This may be Justly thought whimsical. But others Say, that by engaging their own Gentlemen and Peasants and Germans etc they shall rivet their People to the public Cause — this has more weight in it. But that it may have this Effect it is necessary that all who shall be sent be respectfully treated.

JAMES WARREN TO JOHN ADAMS.   ADAMS MSS.

WATERTOWN, *July* 7, 1775

MY DEAR SIR, — I am much obliged to you for your favours by the sage, brave, and amiable General Washington, by Major Mifflin, and by the express which came to hand the night before last. I am much pleased with General Washington. He fully answers the character you have given of him. Major Mifflin I have not yet found out, tho' I am told he was once in the room while I was at the General's. I shall take particular care to know him soon, perhaps this day, as I am to dine with the General. General Lee I have seen but a minute. He appears to me a genius in his way; he had the marks about him of having been in the trenches. I heartily rejoice at the appointment of these two generals, and I dare say it will give you pleasure to hear that every body seems to be satisfied with it. I have not heard a single word uttered against it. This is more than I expected with regard to the second. Since their arrival every thing goes well in the army. They are quiet, busy, and forming fast to order. Our business lessens upon our hands, and we find a great relief from the General's arrival. I am told they are very active, etc. You will have a return of the army from the General I suppose, who will be able to give it with more accuracy than any body. The general estimation of our army is about 16 or 17000, ten of which are at Cambridge etc., the remainder at Roxbury. We can't with any certainty determine the numbers of the enemy. We suppose from the best grounds we have that when the [New] York troops arrive, which are daily expected, they will amount to 9,000 at least, perhaps more, including the black and white negroes engaged in their service in Boston. The battle of Charlestown gave them a great shock. It is now pretty certain that near 1500, and chiefly of their best troops, among which were about 90 officers, were killed and wounded, about 1000 of which were killed. This is amazing, but I believe true. I will endeavour to get and inclose the return exact as we have it. Your appointment of the other generals I can't say is so well approved of. We can't investigate the principle you went on, tho' I think I can trace an influence that marks some of them. But I will say no more on that head; you have enough of it in a letter I wrote in conjunction with H[eath] and G[erry]. The general was very sorry and somewhat embarrassed with the neglect of Thomas. I am told Heath behaves very well, and is willing to give place to him. I am much obliged to you and my friend Adams for thinking of me. I am content to move in a small sphere. I expect no distinction but that of an honest man who has exerted every nerve. You and I must be content without a slice from the great pudding now on the table. The condition of the poor people of Boston is truly miserable. We are told that James Lovel, Master Leach [1] and others are in gaol for some trifling offences, the last for drinking success to the American army. Their offences may be capital. It is reported that Doctors Elliot and Mather [2] are on board a man of war. From those circumstances you may form an idea of their situation.

I am very sorry for the trouble given you by your companions and eyes. I hope to hear the last are better, if not the first. I am much pleased with your doings in general, and the prospects you hold up to me. Is it not our duty to pray that the infatuation of Britain may last one year more at least. The powder you sent us arrived yesterday, and was viewed as it passed with a kind of pleasure I suppose you felt in sending it. The want of that article is the only obstacle I have in getting through a project of mine for a fleet. I made the motion early in the Sessions, and though opposed by Pickering,[3] etc., this is the only reason that prevailed.

1 John Leach (1724?–1799) kept a "navigation school" in Boston before the Revolution. His diary during his confinement is in *N.E. Hist. Gen. Register*, XIX. 255.
2 Samuel Mather (1706–1785).
3 John Pickering (1740–1811). See *Journals of the Provincial Congress* (Mass.), 308, 318, 361.

We talk of rising tomorrow. I hope we shall. I long to ramble in the fields a day or two, and more especially since they have been watered with delightful showers. . . .

JAS. WARREN

. . . I can't send you a list of the officers of our army. I hope you wont make establishments for them in proportion to what you hint is done for the Generals. High Establishments will not be relished here, and I think bad policy in every view, and will lead us fast into the sins, folly and sufferings of our old impolitic and unnatural mother. There is a printed account of the battle got out of Boston giving a gorgeous account of their victory over the rebels, with a great slaughter made among them, and with a loss of only 170 on their side. This lying paper I cannot obtain for you.[1]

JOHN ADAMS TO JAMES WARREN

PHILADELPHIA, *July* 10th, 1775

DR SIR, — I have just Time to inclose you a Declaration and an Address.[2] How you will like them I know not. A Petition was sent yesterday by Mr. Richard Penn in one ship and a Duplicate goes in another Ship this day. In exchange for these Petitions, Declarations and Addresses I suppose We shall receive Bills of Attainder and other such like Expressions of Esteem and Kindness.

This Forenoon has been spent in an Examination of a Mr Kirkland,[3] a worthy Missionary among the Oneida Indians. He was very usefull last Winter among all the Six Nations, by interpreting and explaining the Proceedings of the Continental Congress and by representing the Union and Power of the Colonies as well as the Nature of the Dispute.

The Congress inclines to wait for Despatches from General Washington before they make any Alteration in the Rank of the Generals, least they should make some other Mistake. But every Body is well inclined to place General Thomas in the Stead of Pomroy.

[1] It is dated June 26. A copy is in the Massachusetts Historical Society.
[2] Nos. 52 and 57 of the "Bibliographical Notes" in *Journals of the Continental Congress*, III. 508.
[3] Samuel Kirkland (1741-1808).

You must not communicate without great Discretion what I write about our Proceedings, for all that I hint to you is not yet public. I am etc.

John Adams to James Warren

Philadelphia *July* 11 1775

Hond and Dr Sir, — I have the Pleasure of inclosing you a Declaration. Some call it a Manifesto. And We might easily have occasioned a Debate of half a Day whether it should be called a Declaration or a Manifesto.

Our Address to the People of Great Britain[1] will find many Admirers among the Ladies, and fine Gentlemen; but it is not to my Taste. Prettynesses, Juvenilities, and much less Puerilities become not a great assembly like this the Representative of a great People.

July 23 We have voted Twenty-two thousand Men for your Army. If this is not enough to encounter every Officer and Soldier in the british Army, if they were to send them all from Great Britain and Ireland, I am mistaken.

What will N. England do with such Floods of Paper Money? We shall get the Continent nobly in our Debt. We are Striking off our Paper Bills in Nine different sorts, some of twenty Dollars, some of Eight, 7, 6, 5, 4, 3, 2, 1. We shall be obliged to strike off four Millions of Dollars I fear.

Secret as usual. Our Fast[2] has been kept more strictly and devoutly than any sunday was ever observed in this City. The Congress heard Duché[3] in the Morning and Dr Allison[4] in the Evening, good Sermons.

By the way do let our Friend Adams's son[5] be provided for as a Surgeon.

---

1 The committee to prepare it was composed of Richard Henry Lee, Robert R. Livingston and Edmund Pendleton. It is not known which member drafted the Address.
2 Appointed for July 20.   3 Jacob Duché (1737–1798).
4 Francis Allison (1736–1779).
5 Samuel Adams (1751–1788), who studied medicine with Dr. Joseph Warren. The returns show a surgeon of this name in Colonel Fellows' regiment, 1775; in Colonel Phinney's regiment, 1776, and in the continental Hospital, 1777–1780, and possibly later.

JAMES WARREN TO JOHN ADAMS. ADAMS MSS.

WATERTOWN, *July* 11, 1775

MY DEAR SIR, — I wrote you several days ago, and wrote in a hurry, expecting the General's express would be along before I could finish. But he has been detained, and [I] am told will be on his journey this morning. I was much chagrined last evening when sitting under a tree by the bridge Fessenden rode up from Philadelphia without a single letter for me. He says you complain that you have no letters. I have endeavoured to do my part. I expected we should have rose before this,[1] and I should have got a range over the fields before our election, but I begin to dispair. One thing after another continually crowds upon us. The General thinks he should have more men.[2] I am of the same opinion. How to get them is our difficulty. We are now raising 1700 for the express purpose of guarding the sea coasts. The people are so engaged at this busy season that the militia, if called, would come with reluctance, and tarry but a short time, just long enough to put the camp in confusion. What course we are to take in consequence of an application from the General which now only detains us, I know not. I could wish to have seen more men from the southward. I always forgot to tell you I have seen your letter to Gerry, expressing Mr. Gadsden's[3] opinion about fixing out armed vessels and setting up for a naval power. I thought it very happy to have so great an authority confirming my own sentiments, and having proposed in Congress just such a project the beginning of the session, borrowed the letter to support it. But yet I have not been able to effect it. Pickering and his politics, the want of faith and ardor in Gerry, etc., and above all the want of powder has prevented it. The last is an objection, though I think it would be like planting corn. Ten very good going sloops, from 10 to 16 guns, I am persuaded would clear our coasts. What would 40 such be to the Continent. Such a determination might make a good figure on your Journals. We are all still; not a word of news since my last. The troops were

1 The Provincial Congress adjourned July 13.
2 *Washington to Warren*, July 10, 1775, in *Writings* (Ford), III. 5.
3 Christopher Gadsden (1724–1805).

crossing the ferry yesterday in great numbers. Things will not remain long in this situation. I expect another action soon. God grant us success. I believe he will. . . .

JAS. WARREN

SAMUEL ADAMS TO JAMES WARREN

PHILADA., *July* 12, 1775

MY DEAR SIR, — Give me leave to recommend to your friendly Notice and to desire you would introduce into the Circle of our Friends Mr. Hugh Hughes[1] of New York, a worthy sensible Man, whose Virtue has renderd him obnoxious to all the Tories of that City. I know I cannot say more *to you* in favor of any Man. He is perhaps as poor as I am but he "goes about doing good." I am sincerely, your affectionate Frd.

S. ADAMS

Pray write me particularly *of Men* as well as Events.

JAMES WARREN TO JOHN ADAMS. ADAMS MSS.

WATERTOWN, *July* 20, 1775

MY DEAR SIR, — I yesterday returned from Plymouth where I had opportunity of spending only three or four days, in such a scurry of private business as would scarcely admit of a single meditation in the calm retirements of the fields. I breakfasted in the morning with your sensible and amiable lady. She showed me a letter from you. I read it with pleasure. I arrived here about 12 o'clock. You will say a late hour for election day. I found here two of your letters, one of them inclosing the two pamphlets, and your friend Mr. Collins called upon me this morning and delivered two more. I think myself greatly obliged to you for your friendship, confidence, and the marks of partiality I meet with in every letter I receive from you. I had but an hour's conversation with your friend. From the best judgment I can make in so short an acquaintance he is worthy of your friendship. I admire his open frankness and judicious observations and sentiments. He has prom-

1 Afterwards Assistant Quartermaster General. He died in 1810.

ised to dine with me tomorrow or next day. Our new Assembly met yesterday, and only chose Speaker and clerk,[1] and postponed the choice of Councillors till tomorrow morning. I fear with all this deliberation we shall not get such a board as will please you. Boston is the only place to hold election in. I hope the next will be there; but if we might do as we would, it is astonishing how few sterling men are to be found in so large a Province as this is. I am not able to give my opinion of the Pamphlets you sent me, not having had time to read them. I was late last evening settling the list of Councillors; this morning I had many things to do, and then to go to meeting. The Fast is observed here with a strictness and devotion that shows the opinion the people have of the authority that appointed it, as well as their reverence for him who overrules all events, and has so signally appeared in our favour. So few occurrences have taken place since my last in the military way that your curiosity will not be sufficiently satisfied with an account of them. I will endeavour to recollect them all. The attempt on Long Island,[2] the taking off all the stock and afterwards returning to burn the buildings (which you will have in the papers,) was certainly a bold, intrepid manoeuvre, and as such astonished our enemies. The barges full of armed men were afraid to attack our whale boats, at a proper distance, and the armed vessels, either agitated with fear, or destitute of judgment, did it without execution. The next thing that took place, was the possessing and fortifying a post by Brown's House, very near their lines. This has been effected with the loss only of one man, and he not employed there, tho' they worked in open sight of them, and exposed to an incessant fire from their cannon, which our people treated with the extremest contempt, not so much as once leaving their work, or returning a shot. No general movements have taken place. There was an appearance of it the day before yesterday on Roxbury side; but they did not venture out. General Thomas, who as yet continued in that command, made an excellent disposition to receive them, and was disappointed. Roxbury is amazingly strong. I believe it would puzzle 10,000 troops to go through it, I mean of the best in the world. I am just told that our boats have this day been

[1] James Warren and James Freeman.   [2] Adams, *Familiar Letters*, 80.

to the Lighthouse and burnt it in spite of the firing from a man of war and a number of boats. I hear it was executed by 300 Rhode Islanders. I don't learn that they suffered any loss. It is said they are more afraid of our whale boats than we are of their men of war. A few armed vessels, I am abundantly convinced, would produce great consequences. I want to see the Riflemen, and should be pleased to see the Hussar at the head of his troop. You need not fear our treating them with the utmost tenderness and affection. There is a strong spirit of love and cordiality for our friends of the other colonies prevailing here. The finger of Heaven seems to be in every thing. I fear nothing now so much as the small Pox in our army. (There is some danger of it, tho' I hope it will be stop'd), and proposals of a conciliatory nature from England. The first would be dreadful, but the last more so. I see the difficulties you have to struggle against, and the mortification you are obliged to submit to. I did not expect another petition. I hope however your sentiments and plans will finally prevail. The infatuation of Britain may supply the firmness of your brethren, and effect what their timidity and ridiculous moderation would otherways prevent. If the Canadians should relish an army of ours there, as I am told they will, I think it would be a grand move. Captain Darby,[1] who we sent with the account of the battle of the 19th of April, returned two days ago. He was there eight days, and came away before Gage's packet arrived. He says trade and the stocks were amazingly affected in that short time. Lord Dartmouth sent three times for him. He refused to go, and when he threatened him he decamped, got on board, and came without either entering or clearing. I shall enclose you a letter bro't by him from Sheriff Lee,[2] and one of the latest papers. By the letter I fancy General Gage is to expect no other reinforcement this fall. They are very sickly, and are greatly reduced. The Tories in Boston I believe are low enough, are bowed down with the load of guilt they have by their wickedness accumulated, and the apprehensions of what is to

[1] John Derby. He arrived July 18, and set out at once for Philadelphia. He had sailed from Salem April 29, and reached London May 29. General Harvey asked whether notice should not be taken of this messenger of rebellion. Hutchinson, *Diary and Letters*, 1. 461, 464.
[2] William Lee (1737-1795), a brother of Francis Lightfoot, Richard Henry and Arthur Lee. See Ford, *Letters of William Lee*, in three volumes.

CAPTAIN JOHN DERBY
From a silhouette in the possession of Dr. Frederick Cheever Shattuck

come. I am concerned for your health in this hot season. Pray take care of it. I have dispensed with attendance on public worship this afternoon in order to write to you, having no other time. Colonel Read [1] was kind enough to give me notice of this opportunity. Pray present my best respects to all my friends, among which I presume to rank Mr. Hopkins and Ward. Your own goodness will induce you to continue your favours. I shall lose no opportunity of writing as long [as] you continue to be pleased with it. When you are tired with my incorrect ramblings you will I hope very honestly tell me of it. I shall think it not strange, and shan't think of resentment. I never write well. I am sure I can't here crowded with business and surrounded with company. Your usual candour must be called into exercise; it is greatly relied on. I am, as I believe I shall be, your sincere friend

JAS. WARREN

JOHN ADAMS TO JAMES WARREN

PHILADELPHIA, *July* 23d, 1775

DR. SIR, — I have many things to write you which thro. Haste and Confusion I fear, I shall forget.

Upon the Receipt of General Washington's Letter,[2] the Motion which I made Some Days before for appointing General Thomas first Brigadier was renewed and carried, so that the return of the Express will carry his Commission. I hope that this will give all the satisfaction which is now to be given. You ask me upon what Principle We proceeded in our first Arrangement. I answer upon the Principle of an implicit Complyance with the order in which the General officers were chosen in our Provincial Congress last Fall. Not one of us would have voted for the Generals in the order in which the General Officers were chosen in our Provincial Congress

---

1 Joseph Reed.

2 "General Thomas is much esteemed and earnestly desired to continue in the service: and as far as my opportunities have enabled me to judge I must join in the general opinion that he is an able good officer and his resignation would be a public loss. The postponing him to Pomroy and Heath, whom he has commanded, would make his continuance very difficult, and probably operate on his mind." *Washington to the Continental Congress*, July 10, 1775. *Writings* (Ford), III. 15. Congress appointed Thomas "in room of General Pomeroy, who never acted under the commission sent him," July 19. *Journals of the Continental Congress*, II. 191.

last Fall; Not one of us, would have voted for the Generals in the order in which they were placed, if We had not thought that you had settled the Rank of every one of them last Fall in Provincial Congress and that We were not at Liberty to make any Alteration. I would not have been so shackled however, if my Colleagues had been of my Mind.

But, in the Case of the Connecticutt officers, We took a Liberty to alter the Rank established by the Colony and by that Means made much Uneasiness; so that We were sure to do Mischief whether We conformed or deviated from Colony arrangements. I rejoice that Thomas had more Wisdom than Spencer [1] or Woorster, and that he did not leave the Camp nor talk imprudently. If he had we should have lost him from the Continental service; for I assure you, Spencer by going off, and Woorster by unguarded Speeches have given high offence here, it will cost us Pains to prevent their being discarded from the service of the Continent with Indignation. Gentlemen here had no private Friendships Connections, or Interests which prompted them to vote for the arrangement they made but were influenced only by a Regard to the Service; and they are determined that their Commissions shall not be despised.

I have read of Times, either in History or Romance, when Great Generals would cheerfully serve their Country, as Captains or Lieutenants of Single Companies, if the Voice of their Country happened not to destine them to an higher Rank; but such exalted Ideas of public Virtue seem to be lost out of the World. Enough of this.

I have laboured with my Colleagues to agree upon proper Persons to recommend for a Quarter Master General, a Commissary of Musters and a Commissary of Artillery [2] — but in vain. The Consequence has been that the appointment of these important, and lucrative officers is left to the General, against every proper Rule and Principle, as these offices are Checks upon his. This is a great Misfortune to our Colony; however, I hope that you and

---

1 Spencer refused at first to serve under Putnam, but later consented to the arrangement.
2 Thomas Mifflin was appointed Quartermaster-General August 14, 1775; Ezekiel Cheever, Commissary of Artillery Stores, August 17.

others, will think of proper Persons and recommend them to the General.

There is, my Friend, in our Colony a great Number of Persons well qualified for Places in the Army, who have lost their all, by the outrages of Tyranny, whom I wish to hear provided for. Many of them will occur to you. I beg leave to mention a few. Henry Knox, William Bant[1] young Hichbourne the Lawyer[2] William Tudor, and Perez Morton.[3] These are young Gentlemen of Education and Accomplishments, in civil Life, as well as good Soldiers; and if at this Time initiated into the service of their Country might become in Time and with Experience able officers, if they could be made Captains or Brigade Majors, or put into some little Places at present I am very sure their Country would loose nothing by it, in Reputation or otherwise. A certain Delicacy which is necessary to a good Character may have prevented their making any applications, but I know they are desirous of serving.

I must enjoin Secrecy upon you, in as strong Terms as Mr. Hutchinson used to his confidential Correspondents; and then confess to you that I never was since my Birth, so compleatly miserable as I have been since the Tenth of April. Bad Health, blind eyes, want of Intelligence from our Colony, and above all the unfortunate and fatal Divisions, in our own Seat in Congress, which have lost us Reputation, as well as many great Advantages which We might otherwise have obtained for our Colony have made me often envy the active Hero in the Field, who, if he does his own Duty, is sure of Applause, tho he falls in the Execution of it.

It is a vast and complicated System of Business which We have gone through, and We were all of us unexperienced in it. Many Things may be wrong, but no small Proportion of these are to be attributed to the Want of Concert and Union among the Mass. Delegates.

We have passed a Resolution that each Colony make such Provision as it thinks proper and can afford, for defending their Trade

1 One of the name was a member of an independent Company formed at Boston, in 1776.
2 Benjamin Hichborn, who was taken by the British on his return from Philadelphia, and whose experiences are related by Dr. Belknap in 1 *Proceedings*, IV. 79.
3 (1751–1837).

in Harbours Rivers, and on the Sea Coast, against Cutters and Tenders.[1] We have had in Contemplation a Resolution to invite all Nations to bring their Commodities to Market here,[2] and like Fools have lost it for the present. This is a great Idea. What shall we do? Shall we invite all Nations to come with their Luxuries, as well as Conveniences and Necessaries? or shall We think of confining our Trade with them to our own Bottoms, which alone can lay a Foundation for great Wealth and naval Power? Pray think of it.

I rejoice that the Generals and Coll. Reed and Major Mifflin are so well received. My most respectfull Compliments to them all.

I thank you and Mrs. Warren a thousand Times for her kind and elegant Letter. Intreat a Continuance of her Favours in this Way, to your old Friend

[*No signature.*][3]

JOHN ADAMS TO JAMES WARREN [4]

PHILADELPHIA, *July* 24th, 1775

DEAR SIR, — In Confidence. I am determined to write freely to you this time. A certain great Fortune and piddling Genius, whose Fame has been trumpeted so loudly, has given a silly Cast to our whole Doings.[5] We are between Hawk and Buzzard. We ought to have had in our Hands a month ago the whole Legislative, executive and judicial of the whole Continent, and have completely

---

1 *Journals of the Continental Congress*, III. 189.
2 *Ib.*, 200. On the following day, July 22, the question was "postponed to be taken up at some future day."
3 Endorsed "Favored by Mr. Hitchbourne."
4 This is taken from a copy of the letter, in an unidentified writing, in the Warren papers. This copy also gives the letter from John Adams to his wife, taken like the other from Hichborn, and the facetious paragraph from Benjamin Harrison's letter to Washington which has given rise to so much gossip since, and which Jared Sparks omitted in his *Correspondence of the Revolution*. The two Adams letters are given in *Works of John Adams*, II. 411 *n.* with an explanation of the entrusting them to Hichborn. The letters were printed in Draper's *Massachusetts Gazette*, August 17, 1775, and while the text now given differs from that used in the *Works*, it does not differ materially. In a letter from Hannah Winthrop to Mercy Warren, September 30, 1775, she wrote: "I have taken pains to procure the Letters for you, but have not been able. As for the Versification, it was in a hand Bill, and so scurrilous as not to be worth notice." No copy has been found.
5 John Dickinson, a conservative in this Congress.

modeled a Constitution; to have raised a naval Power, and opened all our Ports wide; to have arrested every Friend to Government on the Continent and held them as Hostages for the poor Victims in Boston, and then opened the Door as wide as possible for Peace and Reconciliation. After this they might have petitioned, and negotiated, and addressed etc. if they would. Is all this extravagant? Is it wild? Is it not the soundest Policy?

One Piece of News, Seven thousand Weight of Powder arrived here last Night. We shall send some along as soon as we can, but you must be patient and frugal.

We are lost in the Extensiveness of our Field of Business. We have a Continental Treasury to establish, a Paymaster to choose and a Committee of Correspondence or Safety, or Accounts, or something, I know not what, that has confounded Us all Day.

Shall I *hail* you Speaker of the House or Counsellor or what? What kind of an Election had you? What sort of Magistrates do you intend to make?

Will your new Legislative and executive feel bold or irresolute? Will your Judicial hang and whip and fine and imprison without scruples? I want to see our distress'd Country once more — yet I dread the Sight of Devastation.

You observe in your Letter the Oddity of a great Man.[1] He is a queer Creature. But you must love his Dogs if you love him, and forgive a thousand whims for the Sake of the Soldier and the Scholar.

SAMUEL ADAMS TO JAMES WARREN

PHILADA., *July* 24, 1775

MY DEAR SIR, — I am exceedingly obligd to you for your Letter of the 9th of July. It affords me very great Satisfaction to be informd by you, that "no Suspicions, no Uneasiness at all prevails with Regard to our old Generals."[2] I assure you I have been otherwise informd since I received your Letter. Indeed I do not always rely much upon the Information we have, being often

---

[1] Charles Lee.   [2] Adams, *Familiar Letters*, 89.

obligd even to the Citizens for the Intelligence they are pleasd to give us of the State of our Army, the Character of our officers and the Scituation of our oppressd Friends in Boston. However ill a Choice was made of Delegates for the Continental Congress by our Colony it would certainly have been good Policy, to have as far as possible supported their Reputation and given them some Degree of Weight by putting it in their Power at least to ascertain Matters of Fact within their own Colony. But I am disposd to make Allowance for the Multiplicity of Affairs you must attend to, and will cease to complain lest I should charge our Friends foolishly. I have many things to say to you. I expect we shall soon make a short Adjournment.[1] If so, I shall then have the Opportunity of seeing you. In the meantime I have one favor to ask of you. I have an only Son, for whom my Anxiety is great. He was educated at Harvard College and afterwards was Pupil to our worthy deceased Friend Dr. Warren. Warren spoke well of this young Fellow as being capable in his Business. If he is not already provided for as a Surgeon in the Army, I shall be much obligd to you if you will use your Influence for his Promotion as far as he shall appear to have merit. I am your Friend,

S. ADAMS

JOHN ADAMS TO JAMES WARREN

July 26, 1775

DEAR SIR, — I can never Sufficiently regret that this Congress have acted so much out of Character as to leave the Appointment of the Quarter Master General, Commissary of Musters and Commissary of Artillery to the General; As these officers are Checks upon the General, and he a Check upon them, there ought not to be too much Connection between them. They ought not to be under any dependance upon him or so great obligations of Gratitude as those of a Creature to the Creator.

---

1 "The arduous Business that has been before the Congress and the close Application of the Members, added to the necessity and importance of their visiting their several Colonies and attending their respective Conventions, have induced them to make a recess during the sultry Month of August." *Samuel Adams to his Wife*, July 30, 1775. *Writings*, III. 221. See also, Adams, *Familiar Letters*, 90.

We have another office of vast Importance to fill, I mean that of Paymaster General; and if it is not filled with a Gentleman, whose Family, Fortune, Education, Abilities and Integrity, are equal to its Dignity, and whose long Services in the great Cause of America have abundantly merited it, it shall not be my Fault. However I can't foretell with Certainty whether I shall be so fortunate as to succeed.

I see by Edes's last Paper that Pidgeon[1] has been Commissary for the Mass. Forces and Joseph Pearce Palmer,[2] Quarter Master General. No Body was kind enough to notify me of these appointments or any other.

We shall establish a Post office,[3] and do what We can to make salt Petre and to obtain Powder.[4] By the Way about Six Tons have arrived here within 3 days and every Barrell of it, is ordered to you.

I want a great deal of Information. I want to know more precisely than I do the Duties and necessary Qualifications of the officers — the Quarter Master, Commissary of Stores and Provisions, the Commissary of Musters and the Commissary of Artillery, as well as the Paymaster General, the Adjutant General, the Aid de Camps, the Brigade Majors, the Secretaries, etc.

I want to know more exactly the Characters and [bio]graphy of the officers in the Army. I want to be precisely informed when and where, and in what Station, General Ward has served, General Thomas, the two Fry's,[5] Whitcomb,[6] etc., and what Colonells We have in the Army and their Characters.

I am distressed to know what Engineers you have, and what is become of Gridly[7] and Burbank,[8] what service they have seen and what are their Qualifications. Yours, etc.

[*No signature.*]

---

1 John Pigeon. He had been the Commissary General of the Massachusetts forces certainly since April. 1 *Proceedings*, xv. 92.
2 (1751–1829).   3 *Journals of the Continental Congress*, III. 208.   4 *Ib.*, 218.
5 James Frye (1709–1766) and Joseph Frye (1711–1794). They were cousins, and had served in the expedition against Louisburg.
6 John Whitcomb (*c.* 1720–1812).   7 Richard Gridley (1711–1796).
8 Silas Burbank, of Scarborough?

JOHN ADAMS TO JAMES WARREN

July 26, 1775

DR. SIR, — I shall make you sick at the Sight of a Letter from me.

I find by Edes's Paper that Joseph Pearse Palmer is Quarter Master General. I confess I was surprized.

This office is of high Rank and vast Importance. The Deputy Quarter Master General whom we have appointed for the New York Department, is a Mr. Donald Campbell,[1] an old regular officer, whom We have given the Rank of Collonell. The Quarter Master General cannot hold a lower Rank perhaps than a Brigadier.

Mr. Palmer is a young Gentleman of real Merit and good Accomplishments; but I should not have thought of a less Man than Major General Fry for the Place. It requires an able experienced officer. He goes with the Army and views the Ground and marks out the Encampment, etc., besides other very momentous Duties.

I have written to Mr. Palmer, and informed him that the Appointment of this Officer is left with the General.

My dear Friend, it is at this critical Time of great Importance to our Province, that We take Care to promote none to Places but such as will give them Dignity and Reputation. If We are not very solicitous about this We shall injure our Cause with the other Colonies. Yours,

[*No signature.*]

I hope before another Year We shall become more familiarly acquainted with this great piece of Machinery an Army.

We have voted three Millions of Dollars. Six Tons of Powder are arrived and We have ordered every Pound of it to you.

12 o'clock, July 26, 1775. this Moment 130 full Blls making Six Tons and an half of Powder is brought into the State House yard in Six Waggons — to be sent off to you.

[1] *Journals of the Continental Congress,* III. 186.

JOHN ADAMS TO JAMES WARREN

PHILADELPHIA, *July* 27, 1775.

DEAR SIR, — The Congress have this Day made an establishment of an Hospital and appointed Dr. Church Director and Surgeon, and have done themselves the Honour of unanimously appointing the Honourable James Warren, Esqr. of Plymouth in the Massachusetts Bay, Paymaster General of the Army. The Salary of this officer is one hundred Dollars per Month. It is an office of high Honour and great Trust.

There is another Quantity of Powder arrived in New Jersey, about 5000 Weight from So. Carolina, and it is said that another Boat has arrived in this River with about Six or Seven Tons. It will be ordered to the Generals Washington and Schuyler.

We have voted fifty Thousand Dollars, for Powder to be got immediately — if possible.

I begun this Letter merely to mention to you a Number of young Gentlemen bound to the Camp: Mr. George Lux, Son of a particular Friend of my Friend Chase; Mr. Hopkins and Mr. Smith, all of Baltimore in Maryland. Mr. Cary is with them, son of Mr. Cary of Charlestown [1] — neither Father nor Son want Letters. Your fast day Letter to me is worth its Weight in Gold. I had by that Packett Letters from you, Dr. Cooper, Coll. Quincy and Mrs. Adams, which were each of them worth all that I have recd from others since I have been here.

[*No signature.*]

SAMUEL ADAMS TO JAMES WARREN

PHILADA., *July* 29, 1775

MY DEAR SIR, — I have received your favor of the 20th Instant by Express. I observe that our new House of Representatives is *organized*, and am exceedingly pleasd with the Choice they have made of their Speaker. I find that two of the former Boston Mem-

[1] Richard Cary (1717-1790) and his son Richard (1747-   ), an aid to Washington in 1776.

bers are left out.[1] C— is kickd up Stairs,[2] etc., etc. I have not Leisure at present to write to you particularly. I expect soon to see you. I must inform you that you were yesterday unanimously chosen Paymaster General, with the pay of 100 Dollars per month, if I do not misremember.

The Bearer hereof is a Maryland young Gentleman by the name of Lux. His father is a Gentleman of Character as a Mercht. in Baltimore who is a friend to American Liberty and I am informed has shown Benevolence to the poor of my Native Town. I am therefore bound in Gratitude to desire your Notice of him so far as to recommend him to some of our military officers. He proposes to joyn the Army. Excuse this unconnected Epistle and be assured that I am your unfeigned friend,

SAML. ADAMS

Dr. Church is Director General and Chief Physician of the Hospital with the Power of appointing Surgeons, etc. I wish my Son could get Employmt in the Army. He has lost his Friend under whose care he was educated; Mr. Lux has several Companions with him, young Gentlemen who are in quest of Laurels.

JOHN ADAMS TO JAMES WARREN

PHILADELPHIA, *July* 30th, 1775

DEAR SIR, — For the Honour of the Massachusetts I have laboured in Conjunction with my Brethren to get you chosen Paymaster General and Succeeded so well that the Choice was unanimous! But whether We did you a Kindness or a Disservice I know not. And whether you can attend it or will incline to attend it, I know not. You will consider of it however.

Pray, who do you intend to make Secretary of the Province?[3] Has not our Friend deserved it? Is he not fit for it? Has any other Candidate So much Merit or so good Qualifications? I hope his temporary Absence will not injure him.

---

1 Thomas Cushing, who had led the delegation in the Third Provincial Congress, and Oliver Wendell.
2 Thomas Cushing, now chosen to the Council.
3 A Secretary was not appointed until August 28, when Samuel Adams was chosen to the office.

This Letter goes by my good Friend Mr. William Barrell a worthy Bostonian transmuted into a worthy Philadelphian. But whether you will grasp this Letter or the Hand that writes it first Is uncertain, both about the same Time I hope.[1]

[*No signature.*]

JAMES WARREN TO JOHN ADAMS. ADAMS MSS.

WATERTOWN, *July* 31, 1775

MY DEAR SIR, — I had the pleasure of your favours of the 23d. instant yesterday. I am glad to find that you have appointed Thomas the first brigadier. This I think will satisfy both him and the army. I have been obliged to take pains to keep him in the camp. He seldom talks imprudently, and I believe has never done it on this occasion. Spencer is a man I have no knowledge of. He left the camp on the first hearing of the arrangement with resentment. He has since returned, and I am told behaves very well. I am convinced of the necessity of supporting your own dignity, and the importance of your commissions. If you suffer them to be despised they will soon depreciate, and become of little value. While Thomas talked of leaving the camp I must do him the justice to say he exhibited a degree of the virtue you admire. He said he would soon return, and serve as a volunteer. I have lately felt great uneasiness on your account. Your want of health, and the disorder in your eyes yet continuing at a time when you are engaged in such a variety of great and complicated business, I should think sufficient, without external embarrassments, and the pain you must feel from dissentions which injure the general interest of the whole, and that of your Colony in particular. It seems to be the misfortune of every man of enlarged ideas and extended views, of integrity and disinterested virtue, to be plagued with either the narrow, contracted notions, or interested designs of those he is connected with in public life. This is exactly your case. I have been sensible of it a good while, and have a more perfect idea of it than I can express. The hint you give of inviting all nations to trade with us is indeed a grand idea, and I can easily

[1] Only a fragment of a second leaf of this letter remains.

conceive how bitterly you regret the loss of it. Such a step would have been worthy of such a body. It would have been in the true stile of a Sully, and have produced mighty consequences. I can easily conceive also the narrow principles that operated against and finally destroyed them. The two questions you ask, to what articles the trade should extend, and what bottoms it should be carried on upon, require a nice determination. Perhaps it would not answer our immediate purposes so well by being confined to our own bottoms, but if it be not, and we should finally be detached from Britain, we might have some difficulty in making an alteration so advantageous to ourselves in gaining great wealth and naval power. I hope to hear you *viva voce* on this subject.

After a most profound tranquility for a state of war, several skirmishes of some consequence took place last night. The regulars had advanced a little without Charlestown Neck, which gave umbrage to our troops. Some firings happened. In the night, which was dark, a number of the Riflemen got within their outer guards, and but for an unlucky circumstance (they happened at that instant to be relieving their guards) had brought off their main guard intire. However, a smart action ensued. They brought off two or three of them, and several arms, and killed several of their men. One of ours was taken by them, supposed to have lost his way. About the same time, the regulars, about sixty of them, pushed out suddenly on Boston Neck, drove back a few of our centinels, and by the negligence of our main guard, and the cowardice of the captain [1] burnt the George Tavern, and retired without loss. This is esteemed the greatest disgrace we have suffered. The most capital action was at the light house. You will recollect that we burnt it some time ago. They had for some time been very industrious in rebuilding it, and had it in such forwardness as actually to shew a light on Saturday night. About twenty-five whale boats and two hundred men, commanded by Major Tupper, set off last night, and arrived about daylight, attacked

[1] Captain Christopher Gardner, of Colonel Varnum's regiment. He was tried by court martial for deserting his post, and unanimously sentenced to be cashiered, "as incapable of serving his country in any military capacity." 1 *Proceedings*, xv. 135, 136.

the guard and workmen, and one small tender soon carried it, after killing two or three, and wounding four or five more. They took all the rest, burnt and destroyed the light house, took thirty six prisoners, and all their arms. Among the prisoners are four Marshfield Tories, and three or four others. The rest are marines and soldiers. One of the Whites of Marshfield is wounded, it is said mortally.[1]

August 2. I went yesterday for the first time this session to wait on the General. I had rather delayed it, as you had mentioned me to him as a person he might consult with, to see if he had any occasion to call on me. However, out of respect to him, and to see if I could serve the persons you recommend, I went. I find the Colony, as you predicted, will suffer by referring the appointments you mention to him. They will, I think, go to the southward. I am amazed that the impropriety of his appointing was not sufficient to determine every one of your body, and I should have thought both considerations would have clearly determined your brethren. He has not yet made the appointments. When I was coming off, I took the freedom to mention the sufferings and abilities of a number of gentlemen, and to ask the liberty to mention them, if he had any occasion for them even in places of no great importance. He said there were many gentlemen that had come some hundred miles, and as we had so large a share of the places, they must be provided for, and that we had among ourselves in effect the power of supplying all vacancies in the army, which is true, but won't aid our friends. Ever since the action on Sunday evening there has been a continual firing with cannon or small arms. The Riflemen have killed several of them, and among the rest an officer, who one of them shot from his horse yesterday at a distance of two hundred and fifty yards. The prisoners taken at the light house were yesterday carried through this town in their way to the gaols in the upper counties. Our Assembly are drudging on in the old way, shackled with forms and plagued with the concurrence and consent of several branches. A question was started and warmly contested whether our Constitution consisted of two or three branches, and was determined in favour of the latter, rather

[1] 1 *Proceedings*, XII. 196; Adams, *Familiar Letters*, 92.

from a supposition that it was your design than from the express words of your resolve. It was but last evening I heard of this opportunity and have not time to say many things I could wish for. I expect the express, and must be ready. The General was kind enough to direct he should call.

You will remember that our army, I mean our forces are inlisted only to the last of December. We must perhaps have a winter as well as summer campaign. I am well informed that Newfoundland is supplied with provisions from New York. A late instance. A vessel arrived there from [New] York, cleared out for the West Indies. This may be worth enquiring into. You mention nothing of an adjournment; from others we are made to expect it, and to suppose you are on your way home. Your good lady and family were well a few days ago. I sent a letter to the care of Major Mifflin some days ago for you, perhaps from Mrs. Adams. It was sent to me, and so directed. He promised good care of it. Mr. Adams' son is provided for in the manner he wishes. Pray make my regards to him. Nothing but want of time prevents my writing to him. Please to give my regards to Mr. Paine. I acknowledge the receipt of a letter from him. Shall write him per first opportunity. I am your sincere friend

J. W.

A treaty has subsisted for some time between the Selectmen of Boston and Gage, relative to the poor. Application was made to us. We provided for them at Salem, and insisted on having the donations with them. They are on their way there, but without the donations. Last Friday he took a sudden resolution to suffer the inhabitants to come out. A number of them landed at Chelsea. The General advised us of it. My apprehension of the small pox, etc., sent a committee there on Sunday. Many persons have come out. All agree in their account of the distresses of the inhabitants and soldiery, that they are very sickly, and many of them dye. It is said that not less than 1800 of the troops are unfit for service. John Brown is out, and was here yesterday. He says Gage has determined to detain about thirteen until one Jones [1]

[1] Josiah Jones.

and Hicks,[1] now in Concord gaol, shall be sent in. Among which are Boylston[2] and John Gill. What is to be done, can't say. Have just received a letter from Mrs. Adams which I enclose.

GEORGE WASHINGTON TO JAMES WARREN

SIR,—I should be very glad to procure Mr. Hitchbourne's Release agreeable to your Favour of yesterday if I could think of any Mode in which it was practicable. To propose it on any other Footing than an Exchange would I fear expose the Application to Contempt. As I observe he is included in the Note delivered me this Morning by a Committee from the General Court. I apprehend it had best be left on that Footing and is most likely to be successful.

It is very surprizing if the Letters intercepted are of Consequence that these Gentlemen should act so imprudent a Part. If their suffering only affected themselves I should not think it improper that they should feel a little for their Misconduct or Negligence.

I am with much Truth and Regard, Sir, your most Obedt and very Hbble Servt,

[GEORGE WASHINGTON][3]

Camp at Cambridge, Head Quarters, Augt 6, 1775.

JAMES WARREN TO JOHN ADAMS. ADAMS MSS.

WATERTOWN, *August* 9th, 1775

MY DEAR SIR,—I have very accidentally heard of this opportunity by Mr. Brown, and have so short notice of it that I can do little more than acknowledge the receipt of your favour of the 26th July, which I received the day before yesterday. When my mind was tortured with anxiety and distress, the arrival of powder in this manner is certainly as wonderful an interposition of Providence in our favour, as used to take place in favour of the Jews

---

1 John Hicks, printer of the *Boston Post-Boy*.
2 Thomas Boylston, a merchant of Boston.
3 The signature has been cut out of the letter and the body of the paper is in the handwriting of Joseph Reed.

in the days of Moses and Joshua. We have very little news here. No remarkable military events have taken place in the army here. In short the General has been obliged from principles of frugality to restrain his Riflemen. While they were permitted liberty to fire on the enemy, a great number of the army would go and fire away great quantity of ammunition to no purpose. Four captains and a subaltern were killed the beginning of last week chiefly by the Riflemen, and I am persuaded they will do great execution. There was but one company of them here last week. On Sunday a very fine company came in from Virginia. Yesterday morning went through this town three companies more; as many are expected this morning. I never saw finer fellows. What a view does this and the concourse of gentlemen from all the Colonies give us of Bernard's and Hutchinson's small faction. Last evening arrived here a gentleman from Machias, with an account of their having taken two other tenders, so that they now have five prizes, three tenders and two sloops taken from Jones. Twenty-eight prisoners are on the road, and will be here this day, among whom is old Ichabod Jones.[1] The rest are lieutenants of men of war, midshipmen and seamen. Five sloops after wood and fresh provisions are taken by Cargill and others, and carried into Penobscot. This is doing great service. They are reduced to great straits for wood as well as fresh provisions in Boston. It is said it would fetch three guineas a cord. They have already burnt all the fences, etc. All accounts from Boston agree that they are dismantling the Castle, and intend to destroy the works there; which, with other circumstances, induce many to suppose they have an intention to leave the town. Many people have lately come out. He has restricted them to £5 sterling in money, a small matter of furniture, and absolutely forbid them bringing out plate. What the policy should be, unless he designs to plunder, destroy, and then leave, we can't devise. Boylston, John Gill, Lovel, the Selectmen, etc., to the number of thirteen, are kept, it is said till Jones and Hicks, two insignificant prisoners we have in Concord gaol, are suffered to go into Boston. We have resolved they shall go. The General has

---

[1] Of Machias. See *Journals of the Provincial Congress* (Mass.), 395 *n*., 399. He afterwards fled to the British. *Journals of the House of Representatives* (Mass.), 1775, 88.

sent in the resolve by a trumpet.[1] We have no answer yet, tho' that was done last Sunday. I am very sorry I should omit any information you had occasion for. It is not wholly and only negligence. Such has been the confusion here that it was difficult to ascertain who held many of the offices. This was the case with young Palmer. I often asked, and never was satisfactorily resolved whether he was Quartermaster General or his Deputy. He was however the first, and still acts as such in the Massachusetts forces, and has expectations of being appointed by the General. I can't learn that any of those appointments you so justly regret to have referred to other hands than your own are yet made. As to Pigeon, I knew he was a commissary, but his temper is so petulant, that he has been desirous of quitting for some time, and, indeed, I have wished it. I am taking pains to give you the information you want of the biography of the officers in the army, etc. I have applied to General Thomas and one other General for that purpose. As for engineers, I wish we were in a better way. G[ridle]y is grown old, is much governed by a son of his, who vainly supposed he had a right to the second place in the regiment, that is before Burbank and Mason. The Congress thought otherways; he was sulky. We had much trouble with them, and I understand the General has his share yet. . . .

We have a short adjournment in contemplation, and expect it the latter end of this week. You will hear of the accident which befel the letters sent by Hitchborne. He very injudiciously kept them, when he had all the opportunity he could wish to destroy them. I wish to hear whether the letter to me was from you or Mr. S. Adams. I lost the pleasure of it, and they boast of great discoveries made from that and the two letters to General Washington. . . .

J. WARREN

Many of the Tories are preparing to leave Boston. Sewall and family, and some others, are going home, and some know not where to go. I believe they are almost ready to call on the rocks and mountains to cover them. . . .

1 *Journals of the House of Representatives* (Mass.), 1775, 32, 47.

HANNAH WINTHROP TO MERCY WARREN

ANDOVER, *Aug.* 17, 1775.

DEAR MRS. WARREN, THE FRIEND AND SISTER OF MY HEART, — What a great Consolation is it that tho the restless ambition and unbounded Avarice and wicked machinations of some Original Characters have deprivd us of many of the pleasures of life yet are they not able to take from us the heartfelt Satisfaction of mutual affection and Friendly Converse. Your Favor Truly Delineates human nature in a disagreeable light. The Contrast is very striking! What have we to expect from such Vitiated Persons as you present to view in the British Generals. I hope their Wicked inclinations will be restraind. I am Charmed with the Portrait you give of General Washington. Must not we expect Success under the direction of so much goodness. But my heart Bleeds for the people of Boston, my Blood boils with resentment at the Treatment they have met with from Gage. Can anything equal his Barbarity. Turning the poor out of Town without any Support, those persons who were possessd of any means of Support stopd and Searchd, not sufferd to carry anything with them. Can anything equal the distress of parents Seperated from their Children, the tender husband detain in Cruel Captivity from the Wife of his Bosom, she torn with anxiety in fearfull looking for and expectation of Vengeance from the obdurate heart of a Tyrant supported by wicked advisers. Can a Merciful Heaven look on these things and not interpose. Is there not a day of retribution at hand! Should these things continue what a horrid Prospect would a Severe Winter afford and how many must fall a Sacrifice to the unrelenting rigors of Cold and Want. Be ye clothd and be ye warmd will be of little Efficacy to the trembling nakd limbs or the hungry Soul of many a one who once livd in Affluence. I believe human Nature never produced but one Parallel Tyrant, Cesar Borgia, the Series of whose Cruelties will at any time make human Nature Shudder. You kindly enquire after my Sister. I have seen her but once since the Charlestown Conflagration. She is poorly accomodated at Stoneham. I found her and my Brother Mason [1]

[1] Thaddeus Mason (1706–1802), who married for his third wife Anne Fayerweather.

too much affected with their Loss. I really think their prospects peculiarly discouraging. He has been out of business for a Twelvemonth past, a Large Family to provide for. He advanced in life and losing his habitation by the hands of as barbarous an enemy as ever appeard on the theatre of life to torment mankind. Where is the Historic page that can furnish us with such Villainy. The Laying a whole town in ashes after repeated promises that if they would protect their troops in their return from Concord, it should have been the last place that should suffer harm. How did they give shelter to the wounded expiring soldiers; their houses their beds were prepared to receive them, the women readily engaged in pouring balm in to their wounds, making broths and Cordials to support their exhausted spirits, for at that time the Softer Sex had not been innured to trickling blood and gaping wounds. Some of the unhappy Victims died. They gave up the ghost Blessing the hands that gave relief, and now in return for their kindness they take the first opportunity to make 500 householders miserable involving many a poor widow and orphan in one common ruin. Be astonished o heavens at this and let the inhabitants of America tremble to fall into the hands of such a merciless foe.

But a more pleasing theme presents to me and I most Sincerely rejoice in the Late Appointment of your dear Consort to an Honorable and I hope profitable employment. The Assiduity and Fortitude with which he has Labord in the Fair field of Patriotic Virtue thro much self denial and Toil I think merits very highly of his Country and it must give pleasure to every Friend of Liberty to see such Abilities and unabating Services meet with some recompence before the Warfare is finished. May He long live a Blessing to his Country and reap the fruits of his Labors in a quiet and peaceable resting place. I now write from the Solitude of Andover and tho reducd to humble life yet by no means is my firm persuasion staggered in the glorious Cause we are Struggling in, the Cause of Virtue truth and justice. Your Faith that the united Efforts will be Blest with Success animates me. I catch a spark of that heavenly Flame which invigorates your breast knowing your Faith has a permanent Foundation and your acquaintance with those in the Cabinet must enable you to form a better Judgment than those who have not those advantages. After I have made an apology for this Scrawl hope you will consent I should finish it with my sincere regards to Coll. Warren. I subscribe your Ever Affectionate,

Hannah Winthrop

John Adams to Mercy Warren

Braintree, *Aug.* [26], 1775

Madam, — I have been the happiest Man these two Days past, that I know of in the World. I have compared myself in my own Mind, with all my Friends and I cannot believe any of them so blest as myself.

In the first Place, Rest, you know, is Rapture to a weary Man and I was quite weary enough to enjoy a State of Rest for a Day or two in all its Perfection, accordingly I have Slept by the best Computation, Sixteen Hours in the four and twenty.

In the next Place for the two last Days I have been entirely free from the Persecution of the "Fidgets and Caprices, Vanity, Superstition, and Irritability," which are Supposed by Some to assault me, now and then both from within and without. This is rare Felicity indeed.

Thirdly I have been allowed the Pleasure of rambling all alone, through the Fields, Groves and Meadows, and over the lofty Mountains, of peaceful happy Braintree, that wholesome Solitude and Nurse of Sense,

> Where Contemplation prunes her Ruffled Wings
> And the free Soul looks down to pity kings.

Fourthly and lastly, I have enjoyed the Conversation of the amiable Portia and her little prattling Brood of Children. This is a Pleasure of which I can Say no more. Mrs. Warren can conceive it; I cannot describe it.

Now taking all these Circumstances together neither Mr. Warren nor Mr. [erased], nor Mr. any Body that I can recollect, has been in a Situation equal to mine.

These have been vexed with the Society of Statesmen and Heroes; I have been disturbed with no such Animal. These have been interrupted with Cares; I have banished all of them from my Habitation from my Head and Heart. These have been wearied with Business; I would have no Business but have been wholly at Leisure. In short, I have some Idea now of the Happiness of the Inhabitants of Arcadia, Paradise, and the Elisian Fields.

Why will the cruel Thought intrude itself? Is this to last only untill Monday Morning four o'clock?[1] Avaunt this gloomy Thought, this impertinent Intruder; I wont Suffer myself to think that it is ever to End untill the Moment arrives and then I must endeavour to forget for a while, that I have ever been so happy.

I hope, Madam, I shall not be left to Stain this Paper with any Thing concerning Politicks or War. I was determined to write you before I went away and there is no other Subject in the whole Compass of Art, Science, or Nature, upon which I could have written one Line without diminishing my Happiness.

I wish you, Madam, a Speedy Return, with your worthy Partner, to your Family, and a Happiness there as exquisite as mine has been here and much more lasting. I am with unfeigned Esteem and Affection your and Mr. Warren's Friend and humble Servant,

JOHN ADAMS

Saturday Evening

ABIGAIL ADAMS TO MERCY WARREN

BRAINTREE, *Aug.* 27, 1775

MY DEAR MRS. WARREN, — It was with pleasure I received a line from my Friend to-day informing me of her better Health. I was really anxious for her, more so on account of the Great mortality which prevails around us. I arrived at my own habitation a fryday and found my family all well — a blessing which I hope will be continued to me.

The peaceful tranquility of my own habitation was enhanced to me by a few days absence, amidst a more Noisy and tumultuous

[1] The Continental Congress had adjourned to September 5.

Scene than I Love — tho I injoyed many hours of pleasure in the Society of my Friends.

I have not heard any of the allarms you mention, only the artillery of the clouds which has been pretty heavey this afternoon but produced us many refreshing Showers — in which I rejoice for many reasons. My Friend will leave me tomorrow morning and will have a much more agreeable journey for the rain. I find I am obliged to summon all my patriotism to feel willing to part with him again. you will readily believe me when I say that I make no small sacrifice to the publick.

You write me that you have been to Head Quarters, and there seen the Letters.[1] Pray what did you think of them? Money must be much plentier than provisions with Gage or he would not think of setting so high a value upon them.

I shall send this by Mr. Adams who will call upon you as he has alterd his mind with regard to going to Deadam. I shall be very glad to see my Friend Next week, any week or any time she may be assured of a hearty welcome from her affectionate,

PORTIA

MERCY WARREN TO JOHN ADAMS.   ADAMS MSS.
WATERTOWN, *September* 4, 1775

. . . .

The ships which arrived last Fryday are from Halifax, with a few potatoes and a little wood. The people there are in expectation of an attack from a body of troops, which they hear are to be sent down under the command of Preble,[2] and are preparing for defence. If they suffer such terrors from the name of a worn-out American veteran what must be their apprehensions from the active, vigorous, spirited heroes who are rising up from every corner of the United Colonies to oppose the wicked system of politicks which has long governed a corrupt court.

But I ask pardon for touching on war, politicks, or any thing

---

[1] The intercepted letters.
[2] Jedidiah Preble, of Falmouth (Portland). A biographical sketch of him, with letters and "fragments" of his "Diary" during the Revolution, are in Preble, *Genealogical Sketch of the First Three Generations of Prebles in America*, 40.

relative thereto, as I think you gave me a hint in yours not to approach the verge of any thing so far beyond the line of my sex.

The worthy bearer[1] of this will inform you of all the intelligence stirring. Tranquility still reigns in the camp. We scarcely hear the distant roar of cannon for twenty four hours past.

By a person from Boston last Saturday we learn they are building a floating battery in town in order to bombard Prospect Hill. What a contemptible figure do the arms of Britain make....

MARCIA

Swift of Boston[2] is really dead.

JAMES WARREN TO JOHN ADAMS.   ADAMS MSS.

WATERTOWN, *September* 11, 1775

MY DEAR SIR, — I please myself with the probability that before this you are safely arrived at Philadelphia, after having fine weather for journeying. I hope you will not be disappointed in your wishes with regard to the spirit and temper of the Congress. I should have wrote you before, if I had been well; but from a cold I took in the long storm we had here, have been much indisposed since you left us. Am now much better. Nothing very material has occurred. The military operations are much in the same way as when you was last here. The works on Ploughed Hill are thought to be impregnable. They fired at them and Roxbury till they tired themselves, and have now in a manner ceased. We seldom hear a cannon, tho' these natural effusions of resentment and disappointment now and then give us an instance, harmless enough, for they never injure us. All seems to be in a tranquil state for a war. The greatest difficulty seems to be to govern our own soldiery; I may say the Riflemen only, for I hear of no other. Yesterday the General was obliged to order no less than twenty-four of them under guard.[3] They are the most disorderly part of the army, if not alone so. I have not been at head quarters since Saturday, but am told that for some crime one of them was ordered under

[1] Stephen Collins.   [2] Samuel Swift, the lawyer?
[3] September 11 a court martial was ordered to try these men, who were accused of mutiny. Thirty-two were sentenced to pay twenty shillings each, and one was sentenced to six days' imprisonment in addition to the fine. 1 *Proceedings*, xv. 154.

guard. An attempt was made by a number to rescue him. Upon which they were also ordered to be put under guard; upon which a whole company undertook to rescue them, and the General was obliged to call out a large detachment from the Rhode Island Troops to apprehend them, who though prepared for resistance, thought proper to submit, and the ringleaders are now in custody. I believe he will choose to make examples of them. I should, were I in his place. We have in a few days past a great deal of foreign news, and all seems to agree that both England and Ireland are in great confusion. It is said the Irish Parliament have resolved that no more troops, or provisions for troops, shall come from there to America, and that several of the recruiting parties there have been killed; that the whole kingdom is in an uproar, and in such an opposition to administration as will intitle them equally with the Americans to the character of rebels. The vessel that brings this account has been stopped by the men of war at Rhode Island in her way to Providence, and perhaps many other particulars smothered. Callihorne[1] is arrived at Boston, and several letters have been received, and some of them sent out of Boston, giving assurances that no more troops will be sent to America, and that the dispute will be soon settled. Oliver Wendel[2] told me he had seen one to that purpose from a man whose intelligence he could depend on. Other letters I hear of, which say the people had obliged the King to promise not only to send no other troops out but to recall the fleet and army already here. If all this be true how seasonably will your last petition arrive to serve as a mantle to cover the nakedness of the Ministry, and to screen them from the shame of being forced to a retreat by the virtue of the Americans. Depend on it, they will catch at it, like a hungry fish at a bait, and we must be content with a harvest blasted with mildew, and cut before it is ripe, and consequently of little value. Does no powder arrive? I wish we may be able to give them at least one blast more that they may leave us thoroughly impressed with a sense of American bravery and prowess, if they do go. I know you won't fail to do every thing in your power to furnish us. Money, if possible, grows scarcer than powder. The last dollar, perhaps, will be gone to-

[1] Callanan? [2] (1733–1818). *N.E. Hist. Gen. Register*, I. 186.

morrow, and then I expect we shall all be din'd with clamours and complaints. We have enough of them already from the largeness of the bills. 1200 men march this afternoon and to-morrow under Colonel Arnold for Newbury Port, to embark for Kennebeck on their way to Quebec. I wish they may not be intercepted in their passage. Were I to conduct the matter I think I should march them all the way by land. Two frigates and a number of schooners, I am told, left Boston yesterday, probably to intercept them. A few deserters came over to us, and several of our riflemen have deserted to the enemy. A ship from Piscataqua for the West Indies, owned by Mr. Langdon, was taken by the *Lively*, and has been retaken by an armed vessel from Beverly, and carried into Cape Anne. The prisoners were bro't to Head quarters on Saturday. I don't find your friend P. Henry in the list of delegates from Virginia. How does it happen? It gives me concern; you know I have a great opinion of him.

Our Council are yet sitting, tho' they talk of an adjournment tomorrow. They seem to have been very busy. I can hardly tell you what has been done since you left us. Colonel Prescott, sheriff of this county, Colonel Dwight, Worcester, Dr. Winthrop, Judge of Probate, his son Reg'r Foster appointed for Worcester. No appointments for the Superior Court; they seem as much at a loss as ever. . . .

J. W.

Six regulars put off from Boston in a boat and were unable to row back against the wind, which blew hard at N. W. this day. They drifted on Dorchester, and were taken.

JOHN ADAMS TO JAMES WARREN

PHILADELPHIA, *Sept.* 17, 1775

DR SIR, — I have nothing in particular to write. Our most gracious K— has given a fresh Proof of his Clemency in his Answer to the City. But no more of Politicks at present. If this Scratch of a Pen should fall into the Hands of the wiseacre Gage, as long as I confine myself to Matrimony and Horsemanship, there will be no Danger.

Be it known to you then that two of the most unlikely Things, within the whole Compass of Possibility, have really and actually happened. The first is the suden Marriage of our President, whose agreeable Lady honours us with her Presence and contributes much to our good Humour as well as to the Happiness of the President. So much for that.[1]

The next Thing is more wonderfull still.

You know the Aversion which your Secretary,[2] has ever entertained to riding, on Horseback — he never would be persuaded to mount a Horse. The last time we were here I often laboured to persuade him, for the Sake of his Health but in vain. Soon after we set out on the last Journey, I reflected that some Degree of Skill and Dexterity in Horsemanship, was necessary to the Character of a Statesman. It would take more Time and Paper than I have to Spare to shew the Utility of Horsemanship to a Politician; so I shall take this for granted. But I pointed out the particulars to him, and likewise shewed him that Sociability would be greatly promoted by his mounting one of my Horses.

On Saturday the second day of September, 1775, in the Town of Grafton He was prevailed on to put my Servant with his, into Harrison's Chaise and to mount upon my Horse, a very genteel and easy little Creature. We were all disappointed and Surprised. Instead of the Taylor riding to Brentford We beheld, an easy, genteel Figure upon the Horse, and a good deal of Spirit and Facility, in the Management of the Horse, insomuch that We soon found our Servants were making some disagreeable Comparisons, and since our arrival here I am told that Fessenden (impudent Scoundrel) reports that the Secretary rides fifty per cent better than your Correspondent.

In this manner, We rode to Woodstock, where we put up for the Sabbath. It was soon observed that the Secretary could not sit so erect in his Chair as he had Sat upon his Horse, but Seemed to be neither sensible of the Disease or the Remedy. I soon perceived and apprised him of both. On Sunday Evening, at Mr. Dexter's,

1 The *New England Chronicle*, September 7, 1775, contains a notice of the marriage of John Hancock to Dorothy Quincy, at the seat of Thaddeus Burr, in Fairfield, Connecticut.
2 Samuel Adams. See Wells, *Life of Samuel Adams*, II. 323.

where we drank Coffee and spent an agreeable evening I persuaded him to purchase two yards of flannell, which we carried to our Landlady, who, with the assistance of a Taylor Woman in the House, made up a Pair of Drawers, which the next morning were put on, and not only defended the Secretary from any further Injury, but entirely healed the little Breach which had been begun.

Still an Imperfection remained. Our Secretary had not yet learned to mount and dismount. Two Servants were necessary to attend upon these occasions, one to hold the Bridle and Stirrup, the other to boost the Secretary. This was rather a ridiculous Circumstance still. At last, I undertook to instruct him the necessary Art of mounting. I had my Education to this Art, under Bates, the celebrated Equerry, and therefore might be Supposed to be a Master of it. I taught him, to grasp the Bridle with his Right Hand over the Pummell of his Saddle, to place his left Foot firm in the Stirrup; to twist his left Hand into the Horses Main, about half Way between his Ears and his Shoulders, and then a vigorous Exertion of his Strength would carry him very gracefully into the Seat, without the least Danger of falling over on the other Side. The Experiment was tryed and Succeeded to Admiration. Thus equipped and instructed, our Horseman rode all the Way from Woodstock to Philadelphia, Sometimes upon one of my Horses, Sometimes on the other, and acquired fresh Strength, Courage, Activity and Spirit every day. His Health is much improved by it, and I value myself, very much upon the Merit of having probably added Several years to a Life so important to his Country, by the little Pains I took to persuade him to mount and teach him to ride.

Sully and Cecil were both Horsemen and you know I would not have our Americans, inferior to them in the Smallest Accomplishment.

Pray Mrs. Warren to write to me. I would to her, if I had half so much Time.[1]

[No signature.]

---

[1] Endorsed "Favored by Mr. Andrew Cabot."

JOHN ADAMS TO JAMES WARREN

PHILADELPHIA, *Septr.* 19, 1775

DEAR SIR, — I have but a Moment's Time to write and nothing of Importance to say.

Mr. Randolph our former President is here and Sits very humbly in his Seat, while our new one continues in the Chair, without Seeming to feel the Impropriety.[1] Coll. Nelson,[2] a Planter, Mr. Wythe,[3] a Lawyer and Mr. Francis Lightfoot Lee,[4] a Planter, are here from Virginia, instead of Henry, Pendleton [5] and Bland.[6] Henry is General of Virginia — the other two are old and infirm. I am well pleased that Virginia has Set the Example of changing Members and I hope that Massachusetts will follow it, and all the other Colonies. I should be glad upon a new Election to be relieved from this Service. this Climate does not agree with my Constitution So well as our own, and I am not very well fortified you know against the Inclemencies of any.

This Congress, I assure you, feels the Spirit of War, more intimately than they did before the Adjournment. They Set about Preparations for it with Seriousness and in Earnest.

[*No signature.*]

JAMES WARREN TO JOHN ADAMS.   ADAMS MSS.

WATERTOWN, *September* 19, 1775

MY DEAR SIR, — I had fixed a determination in my own mind, to omit no opportunity of writing either to you, or my friend Mr. S. Adams; but I have indeed so little to say at this time, that I should have thought it hardly worth while to trouble you with a letter had it not been to inclose one from Mrs. Adams who, with the children, I had the pleasure yesterday to hear were recovered. I have been much concerned about them. I presume the inclosed

---

1 May 24, Peyton Randolph, President, was under a necessity of returning to Virginia, to take his place as Speaker of the House of Burgesses, and the *Journals* of the Congress state "the chair was vacant." John Hancock was then unanimously chosen President. Randolph never occupied the chair again, and died October 22, 1775.

2 Thomas Nelson (1738–1789).   3 George Wythe (1726–1806).   4 (1734–1797).
5 Edmund Pendleton (1721–1803).   6 Richard Bland (1710–1776).

will give you the state of the family, and make it unnecessary for me to add more. I have been here ever since you left us, without once hearing from you. I wrote to you a week ago, and took pains to collect every thing I could think of as new, foreign and domestic. Your intelligence from abroad is so much better than ours at this time that I expect no success in handing you our foreign news; and of the domestic kind we have very little. We suffer extremely for want of it. When we meet in the street we have not a word more to say than to inquire after each other's health, or make an observation on the weather. These are circumstances so different from what we have been used to, that we are quite out of our element. Scarcely any one thing has happened since my last worthy of your notice. We have frequent desertions to us, seldom two nights without an instance of that kind; the night before last were four or five sailors. By the best accounts given by gentlemen out of town, the soldiery are dispirited by their confinement, their want of supplies, and above all by their vast fatigue. They live in continual horror of being attacked. Their guards are therefore large, and must be numerous from the extensiveness of their works. It is supposed that frequent shews of attacking them, would soon wear them out. I mentioned this at Head-quarters yesterday. I hope they will take that method to harrass them. A servant of General Howe deserted about ten days ago. I heard him tell the General that his master constantly set up till one o'clock, and then slept till morning in his boots and cloaths. They seem to be making but little preparation for winter. It was reported that they were pulling down the houses from the Haymarket to the fortification, in order to erect works to retreat to if they could not hold those they now have. They really have begun to pull down the houses; but it is generally thought to be only for fuel, of which they are in great want, and they choose that place as the clearing would be most convenient for new works, if they should have occasion for more. We have had scarce a gun fired for ten days before Sunday morning, when a number of the Rebels[1] appearing without their works on Boston Neck, our people fired four cannon on them, which drove them in, killed two and wounded five of

[1] It is under this term that Warren described the British.

their men, as we have learned by deserters. They returned a smart fire without any success. And yesterday again Roxbury side had a very heavy cannonade with as little, only one officer very slightly wounded. This is indeed very remarkable, as our people expose themselves without reserve, having been so enured to shot and shells that do no execution, that they totally disregard them. Cobble Hill is to be possessed and fortified this or tomorrow night. Putnam is to be gratified with the command. This must open a warm scene, and will furnish us abundantly with the musick of cannon, and topicks of conversation. The constant expectation I have had of receiving the money from Philadelphia has confined me to this place, contrary to both my inclinations and interest, supposing it would not do to be absent when it came. It is not yet arrived. This delay is astonishing, and I fear will cause irreparable injuries to the army. The soldiers that are not paid for the month of August are very uneasy. The General can't fulfill his promise to them. The Quarter master General and Commissary General are both out of money, their credit suffering, and their provisions for the army at a stand, and this at a time when the season is approaching that transportation from distant places will be difficult. Do apologize to my friend Adams for my not writing to him. It is really owing to the poverty of the times. I had no subject without I had entered on metaphysics, mathematics, or some subjects foreign from politics or news, which alone engage my attention. I will, however, write him soon, subject or no subject. The Council adjourned for a week. The Assembly meets tomorrow. Whenever any thing occurs, you shall hear it, and [I] shall on my part be glad to hear of your doings. I want to hear of high spirited measures. It is in my opinion ridiculous to hesitate now about taking up crown officers, and fifty other things. You won't lose sight of powder and money. . . .

I forgot to tell you that they are exercising their wit, and diverting themselves in Boston by versifying the letters taken from Hitchburne, as I hear. I have not been able to get sight of it.

JOHN ADAMS TO JAMES WARREN

PHILADELPHIA, *Septr.* 26, 1775

DR SIR, — This afternoon and not before I received a Line from the excellent Marcia, which [is] the first and only Letter I have received from the Family to which She belongs Since I left Watertown. Be pleased to thank her for this Favour and to let her know that She must certainly have misinterpreted Some Passage in my Letter, Since I never thought either Politicks or War, or any other Art or Science beyond the Line of her Sex: on the contrary I have ever been convinced that Politicks and War, have in every Age been influenced, and in many, guided and controuled by her Sex. Sometimes it is to be feared by the unworthy Part of it; but at others, it must be confessed by the amiable and the good. But if I were of opinion that it was best for a general Rule that the fair should be excused from the arduous Cares of War and State; I should certainly think that Marcia and Portia, ought to be Exceptions, because I have ever ascribed to those Ladies, a Share and no Small one neither, in the Conduct of our American Affairs.

I have nothing new to communicate. Every Thing, has been done, and is now doing, to procure the *Unum Necessarium*.[1] I wish I could give you a more agreable account of the Salt Petre Works in this City. I fear they have chosen injudiciously a Place for their Vatts Vaults and Buildings, a low marshy Place which was lately overflowed by the Storm. Still We have Sanguine Accounts of the Skill and Success of Some operators.

Coll. Dyer produces a Sample of excellent Salt Petre made by two De Witts, one of Norwich the other of Windham, and he is confident that they can and will make large Quantities. Coll. Harrison of Virginia, whose taste in Madeira I know, and in girls I believe,[2] and in Salt Petre I hope, to be much Superiour to his Judgment in Men, is very confident that they are making large Quantities from Tobacco House Earth in his Colony.

We are hourly expecting Intelligence from Canada, as well as Massachusetts, and from London.

[1] Gunpowder.
[2] A hit at a paragraph in the intercepted letter from Harrison to Washington.

My dear Sir, Let me intreat you to do every Thing in your Power to get ready the Accounts of all that our Province has done and expended in the Common Cause, for which they expect or hope to be reimbursed by the United Colonies. It has ever appeared to me a Thing of much Importance, that We should be furnished with those accounts as soon as possible. From present appearances, our Session will not be long and if We should not be furnished with the Necessary Papers very soon, We shall not be able to obtain any Reimbursement this Fall; and the next Spring We may be involved in So many Dangers as well as new Expences as to render our Chance for obtaining Justice, more precarious. You know that your Delegates have been here almost the whole Time since the Commencement of Hostilities, and therefore can say nothing of their own Knowledge concerning your Exertions or Expences but must depend altogether upon Information from the General Court.

This is really a Strong Reason for a Change in the Delegation.

We have been absent so long from our native Country as to be a kind of Aliens and Strangers there. If it is good Policy to re-elect one of the old Delegates, because he is personally knowing to what has passed here; it is equally good Policy to elect Some new ones, because they are Witnesses of what has passed with you. For my own Part, as my political Existence terminates with the Year, I sincerely wish to be exempt in the next Election. I long to be a little with you in the General Court, that I may see and hear, and feel with my Countrymen, and I ardently wish to be a little with my Family and to attend a little to my private affairs. To be frank and candid to a Friend, I begin to feel for my Family. To leave all the Burthen of my private Cares, at a Time when my affairs are in so much Perplexity, to an excellent Partner, gives me Pain for her. To leave the Education of a young Family entirely to her, altho I know not where it could be better lodged, gives me much Concern for her and them.

I have very little Property, you very well know, which I have not earned myself by an obstinate Industry, in opposition to the Malice of a very infirm Constitution, in Conjunction with the more pernicious Malice of Ministerial and gubernatorial Enemies.

Of the little Acquisitions I have made, five hundred Pounds Sterling is sunk in Boston in a Real Estate, four hundred Sterling more is completely annihilated in a Library that is now wholly useless to me and mine,[1] and at least four hundred Sterling more is wholly lost to me in Notes and Bonds, not one farthing of the Principal or Interest of which can I obtain, and the Signers are dying, breaking, flying every day.

It is now compleatly two years since my Business has been totally ruined by the public Confusions. I might modestly estimate the Profits of my Business before this Period at three hundred sterling a Year, perhaps more. I think therefore I may fairly estimate myself a sufferer immediately to the Amount of two Thousand Pounds sterling. I have purchased Lands, which these Causes have prevented me from paying for, and the Interest is running on without a Possibility of my paying it and I am obliged to hire Labour yearly upon my Farm to no small amount.

In the mean Time all that has been granted me by the general Court for the sessions of this Congress last Fall and this Spring has not defrayed my necessary Expences however strange it may appear.

The Conclusion from all this is, that I am rushing rapidly into Perplexities and Distresses in my private affairs from which I can never extricate myself. By retreating from Public Life, in some Measure I might preserve myself and Family from a Ruin, which without it will be inevitable. I am willing to Sink with my Country, but it ought not to be insisted on that I should sink myself without any Prospect of contributing by that Means to make it Swim. I have taken my Trick at Helm when it was not easy to get Navigators who would run the Risque of the Storm. At present the Course is plain whatever the Weather may be, and the prospect of that is much better than it was when I was called to assist in steering the Ship.

[*No signature.*]

[1] What is left of the library, much increased during his diplomatic service, is in the Public Library of the City of Boston. A catalogue was printed in 1917.

John Adams to Mercy Warren

PHILADELPHIA, *Septr.* 26, 1775

MADAM, — Your Favour by my Friend Collins never reached me till this Evening. At Newport, concluding to go by Water, he put it into the Post Office least it Should meet with a Fate as unfortunate as Some others. I call them unfortunate after the manner of Men. For, altho they went into Hands which were never thought of by the Writer, and notwithstanding all the unmeaning Noise that has been made about them, they have done a great deal of good. Providence intended them for Instruments to promote valuable Purposes, altho the Writer of them, thought so little of them that he never could have recollected one Word in them, if they had been lost. The most that I care about them, is the indecent Exposure of the Name of a Lady,[1] who cannot be put to Pain, without giving me Uneasiness by Sympathy.

I boasted, Madam, of my Happiness, in my last to you, because I knew you could excuse the Appearance of Vanity and because I knew very well that the Person who so deservedly holds the first Place in your Heart, could Say by Experience, that an Happiness so perfect was not merely ideal. . . .

[*No signature.*]

John Adams to James Warren

PHILADELPHIA, *Septr.* 28, 1775

DR SIR, — I write at this Time only to remind you that I have recd no Letters.

Let me intreat the earliest Attention of our Houses to the Accounts and Vouchers of our Province. Accounts must be exact and Vouchers genuine, or we shall suffer. The whole Attention of every Member of both Houses would be not unprofitably employed upon this Subject untill it is finished.

The accounts I mean are of Ammunition; such as Powder, Ball, Cartridges, Artillery, Cannon Field Pieces, Carriages, Camp Equipage, Cantins, Kettles, Spoons, etc., Tents, Canvas, etc., etc.,

---
1 Mrs. Adams.

Philadelphia Sept. 30. 1775

Dr Sir   Mr Lynch Coll Harrison, and Dr Franklyn are preparing for a Journey to Watertown and Cambridge, one of whom will do me the Favour of taking this Letter. —

Mr Lynch, you have seen before — he is an opulent Planter of great Understanding and Integrity and the best Affections to our Country and Cause

Coll Harrison, is of Virginia and the Friend and Correspondent of the General; but it seems by a certain Letter, under some degree of Prejudice against our dear New Englandmen. These Prejudices however, have arisen from Misrepresentation and may be easily removed —

Dr Franklyn needs nothing to be said — There is no abler or better American, that I know of —

I could wish a particular Attention and Respect to all Three —

I know you will be pleased to be introduced to these Gentlemen, because it will give you an opportunity of serving your Country — I am your Friend

John Adams —

etc., Provisions, Bread, Meat, Meal, Peas, everything in short. In fine it is idle for me to enter [in]to detail. The Pay and Cloathing of the Troops, etc., etc. But I must entreat to have these Accounts and Vouchers. I do beseech that it may be remembered that I was importunate on this Head with several Gentlemen, when I was with you.

[*No signature.*]

JOHN ADAMS TO JAMES WARREN

PHILADELPHIA, *Septr.* 30, 1775.

DR SIR, — Mr. Lynch, Coll. Harrison and Dr. Franklyn are preparing for a Journey to Watertown and Cambridge,[1] one of whom will do me the Favour of taking this Letter.

Mr. Lynch,[2] you have seen before — he is an oppulent Planter of Great Understanding and Integrity and the best Affections to our Country and Cause.

Coll. Harrison[3] is of Virginia, and the Friend and Correspondent of the General, but it seems by a certain Letter under some degree of Prejudice against our dear New Englandmen. These Prejudices however, have arisen from Misrepresentation and may be easily removed.

Dr. Franklin needs nothing to be said. There is no abler or better American, that I know of.

I could wish a particular Attention and Respect to all Three.

I know you will be pleased to be introduced to these Gentlemen, because it will give you an Opportunity of serving your Country. I am your Friend,

JOHN ADAMS

1 On the 29th, after spending most of the morning in debate on the motion, Congress appointed a committee of three "to repair immediately to the camp at Cambridge," to confer with General Washington, executives of the New England governments, and others, "touching the most effectual method of continuing, supporting, and regulating a continental army." On the next day a ballot was taken for members of the committee. Lynch and Franklin were chosen, and Harrison and Dyer had a tie vote. On a subsequent ballot Harrison received a majority. *Journals of the Continental Congress*, III. 265, 266. Congress began to consider the report of the committee November 4. *Ib.*, 320.

2 Thomas Lynch (*c.* 1720–1776).   3 Benjamin Harrison (1740–1791).

John Adams to James Warren

PHILADELPHIA, *Oct.* 1, 1775

DEAR SIR, — This morning I received your kind Favours of the 11th and 19th Ult. — with the Inclosures. Draper's Paper is a great Curiosity and you will oblig me by sending it as often as possible.

The foreign News you mention, is all a Delusion my Friend. You may depend upon it, every Measure is preparing by the Ministry to destroy Us if they can, and that a Scottish Nation is Supporting them.

Heaven helps those who help themselves, and I am happy to find a Disposition so rapidly growing in America to exert itself.

The Letters, by your Packett from my Family, have given me Serious Concern indeed. I am much at a Loss what Course to take. I have thoughts of returning home. I fear, my dear Mrs. Adams's Health will sink under the Burthen of Care that is upon her. I might well enough be spared from this Place, where my Presence is of no Consequence, and my Family might derive some advantage from my being there, and I might have an Opportunity of attending a Conference between a Comtee of this Congress and the Council of Mass., where perhaps I might be of more service than I can [be] here. However I am not determined. My Friend, your Secretary [1] is very much averse to my going. I don't know what to do.

The Comtee who are going to the Camp, are Dr. Franklin, Mr. Lynch and Coll. Harrison, who I hope will be received with Friendship and Politeness, by all our Friends.

I assure you, Sir, there is a serious Spirit here. Such a Spirit as I have not known before.

The Committee, by whom this Letter will go, are determined Americans. I fear that two of them, I mean Mr. L and H. may have received some unfavourable Impressions from Misrepresentations, concerning our Province; but these will be easily removed, by what they will see and hear, I hope. I wish that every Civility may be shewn them, which their Fortunes, Characters and Stations demand.

[1] Samuel Adams.

Our News from England, is, Troops from England, Scotland, Ireland, and Hanover. Poor Old Britania! I am, your Friend,

JOHN ADAMS

JAMES WARREN TO JOHN ADAMS.   ADAMS MSS.

WATERTOWN, *October* 1, 1775

MY DEAR SIR, — An event has lately taken place here which makes much noise, and gives me much uneasiness, not only as it affects the character, and may prove the ruin of a man who[m] I used to have a tolerable opinion of, but as it may be the cause of many suspicions and jealousies, and what is still worse, have a tendency to discredit the recommendations of my friends at the Congress. Dr. Church has been detected in a correspondence with the Enemy, at least so far that a letter wrote by him in curious cypher and directed to Major Cane [1] (who is an officer in the Rebel army and one of Gage's family), has been intercepted. The history of the whole matter is this. The Doctor, having formed an infamous connection with an infamous hussey to the disgrace of his own reputation, and probable ruin of his family, wrote this letter last July, and sent it by her to Newport with orders to give it to Wallace,[2] or Dudley,[3] to deliver to Wallace for conveyance to Boston. She, not finding an opportunity very readily, trusted it with a friend of hers to perform the orders, and came away and left it in his hands. He kept it some time, and having some suspicions of wickedness, had some qualms of conscience about executing his commissions, after some time consulted his friend. One result was to open the letter, which was done. The appearance of the letter increasing their suspicions, the next question after determining not to send it to Boston was, what should be done with it. After various conferences at divers times, they concluded to deliver it to General Washington. Accordingly the man came with it last Thursday.[4] After collecting many circumstances, the man was

---

[1] Maurice Cane, lieutenant colonel in the Sixth Regiment.
[2] James Wallace, commanding the ship *Rose*, stationed at Newport.
[3] Charles Dudley, collector of the customs.
[4] This person was named Godfrey Wainwood, an inhabitant of Newport. See *Writings of Washington* (Ford), III. 163.

employed to draw from the girl, by using the confidence she had in him, the whole secret, but without success. She is a subtle, shrewd jade. She was then taken into custody and brought to the General's quarters that night. It was not till the next day that anything could be got from her. She then confessed that the Doctor wrote and sent her with the letter as above. Upon this, the General sent a note desiring Major Hawley [1] and me to come immediately to Cambridge. We all thought the suspicion quite sufficient to justify an arrest of him and his papers,[2] which was done, and he is now under a guard. He owns the writing and sending the letter, says it was for Flemming [3] in answer to one he wrote to him,[4] and is calculated by magnifying the numbers of the army, their regularity, their provisions and ammunition, etc., to do great service to us. He declares his conduct tho' indiscreet was not wicked. There are, however, many circumstances, new and old, which time won't permit me to mention, that are much against him. The letter, I suppose, is now decyphering, and when done will either condemn, or in some measure excuse him.[5] Thus much for this long story.

A strong S.W. wind put into Marblehead last week a New Providence man,[6] with a large number of turtle, etc., etc. They boarded, took and carryed him to Salem, and prevented the scoundrels from enjoying and feasting on callipee, callipack,[7] and a desert of pine apples, etc. A few fisher men also have taken a brigantine from Quebec with cattle, sheep, oatmeal, etc., a present

1 Joseph Hawley.
2 A confidant had been through Church's papers before Washington's agent reached them.
3 "Brother" of Church. A letter to Colden in February, 1776, says "Fleming the printer." This was John Fleming, partner of John Mein, printers and booksellers in Boston.
4 This letter of Fleming is in *Journal of the House of Representatives* (Mass.), October 27, 1775.
5 In a short note of October 2nd Warren says: "I have just heard that the letter is decyphered, and is much against the writer." *Adams* MSS. It was decyphered by West. The text appeared in the *New England Chronicle*, January 4, 1776. A council of war was held on October 3-4, a record of which is in the Washington Papers, Library of Congress. It is printed in *Journals of the House of Representatives* (Mass.), October 27, 1775.
6 Schooner *Industry*, Francis Butler, Master. Her invoice is given in *Journals of the House of Representatives* (Mass.), 1775, 129.
7 Calipee is that part of turtle which is next the lower shell; calipash, that which is next the upper shell — West Indian words, conjectured to have been from the Spanish *carapacho* (carapace), itself of unknown origin.

from the Tory merchants, etc., to the sick and wounded in Boston, and some forage for the Light horse. She is carried in to Cape Ann. There are two letters from one Gamble,[1] an officer, one to General Gage, the other to Sherriff,[2] which tell them that they are to expect no aid to Government from there; that Carleton dare not issue his orders to the militia, supposing they could not be obeyed; that the Canadians, poisoned from New England, had got in use the damned abused word Liberty. I can't recollect the time she sailed, her bills [of] lading dated September 5, but the master says that Carlton has had no success in recruiting. He went off the night he came away, for St. Johns, with about seventy five raggamuffins, the whole posse he could collect; that there were at Quebec 10,000 barrels powder. I long for them more than turtle or pine apples. Arnold was last Monday with his detachment, sixty miles up Kennebeck, every thing as it should be. We please ourselves with fine prospects of success. I say nothing about St. Johns, etc. presuming you know as much or more about it than I do. The money arrived safe here last Fryday, and I assure you gives a new face to our affairs, which by a greater delay must have run into confusion.[3] I thank you for your short letter; would have thanked you more if it had been longer. . . .

Is it worth while to wonder that some people can't feel improprieties? However ambition and variety I think, must predominate and mark strongly the character of a man who can act such a part, if he has any sense at all. I am glad to find the Congress in such a temper. . . .

I must write General Court news, and plans on foot for fixing armed Vessels, animated by our late success. . . .

[1] Captain Thomas Gamble, of the 47th Regiment.
[2] William Sheriff.
[3] Writing to Mrs. Adams on September 27th, Warren said: "I have been detained here three weeks, expecting every minute the remainder of the money to be sent from Philadelphia. The delay is unaccountable to every one here. We are all agreed that there is some wickedness at the bottom, but know not where. It is suspected to be in one of the Treasurers, whose principles I am told would not recommend him to the place he holds." *Adams* MSS. The two treasurers were Michael Hillegas and George Clymer. *Journals of the Continental Congress*, II. 221.

John Adams to James Warren

PHILADELPHIA, *Oct.* 2, 1775

DR SIR, — I believe you will have a surfeit of Letters from me, for they will be as inane as they are numerous.

The Bearer of this is Major Bayard [1] a Gentleman of this City, of the Presbyterian Persuasion, of the best Character, and the clearest affections for his Country. I have received so many Civilities from him, that I could not refuse myself the Pleasure of introducing him to you.

Our Obligations of Secrecy are so braced up, that I must deny myself the Pleasure of Writing Particulars. Not because some Letters have been intercepted, for notwithstanding the Versification of them, they have done good, tho they have made some People grin.

This I can Say with Confidence, that the Propriety and Necessity of the Plan of Politicks so hastily delineated in them is every day, more and more confessed even by those Gentlemen who disapproved it at the Time when they were written.

Be assured, I never Saw So Serious and determined a Spirit as I see now every day.

The high Spirited Measures you call for will assuredly come. Languid and disastrous Campaigns are agreeable to Nobody.

Young Mr. Lux desires his Compts. to you and your Lady. He is vastly pleased with his Treatment both from you and her. Remember me to her. I have Shocking Letters from her Friend at Braintree, such as have put my Phylosophy to the Tryal. I wait only for another Letter to determine whether I shall come home.[2]

[*No signature.*]

Samuel Adams to James Warren

PHILADA., *Octob.* 3, 1775

MY DEAR SIR, — I take the Liberty of recommending to your Notice Mr. Bayard, a worthy Inhabitant of this City, who with his Friend Mr. Henry intends to make a Visit to the American

---
[1] Colonel John Bayard? *N.Y. Gen. and Biog. Record*, XVI. 53.
[2] This refers to the two letters of Mrs. Adams of September 8 and 16, in *Familiar Letters*, 94, 96.

Camp. They are both honest Whigs, and as such I am sure they will be duly regarded by you.

This day Dr. Franklin setts off for Cambridge, being deputed by the Congress in Conjunction with Mr. Lynch of South Carolina and Coll. Harrison of Virginia to consult with the General and some Gentlemen of the four New England Colonies, concerning the most effectual Methods of continuing supporting and regulating the Continental Army. This Embassy I conjecture will be attended with great and good Consequences.

The Intelligence received by the July Packett, which arrivd at New York a few days ago, has convincd some, who could not be prevaild upon to believe it before, that it is folly to supplicate a Tyrant, and that under God, our own virtuous Efforts must save us. I hope, that our Troops will before long force their Way into Boston. If such a Design should be in Contemplation I dare say you will encourage it to the utmost of your Power.

Mr. Lynch is a Man of Sense and Virtue. Coll. Harrison's Character may be drawn from his Confidential Letter publishd not long ago in Madam Draper's Gazette. I hope these Gentlemen will be treated with all the Respect which is due to the publick Character they sustain. I mentiond to my valuable friend Coll. Lee [1] (Brother of my trusty Correspondent Dr. Lee [2] of London) his going upon this Embassy. Indeed he could not have been well spared from the Congress, and therefore I was the more easily satisfied with his Objection, which was the Want of Health. You would have been exceedingly pleasd with him.

In your Letter to Mr. J. A. you promise to write to me. I shall be happy in receiving your Letters by every Opportunity. If I am not much mistaken, a short time will afford you a delightful Subject to write upon. Our army must not long remain inactive. They must improve the golden Season, before the Rebels can be reinforced, which probably will be this Fall.

We are expecting every Moment important News from General Schuyler. May God prosper our Designs in that Quarter.

I wish you would inform me, how Affairs are carried on in General Assembly. Adieu. S. A.

[1] Richard Henry Lee. [2] Arthur Lee.

JOHN ADAMS TO JAMES WARREN

PHILADELPHIA, *Octr.* 7th, 1775

DR. SIR, — The Debates and Deliberations in Congress are impenetrable Secrets; but the Conversations in the City and the Chatt of the Coffee house are free and open. Indeed I wish We were at Liberty to write freely and Speak openly upon every Subject, for their is frequently as much Knowledge derived from Conversation and Correspondence as from Solemn public Debates.

A more intricate and complicated Subject never came into any Man's thoughts than the Trade of America.[1] The Questions that arise when one thinks of it, are very numerous.

If the Thirteen united Colonies should immediately Surcease all Trade with every Part of the World what would be the Consequence? In what manner, and to what degree, and how soon would it affect, the other Parts of the World? how would it affect G. B., Ireland, the English West India Islands, the French the Dutch the Danish, the Spanish West India Islands? how would it affect the Spanish Empire on the Continent? how would it affect the Brazills and the Portuguese Settlements in America? If it is certain that it would distress Multitudes in these Countries, does it therefore follow that it would induce any foreign Court to offer Us assistance, and to ask us for our Trade or any Part of it? If it is questionable whether foreign States would venture upon Such Steps, which would perhaps be Violations of Treaties of Peace, and certainly would light up a War in Europe, is it certain that Smugglers, by whom I mean private Adventurers belonging to foreign Nations would come here, through all the Hazards they must run? Could they be suffered to clear out for America in their own Custom houses? Would they not run the risque of Seizure from their own Custom House officers, or of Capture from their own Men of War? Would they not be liable to be visited by British Men of War, in any Part of the Ocean, and if found to have no Clearances be seized? When they arrived on any Part of the Coast of N. America would they not be seized by Brittish Cutters,

---

[1] See Adams' "Notes of Debates," October 4 and 5, in *Journals of the Continental Congress*, III. 476.

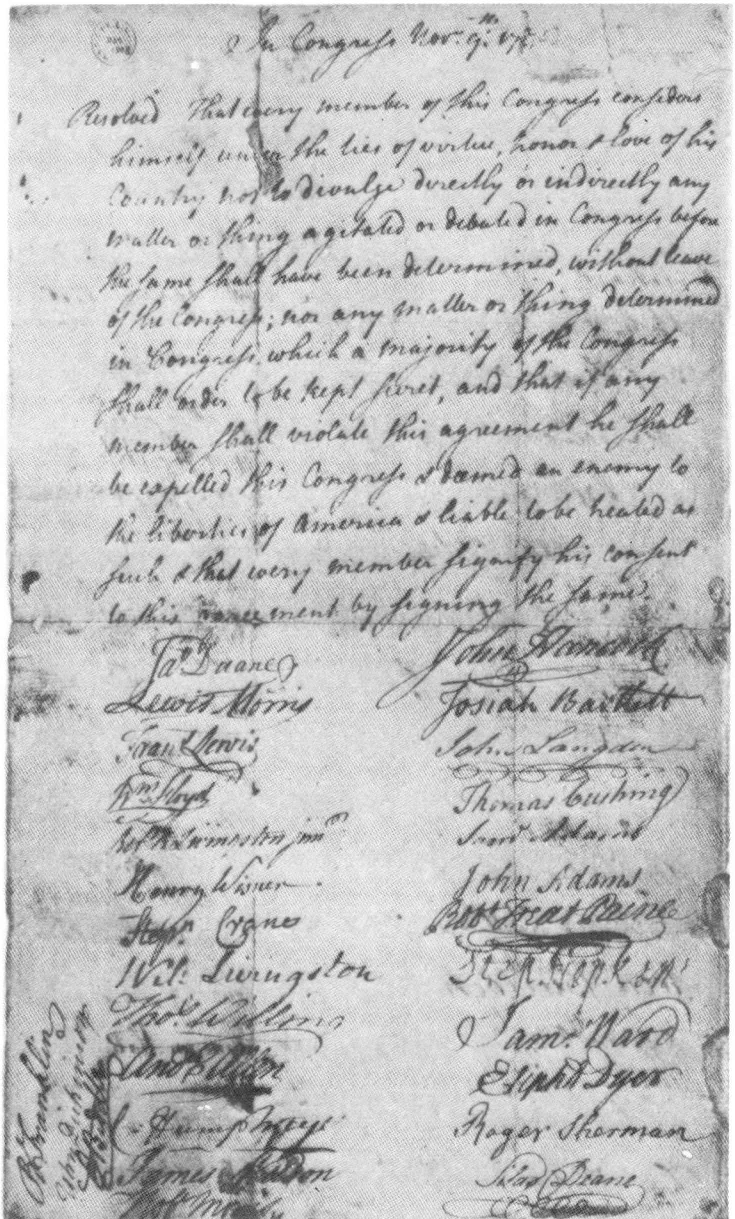

In Congress Nov. 9th 1775

Resolved That every member of this Congress considers himself under the ties of virtue, honor & love of his Country not to divulge directly or indirectly any matter or thing agitated or debated in Congress before the same shall have been determined, without leave of the Congress; nor any matter or thing determined in Congress which a majority of the Congress shall order to be kept secret, and that if any member shall violate this agreement he shall be expelled this Congress & deemed an enemy to the liberties of America & liable to be treated as such & that every member signify his consent to this agreement by signing the same.

Jas. Duane
Lewis Morris
Fran. Lewis
Wm. Floyd
Robt. R. Livingston junr.
Henry Wisner
Steph. Crane
Wil. Livingston
Thos. Willing
Andw. Allen
C. Humphreys
James Wilson
Robt. Morris

John Hancock
Josiah Bartlett
John Langdon
Thomas Cushing
Saml. Adams
John Adams
Robt. Treat Paine
Step. Hopkins
Sam. Ward
Eliphalet Dyer
Roger Sherman
Silas Deane

B. Franklin
John Dickinson

Th: Sim

Wm Paca
Samuel Chase

Richard Henry Lee

Th: Jefferson
Benj Harrison
Ths Nelson jr
G Wythe
Francis Lightfoot Lee
John Penn
Will Hooper
Joseph Hewes   Nov. 10

Tho Lynch
Chris Gadsden
Edwd Rutledge
Archd Bulloch
John Houstoun
Thomas Lynch Jr
Arthur Middleton
Fras Hopkinson   28 June

Robt Read
Geo Read
Caesar Rodney
John Jay

Rich: Smith (Jersey)
Philad 18 Jany 1776

Saml Huntington
Robt Alexander
Oliver Wolcott
Rogers
Elbridge Gerry

T Stone
Jona D Sergeant
G. Wolcott
Wm Whipple
Mat Tilghman
Carter Braxton
Ths Heyward jun.
May 20 Lyman Hall
20   Button Gwinnett
William Ellery
Jas Witherspoon

Abra: Clark

Geo Walton
John Hart
B Rush. 22 July 1776
M. Williams, 20 Feb 1776
Geo Clymer
Geo Smith
Jonath:n Elmer

Mann Page Jun.r
Nathan Brownson Feb.y 1778
Matthew Thornton

James Lovell
Th: Burke
M. Smith

W.m Duer June 5.th 1777 —
Nich.s Vandyke
H. Marchant
Geo: Frost

Cruizers, Fenders, Frigates without Number? But if their good Fortune should escape all these Risques, have We harbours or Rivers, sufficiently fortified, to insure them Security while here? In their Return to their own Country would they not have the same Gauntlett to run? In short, if We Stop our own Ships, have we even a Probability that the Ships of foreign Nations, will run the Venture to come here, either with or without the Countenance and Encouragement of their several Courts or States public or private open or secret? It is not easy for any Man precisely and certainly to answer this Question. We must then say all this is uncertain.

Suppose then We assume an intrepid Countenance, and send Ambassadors at once to foreign Courts, what Nation shall We court? Shall We go to the Court of France, or the Court of Spain, to the States General of the United Provinces? to the Court of Lisbon, to the Court of Prussia or Russia or Turkey or Denmark, or where, to any, one, more, or all of these? If we should, is there a Probability, that our Ambassadors would be received, or so much as heard or seen by any Man or Woman in Power at any of these Courts. He might possibly, if well skill'd in intrigue, his Pocketts well filled with Money and his Person Robust and elegant enough, get introduced to some of the Misses and Courtezans in Keeping of the statesmen in France, but would not that be all.

An offer of the Sovereignty of this Country to France or Spain would be listened to no doubt by either of those Courts, but we should suffer any Thing before we should offer this. What then can We offer? An Alliance, a Treaty of Commerce? What Security could they have that we should keep it? Would they not reason thus: These People intend to make Use of us to establish an Independency, but the Moment they have done it Britain will make Peace with them, and leave us in the Lurch, and we have more to dread from an Alliance between Britain and the United Colonies as an independant state, than we have now they are under one corrupted Administration. Would not Spain reason in the same manner, and say further our Dominions in South America will be soon a Prey to these enterprizing and warlike Americans, the Moment they are an independent State? Would not our Proposals and Agents be treated with Contempt? and if our Proposals were made and rejected, would not this sink the Spirits of our own People Elevate our Enemies and disgrace Us in Europe?

If then, it will not be safe to Stop our own Ships entirely and trust to foreign Vessels coming here either with or without Convoy of Men of War belonging to foreign States, what is to be done? Can our own People bear a total Cessation of Commerce? Will not such Numbers be thrown out of Employment and deprived of their Bread, as to make a large discontented Party? Will not the Burthen of supporting these Numbers, be too heavy upon the other Part of the Community? Shall we be able to maintain the War, wholly without Trade? can we support the Credit of our Currency without it?

If We must have Trade how shall We obtain it?

There is one Plan, which alone, as it has ever appeared to me, will answer the End in some Degree, at first. But this is attended with So many Dangers to all Vessels, certain Loss to many, and So much Uncertainty upon the whole, that it is enough to make any Man thoughtfull. Indeed it is looked upon So wild, extravagant and romantic, that a Man must have a great deal of Courage and much Indifference to common Censure, who should dare to propose it.

"God helps those who help themselves," and it has ever appeared to me since this unhappy Dispute begun, that We had no Friend upon Earth to depend on but the Resources of our own Country, and the good sense and great Virtues of our People. We shall finally be obliged to depend upon ourselves.

Our Country furnishes a vast abundance of materials for Commerce. Foreign Nations have great Demands for them. If We should publish an Invitation to any one Nation or more, or to all Nations, to send their ships here and let our Merchants inform theirs that We have Harbours where the Vessels can lie in Safety, I conjecture that many private foreign Adventurers would find Ways to send Cargoes here thro all the Risques without Convoys. At the Same Time our own Merchants would venture out with their Vessels and Cargoes, especially in Winter, and would run thro many Dangers, and in both these Ways together, I should hope We might be supplied with Necessaries.

All this however Supposes that We fortify and defend our own Harbours and Rivers. We may begin to do this. We may build Row Gallies, flatt bottomed Boats, floating Batteries, Whale Boats, Vesseaux de Frize, nay, Ships of War, how many, and how large I can't say. To talk of coping Suddenly with G. B. at sea would be Quixotism indeed, but the only Question with me is, can We defend our Harbours and Rivers? If We can We can trade.

[*No signature.*]

SAMUEL ADAMS TO JAMES WARREN

PHILADA., *Octob. 7*, 1775

DEAR SIR,—Yesterday Capt. Read arrived here from London which place he left the 5th of August and Falmouth the 11th.

He brings Advice that there is not the least Appearance of a Relaxation of Ministerial Measures; That the [King] speaks of them with the utmost Satisfaction; that 2000 Troops are raising to be sent to America immediately, either to Boston or New York. The Parliament is to meet in November when a Bill will be brought in to enable our most gracious Sovereign to send for and employ 16,000 Hessians, to subdue his Subjects in America. The Necessity of the times requires the utmost Activity and Vigor on this side of the Atlantick.

Pray get ready our Colony Accounts with all convenient speed. I am now in Congress and can add no more than that I am with the warmest Affection, your Friend,

SAML. AD.

JOHN ADAMS TO JAMES WARREN

October the 8, 1775

DEAR SIR,—You will not think your Time misspent in Perusing any Plans for the Service of your Country, even altho they may prove, upon Examination chimerical. There are two Channells only, through which Vessels of large Burthen, can pass, to and from Boston; one, is between the West Head of long Island and the Moon: It is a mile Wide, but incumbered with Rocks and too shallow for a Man of War of more than twenty Guns. The other is between Long Island and Deer Island, a mile and a half from Point to Point, the only Channell thro which capital Ships can pass, leads through the Narrows, between Gallop's Island and Lovell's Island where it is not wider, than the length of a fifty-Gun Ship. In the Interval between Gallop's and George's, is Nantaskett Road, where five Men of War are now Stationed; for what other End, do you suppose, than to guard the Narrows from being obstructed?

The Moon communicates with Squantum, at low Water, even without a Canoe. A Fort therefore, upon Squantum may be so placed as to Secure a Retreat from the Moon to Squantum and from that to the Main; one upon the East Head of the Moon, and another on the West Head of long Island, Secures the Communication, and covers a Retreat from the latter to the former; another, on the Summit of Long Island, covers the shore on each side. A Strong Battery at the East Head of long Island commands the ship Channell, the Narrows, and Nantaskett Road, consequently by sinking Hulks or Vesseaux de Frise in the Narrows, We might prevent any Vessell of great Force from going out or coming in.

In the Month of February last a Plan of the Town and Chart of the Harbour of Boston, was published in London. I think in a Magazine.[1] I wish you would examine this Project by that Plan, and give me your opinion. I dont trouble Washington with any of these Schemes, because I dont wish to trouble him with any Thing to no Purpose. But if I could command a Thousand Tons of Powder and an hundred Pieces of heavy Cannon I would Scribble to him till he would be weary of me. Mean Time It may not be amiss for me to amuse myself with some of my Friends, in Speculations of this kind; because some good may some time or other Result from them.

Can no Use be made of Rowe Gallies, with you? Eight or Ten are compleated here. Can they be used in the Vineyard Sound? Would not their heavy Metal demolish a Cruizer now and then? There is a Shipwright escaped from Boston, who [has] been several Years a Prisoner in a Turkish galley and has a Model of one. Coll.

---

1 *The Gentleman's Magazine*, XLV. 41.

Quincy knows him — or I could procure you Directions from this Place how to construct them.

We have just received by an express from Schuyler, very promising Intelligence concerning the operations of the Northern Army. Ethan Allen is in the Heart of the Country joined by 200 Canadians. Montgomery was beginning to bombard St. Johns.

If We should be successful in that Province, a momentous, political Question arises — What is to be done with it? A Government, will be as necessary for the Inhabitants of Canada as for those of the Massachusetts Bay, and what form of Government, shall it be? Shall the Canadians, choose an House of Representatives, a Council and a Governor? It will not do to govern them by Martial Law, and make our General Governor. this will be disrelished by them as much as their new Parliamentary Constitution or their old French Government.

Is there Knowledge and Understanding enough among them, to elect an Assembly, which will be capable of ruling them and then to be governed by it — who shall constitute their Judges and civil Officers.

This appears to me as serious a Problem as any We shall have to solve. [Six lines are here erased in the original letter] when I was at Watertown a Comtee of both Houses was appointed to Correspond with Us.[1] We have not recd any Letter from it.

Another was appointed to enquire after Virgin Lead and leaden ore and the methods of making Salt,[2] and acquaint Us with their Discoveries. We have not heard from this Comtee.

Please to send the enclosed News Paper to my Wife when you have read it.

[No signature.]

[1] "*Resolved*, that William Sever, Jedidiah Foster, and Joseph Palmer, Esqrs. together with such as the honorable House shall join, be a standing Committee for the Purpose of transmitting from Time to Time, to our Delegates at the honorable Continental Congress, all such Transactions of the Great and General Court; together with all such other Transactions and Events, as may affect the Publick, and which may appear to said Committee, proper and expedient, that the said honorable Congress should be made acquainted with." *Journals House of Representatives* (Mass.), August 22, 1775.

[2] The Council appointed on the Committee on lead and salt, Benjamin Greenleaf, Eldad Taylor and Joseph Palmer; to whom the House joined, Col. Freeman, Capt. Greenleaf, Dr. Whiting and Mr. Story. *Ib.*

John Adams to James Warren

Philadelphia, *Octr.* 10, 1775

Dr. Sir, — Mr. Jonathan Mifflin, a young Gentleman of this City a relation of our Friend the Quarter Master General will hand you this Letter.

I believe you will have enough of my Correspondence this Time, for it has certainly been filled with mere Impertinence and contains nothing of War or Politicks which are so agreeable to your Taste.

Our Expectations are very Sanguine of Intelligence from Schuyler that Canada is ours. Our advices from England breath nothing but Malice, Revenge and Cruelty.

Powder and Salt Petre are Still the Cry from one End of the Continent to the other. We must, and, God willing, We will have them.

I long to hear concerning our Friends in Boston. My Friends cannot be too particular. I want to know the Condition of every Individual; I want to know also every Event however minute which Turns up in our Camp or Lines. We have most formidable Descriptions of Gage's Fortifications in Boston. Ninety Pieces of Brass Field Pieces from four to eight Pounders have certainly been cast in the Tower for America, and Carriages, Wheel-barrows, Flat bottomed Boats, etc. I am, etc.

[No signature.]

Samuel Adams to James Warren

Philada., *Octob.* 10, 1775

My Dear Sir, — Since my last I have receivd Intelligence from London, that the British Ministry after having receivd the Advice of the Engagement on Bunker's Hill held various Councils on American Affairs and had resolvd to persevere in their Attempts to enslave us. 50 or 60 brass field pieces 6 and 9 pounders some thousand stands of small Arms with Ammunition had been shipd from the Tower of London for Quebeck to arm the Canadians. Five Regiments from Ireland, viz. 17th 27th 28th 46th and 55th were orderd to Boston. 4 Companies of the Train of Artillery are to go with the Ordnance and Stores to Quebeck. Several Ships of War were also orderd to America. What was intended for Quebeck were to sail in a fortnight from the Date of the Letter which was the 8th of August. The Regiments from Ireland were intended to be at Boston in October. The Parliamt. was to meet in Octr. and so soon, that a Sanction might be given as early as possible to the Measures that have been taken as well as others to be adopted. General Gage had been appointed Governor General of all North America, but afterwards it was concluded that Leave should be given him to return home. This was to make Room for Genl. Amherst, who is to take the Command in the Spring with a promise of 20,000 Men — 2000 Highlanders 3000 Irish Roman Catholicks, and the rest, if they cannot be raised in England, to consist of Hannoverians, Hessians and other Germans.[1] The Plan said to have been laid before Ministry last Spring, which was to divide the Troops then sent out, a part of them to go to New York, is now to be followed. General Gage's Necessity then obligd him to alter that plan and to collect all his troops together at Boston. Govr. Carleton had orders to enter upon the New England Frontiers with the Canadians, and Tryon with the Forces at New York was to meet and cooperate with him. This it is said was the Design of his return to his Government.

The idea is not given up, and to facilitate the plan a Number of flat bottom boats were to be constructed and so contrivd as when they touch the Shore, to throw down a platform that will land at once 6 armed Men. They may be used to fire field pieces or Swivel Guns. When they are compleated they are to be taken to pieces and sent to Canada to be used on the Lakes. It was reported in England that the Officers just arrivd from Boston said, the Intention was to dispossess the Americans of Dorchester Neck which was all they thought of doing this Campaign, supposing

[1] The intelligence in Boston was better. "The *Cerberus* Man of War, which carried you the News of Charlestown Battle, is Returned here after a Short Passage. She brings us very pleasing Accounts, such as have put new Life into Every Body; Gen'l Gage goes home in the *Pallas*, a Transport Ship, and Gen'l Howe is advanced to the Chief Command, a Man almost adored by the Army, and one that with the Spirit of a Wolfe, possesses the genius of a Marlborough." *Samuel Paine to William Paine*, October 2, 1775. *N.E. Hist. Gen. Reg.*, xxx. 371.

that by the Spring they should have Reinforcements sufficient to attempt any thing; especially as they concluded the Americans would be obligd from the Severity of the Winter to break up their Encampment, while the Soldiers would be in good Quarters in Boston. They also said that the Officers were much disgusted with the Service, and that it was with the utmost difficulty the Soldiers were compelld to fight.

By late accounts from the Northern Army things wear a promising Aspect there. Genl. Schuyler's Success will frustrate the designs of Ministry in Canada.

Letters have been intercepted here which discover a plot of which I have not now time to write you, as the Bearer, Mr. Mifflin, of whose going I was apprizd but a few Minutes ago, is now waiting. I am impatient to hear the particulars of a report we have just heard concerning Dr. Church which astonishes me.

Be kind enough to forward the inclosd Letter. Excuse this indigested account of Matters, which however comes from good Authority and be assured that I am with due regards to your good Lady and Friends most affectionately. Yours,

S. A.

John Adams to James Warren

Octr. 12, 1775

DR. SIR, — I would write often if I had anything to communicate; But obligations of Honour forbid some Communications and other Considerations prevent others. The common Chatt of a Coffee house is too frivolous for me to recollect or you to read. I have inclosed a Paper upon which I will make no Remark: But leave you to your own Conjectures — only I must absolutely insist that it be mentioned to nobody. It may gratify your Curiosity and give some Relief to your Cares.

I most earnestly pray that all my Friends would exert themselves to furnish me with Intelligence of a particular Nature. I mean with a List of all the Depredations committed upon our Trade; a List of all the Vessels which have been taken by the Cutters, Cruizers, etc.; the Names of the Vessels, Masters, owners;

Burthen of the Ship, the Nature of the Cargo's, and the Value of both. Nothing will contribute so much to facilitate Reprizals, as an exact Account of our Losses and Damages. I wish our General Court would take it up, and examine it thoroughly.

We have no Accounts nor Vouchers yet. Nor one Line from the Comtee appointed to correspond with Us. I am very happy — how it is I know not — but I am very happy.

[No signature.]

[ENCLOSURE][1]

As the Article of Powder is much wanted to carry on the operations vs. the Ministerial Army, and as the british Ministry have taken Every Step that human Nature could devise to prevent the Americans obtaining so essential an Article; it is humbly Submitted to the wisdom of the Cont. Congress, whether it will not be prudent to Supply themselves with that Article at the Expence of the said Ministry by taking it wherever they can get it. It is therefore recommended that 2 Vessells properly mann'd be sent to the Island of Antigua one of which may anchor at old Road on the South Side of the said Island (where there are only a few Houses) in the Evening under Dutch Colours; passing for a Vessell bound on a forced Trade, to the French Islands; in the night they may land, and take away all the powder; there being not above one or two Persons, in the fort to prevent it. As soon as the Powder is obtained the Vessell may proceed down to Johnsons Point Fort, at the S. W. point of the Island; and take what is there; there being only a single Matross in the said Fort; the other Vessell must be commanded by a prudent Man, well acquainted with the Bar and Harbour at St. Johns; if any Man of War be anchored without the Bar; it will not be prudent to attempt any Thing, but should there be none; the Vessell may then go over the Bar, and anchor close under the fort; as is commonly the Custom. There are generally 10 or 12 Soldiers in James Fort Situated on a Point on the larboard Hand, Seven miles distant from the Town; the Magazine is in a hollow; on the Left Hand just after entering the Gate, and commonly contains from 500 to 1000 Blls. of Powder, or more.

[1] In the writing of John Adams.

2 miles from thence to the northward is a Small fort called Corbresons point fort; and 2 miles from this northward is another Small fort called Dickensons bay fort, in either of which there is not above a Single Matross. All this Powder may be easily obtained without any Opposition, if conducted with Prudence; it will be necessary that the Captn should have some Money, to distribute among the Soldiers, to assist in taking it away; He may go into the Fort in the afternoon (and See how the Land lies) under pretence of Sailing that night, and thereby guide his operation.

The same Thing may be done by other Vessells at Montserrat, Nevis, Charles fort at Sandy point, St. Kitts, also at St. Martens; without any Risque.

I would advise the continental Congress to make a general Sweep of all the Powder, at St. Eustatius, it may first be taken and then paid for afterwards as the Dutch refuse to sell it to us; I am well persuaded the whole of this Plan may be executed, and that near 3000 Blls of powder may be obtained in the Course of 3 or 4 months.

John Adams to James Warren

PHILADELPHIA, *Octr.* 13, 1775

MY DEAR SIR, — Your obliging Favour of the fifth Inst.[1] I this Moment received and give me Leave to assure you that no Letter I ever received gave me greater Pleasure. In truth, sir, I have been under some Apprehensions, that a certain Passage, in a very unfortunate as well as inconsiderate Letter, might have made some disagreeable Impressions on your Mind; I was indeed relieved in some Degree by Accounts which I had from Gentlemen who knew your sentiments, especially such as were present when you first heard it read. The candid, genteel and generous Manner in which it was heard and animadverted on, gave me great Satisfaction: I had thoughts of writing you on the Subject, but was hindered by certain Notions of Delicacy, perhaps as whimsical as any Thing alluded to in that Letter. But I rejoice exceedingly, that this incident has induced you to write.

[1] Not found.

I frankly confess to you that a little whim and Eccentricity so far from being an objection to any one in my Mind,[1] is rather a Recommendation, at first Blush, and my Reasons are, because few Persons in the World, within my Experience or little Reading, who have been possessed of Virtues or Abilities, have been entirely without them, and because few Persons, have been remarkable for them, without having something at the same Time, truly valuable in them.

I confess farther that a Fondness for Dogs, by no means depreciates any Character in my Estimation, because many of the greatest Men have been remarkable for it; and because I think it Evidence of an honest Mind and an Heart capable of Friendship, Fidelity and Strong Attachments being the Characteristicks of that Animal.

Your opinion of my Generosity, Valour, Good Sense, Patriotism and Zeal for the Rights of Humanity is extreamly flattering to me; and I beg leave to assure you, in the strongest Manner and I flatter myself that my Language and Conduct in public and private upon all Occasions, notwithstanding the wanton Expressions in the intercepted Letter, have demonstrated that this Opinion is reciprocal. Your Sincerity, sir, I never doubted, any more than I did my own, when I expressed or implied an Opinion of your Attainments as a Schollar and a Soldier. Indeed I might have expressed a much higher opinion of these than I did, with the same Sincerity. But enough of this.

At the Story of the Surgeon General [2] I stand astonished. A Man of Genius, of Learning, of Family, of Character, a Writer of Liberty Songs and good ones too, a Speaker of Liberty orations, a Member of the Boston Committee of Correspondence, a Member of the Massachusetts Congress, an Agent for that Congress to the Continental Congress, a Member of the House, a Director General of the Hospital and Surgeon General — Good God! What shall We say of human Nature? What shall We say of American Patriots? or rather what will the World Say? The World however will not be too severe. Indeed, Sir, We ought to expect in a Contest like this, however we may detest, such Examples as this.

[1] A hit in favor of Charles Lee.   [2] Church.

History furnishes Instances more or less, in all Quarrels like this. The Drs. Brother Poet Waller in the Struggle with a Stuart, was his Antitype. We cannot be too cautious of the Persons We entrust, in such Times as these: Yet We ought not to let our Caution degenerate into groundless Jealousy. There is a Medium between Credulity on one hand and a base suspicious Temper on the other from which We need not be induced to deviate even in such Times as these and by such Examples as the Drs.

The Nature of the Conspiracy and the Duration and Extent of it seem as yet in much obscurity. I hope Time and Care will bring the whole Truth to light that exact and impartial Justice may be done, if that is possible.

Before this Reaches you, a Comtee. from Congress will tell you News from hence. I wish, sir that I could write freely to you concerning our Proceedings; But you know the obligations I am under to be upon the Reserve: and the danger there would be as I know not the Carrier of this Letter, if I was at perfect Liberty. But this I must say, that I see no danger of our "displaying Timidity." This Congress, is more united, and more determined than ever. And if the petrified Tyrants would but send us their Ultimatum, which is expected soon, you would see Us, in Earnest.

As to confiscating Estates, that is but a small Part of what will be done when We are engaging seriously.

You began upon a Subject, towards the Close of your Letter of infinite Importance; I read with avidity your Thoughts and was much chagrin'd that you gave me so few of them. The Intricacy and Multiplicity of the Questions involved in it, require more extensive Knowledge and a larger Mind than mine to determine them with Precision. There is so much Uncertainty too, that I believe no Man is capable of deciding with Precision; but it must be left to Time Accident and Experience, to begin and improve the Plan of our Trade.

If We should invite "all the Maritime Powers of the World into our Ports," would any one of them come? At least, untill they should be convinced that We were able, and determined to fight it out with G. B. to the last? Are they yet convinced of this, or will they be very soon? Besides, if they should, Would it be Sound

Policy in Us to admit them? Would it not be sounder to confine the Benefit and the Bargain to one or a few?

Is it not wiser to send our own Ships to all maritime Powers, and admit private adventurers from foreign Nations, if by any Means We can defend them against Cutters and Cruizers, or teach them to elude them. I have upon this Subject a System of my own but am not bigoted to it, nor to any other. You will oblige me vastly by your Sentiments at large.

[*No signature.*]

JOHN ADAMS TO JAMES WARREN

Octr. 13, 1775

Yours of October 1 and 2d I received this Morning with the Letters inclosed. These were from my afflicted Wife giving me such a continued History of her Distresses, as has affected me too much to write you a long Letter.

The Misfortune, or what shall I call it, of the Surgeon General had been represented here in several Letters in very glaring Colours, until one arrived from the secretary to the general, couched in Terms of more Temper and Candour. By your Account, and indeed by the Letter itself it appears an unaccountable Affair. Balaam praying for Leave to curse Israel, is the Emblem. A manifest Reluctance at hurting his Country, yet desirous of making a Merit, with the other Side — what shall we think? Is there reason to believe that other Letters have gone the same Way? I was so little acquainted with the World that I never heard a Suspicion to the Disadvantage of his Moral Character untill I was lately with you at the Adjournment. I should scarcely have joined in a certain Recommendation, if I had heard before what I heard then; for Honour and Fidelity violated in Such gross Instances in private Life are slender securities in public. Be not concerned about your Friends at the Congress. Their Recommendations will not be discredited by this Event. Gentlemen here have behaved universally with the Utmost Politeness, upon this Occasion, they say they pitty us, for the Suspicions that there is danger may arise among us of one another, and the Hurt to that Confidence in one another which ought to be. But any Man ought to be kick'd for a Brute that shall reproach Us in Thought, Word or Deed on this Account.

Our accounts from Schuyler's Army are as agreable as yours from Arnold. We are in hourly Expectation.

Rejoice to hear of your Successes by Sea. Let Cargill[1] and Obrien[2] be put into continental service immediately I pray.

We begin to feel a little of a Seafaring Inclination here.

The Powder at Quebec, will place us all upon the Top of the House.

Your Letters are very usefull to me, and I cannot have too many or too long.

I believe We shall take some of the twenty Gun Ships before long. We must excite by Policy that kind of exalted Courage, which is ever victorious by sea and land — which is irresistable. The Saracens, had it — the Knights of Malta — the Assassins — Cromwell's soldiers and sailors. Nay, N. England men have ever had it hitherto. They never yet faild in an Attempt of any Kind.

[*No signature.*]

SAMUEL ADAMS TO JAMES WARREN

PHILADELPHIA, *Octob.* 13, 1775

MY DEAR SIR, — It is now more than a Month since we arrivd in this City. I have receivd but one Letter and for that I am much indebted to you. I thought our Assembly had appointed a Committee to transmit Intelligence to us. We hear nothing from them. Have they no Intelligence of Importance to send to us? If so, let them inform us even of that, and we will pay the Postage of their Letter. But surely it is of some Importance that we should know whether C[hurch] is a Traitor or not — that on the one hand we might joyn like disinterested Patriots in execrating him, or, on the other hand, in vindicating the Character of an unfortunate Friend. Our pride is sorely mortified when there are Grounds to suspect that so eminent a Countryman is become a Traitor. The Fool will say in his heart, there is no such thing in the World as

---

1 The exploit is that on p. 100, *supra*.
2 Jeremiah O'Brian. In March, 1776, he was commissioned captain of the sloop *Machias Liberty*. See Currier, *History of Newburyport*, I. 612.

publick Spirit. The most virtuous Citizen will be suspected of concealing his dishonest Designs under a Cloak of Zeal for his Country and the brightest Examples will lose their Influence.

I am very sollicitous that our Army, if it be practicable, should make a resolute Attack upon the Rebels before a Reinforcement to them shall arrive, which I think may be depended upon very soon. Genl. Gage I understand is already gone for England. This verifies a part of the Intelligence which I gave you in my last Letter. Howe will remain in Command till the Spring, when Amherst will come out as strong as they can make him. It is said that ——[1] usd his utmost Power of Dissimulation (and he is as great a Master of it as Mansfield or Hutchinson) to prevail on him to undertake the Command. Among the officers of the British Army, the slavish Maxim "the Will of the Prince is Law" too much prevails. They will suffer the arbitrary and cruel Commands of their Sovereign to supersede the Dictates of Honor, Morality, and Conscience. I fear there are few, if more than one Effingham [2] to be found in Britain. I have thought there was more of the true principle of Honor in the British Army, than among any other publick Class. If this be a Truth it is a melancholy one, for it is greatly to be apprehended that there is not Virtue enough in the Nation to save it. We know by long Experience that there is not Virtue enough there to save America. Why then should America expect it from Britain. This fond Hope of a Change from violent to lenient Measures in Britain is the Rock which endangers the Shipwreck of America.

This Instant is arrivd an authentick Account of Dr. Church's Affair and a Copy of the Letter he had intended to send into Boston. To me it appears to be a very unintelligible Letter. I have not indeed thoroughly examined it. I have only heard it read. I do not recollect that it in any measure was calculated to expose the Weakness of our Army, which a Traitor, would gladly have seizd the Opportunity of doing, especially as he might have done it at that time with great Truth. The Union of Individual Colonies

[1] Thus in the MS. Perhaps the King is intended.
[2] Charles Howard, Lord Howard of Effingham (1536–1624), lord high admiral at the defeat of the Spanish "armada."

and of the Continental Congress, and their firmness and Resolution are picturd in high Colours. He informs of the Arrival of large Quantities of Gunpowder at a time when he knew there was the greatest Scarcity and was solliciting his Friends here to take every Method for providing as he expressd it that "unum necessarium." Other parts of his Letter wear a different Complection, such as his mentioning the Defeat of our Army at Bunker Hill as "lucky"; his attempting three times in vain to send in his Letter, the messenger in the third Attempt being taken up (which I do not recollect to have heard before) and the Manner in which this Letter was conceald. But I will quit this disagreeable Subject and conclude with assuring you that I am very affectionately yours,

S. A.

John Adams to James Warren

Octr. 18, 1775

Dr. Sir,—The Letter of Dr [Church] is the oddest Thing imaginable. There are so many Lies in it, calculated to give the Enemy an high Idea of our Power and Importance, as well as so many Truths tending to do us good that one knows not how to think him treacherous: Yet there are several Strokes, which cannot be accounted for at least by me, without the Supposition of Iniquity.

In Short I endeavor to suspend my Judgment. Don't let us abandon him for a Traitor without certain Evidence.

But there is not so much Deliberation in many others, or so much Compassion.

The Congress declined entering into any Discussion of the Evidence, or any Determination concerning his Guilt or the Nature of his Offence.

But in general they had a full Conviction that it was so gross an Imprudence at least and was so Suspicious, that it became them to dismiss him from their Service, which they did instantly.

Yesterday they chose a Successor, Dr. Morgan [1] an eminent Surgeon of this City. We as usual had our Men to propose, Dr.

---

[1] John Morgan (1725-1789). He was dismissed from his office in January, 1777, and a sharp controversy followed, in which he held the advantage.

Hall, Jackson, and Dr. Forster. But Dr. Forster's Sufferings and services, and Dr. Jackson's great Fame, Experience and Merits were pleaded in vain.

There is a fatality attends our Province. It Seems destined to fall into Contempt. It was destined that We should make Mistakes I think, in our Appointment of General Delegates, Surgeons, and every Thing else, except Paymaster and Judge Advocate. I hope they will not turn Cowards, Traytors, nor Lubbers; if they do I shall renounce all.

Dr. Morgan will be with you soon. He is Professor of Medecine in the Colledge here, and reads Lectures in the Winter. He is a Brother of Mr. Duché and of our Mr. Stillman. I may write you more particularly about him another Time.

Let me close now with a matter of some Importance. Congress have appointed Deane, Wythe and your servant a Committee to collect a just Account of the Hostilities committed by the ministerial Troops and Navy, in America, since last March; with proper Evidence of the Truth of the Facts related, the Number and Value of the Buildings destroyed by them, also the Number and Value of the Vessels inward and outward bound, which have been Seized by them, since that Period, also the Stock taken by them from different Parts of the Continent: We shall write to the Assemblies of New England and Virginia at least, but we shall likewise write to many Individuals requesting their Assistance and to you among others. I wish you would think a little and consult with others concerning this Business for it nearly concerns our Province to have it well done.

[*No signature.*]

JOHN ADAMS TO JAMES WARREN

Octr. 19, 1775

MY DEAR SIR, — It was the latter end of August that I left you. All September has run away, and 19 days in Octr. and We have had no regular Intelligence from Watertown or Cambridge. Your Goodness I acknowledge. But there was a Committee of both Houses appointed, to correspond with your Delegates; and We were to be informed of every Thing that occurred in Boston, Cambridge, Roxbury, Watertown, etc., especially of every Thing which passed in Either House; But have never received a single Letter not even a Scratch of a Pen from this Comtee. or any Member of it, unless you are one, which I dont know that you are. Should be glad to hear if this Committee, is all defunct or not.

I have, in almost every Letter I have written, to any of my Friends, entreated that We might have accounts and Vouchers sent Us, that We might obtain a Reimbursement of some Part at least of the inordinate Expence that has fallen upon Us. But have received No answer from any one, concerning it. I wish to be informed, however, what the Difficulty is, that lies in the Way, if We cannot have the Accounts, etc. The Continental Money goes away so fast, that I greatly fear We shall have none left in the Treasury, before We get the Proper Evidence and Information to obtain a Reimbursement for our Province. Dollars go but little Way in Maintaining Armies — very costly Commodities indeed. The Expence already accrued will astonish Us all I fear.

Congress has appointed a Comtee — Deane, Wythe and your servant — to collect a Narration of Hostilities, and Evidence to prove it, to ascertan the Number and Value of the Buildings destroyed, Vessells captivated, and Cattle plundered, etc., every where. I hope We shall tell a true Story, and then I am sure it will be an affecting one. We shall not omit their Butcheries, nor their Robberies, nor their Piracies. But we shall want Assistance from every Quarter. I want the Distresses of Boston painted by Dr. Cooper's Pencil.[1] Everything must be supported by Affidavits. This will be an usefull Work for the Information of all the Colonies of what has passed in Some, for the Information of our Friends in England, and in all Europe, and all Posterity. Besides it may pave the Way to obtain Retribution and Compensation, but this had better not be talked of at present. The Committee will write

[1] The Committee of Safety of the Massachusetts Provincial Congress was instructed to "draw up and transmit to Great Britain, a fair and impartial account of the late battle of Charlestown, as soon as possible." The Committee, being exceedingly crowded with business, desired the Rev. Dr. William Cooper, the Rev. Mr. William Gordon and the Rev. Mr. Peter Thacher to draw up a true statement. *Journals of the Provincial Congress* (Mass.), 594. No report appears to have been made. The Continental Congress took up the matter with an equal want of results. See p. 162, *infra*.

to the Assemblies, and to private Gentn. No Pains or Expense will be Spared I hope to render the Execution of this Commission compleat. It concerns our Province very much.

[*No signature.*]

JOHN ADAMS TO JAMES WARREN

Octr. 19, 1775

DR. SIR, — What Think you of an American Fleet? I don't Mean 100 ships of the Line, by a Fleet, but I suppose this Term may be applied to any naval Force consisting of several Vessels, tho the Number, the Weight of Metal, or the Quantity of Tonnage may be small.

The Expence would be very great — true. But the Expence might be born and perhaps the Profits and Benefits to be obtained by it, would be a Compensation. A naval Force might be created which would do something. It would destroy Single Cutters and Cruisers. It might destroy small Corvets or Fleets of these like Wallace's at R. Island and Ld. Dunmores at Virginia. It might oblige our Enemies to sail in Fleets. For two or three Vessels of 36 and twenty Guns, well armed and manned might attack and carry a 64 or a 70 or a 50 Gun Ship.

But, there is a great Objection to this. All the Trade of Pennsylvania, the Lower Counties, a great Part of Maryland and N. Jersey Sails in between the Capes of Delaware Bay. And if a strong Fleet should be posted in that Bay, Superiour to our Fleet it might obstruct all the Trade of this River.

Further the Trade of Virginia and the rest of Maryland floats into Cheasapeak Bay between the Capes of Henry and Charles where a Fleet might stop all. Besides Virginia and Maryland have no Navigation of their own nor any Carpenters to build ships. Their whole Trade is carried on in British Bottoms by British, most of it by North British Merchants. These Circumstances distinguish them quite from New England, where the Inlets are innumerable and the Navigation all their own.

They agree that a Fleet, would protect and secure the Trade of New England but deny that it would that of the Southern Colonies.

Will it not be difficult to persuade them then to bear the Expense of building a Fleet, merely for N. England. We are Speculating now about Things at a Distance. Should we be driven to a War at all Points, a Fleet a public Fleet as well as privateers might make prey enough of the Trade of our Enemies to make it worth while.

[*No signature.*]

JOHN ADAMS TO JAMES WARREN

Octr. 19, 1775

DR. SIR, — I want to be with you, Tête à Tête, to canvass, and discuss the complicated subject of Trade. I say nothing of private Consultations or public Debates, upon this important Head. When I write you Letters you must expect nothing from me but unconnected Scraps and broken Hints. Continual Successions of Company allow me Time only to Scrawl a Page of Paper, without Thought.

Shall we hush the Trade of the whole Continent and not permit a Vessell to go out of our Harbours except from one Colony to another? How long will or can our People bear this? I say they can bear it forever. If Parliament should build a Wall of Brass, at low Water Mark, We might live and be happy. We must change our Habits, our Prejudices our Palates, our Taste in Dress, Furniture, Equipage, Architecture, etc., but We can live and be happy. But the Question is whether our People have Virtue enough to be mere Husbandmen, Mechanicks and Soldiers? That they have not Virtue enough to bear it always I take for granted. How long then will their Virtue last? till next Spring? If We Stop all Trade G. B. I. and W. I. will not be furnished with any Thing.

Shall We then give Permission for our Vessells to go to foreign Nations, if they can escape the Men of War? Can they escape the Men of War? How many will escape in Proportion? If any Escape, will they not venture to Britain, Ireland, and W. I. in defyance of our Association? If they do not will not the British Dominions furnish themselves with our Produce from foreign Ports, and thereby avoid that Distress, which We expect will overtake them?

Will not the W. I. Islands especially, who cannot exist without our Provisions for 6 Months, unless Glou[cester(?)and] Walker were ignorant.

If We should invite other maritime Powers, or private adventurers from foreign Nations to come here, Will they venture? They run the risque of escaping Men of War, and the Dangers of an unknown Coast. Maps and Charts may give Strangers a confused Idea of the Geography of our Country, and of the Principal Inlets of Harbours, Rivers, Creeks, Coves, Islands, etc., but without skillful Pilots, the danger of Shipwreck will be 10 to one.

This vast object is never out of my Mind. Help me to grapple it. The W. I., Barbadoes particularly, begin, We are told here by a late Vessel, to be terrified out of their Wits.

[*No signature.*]

ABIGAIL ADAMS TO MERCY WARREN

BRAINTREE, *October* 19, 1775

I thank my Friends for their kind remembrance of me last week. The Letter enclosed was dated one day after that I received a week before and contain no publick intelegance. I have been Expecting Letters by the Gentlemen who I hear have arrived, but fear I have not any as there are none come to hand. I thought I should hear oftener from Philadelphia this fall, than I had ever done before; but I never before had so few Letters, or found the communication so difficult.

I wish, my Friend, you would be kind enough to write me often whilst you tarry at Watertown, and let your Letters be of the journal kind; by that mean I could participate in your amusements, in your pleasures, and in your Sentiments which would greatly gratify me, and I should collect the best of inteligance.

Pray, Sir, is this request unreasonable? I would not ask anything willingly which might be deemd so? If it is not, will you use your influence in obtaining for me this favour? It is Matter of Speculation what the errant of these Gentlemen is. Some Suppose one thing, some an other.

What do you immagine will be the consequence if a certain

Letter writer[1] should escape without very severe punishment? Would there or not be Suspicions in the minds of people prejudicial to those in power? The Country appear much exasperated, and would say he was not the only traitor.

You have not wrote me what you think of the intercepted Letters, nor of the ridiculous pharaphrase. I wish you would be kind eno to return the coppy of the Letters when ever you have done with them.

I hear Mrs. Miflin is come to the Headquarters, if you see her, please to present my compliments to her. I want to know all that passes, curiosity you see natural to me as a ———, but I know who has as much and therefore can excuse a reasonable share of it in her Friend.

My best regards attend Mrs. Wintrope when you see her, When do you expect to return? I hope I shall see more of you then and have the pleasure of both your company's much oftener. I fear I shall not see you at Watertown. I feel but little inclination to go into company. I have no Son big enough to accompany me, and two women cannot make out so well, as when they are more naturally coupled. I do not fancy riding thro Roxbury with only a female partner. So believe you will not see Your

PORTIA

SAMUEL ADAMS TO JAMES WARREN

PHILADA. *Octob.* 19, 1775

MY DEAR SIR, — This Letter will be delivered to you by Capt. Gist,[2] a Gentleman who I am well informed is meritorious in his endeavors with others in the Colony of Maryland to inspire the Inhabitants there with Military Virtue. You will excuse the Freedom I take in recommending him to your Notice. It is for the Sake of my Country.

Our Affairs are at this Moment in a critical Situation. I am impatient to hear from Schuyler and Arnold. By Accounts receivd last Evening from Quebeck, the Lt. Governor[3] of that Colony

---

1 Church.   2 Mordecai Gist (1743–1792).   3 Hector Theophilus Cramahe.

(Carleton being absent) had raisd a Number of Companies of Canadians to defend the Country. There was however no Expectation of an Expedition to Quebeck at that time, viz. the 28th September.

"Tis not in Mortals to command Success." If we fail we may yet console ourselves, in reflecting that we have done all that was in our power to save our Country. *Voluisse sat est.* I am in haste, Yours Affectionately,

S. A.

JAMES WARREN TO JOHN ADAMS. ADAMS MSS.

WATERTOWN, *October* 20, 1775

MY DEAR SIR, — After an interval much longer than I ever designed should take place, I now sit down to write again. The multiplicity of business, and the crowd of company here, must be my excuse. Every body either eats, drinks or sleeps in this house, and very many do all, so that for a week past I could get no opportunity to write, morning, noon, or night. The committee of Congress arrived here last Sunday. Colonel Harrison went through [the] town without my seeing him. Doctor Franklin and Mr. Lynch stop'd at Davis. I waited on them, and they came over and drank coffee with us. The next day I dined with them all at Head quarters, and yesterday they and the general officers, and the gentlemen of character from the southward on a visit here, were entertained by the House at Coolidge's,[1] on the best dinner we could get for them, turtle, codfish, etc. Every kind of civility and mark of respect is shewn them here, and if they don't leave us better satisfied than they came to us, it will not be our faults. From the little conversation I have had with them, which has been as much as could be got in a crowd, I presume they will. I am much pleased with them. Doctor Franklin, who[m] I never saw before, appears venerable in the characters of a gentleman, a physician, and statesman. I think Mr. Lynch very sensible and judicious, and all of them firmly attached to the good cause, and I flatter myself their zeal will not be abated by this visit. In my last

[1] Nathaniel Coolidge, whose house was near the south end of Mill Bridge.

short billet I forgot to congratulate you on your appointment to the Supreme Bench of justice here, and I expect the first seat, as no doubts are made of it, tho' they are not yet ranked. Four only are appointed, Mr. Adams, Mr. Cushing, Mr. Read, and Mr. Sergeant. The Board voted by ballot for those that should be nominated, and with the four mentioned voted Mr. Sever, but from his diffidence, etc., he prevailed not to be nominated. Where the next appointment will fall I can't tell. Some of Paine's friends had it in contemplation to have him nominated, but gave it up after you was appointed, very naturally supposing he could not be ranked before you, and he having previously declared to them that he would not serve in an inferiour station, As every body must know he was your superiour. I am told they have a design to nominate him King's Attorney. How far his acceptance of that place is to be reconciled to his declaration you may judge. Lowell seems to stand no chance, at least till he has served an apprenticeship in Purgatory. This appointment if you accept it will cooperate with your wishes expressed in several letters to leave the Congress. Indeed we want you here, for this and divers other reasons; but how to be reconciled to your leaving the Congress I can't tell.[1] I shall certainly, when such an event takes place, lose some share of my confidence in, and reverence for that august body. We have passed a bill for the judges holding their commissions *quam diu se bene gesserint*, but could not compleat their independency by established salaries.[2] As for the town of Boston, it continues in the same miserable situation. A few deserters come out, and of late several of the inhabitants have stole out in boats, among the rest our friend Hitchburne the night before last. One man who got out last night has just called on me. He says one reason of their running all hazards to get out is the threats of forcing them to take arms. They all give the same general account that fresh provisions are very scarce, 11*d*. sterling per pound, and no vegetables; the meat excessive poor; that the troops have not been served with it but twice during the summer and fall; that

[1] The appointment was taken advisedly, but resigned in 1777. See *Works of John Adams*, IX. 390, 457.
[2] See "Journal of Josiah Quincy, Jr.," in *Proceedings*, XLIX. 448.

their duty is very severe, and they continue sickly, about 1500 in the hospitals; that they suppose Canada is in our hands, and are not elated with any certain expectation of reinforcements. They are apprehensive of an attack, were hove into great confusion a few nights ago by Admiral Putnam, who went down into the Bay with our floating batteries, etc., and fired some shot into the town, which interrupted their ball, and the acting of a play they were then engaged in, and their repose for the night. A misfortune attended this expedition, which contributed to their relief and cost us the loss of two men killed and six wounded. A gun split in one of the batteries, and destroyed her also. Gage sailed about ten days ago, and is succeeded by Howe. Gill, Leach and Edes's son [1] are out of gaol. Lovel still remains. It is said he refuses to come out, but I doubt that. Several armed vessels are fixing by the General, and we have passed a bill to encourage individuals to fix out others. We have just received an account that they have been cannonading Falmouth, Casco Bay, and that Wallace, the pirate at Newport, has insisted on the removal of the troops from Rhode Island, or he will destroy Newport, and shewn instructions to the Committee there to destroy four towns, among which are Plymouth and Machias. The others I can't learn. This account the Governour, Cooke,[2] has just received. Please to tell Colonel Hancock I have the honour to be ranked a damned rebel with him. Upon hearing we were concerned in a brigantine bound to London the beginning of September, they sent out a cruiser on purpose for her, took her, carryed her in, condemned her and cargo, and ordered them sold. Our accounts, or rather the delay of them, has given me infinite pain. We are determined to exert ourselves, and prepare them as soon as possible. In the mean time shall forward you an application which tho' a lumping one is not, perhaps, far from the truth. I wish it may have a favourable reception. It is impossible to describe the field of business before us, rendered still more difficult and embarrassing by the multitude of new questions out of the common road. When are we to see the resolves upon which is grounded the credit of your bills? The misers will soon be started upon that question. I will thank you for the

[1] John Gill, John Leach and Peter Edes.   [2] Nicholas Cooke (1717-1782).

establishment of my office. You wrote me it was one hundred dollars per month.[1] Colonel Hancock had every other establishment here but that. Our army are in much the same state they have been for some time past, as vigorous spirited as ever, and more healthy than they have been, well secured by impenetrable lines. So far we are prepared for the defensive. When we are to be so for the offensive I know not. I suppose that depends much on having a large quantity of a certain article, with which we have never yet abounded. We have no news from Colonel Arnold since he left Norridgwalk. I flatter myself he is before this in Quebeck, where are large quantities of warlike stores, not less than 10,000 barrels powder. They would be a grand acquisition, but I can hardly hope that they will be so stupid as not to take care to prevent it by setting them afloat. We have no late news from St. Johns. We begin to grow impatient.

The 21st. The conference I am told is to be finished this day. I know little about it. There seems to be such a reservedness among those concerned here, that my pride won't permit me to ask many questions. By the way, the Committee of Council are Colonel Otis,[2] Mr. Sever,[3] and Mr. Spooner,[4] to whom has since been added Bowdoin,[5] who lately came to town and took his seat at the Board. I believe your committee were very soon convinced that the soldiers never had less wages. The bounty given on an average last war, I suppose might be set at £8; sometimes we gave £12, and one year £14, tho' at first less than £8, which will make at least 20/ per month to be added to 36/, the wages then given. We now give them a coat upon an average about 24/, which will make 3/ to be added to 40/. A blanket they had in both cases. It will from these facts be easy to infer that they then had 13/ at least per month more than now.

I have given you before a minute detail of Church's affair. I have learnt that you are furnished with a copy of the letter, or should not fail to send one. I am told that he continues with great confidence, or rather impudence, to assert his innocence, and,

---
1 *Journals of the Continental Congress*, II. 94.
2 James Otis (1725–1783).
3 William Sever (1729–1809). His wife was Sarah Warren.
4 Walter Spooner (1720–1803).   5 James Bowdoin (1727–1790).

against common sense and the most flagrant evidence, to pretend he was serving his country. This is, indeed, Hutchinson like, affronting to our understandings. I have never seen him; I never wish to again. You know I hate an apostate, I hate a traitor. How he is to receive an adequate punishment is I suppose a question for your determination. I am sensible of the deficiencies in your code of laws, and the objections to *post facto* laws; but something must be done, and he made an example of, or the people will suppose us all traitors, and lose their confidence in what we say or do. Our House are adjusting the ceremonies of proceeding in order of expulsion, and then will end our tether.[1]

I believe it is time to think of concluding this letter, or never expecting you to wish for another; but before I do, I must and do thank you heartily and fervently for your several letters received by Major Bayard, the gentlemen of your committee, and yesterday by Mr. Mifflin. Tho' you communicate no secrets, I can see and taste the traces of that extensive system of policy which always marks your way, and which I hope will be adopted. Your last has led me into a sea so extensive and deep, that my small abilities have not yet been able either to fathom the bottom or descry the shore. However, I shall rally them, and if I have vanity enough to suppose I can strike out one particle of light on so grand and important a subject, shall certainly attempt it in my next, which will soon follow this, if opportunity presents. In the mean time your maxim "God helps those who help themselves" recurs to mind. We are in a storm and must make a port. We must exert ourselves in some of the ways you mention. I think we must have trade and commerce. I see no difficulty in admitting it in our own bottoms consistently with the association, if individuals will hazard their interest, and opening our ports to foreigners, one or more. If you could see me at this instant, you would think that the embarrassments and hurry of business on hand would by no means admit of discussions of this kind. The great objects some of us would wish to confine our House to are, the manufacturing salt petre and fire arms, the regulating the militia and fixing out

[1] Dr. Church was examined by the House October 27 and the order of expulsion was passed November 2.

armed Vessels. The first is in a good way in Connecticut. We have sent Doctor Whiting [1] there to learn the process and art, and since his return have directed him to try the experiment here. I am not able to inform you of his success. The next I think we shall succeed in. The two others are under consideration, and a bill for the last in great forwardness, so far as relates to individuals. We have a difficulty with regard to the militia from a construction in our House of your resolve, giving them a power to appoint officers. I wish it could be explained.

The 22d. We have just heard that the pirates on the Eastern shore have destroyed two-thirds of Falmouth burnt down, and have orders to destroy every sea port from Boston to Pemmaquid. This is savage and barbarous in the highest stage. What can we wait for now? What more can we want to justifie any step to take, kill and destroy, to refuse them any refreshments, to apprehend our enemies, to confiscate their goods and estates, to open our ports to foreigners, and if practicable to form alliances, etc., etc.

Hitchburne was to see me last evening. He seems distressed to approve his conduct to us relative to the letters. Very little of a publick kind can I learn from him more than we have from others. He says they dread and apprehend the erecting batteries on Dorchester Hill and Noddle's Island. The first will drive them from their lines on the Neck, and the other make it impossible for ships to lay in the harbour, I mean above the Castle. I wish and hope we may be able to effect it. One piece of good news I had like to have forgot. A Vessel is arrived at Sheepscot with a very considerable quantity of powder, cannon, and arms. I believe she belongs to the Massachusetts Bay Colony.

I shall endeavour to see and form a judgment of your plan as soon as I can procure the chart. The row gallies you have at Philadelphia may be very serviceable in smooth water, but if I am rightly informed would not do in a sea. No doubt such might be constructed as would, but I am inclined to think that our cannon armed Vessels, especially as we can be so superiour in men, and are more used to them, will answer the purpose better, if we choose such as sail well.

[1] William Whiting.

I am sensible of the importance of the question you propose about the government of Canada. It is indeed a curious problem, and I am glad it is in such good hands. I never expected you would derive any advantages from the committees you mention. The spirit of indolence is too prevalent. There is in the western parts of this Province a lead mine of three miles in length which affords one half pure lead. It is said the country abounds with sulphur; we want nothing but salt petre. I trust Providence will give us that. I cannot inclose you any of Mother Draper's papers, they are very scarce. I think I have not seen one since that I inclosed you. I shall endeavour, however, to procure you one or two curiosities of a like kind, and inclose without any comment, tho' I feel somewhat inclined to it. . . .

J. W.

JOHN ADAMS TO JAMES WARREN

Octr. 20, 1775

DEAR SIR, — Can the Inhabitants of North America *live* without foreign Trade?

There is Beef and Pork and Poultry, and Mutton and Venison and Veal, Milk, Butter, Cheese, Corn, Barley Rye, Wheat, in short, every Species of Eatables animal and Vegetable in a vast abundance, an immense Profusion. We raise about Eleven hundred Thousand Bushells of Corn, yearly more than We can possibly consume. The Country produces Provisions of all Kinds, enough for the sustenance of the Inhabitants, and an immense Surplusage.

We have Wood and Iron in plenty. We have a good Climate as well as a fertile Soil.

But Cloathing. If instead of raising [a] Million Bushells of Wheat for Exportation and Rice, Tobacco, naval stores Indigo, Flaxseed, Horses Cattle, etc., Fish, Oyl, Bone Potash etc., etc., etc., the Hands now employed in raising surplusages of these Articles for Exportation, were employed in raising Flax and Wool, and manufacturing them into Cloathing, We should be cloathed comfortably.

We must at first indeed Sacrifice some of our Appetites. Coffee, Wine, Punch, Sugar, Molasses, etc. and our Dress would not be so elegant. Silks and Velvets and Lace must be dispensed with. But these are Trifles in a Contest for Liberty.

But is there Temperance, Fortitude and Perseverance enough among the People to endure Such a Mortification of their Appetites Passions and Fancies? Is not the Merchantile Interest comprehending Merchants Mechanicks, Labourers So numerous, and So complicated with the landed Interest, as to produce a general Impatience and Uneasiness, under Restrictions so severe?

By a total Cessation of Commerce sh[ould we drive] away our Mariners? Will they not go [to the other] maritime Nations, the French, the Spaniards, the Dutch? or, which is worse, will they not go to England, and on Board of British Men of War?

Shall We not lose a large Property in Navigation which will rot by the Wharves?

On the other Hand if We give Liberty Trade, will not most of our Vessels be seized? Perhaps all but those of the Tories who may be priviledged.

[*No signature.*]

JOHN ADAMS TO JAMES WARREN

Octr. 20, 1775

DR. SIR, — The Bearer of this is John McPherson Esq. He is a Genius — an old Sea Warriour, Nine or ten Times wounded in Sea Fights.

He has a son in the Service — Aid de Camp to Schuyler — a very sensible Man.

Of Mr. McPherson's Errand to the Camp ask no Questions and I will tell you no false News. It will make a Noise in Time — but for the present for Gods sake let not a Word be said.[1]

I hope all our Friends who have Opportunity will shew him Respect.

[*No signature.*]

1 *Journals of the Continental Congress*, III. 301.

John Adams to James Warren

Octr. 21, 1775

DEAR SIR, — I believe I shall surfeit you with Letters, which contain nothing, but Recommendations of Gentlemen to your Attention, especially as you have so many important Affairs to take up all your Time and Thoughts.

But the Bearers are Gentlemen, who come so well recommended to me that I could not refuse myself the Pleasure of giving them an Opportunity of seeing my Friend Warren, of whom you must know I am very proud. The Name of one of them is John Folwell, the other Josiah Hart, each of them a Captain of a Company of Militia in the County of Bucks in this Province. Mr. Joseph Hart the Father of one of them has exerted himself with much Success in procuring Donations for Boston.

These Travellers visit the Camp from the best Motive — that of gaining Knowledge in the military Art by Experience, that their Country may have the Use of it, whenever there shall be an Opportunity.

You will greatly oblige them by giving them a Letter to General Thomas, and by introducing them to such Persons and Places as will best answer the honest and usefull End they have in View.

I could wish them as well as other Strangers introduced to H. Knox and young Josiah Waters,[1] if they are anywhere about the Camp. These Young Fellows if I am not mistaken would give strangers no contemptible Idea of the military Knowledge of Mass[achusetts men] in the sublimest Chapters of the Art of War.

Salt Petre is certainly making in considerable Quantities in several Places. I wish to know what success Dr. Whiting has.

You wonder that certain *Improprieties* are not felt. Well you may. But I have done finding fault — I content myself with blushing alone, and mourning in Secret, the Loss of Reputation our Colony Suffers, by giving Such *Samples* of her Sons to the World. Myself, remember the worst Sample of all. Pray change it.

[No signature.]

[1] A surgeon's mate in the artillery.

JOHN ADAMS TO JAMES WARREN

Octr. 21, 1775

DEAR SIR, — We must bend our Attention to Salt Petre. We must make it. While B. is Mistress of the Sea and has so much Influence with foreign Courts, We cannot depend upon a Supply from abroad.

It is certain that it can be made here, because it is certain that it has been formerly and more latterly. Dr. Graham, of White Plains in the Colony of New York told me, that he has made some thousands of Pounds Weight, many years ago, by Means of a German Servant whom he bought and found to be good for nothing else.

Messrs. De Witts, one of Windham the other of Norwich, have made a considerable Quantity, a sample of which has been shewn me by Coll. Dyer, and they have made a large Collection of Materials for making more.

Mr. Wisner[1] of New York, informs me that his son has made a Quantity of very good, by the Method published by the Continental Congress.

Two persons belonging to York Town in this Colony have made one hundred and twenty Weight, have recd. the Premium and are making more.

A Gentleman in Maryland made some last June from Tobacco House Earth.

Mr. Randolph,[2] our venerable President, affirms to me that, every Planter almost in that Colony, has made it from Tobacco House Earth. That the Process is so simple that a Child can make it. It consists in nothing but making a Lixivium from the Earth which is impregnated with it, and then evaporating the Lixivium. That there is certainly discovered in Virginia a vast Quantity of the Rocks of Salt Petre. That there are salt Petre Rocks he says all Chemists and Naturalists who have written Agree, and that he was informed by many Gentlemen in Virginia, cautious, incredulous Men, of strict Honour and Veracity, that

1 Henry Wisner (1725–1790), a member of the Continental Congress.
2 Peyton Randolph.

they have been to see the Rocks and tryed them and found them by Experiment to be the very Rock of salt Petre.

The old Gentn. in short, who is not credulous nor inthusiastical but very steady, solid, and grave, is as sanguine and confident as you can conceive, that it is the Easiest Thing in the World to make it, and that the Tobacco Colonies alone are sufficient to supply the Continent forever.

Every Colony, My Friend, must set up Works at the public Expence.

I am determined never to have Salt Petre out of my Mind, but to insert some stroke or other about it in every Letter for the future. It must be had.

[*No signature.*]

JOHN ADAMS TO JAMES WARREN

Octr. 23, 1775

DEAR SIR, — Yours of the 12th instant came to Hand Yesterday. Thank you and your good Lady for your kind Condolence, on the loss of an excellent Mother, a Loss which is and ought to be more particularly affecting, because there is Reason to fear that her kind Exertions for the Relief [of] my Family when in great Distress contributed to her Catastrophe.[1] I dread to hear further from my Family least a pestilential Infection should have seized some other Branch of it. But will hope for better Things.

I don't Think you negligent, my Friend, having had too much Experience of your Care and Attention. I only thought it my Duty to omit no Opportunity to press for Accounts, etc. I wish my other Friends were as little chargeable with Negligence as you.

I want to know a Thousand Things. What are the Prices of European and West India Goods? how the Non Exportation is observed? How the Prices of Provisions? Whether there is any prospect of keeping any Trade alive, and what?

You will receive a Letter from a Comtee. whose Business it is to prepare a compleat Narrative of the War — at least of the Murders, Robberies, Piracies, Treasons, Felonies, Villanies, etc.

[1] Elizabeth (Quincy) Smith, mother of Abigail Adams. She died October 1, 1775.

of the Army and Navy. Mr. Wythe who is one, is a Virginian, a Lawyer of high Rank at the Bar, a great Schollar, a most indefatigable Man and a staunch Virginian, to all appearance.

You will observe the Vote limits Us to last March. This was done without design and I don't intend to be so limited; and therefore I hope the two Houses will appoint a Committee upon a larger Scale and collect Facts at least from the Port Bill, i.e. the time when it took place. I hope neither Time, Trouble nor Expence will be spared upon this Occasion; that an Account of the Expence will be kept by the Province; and altho I have no authority to say it will be paid, yet I believe it will by the Continent.

Compliments to Mrs. Warren. Tell [her] I had rather have received a Letter than a Promise of one, tho' that is valuable.

[No signature.]

John Adams to James Warren

Octr. 24, 1775

DEAR SIR, — When it is said that it is the Prerogative of omniscience to Search Hearts, I suppose it is meant that no human Sagacity can penetrate at all Times into Mens Bosoms and discover with precise Certainty the secrets there; and in this Sense it is certainly true.

But there is a sense in which Men may be said to be possessed of a Faculty of Searching Hearts too. There is a Discernment competent to Mortals by which they can penetrate into the Minds of Men and discover their Secret Passions, Prejudices, Habits, Hopes, Fears, Wishes and Designs, and by this Means judge what Part they will act in given Circumstances for the future and see what Principles and Motives have actuated them to the Conduct they have held in certain Conjunctures of Circumstances which are passed.

A Dexterity and Facility of thus unravelling Mens Thoughts and a Faculty of governing them by Means of the Knowledge we have of them, constitutes the principal Part of the Art of a Politician.

In a Provincial Assembly, where we know a Man's Pedigree and

Biography, his Education, Profession and Connections, as well as his Fortune, it is easy to see what it is that governs a Man and determines him to this Party in Preference to that, to this System of Politicks rather than another, etc.

But here it is quite otherwise. We frequently see Phenomena which puzzle us.

It requires Time to enquire and learn the Characters and Connections, the Interests and Views of a Multitude of Strangers.

It would be an exquisite Amusement, an high Gratification of Curiosity, this same Mystery of Politicks if the Magnitude of the Interests and Consequences did not interest us Some times too much.

[No signature.]

JOHN ADAMS TO JAMES WARREN

Octr. 24, 1775

DEAR SIR, — I have only Time to acquaint you that Yesterday, that eminent American, and most worthy Man The Honourable Peytoun Randolph, Esqr., our first venerable President, departed this Life in an Apoplectic Fit. He was seized at Table, having but a few Moments before set down with a good deal of Company to dinner. He died in the Evening, without ever recovering his senses after the first Stroke.

As this Gentleman Sustained very deservedly One of the first American Characters, as he was the first President of the united Colonies, and as he was universally esteemed for his great Virtues and shining Abilities, the Congress have determined to shew his Memory and Remains all possible Demonstrations of Respect. The whole Body is to attend the Funeral in as much Mourning as our Laws will admit. The Funeral is to be tomorrow. I am the more pleased with this Respect on Account of an Impropriety, which you know was unfelt.[1]

This venerable Sage, I assure you, since he has stood upon the same Floor with the rest of Us has rose in the Esteem of all. He was attentive, judicious and his Knowledge Eloquence, and clas-

[1] The Hancock incident, p. 112, *supra*.

sical Correctness shewed Us the able and experienced Statesman and Senator; whereas his former station had in a great Measure concealed these and shewed Us chiefly the upright and impartial Moderator of Debate.

You would have wondered more at the Want of [sensi]bility which you remarked if you had been here and seen, the Difference.

Mr. Randolph was as firm, stable and consistent a Patriot as any here. The Loss must be very great to Virginia in Particular and the Continent in general — I sometimes wonder that a similar Fate does not befall more of the Members. Minds so engaged and Bodies so little exercised are very apt to fall.[1]

This goes by Mr. Gawen Brown.[2]

[*No signature.*]

Silas Deane, John Adams, and George Wythe to James Warren

Philadelphia, *Octr.* 24, 1775

Sir, — The Congress has resolved,[3] that a just Account of the Hostilities committed by the ministerial Army and Navy, in America, since the month of March last, be collected, with proper Evidence of the Facts; the Number and Value of the Buildings destroyed, the Vessells whether inward or outward bound, seized or captivated and the Stock of all kinds, plundered, in any Part of the Continent, as you will see by an authenticated Copy of the Resolution, here inclosed.

It is apprehended that little need be said to shew the Utility of this Measure. It may be necessary for our Justification, in the Judgment of the People of Great Britain, and foreign Nations; the Information of the Colonies and the Use of History, not to mention any other Purpose.

Our Distance here from the Scenes of Violence makes it necessary for us to apply to several Assemblies, as well as private Gentlemen for Assistance; and from your Character it is presumed, you will chearfully yield us all the Aid in your Power.

---

1 See *Journals of the Continental Congress*, III. 302. 2 *Proceedings*, XLVII. 289.
3 *Journals of the Continental Congress*, III. 298.

It will be requisite that every Fact be supported by Affidavits, authenticated by the highest Authority of the Place, where they shall be taken.

Our Apology for giving you this Trouble, is the manifest Utility of it, to the common Cause of the Colonies, in these Times of public Distress and Danger. We Subscribe ourselves, with great Respect, Sir, your most obedient and very humble Servants,

SILAS DEANE
JOHN ADAMS
GEORGE WYTHE [1]

JOHN ADAMS TO JAMES WARREN

Octr. 25, 1775

SIR, — A Method of collecting Salt Petre from the Air which is talked of here is this. Take of Lime and Ashes equal Quantities, and of horse dung a Quantity equal to both the Ashes and Lime; mix them together into a Mortar, with this Mortar, and a Quantity of long Straw to keep it together build two Walls eighteen Inches thick, and three feet high, about four feet asunder — then make a Center and turn and Arch over semicircularly from the Top of one Wall to that of the other, and this Arch may be made Eighteen Inches thick too. These Walls with the Arch over them may be continued to any length you please. There must be a shed over it to keep off the Rain and the Arch must be wett every Day with Urine. This in summer, will collect so much salt Petre that an ounce may be extracted from every Pound of the Walls in three months. In Winter it will make as fast provided you keep a Fire at one End of the Arch, that the Wind may blow the Fire and Smoke under the Arch and keep it from freezing.

This is one Method as it is affirmed by Gentlemen here.

Sulphur, Nitre and Lead We must have of our own. We must not depend upon Navigation for these. I wish the Comtee. of the General Court for Lead and Salt would transmit their Discoveries to me. I don't know whether you are one of that Comtee. or not. Pray inform me if Obrian and Carghill were or were not com-

[1] The body of the letter is in the writing of John Adams.

missioned by some Vote of the general Court — and whether they cant be put into the Continental service. An order is gone to Genl. Washington to that Purpose if it can be done.

[*No signature.*]

JOHN ADAMS TO JAMES WARREN

Octr. 25th, 1775

DEAR SIR, — Upon the Receipt of the Intelligence of Dr. [Church's] Letter, Dr. Morgan was chosen in his Room.[1] This Letter is intended to be sent by him, and therefore probably will not go in ten days.

John Morgan a Native of this City is a Doctor of Physick, a Fellow of the Royal Society at London; Correspondent of the Royal Academy of Surgery at Paris; Member of the Arcadian Belles Lettres Society at Rome; Licentiate of the Royal Colledges of Physicians in London and in Edinburgh; and Professor of the Theory and Practice of Medecine in the Colledge of Philadelphia.

This Gentleman served an Apprenticeship of six or seven years under Dr. John Redman,[2] an eminent Physician in this City, during which Time he had an opportunity of Seeing the Practice of all the eminent Physicians in this City, as he attended at the Hospital, and for one Year made up the Prescriptions of all. After this he devoted himself four Years to a military Life and went into the service as a Physician and surgeon to the Troops raised by this Colony. After this he went abroad, and spent five years in Europe, under the most celebrated Masters in every Branch of Medicine, and visiting the principal Cities and Seats of Science in Great Britain, Holland, France and Italy. This Gentleman in 1765, delivered a Discourse upon the Institution of Medical Schools in America, at a Commencement, which was published with a Preface, containing an Apology for attempting to introduce the regular Mode of practising Physic in Phyladelphia. Every Winter since he has read Lectures to the students at the Colledge as a Professor, etc.

[1] *Journal of Dr. John Morgan,* 1764 ... *and a Biographical Sketch* (1907).
[2] (1722-1808)

He and our Revd. Chaplain, Mr Duché, who is now promoted to be Rector of the three United Episcopal Churches in this City, married two sisters,[1] Mr Stillman of Boston, the Antipoedobaptist Minister[2] married Dr. Morgan's sister. The Dr.'s moral Character is very good. Thus much, Sir I thought myself well employed in Writing to you, who have a Curiosity after Characters. I wish I could give a Loose to my Pencil and draw Characters for your Inspection by the Dozen. But Letters dont always go safe. Dr. Morgan, sir, deserves particular Honour and Respect, wherever he goes.

[*No signature.*]

JOHN ADAMS TO JAMES WARREN

Octr. 25, 1775

DEAR SIR, — Governor Ward of Rhode Island has a son about five and twenty years old who has been so far carried away in the Absence of his Father, with a Zeal for his Country as to inlist into the Artillery as a private. He never said a Word to the Governor about, or he would have had a Commission. A younger Brother,[3] who solicited of his father Permission to enter the service was made a Captain. Now it is a Pity, that this young Gentleman's Patriotism, should not be encouraged and rewarded, and it is a greater Pity that an Elder Brother should be a private soldier in an Army where his younger Brother is an officer and a Captain. And a greater Pity still that a Governor of a Province and a worthy Member of the Continental Congress, and the Constant Chairman of our Committee of the whole House, should have a deserving son in the Army in the Ranks, when Multitudes of others in Commissions have no such Pretentions.

I wish you would mention this Matter at Head Quarters and see if any Thing can be done for him. The Governor had no Expectation I believe that I should interest myself in this Matter, but the Fact coming accidentally to my Knowledge I determined to write about it immediately, and I know not how to set this Thing in

1 Duché married, July, 1760, Elizabeth, daughter of Thomas Hopkinson; and Morgan married, September, 1765, Mary. They were sisters of Francis Hopkinson.
2 Rev. Samuel Stillman (1737–1807). 2 *Proceedings*, III. 42 *n*. 3 Samuel Ward, Jr.

Motion. I write every Thing to you, who know how to take me. You dont Expect Correctness nor Ceremony from me. When I have any Thing to write and one Moment to write it in I scratch it off to you, who don't expect that I should dissect these Things, or reduce them to correct Writing. You must know I have not Time for that.

[*No signature.*]

JOHN ADAMS TO JAMES WARREN

Octr. 28, 1775

DR. SIR, — Our Association against Importations and Exportations, from and to G. Britain, Ireland and the British West Indies, if We consider its Influence, upon the Revenue, the Commerce, the Manufactures and the Agriculture of the Kingdom, is a formidable Shield of Defence for Us. It is Shearing of its Beams that Luminary, which, in all its Glory might dazzle our feeble Sight.

But a Question arises, whether, our Association against Exportations, can be observed, so as to have its full Effect, upon Britain, Ireland and the West Indies, unless We extend it further? We have agreed not to export to B., I. and the W. Indies. Parliament has made an Act that We shall not export to any other Place. So that Trade is entirely stopped. But will not a Smuggling Trade be opened? That is, will not Adventurers push out Vessels against the Act of Parliament? If they do, When the Vessells are once at Sea, will they not go to the Place where a Famine price is to be had? The Spirit of Commerce is mercenary and avaricious, and Merchants will go Where the Scarcity is greatest, the Demand quickest and the Price highest.

What Security then can we have that Merchants will not order their Vessells to the West India Islands, British or foreign, to Ireland or even to Great Britain, in Defyance of our Association?

Besides is there not reason to apprehend that the concealed Tories of whom there are many in every Colony, and especially in every maritime Town, will send their Vessels to sea, on purpose to be taken by the Enemy, and sent to supply the Army and Navy in America? It is true, their Vessels would be forfeited, and seized, and condemned no doubt; but they might be pleased with this, and would easily obtain hereafter Compensation or Retribution for this meritorious Sacrifice from the Ministry.

In short may not our association be wholly evaded and eluded, if we don't draw it closer?[1] My own opinion upon these great Questions I may possibly give you some time or other. But I wish to have yours.

[No signature.]

JOHN ADAMS TO JAMES WARREN

Octr., 1775

DR. SIR, — What think you of a North American Monarchy? Suppose We should appoint a Continental King, and a Continental House of Lords, and a Continental House of Commons, to be annually, or triennially, or septennially elected, and in this Way make a Supreme American Legislature? This is easily done you know by an omnipotent Continental Congress; and when once effected, His American Majesty may appoint a Governor for every Province, as his Brittannic Majesty used to do, and Lt. Governor and Secretary and judge of Admiralty. Nay, his Continental Majesty may appoint the Judges of the Supream Courts, etc., too; or if his American Majesty should condescend to permit the provincial Legislatures, or Assemblies [may] nominate two, three or four Persons, out of whom he should select a Governor; and 3 or 4 Men for Chief Justice, etc., out of whom he should choose one, would not this do, nicely?

To his Continental Majesty in his Continental Privy Council, Appeals might lie, from all Admiralty Cases, and from all civil Causes personal at least, of a certain Value. And all Disputes about Land, that is about Boundaries of Colonies, should be settled by the Continental King and Council, as they used to be by the British K. and Council. What a magnificent system?

I assure you this is no Chimæra of my own. It is whispered about in Coffee Houses, etc., and there are who wish it.

[1] See resolves passed by the Continental Congress, November 1, in *Journals of the Continental Congress*, III. 314, 316.

I am inclined to think it is done as one Artifice more to divide the Colonies. But in vain. It would be very curious to give you an History of the out-a-Door Tricks for this important End of dividing the Colonies. Last Fall the Quakers and Antipoedobaptists were conjured up to pick a Quarrell with Massachusetts; last Spring the Land Jobbers were stimulated to pick a Quarrell with Connecticutt for the same End. The Quakers and Anabaptists were hushed and abashed, or rather the reasonable conscientious Part of them were convincd in one evening. The Land Jobbers will meet no better success.

[*No signature.*]

JAMES WARREN TO JOHN ADAMS.   ADAMS MSS.

WATERTOWN, *October* 28, 1775

MY DEAR SIR,—I did not hear till yesterday in the afternoon that Colonel Reed had any intention to leave us so soon, and begin his journey to Philadelphia on this day. The first reflection on this occasion was that he would be missed here. I have formed an excellent opinion of him as a man of sense, politeness and abilities for business. He has done us great service. He is, I might add, strongly attached to the public cause of America. But all this you know, and perhaps more of his character than I do. I shall therefore only say that I regret his leaving us, and shall wish for his return. The next reflection was that I must embrace the opportunity to write to you. For that purpose I assigned the evening, but unluckily the House set till eight o'clock and prevented me. Church had a hearing before us yesterday, which took us nearly the whole day.[1] After he withdrew there was a motion for a suspension of any judgment upon him, least it might influence his court or jury upon his trial. Another motion that we should accept a resignation he had made by letter, and accompany it with a resolve that we should save our honour, and not injure him in the trial. The end of the whole matter was appointing a committee to report how to proceed. I have now only time to thank you for your kind letters by Mr. Tracy, which I received a few days

[1] Church's account of this examination is in 1 *Mass. Hist. Collections*, 1. 84.

AS the great business of the polite world is the eager pursuit of amusement, and as the Public diversions of the season have been interrupted by the hostile parade in the capital; the exhibition of a new farce may not be unentertaining.

THE GROUP,

As lately acted, and to be re-acted to the wonder of all superior intelligences, nigh head-quarters at Amboyne.

The author has thought proper to borrow the following spirited lines from a late celebrated poet, and offer to the public by way of PROLOGUE, which cannot fail of pleasing at this crisis.

> *What! arm'd for virtue, and not point the pen,*
> *Brand the bold front of shameless guilty men,*
> *Dash the proud Gamester from his gilded car,*
> *Bare the mean heart which lurks beneath a star,*
> * * * * * * * *
> * * * * * * * *
> *Shall I not strip the gilding off a knave,*
> *Unplac'd, unpension'd, no man's heir or slave?*
> *I will or perish in the gen'rous cause;*
> *Hear this and tremble, ye who 'scape the laws;*
> *Yes, while I live, no rich or noble knave,*
> *Shall walk the world in credit to his grave;*
> *To virtue only, and her friends, a friend;*
> *The world beside may murmur, or commend.*

BOSTON: Printed and Sold by EDES and GILL, in Queen-Street. 1775.

ago, and those by Captain Macpherson, which came to hand yesterday. You have obliged me extreamly; they have edified, comforted, strengthened and encouraged. I feel like a new man. I have not seen the bearer of the last; shall try to see him this afternoon. We have no kind of news. Time won't permit me to say anything on the important subject of your letters, but to compensate you for any observations of mine I shall inclose what I guess will be much more agreeable. The author has stole an hour now and then since we came to town to proceed so far as you'll see, on purpose to unbend your mind a little, by amusements of a poetical kind well knowing you have a taste for them. You have the two acts in print, you wrote for last summer, and two subsequent ones and the Epilogue. The whole are at your disposition. . . .[1]

I forgot to tell you that the powder arrived in our vessel at the eastward has got from ninety tons by various gradations to seven and one half, which I think I gave you as the true account, being what I thought I could rely on; and from thence to fifteen hundred and from thence to six hundred, which I believe is the true one, tho' I can't say that it won't descend to three lbs.

SAMUEL ADAMS TO JAMES WARREN

PHILADA., *Novr.* 4th, 1775

MY DEAR SIR, — I thank you heartily for your very acceptable Letter of the 23 of October by Fessenden. It is very afflicting to hear the universal Complaint of the Want of that most necessary Article, Gunpowder, and especially in the Camp before Boston. I hope however that this Want will soon be supplied, and God grant that a good Use may be made of it. The Congress yesterday was presented with the Colors of the seventh Regiment taken in Fort Chamblee, which is surrendered to Major Brown. The Acquisition of 124 Barrels of Powder gives a happy Turn to our Affairs in that Quarter the Success of which I almost began to despair of.

The Gentlemen who have lately returned [2] from the Camp may, *perhaps all* of them entertain a favorable Opinion of our Colony — I may possibly be partial in saying, not more favorable than it de-

---

[1] *The Group.*   [2] Their report was laid before Congress, November 1.

serves. Be that as it may, the Congress have judgd it necessary to continue the Establishment of the Men's pay, and to enlarge that of the Captains and Lieutenants. In Addition to the Continental Army four new Batallions are to be raised, viz, three for the Defence of South Carolina and one for Georgia.[1] These with 1000 Men before orderd for North Carolina, with the Assistance of provincial Forces, it is hoped will be sufficient to defend the three Southernmost Colonies.

It is recommended to N. Hampshire to form a Government to their own liking, during this Contest;[2] and S. Carolina[3] is allowd to do the same if they judge it necessary. I believe the Time is near when the most timid will see the absolute Necessity of every one of the Colonies setting up a Government within itself.

No Provisions or Produce is to be exported from any of the united Colonies to any part of the World till the first of March except for the Importation of the Unum Necessarium, and for Supplys from one Colony to another, under the Direction of Committees, and a further Exception of live Stock. Under the last Head, and Horses are allowd to be sent to the foreign West Indies. We shall by the Spring know the full Effect of our Non-exportation Agreement in the West Indies. Perhaps Alliances may then be formed with foreign Powers, and Trade opened to all the World Great Britain excepted.

You will possibly think I have set myself down to furnish a few Paragraphs for Edes and Gills paper, and what is more that I am betraying the Secrets of Congress. I confess I am giving my Friend as much Information as I dare, of things which are of such a Nature as that they cannot long be kept secret, and therefore I suppose it never was intended they should be. I mention them however in Confidence that you will not publish them. I wish I was at Liberty to tell you many of the Transactions of our body, but I am restraind by the Ties of Honor; and though it is painful to me, you know, to keep Secrets, I will not violate my Honor to relieve myself or gratify my Friend. [*Nine lines are here erased, apparently after the receipt of the letter.*] But why have I told you

---

1 See the *Journals of the Continental Congress*, November 4 III. 321.
2 *Ib.*, 319, under date November 3.   3 *Ib.*, 326, under date November 4.

so trifling a Story, for which I cannot forgive my self till I have askd forgiveness of you. We live in a most important Age, which demands that every Moment should be improvd to some serious Purpose. It is the Age of George the Third; and to do Justice to our most gracious King, I will affirm it as my Opinion, that his Councils and Administration will necessarily produce the grandest Revolutions the World has ever yet seen. The Wheels of Providence seem to be in their swiftest Motion. Events succeed each other so rapidly that the most industrious and able Politicians can scarcely improve them to the full purposes for which they seem to be designd.

You must send your best Men here; therefore recall me from this Service. Men of moderate Abilities, especially when weakend by Age are not fit to be employed in founding Empires.

Let me talk with you a little about the Affairs of our own Colony. I persuade my self, my dear friend, that the greatest Care and Circumspection will be used to conduct its internal Police with Wisdom and Integrity. The Eyes of Mankind will be upon you, to see whether the Government, which is now more popular than it has been for many years past, will be productive of more Virtue moral and political. We may look up to Armies for our Defence, but Virtue is our best Security. It is not possible that any State should long continue free, where Virtue is not supremely honord. This is as seasonably as it is justly said by one of the most celebrated Writers of the present time. Perhaps the Form of Government now adopted may be permanent; Should it be only temporary, the golden Opportunity of recovering the Virtue and reforming the Manners of our Country should be industriously improvd.

Our Ancestors laid an excellent Foundation for the Security of Liberty, by setting up in a few years after their Arrival, a publick Seminary of Learning; and by their Laws, they obligd every Town consisting of a certain Number of Families to keep and maintain a Grammar School. I should be much grievd if it should be true as I am informd, that some of our Towns have dismissd their School masters, alledging that the extraordinary Expence of defending the Country renders them unable to support them. I hope this Inattention to the Principles of our wise forefathers does not prevail.

If there should be any Danger of it, would not the leading Gentlemen do eminent Service to the Publick, by impressing upon the Minds of the People, the Necessity and Importance of encouraging that System of Education, which in my opinion, is so well calculated to diffuse among the Individuals of the Community, the Principles of Morality, so essentially necessary for the Preservation of publick Liberty. There are Virtues and Vices which are properly called *political*. "Corruption, Dishonesty to one's Country, Luxury and Extravagance tend to the Ruin of States." The opposite Virtues tend to their Establishment. But "there is a Connection between Vices as well as Virtues, and one opens the Door for the Entrance of another." Therefore "Every able Politician will guard against other Vices" and be attentive to promote every Virtue. He who is void of Virtuous Attachment in private Life, is, or very soon will be void of all Regard to his Country. There is seldom an Instance of a Man guilty of betraying his Country, who had not before lost the feeling of moral Obligation in his private Connections. Before C[hurc]h was detected of holding a criminal Correspondence with the Enemies of his Country, his Infidelity to his Wife had been notorious. Since private and publick Vices, though not always apparently, are in Reality so nearly connected, of how much Importance, how necessary is it, that the utmost pains be taken by the Publick, to have the Principles of Virtue early inculcated on the Minds even of Children, and the moral Sense universally kept alive, and that the wise Institutions of our Ancestors for those great Purposes be encouragd by the Government. For no People will tamely surrender their Liberties, nor can they easily be subdued, where Knowledge is diffusd and Virtue preservd. On the Contrary, when People are universally ignorant and debauched in their Manners, they will sink under their own Weight, without the Aid of foreign Invaders.

There are other things which, I humbly conceive, require the most serious Consideration of the Legislative. We have heretofore complaind, and I think justly, that bad Men have too often found their Way into places of publick Trust. "Nothing is more essential to the Establishment of Manners in a State, than that all Persons employd in Places of Power and Trust be Men of *exem-*

plary Characters. The Publick cannot be too curious concerning the Characters of Publick Men." We have also complaind, that a Plurality of Places incompatible with each other have sometimes been vested in one Person. If under the former Administration there was no Danger to be apprehended from vesting the different Powers of Government in the same Persons, why did the Patriots so loudly protest against it? If Danger is always to be apprehended from it, should we not by continuing the Practice, too much imitate the degenerate Romans, who upon the Fall of Julius set up Augustus? They changd indeed their Masters, and when they had destroyd the Tyrant sufferd the Tyranny to continue. Tell me how a Judge of Probate can consistently sit at the Council Board and joyn in a Decision there upon an appeal from *his own* Judgment? Perhaps, being personally interested in *another* Appointment, I may view it with a partial Eye. But you may well remember that the Secretary of the Colony declind taking a Seat at the Council Board, to which he had been elected *prior* to his Appointment, until, in the House of Representatives he had publickly requested their opinion of the Propriety of it, and there heard it explicitly declared by an eminent and truly patriotick Member as his Opinion, that as the Place was not then as it formerly had been, the Gift of the Crown but of the People, there was no Impropriety in his holding it. The rest of the Members were silent. Major H[awle]y has as much of the stern Virtue and Spirit of a Roman Censor as any Gentleman I ever conversd with.[1] The Appointment of the Secretary and his Election to a Seat at the Board were both made in the Time of his Absence from the Colony and without the Solicitation of any of his Friends that he knew of — most assuredly without his own.[2] As he is resolvd never wittingly to disgrace himself or his Country, he still employs his Mind on the Subject, and wishes for your candid and impartial Sentiments.

I fear I have trespassd on your Leisure, and conclude, with assuring you that I am with sincere Regards to Mrs. Warren, your very affectionate Friend

S. A.

[1] See *Proceedings*, XLIX. 79.   [2] Referring to himself.

November 7th Your kind Letter of the 26th of October by Coll. Read was brot to me last Evening. Our Friend Mr. J. A. and myself were highly entertaind with the Papers inclosd in your Letter to him. It is wonderful to me that there should be any Difficulty about the Expulsion of Church. I intend to write to you by Doctor Morgan who will leave this City in a few days. Adieu.
S. A.

JOHN ADAMS TO JAMES WARREN

Novr. 5, 1775

DEAR SIR, — The Committee have returned, and I think well pleased with their Reception as well as with what they saw and heard. Impressions, have been made upon them either by the New England Gentlemen, or at Head Quarters, much to the Advantage of our Cause, I assure you. Their Return has contributed much to Harmony and Unanimity, in all smaller Matters, in the great material Questions there was enough of them before.

I am under great obligations to you for your Attentions to me. Shall answer your Letters as soon as Time will admit, but I assure you I am very busy. I am obliged to trouble you with Enquiries concerning Subjects which you understand very well and I know nothing of.

I want to know what is become of the Whalemen, Codfishers, and other Seamen belonging to our Province, and what Number of them you imagine might be inlisted into the service of the Continent, or of the Province, or of private Adventurers in Case a Taste for Privateering and a maritime Warfare should prevail, whether you think that two or three Battalions of Marines could be easily inlisted in our Province.

What Ships, Brigantines, Schooners, suitable for armed Vessells might be purchased or hired, and at what Prices in our Province, what their Burthen, Depth of Water, Length of Keel, Breadth, hight between Decks, Age, etc., and to whom they belong?

What Places are most suitable, that is safest and best accommodated, for building new Vessells, if any should be wanted; and what shipwrights may be had, and in what Time Vessels compleated?

But above all, what Persons, their Names, Ages, Places of Abode and Characters, may be found in our Province who might be qualified to serve as Commanders and Officers, etc.

These are necessary Enquiries, and I am very ill qualified to make them, yet to tell you a secret in Confidence, it has become my Duty. There is a Disposition prevailing to spare no Pains or Expence, in the necessary Defence of our Rights by sea or Land.

The News you will see in the Papers, give you Joy of the good Prospect to the Northward.

New Hampshire has Permission to establish what Form of Government they like best, and so has S. Carolina and so will every other Colony which shall ask for it which they all will do soon, if the Squabble continues.

New England will now be able to exert her Strength and if I ken it right, it will be found to be that of a full grown Man, no Infant.

Who expected to live to see the Principles of Liberty Spread and prevail so rapidly, human Nature exerting her whole Rights, unshackled by Priests or Kings or Nobles, pulling down Tyrannies like Sampson, and building up, what Governments the People think best framed for human Felicity.

God grant the Spirit, success.

My best Respects to your good Lady, will write her as soon as possible.

[*No signature.*]

JAMES WARREN TO JOHN ADAMS.   ADAMS MSS.
WATERTOWN, *November* 5, 1775

. . . .

The prices of European and West India goods are, notwithstanding our resolves, much advanced. Trade will have its course. Goods will rise and fall in proportion to the demand for them, and the quantity at market, etc., in spite of laws, honor, patriotism, or any other principle. The people however seem to have forgot their expectations, and the injunctions laid on the merchant, and little is said about it.

The non-exportation is sacredly observed, and I believe [has] never been violated in a single instance; and such is the spirit here, that it cannot be violated with any degree of safety. Provisions are plenty and cheap, beef is a drug, and our people complain much that the Commissary sends to Connecticut for all his beef. I think it but fair that he should give this Colony a chance in that article at least, especially as we are to supply the army with hay and wood, which our people say they can't do and keep their cattle now fat over the winter. This has occasioned great difficulty here. The General has offered 5/ per [cwt] for hay, and 20/ per cord for wood, and cannot be supplied. This he imputes to a monopolizing, avaritious spirit, and perhaps not wholly without foundations.[1] The prices are indeed high, but the people have much to say, and among other things ask why that spirit should be confined to those articles, and why cyder is to be had at 4/ per barrel. In the meantime the army has suffered much for want of wood, and the officers have not been able to restrain them from cutting down the fine groves of Cambridge and threatning to pull down houses for fuel. The General has made repeated applications to us. We at last set ourselves seriously to remedy the evil, which perhaps might terminate in breaking up the army. We spent the whole of last Fryday and evening on the subject. We at last chose a committee[2] in aid to the Quartermaster general to purchase those articles and impowered them to enter the wood lots of the Refugees, cut, stack, and procure teams to carry to the camp wood as fast as possible, and hay as soon as they can get it. The teams are passing all day, and I hope this step will be a radical cure.

Your next question is with regard to trade, a subject complicated, vast and unsounded. When I consider the great abundance we have of the necessaries and conveniences of life, that we want nothing but salt petre and I hope we are in a way to get that, I could wish a total stop was put to all trade. But when I consider the temper and genius of the people, the long habits they have been used to, I fear it would produce uneasiness and bad conse-

[1] See his letter to Joseph Reed, November 28, 1775, in *Writings of Washington* (Ford), III. 246.
[2] *Journals of the House of Representatives* (Mass.), November 3, 1775.

quences. I believe therefore you will find it necessary to indulge so much as will not endanger the success of your commercial measures. If the merchant will run the hazard, so much may tend to conciliate the affections of other nations, and unite them with us on principles of interest, the strongest of all principles in these degenerate days. I am sensible many important questions may arise on this head, too many and too important for my abilities, or opportunities to discuss at present. I am extreamly pleased with the appointment of the committee you mention, and with the committee itself. I believe this business will produce great consequences. You may be assured I shall exert myself to have your expectations and wishes complied with, both with regard to time and manner.

Macpherson is yet here, but I dare not ask questions. Nothing transpires, and whether any plan is adopted or not can't inform you. We have no news here; all things remain *in statu quo*. The enemy, I mean their army, are quiet, and we watch them. Barracks are building for our troops, and many of them are ready to receive them. The whole will be compleated in the course of this month; and indeed it is time; the season is rainy and cold. The pirates continue to rove about and threaten our seaports. They made an attempt to go into Plymouth, but were discouraged by the appearance of the harbour, returned and reported to the Admiral that it was not fit to receive King's ships. Our people are, however, preparing for them, if they alter their minds. Our Assembly have established salt petre works at Newburyport, under the direction of a committee, Doctor Whiting, John Peck, Deacon Baker and one Phips,[1] the last of whom is said to be an adept that way, and have given a bounty of 4/ per pound to any man that shall make fifty pounds or upwards, this bounty to continue to next June. We have also taken care to encourage the manufacture of fire arms. Thus far we have done well, but our militia is still in a miserable unsettled situation. This principally or wholly arises from a dispute between the two Houses. We claim an equal right with them in the appointment of the field officers. This claim

[1] Jedidiah Phips, of Sherburn. *Journals of the House of Representatives* (Mass.), November 1, 1775.

we ground on your resolutions, which will bear very fairly that construction, and is certainly the most eligible constitution, and say that if that is not the true construction we, that deserve as large privileges as any people, are not on an equal footing with the other Colonies. The Board contend for the exclusive right, plead the Charter, and assert the prerogative with as much zeal, pride and hauteur of dominion as if the powers of monarchy were vested in them and their heirs, by a divine, indefeasible right. This is indeed curious, to see a Council of this Province contending for the dirty part of the Constitution, the prerogative of the Governor. How it is to end, or when, I know not.[1] I wish they had in the exercise of powers we don't dispute with them, made appointments in some instances less exceptionable than they have. You will hardly expect to hear after what I last wrote you that Paine is appointed a judge, but so it is. At a time when I least expected, he was appointed, it is said, by the influence of Hawley. Spooner, Foster, and I believe Palmer, were the principle conductors. The rank is thus, John Adams, Esqr. Chief Justice, Cushing, Read, Paine, Sargeant.[2] Now we shall see if he will act in an inferiour station to his superiour. The people at the eastward are apprehensive the enemy intend to possess themselves of an advantageous post at Falmouth, and hold that place and secure the harbour. . . .

Doctor Church is expelled by almost an unanimous vote.

Favourable accounts from the western army; doubtless you have the whole.

Is it not time for a test act? Will the Continent have one from the Congress? How long are we to wait for the success of the petition? I long to hear of the [illegible]. A good devise to furnish the

[1] Writing to Mrs. Warren, December 13, Mrs. Winthrop said of a previous letter which had not reached its destination: "It was an endeavor to remove some unfavorable impressions I thought a late dispute had made upon you; and as I had a free conversation with one of the Board, I aimed at giving you the same light he gave me. He assured me their conduct did not proceed from a fondness for the exercise of prerogative, or an attachment to their power; but from a conviction that they were obliged to act as they did in order to conform to the fundamental resolve of the Congress on which this Government was set up; and he did not doubt every member of the Board are as hearty friends to the liberties of the people as ever they were, and willing the dispute be determined in favor of the house. Query, whether misunderstandings do not often proceed from want of opportunity for an *éclaircissement?*" MS.

[2] William Cushing (1732–1810), William Reed (–1780), and Nathaniel Peaslee Sargent (1731–1791). Robert Treat Paine did not accept.

capital article. You will see in our papers Howe's proclamation and an association.

November 7. . . . We shall rise, perhaps tomorrow or next day.[1] We have some thoughts of coming to a new choice of delegates this setting. I could wish to have it put off to hear from you. I can't think of a list without your name in it. If we make any change, who[m] shall we get? I do not expect to be suited. One of the enemies vessels, bound to N[ova] Scotia with a cargo to purchase provisions, taken and carried into Beverly. Another of them on shore at Cape Cod, with one hundred and twenty pipes of wine, etc. So we get a supply of turtle, wine, and all the delicacies that luxury can wish. I congratulate you on the success at Chamblee. The bell rings, I must go.

ABIGAIL ADAMS TO MERCY WARREN

BRAINTREE, *November*, 1775

DEAR MARCIA, — I hope the Historick page will increase to a volume, tis this hope that has kept me from complaining of my friends Laconick Epistles. Our amiable Friend[2] who lately favourd me with a visit, informd you I Suppose of the difficulty I Labourd under, of a Whitlow upon the forefinger of my right Hand, which prevented my writing to my dearest Friend, and to her who holds, one of the first places among the female Friends of Portia.

I have to acknowledge the kind care of both my Friends in the conveyance of Letters. I feel Loth the House should rise whilst the Congress Sits. But was not there some Mistake in the Last Letters, has not your Friend one which must have been meant for me, by a mistake in the Superscription? I enclose the Letter. I read it, not regarding the dear Sir, but could not comprehend how I came to have such a reply to a Subject I had said very little upon. Upon Nabby's taking it into her hand she observed the address.

I am curious to know how you Spend your time? tis very sausy

[1] The House did not rise until the 11th.
[2] Hannah Winthrop. Her visit occurred before November 5.

to make this demand upon you, but I know it must be usefully imployd and I am fearful if I do not question you I shall loose some improvement which I might otherways make.

What becomes of the State prisoner?[1] is he not to have a trial? When weighd in the balance I fear he will be found wanting. A patriot without religion in my estimation is as great a paradox as an honest Man without the fear of God. Is it possible that he whom no moral obligations bind can have any real Good Will towards Man, can he be a patriot who by an openly vicious conduct is undermineing the very bonds of Society, corrupting the Morals of Youth and by his bad example injuring that very Country he professes to patronize more than he can possibly compensate by his intrepidity, Generosity and honour? The Scriptures tell us righteousness exalteth a Nation.

I wish there was more of it to be seen among all orders and professions, but the Continental Connexion will not improve the Morals of our Youth. A little less swearing at our New England puritanism would be full as honorary to our Southern Brethren. I thank you my Friend for your invitation but cannot comply with it tho my inclination is very strong. I want to see my Friends and hear our worthy Dr. Pray be so kind as to present my regards to Dr Winthrop and Lady. She desired me to write to her. I wish my Friend would let her know that I can better reply to a favour from her than begin a correspondence, tho I should esteem it an honour. But Marcia can witness for me how averse I have been to writing.

I lament the Death of the Worthy president as of an honest

---

[1] Church. On November 11 the House adopted the following report and resolution:

"Whereas it appears to this House, that Dr. Benjamin Church, late a Member thereof, by his past Conduct has discovered himself to be Inimical to the United American Colonies, and has laid himself open in their Opinion to a Criminal Prosecution for his past Conduct, in holding a traiterous Correspondence with our Enemies: And whereas the Court-Martial in whose Custody he now is from the Want of a suitable Provision in the Continental Articles of War, may be unable to bring the said Church to condign Punishment; and the setting him at Liberty may be attended with dangerous Consequences to the Cause of America: therefore,

"*Resolved*, That the honorable the Council of this Colony be, and they hereby are desired to take suitable Measures for causing the said Benjamin Church, in Case of his being liberated from his present Confinement, to be apprehended and secured, and that such further Measures with respect to him may be pursued as the Security of this People loudly Demands, and the Laws of this Colony will justify."

Man. Mr. Randolph's character has secured him esteem. How well might some folks have saved their credit and their Bacon too (as the phraze is) by a resignation of a certain place.[1]

O Ambition, how many inconsistent actions dost thou make poor mortals commit!

Adieu, my Friend. I hope soon to have the pleasure of seeing you at Braintree and of a Social Evening beside our fire. How happy should I esteem myself could the dear Friend of my Heart join us. I think I make a greater Sacrifice to the publick than I could by Gold and Silver, had I it to bestow. Does not Marcia join in this Sentiment with her

PORTIA

JAMES WARREN TO JOHN ADAMS.   ADAMS MSS.

WATERTOWN, *November* 14, 1775

MY DEAR SIR, — I last evening received yours by Captain Gist, and this morning by Fessenden. It gives me great pleasure to see things in such a fine way, and you in such choice spirits. I congratulate you on the taking of St. John's. This news Fessenden brings with him from Hartford. This gives us great spirits. He says likewise that Arnold was within twelve miles of Quebec. You must know that our anxiety for him and his party has been great. Last night I was at Head quarters, where accounts were received that one Colonel Enos[2] of Connecticut, with three companies he commanded as a rear guard, had come off and left him, while advanced thirty miles ahead, and perhaps at Chaudière Pond. This officer certainly deserves hanging. It will always give me great pleasure to be able to give you any information. Great numbers of the Whalemen are gone on voyages which we permitted, after having taken bonds for the landing their oil and bone in some port here other than Boston and Nantucket, some of them are in the army, and sea coast service; many of them, and the greater part of our fishermen and seamen at home and in no serv-

---

[1] Probably a hit at Hancock.
[2] Roger Enos (1729–1808). He was court-martialed, but acquitted "with honor," and retired from the army. He later accepted a commission of brigadier general in the Vermont militia.

ice, earnestly wishing to be employed in the privateering business. What numbers might be inlisted on that service I can't readily compute, but I have no difficulty in supposing that at least three battalions might be raised in this Colony. The taste for it runs high here. As to ships and other vessels, I believe there are great numbers very suitable to arm already on hand. Almost every port of any consequence could furnish more or less, either great or small. Perhaps ships might be difficult to find that could mount twenty guns or upwards; but vessels to carry from six to sixteen guns I think we abound in, and I think they would soon furnish us with others. These vessels are of all burthens, drafts of water, and dimensions, and are many of them excellent sailors, and may be either purchased, or hired, on very reasonable terms. I think the General gives only 5/4 per ton per month. I am not acquainted at Haverhill, Newberry, etc., but from what I have heard, vessels might be built there, safe and with great despatch; and perhaps at Kennebeck and North River, etc., etc. We have no want of the best shipwrights. As to the time for compleating them, much will depend on the winter; but they may be ready as soon as wanted in the Spring, if immediately engaged in.. As for your next question, the names, etc., of those fit to command, I am not quite so ready to answer. You know we have not practised privateering so much here as they have in some of the other colonies, and it is a business I never was concerned in; but I have no doubt that many fine fellows can be found, who have been masters of vessels and at some time in their lives served on board men of war and privateers. I have one Captain Samson[1] in my employ, who has served in both, and particularly with Captain Macpherson the last war. Him I would venture a vessel with. There is Souter,[2] who you know. Time won't permit me to recollect many others, but from the nature and circumstances of this Colony, there must be many. I will endeavour to recollect some for my next. I am glad to see the policy of Congress turned this way, and to see you engaged. You must know I think you qualified for any thing you will undertake. I congratulate South Carolina and New Hamp-

[1] Simeon Sampson, of Plymouth, captain of the brigantine *Independence* in 1776.
[2] Daniel Souther, captain of the brig *Massachusetts* in 1776.

shire on the indulgence shewn them by the Congress. I hope they will improve it to the best advantage. I wish for the time when we shall all have the same liberty. Our situation must be more irksome than ever. To be surrounded on all sides with governments founded on proper principles, and constituted to promote the free and equal liberty and happiness of mankind, while we are plagued with a constitution where the prerogative of the crown and the liberty of the subject are eternally militating, and in the very formation of which the last is but a secondary consideration to the first. Indeed, my friend, I am sick of our constitution, more so than ever. [I] have seen enough lately to make me so. I hate the name of our charter, which fascinates and shackles us. I hate the monarchical part of our government, and certainly you would more than ever, if you knew our present monarchs. But many of them you have no idea of; they are totally changed since you left us, divers of them I mean. They have got a whirl in their brains, imagine themselves kings, and have assumed every air and pomp of royalty but the crown and scepter. You might search Princetown, Brookline, Wrentham, Braintree and several other towns, without finding a man you could possibly know, or suppose to have been chose a councillor here by the freemen of this Colony, no longer ago than last July, and for no longer a time than next May. I shall not trouble you with any further and more particular account than I have already given, of a dispute the last session between the two Houses, much to our disadvantage and disgrace, having seen a copy of a letter from Gerry to you by Revere, when the matter seemed to be fully taken up. The Court was adjourned last Saturday to the 29th instant, after having extended your commission for one month, to the last of January. We were not ready to come to a choice, and was afraid to postpone to the first of the next sitting, so near the expiration of the time. I shall be utterly at a loss, for three men do advise me.

November 15th. I expected to have had the roar of cannon this morning, and some news from the army to have given you. Our army were prepared to intrench on Cobble Hill and on Lechmore's Point last night. I suppose the weather has prevented. I hear nothing of it this stormy morning. What numbers of new recruits are arrived, we can't learn. It is generally thought not many of them. Though there has been appearances of fleets in the Bay. I wish this storm may put some of the transports upon the rocks and quicksands.

You will learn by Revere the general state of things here, the movements and success of our land and naval force, particularly an account of the several prizes made. A number of letters and the King's proclamation, taken in one of them, will give you a general view of their whole system with regard to America. I think your Congress can be no longer in any doubts and hesitancy about taking capital and effectual strokes. We shall certainly expect it. It is said that the delicacy of modern civilization will not admit of foreign powers, while you continue to acknowledge a dependency on Britain or Britain's King, having any connection with you. Let us so far accomodate ourselves to their small policy as to remove this obstacle. I want to see trade (if we must have it) open, and a fleet here to protect it in opposition to Britain. Is the ancient policy of France so lost or dwindled that they will lose the golden opportunity. We must have a test, that shall distinguish Whigs from Tories, etc., etc. I have a thousand things to say to you; I want to see you. I want you there, and I want you here. What shall I do without you and my friend Adams at Congress? And yet you are both wanted here. I believe you must stay there; I mean, belong to that body once more. . . . She [Mrs. Warren] sits at the table with me, will have a paragraph of her own; says you "should no longer *piddle* at the threshold. It is time to leap into the *theatre*, to unlock the bars, and open every gate that impedes the rise and growth of the American republic, and then let the giddy potentate send forth his puerile proclamations to France, to Spain and all the commercial world who may be united in building up an Empire which he can't prevent."

> At leisure then may G[eor]ge his reign review,
> And bid to empire and to crown adieu.
> For lordly mandates and despotic kings
> Are obsolete like other quondam things.
> Whether of ancient or more modern date,
> Alike both K[in]gs and Kinglings must hate. *Extempore.*

... I admire the character you give Doctor Morgan. I think it will do honour to the station he is to fill. You need not fear proper regard will be paid to him. I love to see characters drawn by your pencil; the more dozens you give me the more agreeable. I have a great respect for Governor Ward and his family. I will agreeable to your desire mention his son at Head quarters tomorrow. The method of making salt petre you mention, if to be depended on, is simple and easy in the moderate seasons. I could wish to hear more of it, and also of the rocks. I am not of the committee for sulphur, etc. I will look them up, and urge them to forward their discoveries to you. I believe Obrian is commissioned, and Carghill in a sort commissioned. There will be no difficulty in having them in the service of the Continent; the General may easily execute his order. I am very sensible of the mercenary avaritious spirit of merchants. They must be watched. We oblige all to give bonds, but how to guard against throwing themselves in the way to be taken has puzzled us. But such is the spirit here for preserving inviolate the Association, that a man must have indisputable evidence that his being taken was unavoidable, or never shew his head again. Upon this I at present rely. However, very few vessels except whalemen are gone, and very few have any intentions to go, unless to the southern colonies; and their characters must be so well established as to obtain certificates from our committees, who are not yet corrupted. I apprehend more danger from other places. I think the Association can't be too close drawn. We had better have no trade than suffer inconveniences from the interested tricks of Tories, or even merchants, who pretend to be well principled, and yet are governed by interest alone. I believe you have a curious set of politicians in your Coffee-House. The system you mention is an instance of it; a magnificent one, indeed too much so for you and I, who I dare say will ever be content to be excused from the two most superb branches, the first more especially. I hope the tricks of these people will never answer their purposes. The Union is every thing. With it we shall do every thing, without it nothing. . . .

November 16th. No news this morning. I think all things on our side look well and pleasing. I can't however but feel a little uneasy, till our army has got settled on the new plan. The General has many difficulties with officers and soldiers. His judgment and firmness I hope will carry him through them. He is certainly the best man for the place he is in, important as it is, that ever lived. One source of uneasiness is that they are not paid four weeks to a month. There are some grounds for it. I believe they inlisted here in expectation of it, as it has been at all times the invariable custom in our armies and garrisons. I could wish the Congress had settled it so. Where are the articles of confederation? I want to see some settled constitution of Congress. . . .

JOHN ADAMS TO JAMES WARREN

PHILADELPHIA, *Decr.* 3, 1775

MY DEAR SIR, — I have only Time to acquaint you that Congress have ordered the Arrears of Pay to be discharged to the soldiers and one Months Advance Pay to be made.[1] No Bounty nor any Allowance for Lunar Months. I have a Thousand Things to say — but no Time. Our Army must be reconciled to these Terms, or We shall be ruined for what I know. The Expences accumulating upon the Continent are so vast and boundless that We shall be bankrupt if not frugal.

I lately had an opportunity, suddenly, of mentioning two very deserving officers, Thomas Crafts, Junior, who now lives at Leominster, and George Trot, who lives at Braintree, to be, the first a Lt. Coll, the second a Major of the Regiment of Artillery under Coll. Knox. These are young Men under forty, excellent officers, very modest, civil, sensible, and of prodigious Merit as well as Suffering in the American Cause. If they are neglected I shall be very mad, and kick and bounce like fury. Congress have ordered their Names to be sent to the General, and if he thinks they can be promoted without giving Disgust and making Uneasiness in the Regiment, to give them Commissions.[2]

Gen. Washington knows neither of them; they have too much Merit and Modesty to thrust themselves forward and solicit, as has been the Manner of too many. But they are excellent officers,

---

[1] *Journals of the Continental Congress*, III. 394.   [2] *Ib.*, III. 399.

and have done great Things, both in the political and military Way. In short vast Injustice will be done if they are not provided for.[1] Several Captains in the Artillery Regiment were privates under these officers in Paddock's Company. Captain Crafts[2] who is I believe the first Captain, is a younger Brother to Thomas. I believe that Burbeck[3] Mason,[4] Foster,[5] etc. would have no objection.

The Merit of these Men from the Year 1764 to this day, has been very great tho not known to everybody. My Conscience tells me they ought to be promoted. They have more Merit between you and me than half the Generals in the Army.

[*No signature.*]

JAMES WARREN TO JOHN ADAMS.   ADAMS MSS.

WATERTOWN, *December* 3, 1775

MY DEAR SIR, — I returned from Plymouth last Wednesday, after an absence of about ten days. . . . Doctor Morgan, who with his lady had lodged in my chamber the night before, had left a packet containing letters, etc., to your friends, which I have taken proper care of. This gentleman I have not yet seen. He was attended next day by the surgeons of the army, and escorted to Head quarters in state. I propose to see him tomorrow, and shall look on him with all the reverence due to so exalted a character as you give him. Revere returned here on Fryday. No letters by him from you or my other friend at Congress. I have run over my sins of omission and commission, to see if they were unpardonable, and at last presumed to account for it from the nature and magnitude of the business you are engaged in, and the constant application it requires.

I congratulate you on the success of our northern army. We have no late accounts from Arnold, but have sanguine expectations that before this the whole Province of Canada is reduced.

---

1 Both declined. *Writings of Washington* (Ford), III. 275. The State of Massachusetts commissioned them, May 8, 1776, in an artillery battalion raised for the defence of Boston.
2 Edward Crafts, of Gridley's Artillery Regiment.   3 Edward Burbeck.
4 David Mason.   5 Thomas Wait Foster, of Hadley.

You will no doubt have heard before this reaches you that a Lieutenant Colonel[1] and a considerable number of men had come off from Arnold's detachment and returned here.

Our army here have taken possession of and fortified Cobble Hill, which the enemy seem to view without any emotion, not having fired a gun. It is said they confidently rely on our army's dispersing when the terms of their inlistment ends, and leaving the lines defenceless, and an easy conquest to them. Howe I believe has received such intelligence and assurances from one Benja. Marston,[2] who has fled from Marblehead to Boston. This fellow is a cousin of mine. Had ever any man so many rascally cousins as I have. I will not presume any danger of that kind, tho' I own my anxiety is great. Our men inlist but slowly, and the Connecticut troops behave infamously. It was with difficulty the General prevented their going off in great numbers last Fryday. However, they consented finally to return to their duty, till the army could be reinforced.[3]

The General on the first day of our meeting had represented to the Court the difficulties he laboured under and the dangers he apprehended, and desired a committee to confer with him and the other general officers. A committee went down. The result of the conference was that 5000 men should be immediately raised in this and New Hampshire colony, and brought into camp by the 10th instant, to supply the deficiencies in the army by the going of the Connecticut troops, and the furlows the General is obliged to give the new inlisted men by way of encouragement. General Sullivan undertook to raise 2000 of them, and we reported that the rest should be raised in several parts of this Colony, and yesterday sent off more than twenty of our members to effect it,[4] knowing no other way as our militia is in a perfect state of anarchy, some with, and some without officers. If they don't succeed I know not where I shall date my next letter from; but I have such

---

[1] Roger Enos.
[2] Benjamin Marston (1730–1792), son of Benjamin Marston and Elizabeth Winslow. A loyalist, he followed the British army to Halifax in 1776.
[3] *Writings of Washington* (Ford), III. 253, 258.
[4] The names are given in the *Journal of the House of Representatives* (Mass.), December 2, 1775.

an opinion of my countrymen as to believe they will. The only reasons I know of that are assigned by the soldiers for their uneasiness, or rather backwardness to enter the service again are the increase of the officers' wages lately made, and the paying them contrary to their expectation and former usage by calendar instead of lunar months. The last I have given you my opinion of in a former letter, and the first I think was very unluckily timed. I have till lately thought it a favourable circumstance that so many men were raised in these governments. I begin to think otherways, and many reasons operate strongly to make me wish for more troops from the southern governments. I pity our good General who has a greater burthen on his shoulders and more difficulties to struggle with than I think should fall to the share of so good a man. I do every thing in my power to relieve him and wish I could do more. I see he is fatigued and worried. After all you are not to consider us as wholly involved in clouds and darkness. The sun shines for the most part, and we have many consoling events. Providence seems to be engaged for us; the same spirit and determination prevails to conquer all difficulties; many prizes have been taken by our cruisers, and a capital one last week carried into Cape Ann, of very great value, perhaps £20,000 sterling, a brigantine from England with a cargo consisting of almost every species of warlike stores, except powder and cannon,[1] 2,000 very fine small arms with all their accoutrements, four mortars, one [of] which Putnam has christened and called the *Congress*, the finest one in America, flints, shells, musket balls, carriages, etc., etc. These are principally arrived at Headquarters and the great mortar is a subject of curiosity. I hope we shall be able to make good use of them before long. A small cutter has since been taken loaded with provisions from Nova Scotia to Boston, and carried into Beverly,[2] the first by a Continental vessel, the second by a private one. All serves to distress them and aid us. The reinforcing the army has engrossed the whole attention of the General Court since their meeting. The manufactory of salt petre proceeds but

[1] It was the brig *Nancy*, taken by Captain Manley, of the *Lee*.
[2] The *Concord*, James Lowrie, master? She was laden with dry goods and coal, and was taken by Manley, which does not accord with what Warren wrote.

slowly, tho' it is made in small quantities. Our general committee seem to me too much entangled with particular systems and general rules to succeed in practice. They have done nothing. Colonel Orne and Colonel Lincoln have made tryals in the recess and succeeded according to their wishes. They affirm the process to be simple and easy, and that great quantities may be made. They shew samples of what they have made, and it is undoubtedly good. No experiments with regard to sulphur have yet succeeded. We have good proposals with regard to lead. Colonel Palmer has promised me to write you on that subject. I hope soon to hear from you. The confidence in the Congress prevailing among all ranks of people is amazing, and the expectation of great things from you stronger than ever. It gives me great pleasure to see the credit and reputation of my two particular friends increasing here. Their late disinterested conduct, as it is reported here, does them much honour. A certain colleague of yours has lost, or I am mistaken, a great part of the interest he undeservedly had.[1] Major Hawley is not yet down. What he will say to him, I know not. Paine, I hear, is gone to gratify his curiosity in Canada.[2] A good journey to him. He may possibly do as much good there as at Philadelphia, tho' I find some people here would not have pitched on him for the business we suppose he is gone on, and perhaps there are some who would not have done it for any. Many men, you know, are of many minds. . . .

The great loss at Newfoundland of men, etc., I think may be considered as an interposition of Providence in our favour.

Doctor Adams has just called on me to acquaint me that Mr. Craige,[3] who has been apothecary to the army, is like to be superceded, and Mr. Dyre appointed in his room. As he appears to me a very clever fellow, and such changes do us no good, I could wish it might be prevented.

[1] Hancock or Cushing?
[2] John Langdon, Robert Treat Paine, and Eliphalet Dyer had been appointed by Congress, November 2, to confer with General Schuyler, at Ticonderoga. The report was laid before Congress, December 23, and is printed in the *Journals of the Continental Congress*, III. 446.
[3] Andrew Craige.

SAMUEL ADAMS TO JAMES WARREN

PHILADA., *Decr.* [5],[1] 1775

MY DEAR SIR, — Mr. Jonathan B. Smith, who has the Command of a Party ordered to guard and escorte a Sum of Money to your office, will deliver to you this Letter. He is a Gentleman of Merit and a Friend to our common Cause. Your Friends here have been treated with Civility, and I dare say you will esteem him worthy of your particular Notice.

It will afford you Satisfaction to be informed that Congress has granted £133,000 to the Colony of Massachusetts Bay in part of their Account to be exhibited to be paid out of a new Emission already orderd to be made, for which the Colony is to be accountable.

We go on here by Degrees, though not with the Dispatch I could wish. Gentlemen seem more and more to enlarge their views, and we must be content to wait till the Fruit is ripe before we gather it.

A few days ago[2] we had Intelligence from Virginia that their Governor Lord Dunmore had landed a Party of Regulars, who, joynd by a Number of Voluntiers, had attackd and defeated a Number of Provincials. His Auxiliaries consisted of the Inhabitants of Norfolk, a Town inhabited by Scotch Tories, and such weak and timid People as they prevail upon to joyn them.

Lord Dunmore has issued a Proclamation, calling upon the People to resort to the Kings Standard or be deemd Traitors, and declaring the indented Servants and Negroes belonging to Rebels, who will joyn him free.[3] He has also in the same Proclamation declared his Determination to execute Martial Law, thereby tearing up the Foundation of civil Authority and Government in the Colony. The Congress taking this under Consideration, have recommended to the Colony of Virginia the setting up and exercising civil Government, in like Manner as N. Hampshire and South Carolina.[4]

I hope the dispute between the two Houses relating to the Establishment of the Militia has before this time subsided or settled. The Council wrote us a Letter upon the Subject, directing

---

1 The letter describes two resolutions adopted by Congress on December 4.
2 November 7, 1775.   3 Saturday, December 2.
4 *Journals of the Continental Congress*, III. 403.

us to give our opinion of the Sense of Congress on the two Resolves referrd to either with or without consulting our Brethren as we should think best. I had Reasons of weight in my own Mind against requesting the formal Determination of Congress: Mr. J. A[dams] was of the same Mind. Mr. C[ushing] was of a different opinion, nor would he agree with us in writing an Answer joyntly. We therefore wrote seperately, and, if you think it worth while, you may read our Letters which I suppose are in the Council files.

I intreat you my Friend to joyn with your Compatriots in our Colony, in inspiring our Assembly with publick Spirit. There are Persons not far from you who watch for Opportunities to disgrace the Colony in this Regard. I hope they will never give just occasion to say, "I cannot describe the egregious Want of publick Spirit which *reigns* here." It is exceedingly mortifying to me to hear such Paragraphs read. If I ever shall have the inexpressible Pleasure of conversing with you, I will candidly tell you *who* has written in this Stile. Thus much I can now assure you, that one at least of these Letter writers is not a mean Person.[1] I have many things which I wish to say to you with Regard to the internal Police of our Colony but I have not Leisure now to write. You have Scilla and Charybdis to avoid. You cannot but be perplexd. I feel for you; you have need of the Grace of Patience and (though it has been long said that I have fallen out with the Word) I will add *Prudence* too. Persevere in that which your heart has ever been so warmly engagd in, the Establishment of a Government upon the Principles of Liberty, and sufficiently guarding it from future Infringements of a Tyrant. I will only add, there may be Danger of Errors on the Side of *the People* which may be fatal to your Designs. Adieu.

S. A.

JAMES WARREN TO JOHN ADAMS.   ADAMS MSS.

WATERTOWN, *December* 11, 1775

MY DEAR SIR, — Since my last I have not a scrip from you. Whether you intend by withholding the encouragement you used

[1] Joseph Reed may have shown or read Washington's letter to him of November 28.

to give to get rid of the trouble of my many, long and tedious letters, I don't know. However, I am determined to write this once more at least, not out of spite and malice, but to rectify some errors I find I committed in my last, and to remove any impressions of despondency the temper I wrote in and the spirit of the letter might make. Captain Stevenson who was the bearer of it left us last Monday, and I hope will be with you this day. Since which I find I was much mistaken in the account I gave you of the progress of saltpetre in this Colony. It is certainly making in great quantities in many towns, and I believe we shall next spring have as much as we want. One man in Wrentham had a fortnight ago 50 lb., one at Sherburne about as much, Dr. Whittaker has 70 lb., Parson Whitwell 50, and in the County of Worcester great quantities are collecting. All agree that the process is as simple and easy as making soap. Our committee at Newberry Port have succeeded with some improvements to make steadily 12 lb. a day, and as good as I ever saw. So much for saltpetre. We have assigned this afternoon to choose a committee to erect as soon as possible a powder mill at Sutton, and another at Stoughton. Several prizes have been taken in the week past, and among the rest a fine ship from London,[1] with coal, porter, cheese, live hogs, etc., etc.; and a large brigantine from Antigua,[2] with rum, sugar, etc. All the country are now engaged in preparing to make salt petre, fixing privateers, or reinforcing the army. I suppose if the weather had been favourable twelve or thirteen privateers would have been at sea this day in quest of seven sail of ships which came out with this prize, and had similar cargoes. Commissions are making out for two privateers from Salem, two from Newbury Port, one of them to mount sixteen guns. I hear one is fixing at Plymouth, and one at Barnstable. It will be in the power of the Congress another year to command the American sea. We have here great numbers of fine vessels and seamen in abundance.

The 3000 militia called to reinforce the army are all I believe in camp, and I conjecture some hundreds more than are called for. Such was their indignation at the conduct of the Connecticut

[1] The *Jenny*, Captain Forster.
[2] The *Little Hannah*, Robert Adams, master. Both of these prizes were taken by Manley.

troops and zeal for the cause they immediately inlisted and arrived in camp at the time set, tho' the travelling is exceeding bad. The New Hampshire troops I am told are not behind them. The small pox is broke out at Cambridge and one or two other places among those late out of Boston. I hope good care will be taken of them to prevent its spreading. The inlistments in the army go on rather better than they did. Upon the whole the hemisphere is brighter and the prospects more agreeable than they were a week ago. Our army acknowledge they have been well treated, paid and fed, and if you had not raised the pay of the officers, they could hardly have found a subject of complaint. I am sorry it was done, tho' if the soldiers were politicians they might see it was an advantage to [them]. The southern gentlemen seem to have [taken a dislike to *torn*] equality among us, and don't seem [to understand] that many of the soldiers are [*torn*] possessed of as much property as [*torn*]. The people of Boston by their imprudence [*torn*] town so long have given us more trouble [than both] the ministerial army and navy. I don't [*torn*] an eighth part of our whole time since [*torn*] been taken up about them people, and the[y will at] last perhaps ruin us by spreading [the small pox]. What shall we do? Determine not to [receive them], they die. Adieu. . . .

Just as I finished the above I received your short letter of December 5. Shall endeavour to reconcile the troops as far as I have influence to the terms you mention. The greatest difficulty, however, is about the officers' wages lately raised. Craft[s] I know is a deserving man, and fit for the office you mention. Trot I presume is by the character you give him. But what is to be done with Burbeck? He is said to be a good officer, is well esteemed at Head quarters, and is now a lieutenant colonel. Do you design there shall be two lieutenant colonels, as well as two majors in that regiment? What shall be done for our good friend Doctor Cooper? He is a staunch friend to the cause, a great sufferer, and no income to support him. Must he not be provided for in the civil list? Do devise something.

It is reported from Boston that they have taken one of our privateers.[1] I fear it is true.

1 The *Washington*, Captain Martindale.

[*torn*] it is true they have indeed got one of our [privateers, the] brigantine the General fixed from Plymouth. She [*torn*] double fortified six pounders, about twenty swivels [*torn*]. We don't know who took her, or any [*torn*] about it. Tis supposed she made a stout [resistance as] much firing was heard in the Bay. [I was at Head] quarters yesterday, but the General was gone [*torn*] not see him. I met Crafts. He says the [*torn*] offered him the second majority, and that a man [who was f]ormerly his serjeant is to have the first. [He says he wo]n't accept it. Mason is the lieutenant colonel. [*torn*] wishes to be made barrack master and I could [*torn*] if it don't make a difficulty. Brewer[1] is at present appointed, and gave up his regiment for it to accomodate matters, and facilitate the new establishment. I had a vessel arrived on Monday from the West Indies. She has been at almost all the Windward Islands. The master is sensible and intelligent. . . .

SAMUEL ADAMS TO JAMES WARREN

PHILADA., *Decr.* 26, 1775

MY DEAR SIR, — I have receivd your obliging Letter of the 5th Instant by Fessenden for which I am very thankful to you. The present form of our Government, you tell me, is not considerd as permanent. This affords the strongest Motive to improve the Advantages of it, while it continues. May not Laws be made and Regulations established, under this Government, the salutary Effects of which the People shall be so convincd of from their own Experience, as never hereafter to suffer them to be repeald or alterd. But what other Change is expected? Certainly the People do not already hanker after the Onions and the Garlick! They cannot have so soon forgot the Tyranny of their late Governors, who, being dependent upon, and the mere Creatures of a Minister of State, and subservient to his Instructions or Inclinations have *forbid* them to make such Laws as would have been beneficial to them or to repeal those that were not. But, I find *every where* some Men, who are affraid of a free Government, lest it should be perverted and made use of as a Cloke for Licentiousness. The Fear

[1] David Brewer, of Palmer.

of the Peoples abusing their Liberty is made an Argument against their having the Enjoyment of it; as if anything were so much to be dreaded by Mankind as Slavery. But the Bearer Mr Bromfield, of whose Departure I was not apprisd till a few Minutes past, is waiting. I can therefore say no more at present, but that I am,
Your affectionate Friend,

S. A.

December 27th. Mr. Bromfield who went in a Stage Coach set off yesterday before I could close my Letter. I shall therefore forward it by the Post or any other Conveyance that may next offer.

Your last Letter informd me that "the late Conduct of the ———[1] had weakened that Confidence and Reverence necessary to give a well disposd Government its full operation and Effects." I am sorry for it; and presume it is not to be imputed to a Fault in the Institution of that Order, but a Mistake in the Persons of whom it is composd. All men are fond of Power. It is difficult for us to be prevaild upon to believe, that we possess more than belongs to us. Even publick Bodies of Men legally constituted, are too prone to covet more Power than the Publick has judgd it safe to entrust them with. It is happy when their Power is not only subject to Controul while it is exercisd, but frequently reverts into the hands of the People, from whom it is derivd, and to whom Men in Power ought forever to be accountable. That venerable Assembly the Senate of Areopagus in Athens, whose Proceedings were so eminently upright and impartial, that, we are told, even "foreign States, when any Controversy happend among them, would voluntarily submit to their Decisions . . . not only their determinations might be called in Question and, if Need was, retracted by an Assembly of the People, but themselves too, if they exceeded the Bounds of Moderation, were lyable to account for it."

At present, our Council as well as our House of Representatives are annually elective. Thus far they are accountable to the People, as they are lyable, for Misbehavior, to be discarded. But this is not a sufficient Security to the People, unless they are themselves *virtuous.*

[1] Council?

If we wish for "another Change," should it not be a Change of *Manners*? If the Youth are carefully educated, if the Principles of Morality are strongly inculcated in the Minds of the People — the End and Design of Government clearly understood, and the Love of our Country the ruling Passion — uncorrupted Men will be chosen for the Representatives of the People.

These will elect Men of distinguished Worth to sit at the Council Board, and in time we may hope, that, in the Purity of their Manners, the Wisdom of their Councils and the Justice of their Determinations, our Senate may equal that of Athens, which was said to be, "the most sacred and venerable Assembly in all Greece." I confess I have a strong Desire, that our Colony should excell in Wisdom and Virtue. If this proceeds from Pride, is it not a lawful Pride? I am willing that the same Spirit of Emulation may pervade every one of the confederated Colonies. But I am called off, and must conclude with again assuring you that I am with the most friendly Regards to Mrs Warren, very affectionately Yours,

S. A.

Pray write to me often.

SAMUEL ADAMS TO JAMES WARREN

PHILADA., *Jany.* 7, 1776

MY DEAR SIR, — I verily believe the Letters I write to you are three to one I receive from you. However I consider the Multiplicity of Affairs you must attend to in your various Departments and am willing to make due Allowance.

Your last is dated the 19th of December. It contains a List of very important Matters lying before the General Assembly. I am much pleased to find that there is an End put to the Contest between the two Houses concerning the Establishment of a Militia, and that you are in hopes of making an effectual Law for that Purpose. It is certainly of the last Consequence to a free Country that the Militia which is its natural Strength should be kept upon the most advantageous Footing. A standing Army, however necessary it may be at some times, is always dangerous to the Liberties of the People. Soldiers are apt to consider themselves as a Body distinct from the rest of the Citizens. They have their Arms always in their hands. Their Rules and their Discipline is severe. They soon become attached to their officers and disposd to yield implicit obedience to their Commands. Such a Power should be watchd with a jealous Eye. I have a good Opinion of the principal officers of our Army, I esteem them as Patriots as well as Soldiers; But if this War continues, as it may for years yet to come, we know not who may succeed them. Men who have been long governd by military Laws, and inurd to military Customs and Habits may lose the Spirit and Feeling of Citizens. And even Citizens having been used to admire the Heroism which the Commanders of their own Armies have displayd and to look up to them as their Saviours, may be prevaild upon to surrender to them those Rights for the Protection of which against an Invader, they had employd and paid them. We have seen too much of such a Disposition among some of our Countrymen. The Militia is composd of free Citizens. There is therefore no Danger of their making Use of their Power to the Destruction of their own Rights or suffering others to invade them. I earnestly wish that young Gentlemen of a military Genius, and many such I am satisfied there are in our Colony, might be instructed in the Art of War, and taught at the same time the Principles of a free Government, and deeply impressd with a Sense of that indispensible Obligation which every Individual is under to the whole Society. These might in Time be fit for Officers in the Militia and being thoroughly acquainted with the Duties of Citizens as well as Soldiers might be entrusted with a Share in the Command of our Army, at such Times as Necessity might require so dangerous a Body to exist.

I am glad that your Attention is turnd so much to the Importation of Powder and that the Manufacture of Saltpetre is in so flourishing a Way. I cannot think you are restraind by the Resolve of Congress from exporting Fish to Spain. I will make myself more certain by recurring to our Records tomorrow when the Secretary returns; he being at this time (6 o'clock P.M.) at his House three Miles from Town. And I will inform you by a Postscript to this Letter or by another Letter by the Post. I have the Pleasure to acquaint you that a Vessel with five Tons of

Powder *certainly* arrivd at Egg harbour the Night before last, besides two Tons in this River. A Part of it is consignd to the Congress — The Rest is the Property partly of Mr [Thomas Boylston] and partly of a Gentleman in this City. Congress has orderd the whole to be purchasd for publick Use. We are also informd that Six Tons more arrivd a few days ago in New York which I believe to be true. But better still. A Vessel is *certainly* arrivd in this River with between fifty and sixty Tons of Salt petre.[1] This I suppose will give you more Satisfaction for the present than telling you Congress News as you request.

You ask me, "When you are to hear of our Confederation?" I answer, When some Gentlemen (to use an Expression of a Tory) shall "feel more bold." You know it was formerly a Complaint in our Colony, that there was a timid kind of Men, who perpetually hinderd the Progress of those who would fain run in the Path of Virtue and Glory. I find wherever I am that Mankind are alike variously classed. I can discern the Magnanimity of the Lyon, the Generosity of the Horse, the Fearfulness of the Deer, and the *Cunning of the Fox* — I had almost overlookd the *Fidelity* of the Dog. But I forbear to indulge my rambling Pen in this Way lest I should be thought chargeable with a Design to degrade the *Dignity* of our Nature by comparing Men with Beasts. Let me just observe to you that I have mentiond only the more excellent Properties that are to be found among Quadrupeds. Had I suggested an Idea of the *Vanity* of the Ape, the *Tameness* of the Ox, or the *stupid Servility* of the Ass, I might have been lyable to Censure.

Are you Sollicitous to hear of our Confederation? I will tell you. It is not dead but sleepeth. A Gentleman of this City told me the other day, that he could not believe the People without Doors would follow the Congress *passibus aequis*, if such Measures as *some* called spirited were pursued. I was of a different Opinion. It put me in Mind of a Fable of the high-mettled horse and the dull horse. My excellent Colleague, Mr. J. A. can repeat to you the Fable and if the Improvement had been made of it which our very valuable Friend Coll. M[ifflin?] proposd, you would have seen that

---

[1] *Journals of the Continental Congress*, IV. 40.

Confederation compleated long before this time. I do not despair of it since our Enemies themselves are hastening it. While I am writing an Express arrives from Baltimore in Maryland, with the Deposition of Capt. Horn[1] of the *Snow Bird* belonging to Providence.

The Deponent says, that on Monday the 1st Instant he being at Hampton in Virginia heard a constant firing of Cannon; that he was informd a Messenger had been sent to inquire where the firing was, who reported that the Ships of War were cannonading the Town of Norfolk; that about the Middle of the Afternoon they saw the Smoke ascending from Norfolk, as they supposd; that he saild from Hampton the Evening of the same day and the firing continued till the next day. This will prevail more than a long Train of Reasoning to accomplish a Confederation, and other Matters which I know your heart as well as mine is much set upon.

I forgot to tell you that a Vessel is arrivd in Maryland having as part of her Cargo four thousand yards of Sail Cloth — an article which I hope will be much in Demand in America. Adieu my Friend.

S. A.

Martha Washington to Mercy Warren

Cambridge, *January the* 8th, 1776

Mrs. Washington presents her respectfull compliments to Mrs. Warren and thanks her most cordially for her polite enquire and exceeding kind offer. If the Exigency of affairs in this Camp should make it necessary for her to remove, she cannot but esteem it a happiness to have so friendly an Invitation as Mrs. Warren has given. In the mean while Mrs. Washington cannot help wishing for an oppertunity of shewing every civility in her power to Mrs. Warren, at Head Quarters in Cambridge.

The General begs that his best regards may be presented to Mrs. Warren, accompanied with his sincere thanks for her favourable wishes for his honour and success; and joins in wishing Mrs. Warren, the speaker, and their Family, every happiness that is, or can be derived from a speedy, and honourable peace.

1 John Horn.

Cambridge January the 8th 1776

Mrs Washington presents her respectfull compliments to Mrs Warren, and thanks her most cordially for her polite enquiries, and exceeding kind offer — If the exigency of affairs in this camp should make it necessary for her to remove, she cannot but esteem it a happiness to have so friendly an Invitation as Mrs Warren has given — In the mean while, Mrs Washington cannot help wishing for an oppertunity of shewing every Civility in her power to Mrs Warren, at Head Quarters in Cambridge —

The General begs that his best regards may be presented to Mr Warren, accompanied with his sincear thanks for her favourable wishes for his honour and success, and joins in wishing Mrs Warren — the Speaker and their Family, every happiness that is, or can be derived from a speedy, and honourable peace

JOHN ADAMS TO MERCY WARREN

BRAINTREE, *Jany.* 8, 1776

DEAR MADAM, — Your Friend insists upon my Writing to you and altho I am conscious it is my Duty being deeply in Debt for a number of very agreeable Favours in the Epistolary Way, yet I doubt whether a sense of this Duty would have overcome my Inclination to Indolence and Relaxation with which my own Fire Side always inspires me, if it had not been Stimulated and quickened by her.

I was charmed with three Characters drawn by a most masterly Pen, which I recd at the southward. Copley's Pencil could not have touched off with more exquisite Finishings the Faces of those Gentlemen. Whether I ever answered that Letter I know not. But I hope Posterity will see it, if they do I am sure they will admire it. I think I will make a Bargain with you, to draw the Character of every new Personage I have an opportunity of knowing, on Condition you will do the same. My View will be to learn the Art of penetrating into Men's Bosoms, and then the more difficult Art of painting what I shall see there. You Ladies are the most infallible judges of Characters, I think.

Pray Madam, are you for an American Monarchy or Republic? Monarchy is the genteelest and most fashionable Government, and I dont know why the Ladies ought not to consult Elegance and the Fashion as well in Government as Gowns, Bureaus or Chariots.

For my own part I am so tasteless as to prefer a Republic, if We must erect an independent Government in America, which you know is utterly against my Inclination. But a Republic, altho it will infallibly beggar me and my Children, will produce Strength, Hardiness Activity, Courage, Fortitude and Enterprise; the manly noble and Sublime Qualities in human Nature, in Abundance. A Monarchy would probably, somehow or other make me rich, but it would produce so much Taste and Politeness so much Elegance in Dress, Furniture, Equipage, so much Musick and Dancing, so much Fencing and Skaiting, so much Cards and Backgammon; so much Horse Racing and Cockfighting, so many

Balls and Assemblies, so many Plays and Concerts that the very Imagination of them makes me feel vain, light, frivolous and insignificant.

It is the Form of Government which gives the decisive Colour to the Manners of the People, more than any other Thing. Under a well regulated Commonwealth, the People must be wise virtuous and cannot be otherwise. Under a Monarchy they may be as vicious and foolish as they please, nay, they cannot but be vicious and foolish. As Politicks therefore is the Science of human Happiness and human Happiness is clearly best promoted by Virtue, what thorough Politician can hesitate who has a new Government to build whether to prefer a Commonwealth or a Monarchy?

But, Madam, there is one Difficulty which I know not how to get over.

Virtue and Simplicity of Manners are indispensably necessary in a Republic among all orders and Degrees of Men. But there is so much Rascallity, so much Venality and Corruption, so much Avarice and Ambition such a Rage for Profit and Commerce among all Ranks and Degrees of Men even in America, that I sometimes doubt whether there is public Virtue enough to Support a Republic. There are two Vices most detestably predominant in every Part of America that I have yet seen which are as incompatible with the Spirit of a Commonwealth, as Light is with Darkness; I mean Servility and Flattery. A genuine Republican can no more fawn and cringe than he can domineer. Shew me the American who cannot do all. I know two or Three, I think, and very few more. However, it is the Part of a great Politician to make the Character of his People, to extinguish among them the Follies and Vices that he sees, and to create in them the Virtues and Abilities which he sees wanting. I wish I was sure that America has one such Politician but I fear she has not.

A Letter begun in Levity is likely to have . . . [conc]lusion, while I was writing the last Word . . . Paragraph my attention was called off . . . it and most melodious sounds my Ears . . . more Mortars and Musquettry.[1]

[1] The signature has been cut out, thus mangling the text on the reverse.

A very hot Fire, both of Artillery and Small Arms, has continued for half an Hour, and has been succeeded by a luminous Phenomenon over Braintree North Common, occasioned by Burning Buildings I suppose.[1]

Whether our People have attacked or defended, been victorious or vanquished is to me totally uncertain. But in Either Case I rejoice, for a Defeat appears to me preferable to total Inaction.

May the Supreme Ruler of Events overrule in our Favour. But if the Event of this Evening is unfortunate I think We ought at all Hazards and at any Loss to retrieve it tomorrow. I hope the Militia will be ready and our Honour be retrieved by making Boston our own.

I shall be in suspense this Night but very willing to take my Place with my Neighbours tomorrow and crush the Power of the Enemies or suffer under it.

I hope Coll Warren sleeps at Cushing's this night and that I shall see him in the Morning. Mean Time I think I shall sleep as soundly as ever.

I am Madam your most humble servant and sincere Friend,
[*Signature cut.*]

Mrs. Adams desires to be remembered to Mrs. Warren.

SAMUEL ADAMS TO JAMES WARREN

PHILADELPHIA, *January* 10, 1776

MY DEAR SIR,— I wrote to you the 7th Instant by Mr. Anthony by the way of Providence, and should not so soon have troubled you with another Letter but to inform you, that upon looking over the Journals of Congress I find that the Recommendation of the 26th of October, to export Produce for a certain Purpose, is confind to the foreign West Indies; and the Resolution to stop all Trade till the first of March is subsequent to it. This last Resolution prevents your exporting your Merchantable Fish to Spain for the purpose mentiond, which I am satisfied was not intended, because I am very certain the Congress means to encourage the

---

1 See Force, *American Archives*, 4th Ser., IV. 612.

Importation of those necessary Articles under the Direction of proper Persons, from every Part of the World.

I design to propose to my Colleagues to joyn with me in a Motion to extend the Recommendation so as to admit of exporting Fish to any place besides the foreign West Indies.

A few days ago, being one of a Committee to consider General Washington's last Letter to Congress, I proposd to the Committee and they readily consented to report the inclosd Resolutions, which were unanimously agreed to in Congress.[1] The Committee also reported that a certain Sum should be paid to Mr. Lovel out of the military Chest towards enabling him to remove himself and his Family from Boston, but the Precedent was objected to and the last Resolve was substituted in its stead.[2] The Gentlemen present however contributed and put into my hands Eighty-two Dollars for the Benefit of Mr. Lovell, which I shall remit either in Cash or a good Bill. I hope I shall soon be so happy as to hear that he is releasd from Bondage. I feel very tenderly for the Rest of my fellow Citizens who are detaind in that worst of Prisons. Methinks there is one way speedily to release them all.

This day Congress have appointed General Fry a Brigadier General of the Army at Cambridge and Coll. Arnold a Brigadier General for the Army in Canada.

Another sum of Money is orderd to be sent to you for the Use of the Army.

Jany. 13. I have sent to Mrs. Adams a Pamphlet[3] which made its first Appearance a few days ago. It has fretted some folks here more than a little. I recommend it to your Perusal and wish you would borrow it of her. Don't be displeasd with me if you find the Spirit of it totally repugnant with your Ideas of Government. Read it without Prejudice, and give me your impartial Sentiments of it when you may be at Leisure. Your Friend.

S. A.

[1] On James Lovell. *Journals of the Continental Congress*, IV. 32.
[2] Recommending his appointment to an office.   [3] Paine's *Common Sense*.

MERCY WARREN TO ABIGAIL ADAMS.   ADAMS MSS.
February 7, 1776

Just come to hand is a letter from my very worthy friend,[1] who I suppose is by this time arrived at Philadelphia; and another from his good Portia, whose mind seems to be agitated by a variety of passions, passions of the noblest kind, a sense of honnour, of friendship, of parental and conjugal affection, of domestic felicity and public happiness. I do not wonder you had a struggle within yourself when your friend was again called upon to be absent from his family for perhaps many months; but as you have sacrificed private inclination to the public welfare I hope the reward of virtue will be your portion. I believe the person you consent should be absent from you need give himself very little concern about the ill-natured sugestions of an envious world, and I cannot think you have any apprehension that the whispers of Malice will lessen the esteem and affection I have for my friends; and if she is unkindly brooding anything to their disadvantage it has not reached my ear. When it does I shall comply with your request and give you the opportunity you mention. Mean time let me have an explanation of that source of uneasiness you hint at in yours. Follow my example and set down immediately and write, and I will ensure you a safe conveyance by a gentleman who I hope will call on you on saterday on his way to pay a visit to his Marcia. You may trust him with your letter though ever so important, and anything else you will venture to communicate.

I want to know if certain intercepted letters had any consequences at Philadelphia. Was any umbrage taken by any genius great or small?

I wonder where Mr. Adams's letter has been for a whole month. It might have traveled to Quebec and back again since it was wrote. I began to think he was about to drop our correspondence, and indeed I think now I am obliged to you for the continuance. Yet had I received the letter before he went off I believe I should have ventured to answer some of his queries, though they were not put in a manner serious enough for me to suppose he expected

[1] John Adams.

it. However, when you write again, do make my regards and thank him for his of January 8th. Only the fear of interrupting his important moments prevents my doing it myself. But I think he has so many friends to correspond with that it is rather calling him from more useful employment, to attend to my interruptions. Yet there is a proposal in his that may set my pen to work again, perhaps before he returns.

I am very sorry for the ill health of your family: hope they are all recovered. Do put them in mind of the affection of your friend, in a way most pleasing to the little circle. What is become of my dear mrs. Lincoln? Do tell her I have impatiently wished through the whole winter for the pleasure of hearing from her and the family. Do make them my best regards.

I write in a very great hury, or I should touch a little on politicks, knowing you love a little seasoning of that nature in every production; but it is too wide a field to enter this evening, so will only wish that the aquisition of Boston and Quebec may make the opening of the year '76 an era of Glory to the arms of America, and may hand down the name of Washington and Arnold to the latest posterity, with the laurel on their brow. But a reverse I tremble to think off. Let us forbear to name it. So will hasten to subscribe the name of your Affectionate friend,

M. W.

JOHN ADAMS TO JAMES WARREN

Feby. 18, 1776

MY DEAR SIR, — We have at last hit upon a Plan which promises fair for Success.

Dr. Franklin and Mr. Chase of Maryland and Mr. Charles Carroll of Carrollton are chosen a Committee to go to Canada. I must confess I have very great Confidence in the Abilities and Integrity the Political Principles and good Disposition of this Committee.[1]

Franklin's Character you know. His masterly Acquaintance with the French Language,[2] his extensive Correspondence in

[1] *Journals of the Continental Congress*, IV. 151. The *Journal* of Charles Carroll on this mission was printed by the Maryland Historical Society, in 1876.
[2] Franklin would not have made this claim.

France, his great Experience in Life, his Wisdom, Prudence, Caution; his engaging Address; united to his unshaken Firmness in the present American System of Politicks and War, point him out as the fittest Character for this momentous Undertaking.

Chase, is in younger Life, under forty; But deeply impressed with a sense of the Importance of securing Canada, very active, eloquent, Spirited, and capable.

Carroll's Name and Character are equally unknown to you. I was introduced to him about Eighteen Months ago in this City and was much pleased with his Conversation. He has a Fortune as I am well informed which is computed to be worth Two hundred Thousand Pounds Sterling. He is a Native of Maryland, and his Father is still living. He had a liberal Education in France and is well acquainted with the french Nation. He speaks their Language as easily as ours; and what is perhaps of more Consequence than all the rest, he was educated in the Roman Catholic Religion and still continues to worship his Maker according to the Rites of that Church. In the Cause of American Liberty his Zeal Fortitude and Perseverance have been so conspicuous that he is said to be marked out for peculiar Vengeance by the Friends of Administration; But he continues to hazard his all, his immense Fortune, the largest in America, and his Life. This Gentleman's Character, if I foresee aright, will hereafter make a greater Figure in America. His abilities are very good, his Knowledge and Learning extensive. I have seen Writings of his which would convince you of this. You may perhaps hear before long more about them.

These three gentlemen compose a Committee which I think promises great Things.

But We have done more. We have empowered the Committee to take with them, another Gentleman of Maryland, Mr. John Carroll,[1] a Roman Catholic Priest, and a Jesuit, a Gentleman of learning and Abilities. This Gentleman will administer Baptism to the Canadian Children and bestow Absolution upon Such as have been refused it by the toryfied Priests in Canada. The Anathema's of the Church so terrible to the Canadians having had a disagreeable Effect upon them.

[1] A cousin of Charles Carroll.

In Addition to the whole General Lee is ordered into Canada to take upon him the Command of the whole Expedition.[1] His Address, his Fluency in French, his Activity, his great Experience and Skill, We hope will Succeed.

I long to hear from N. England that the three Regiments are marched. It would damp me very much to hear that our People continue to hesitate about Bounties, and Trifles.

The Unanimous Voice of the Continent is Canada must be ours; Quebec must be taken.

I think the most prudent Measures, have now been adopted and We must leave the Event. If We fail now, I shall be easy because I know of nothing more or better that We can do. I did not feel so well Satisfied after the News of the Failure at Quebec. It is true that We want Lee both at Cambridge and New York! But We cannot have him in three Armies at once, and Canada Seems to me, the most dangerous Post, and that there is the greatest Necessity for him there. Schuyler is to command in N. York, with Ld Sterling under him, who is a very good officer.

The Importance of Canada arises from this, and occasions our remarkable Unanimity at present in deciding the Affairs of it: In the Hands of our Enemies it would enable them to inflame all the Indians upon the Continent, and perhaps induce them to take up the Hatchet and commit their Robberies and Murders upon the Frontiers of all the southern Colonies, as well as to pour down Regulars, Canadians, and Indians, together upon the Borders of the Northern

I am, my dear Sir, unfeignedly your Friend.

[*No signature.*]

James Bowdoin to Mercy Warren

Middleborough, *Feby.* 28, 1776

Dear Madam,—I have read with great pleasure the Pamphlet[2] you favoured me with and am much obliged for the loan of it.

1 Congress passed the order on February 17, but on the 28th countermanded it.
2 Paine's *Common Sense.* "You have read the celebrated Pamphlet, *Common Sense*, and the appendix in last Thursday paper. It would gratify me to know your Opinion of the last Paragraph which proposes an act of oblivion, etc. Methinks the Whigs who have suf-

Most of the Author's observations are very just and I think will proselyte many to his doctrine The more it is contemplated, the stronger is the conviction of the truth of it, at least this is the case with respect to myself and my dear Rib, we having been much confirmed in it since reading the Pamphlet.

If the Pamphlet were republished in all the Newspapers (each head of it together without division) it would have an extensively good effect, and greatly tend to confirm the real christian, recover the doubting, and convert the ignorant and unbelieving to the true faith. . . . Your most obedt. hble. Servt.,

JAMES BOWDOIN

JAMES WARREN TO JOHN ADAMS.   ADAMS MSS.
PLYMOUTH, *March* 7, 1776 [1]

. . . .

I two days ago had the pleasure of receiving yours of February 18th. I think you have taken the best possible methods for the security of Canada. Your policy is exquisitely good, and if it fails you will nevertheless have the satisfaction of having done everything that humane policy could dictate. I am glad you have taken these steps; but they don't satisfy me. I want to see more capital ones adopted. I am extremely anxious, perhaps never more so at any time. You know I never feared the arms of Britain, but I always dreaded their negotiations, aided and assisted as they will be by the silly moderation and timidity of some, by the prejudices and interested views of others. Surely the honest, virtuous and sensible will have enough to do to encounter the plausible subtlety of their agents, supported by such confederates. And what adds to the misfortune is that you are to have this business on your hands at a time when you should be attending to the embassies from the

fered the loss of everything dear in life must be possessed of souls more than human to assent to such an article. Query, whether setting aside the horrors of Conscience which must have been the attendant on Toryism, they would not be in vastly more preferable circumstances than those who have struggled thro all difficulties and dangers, and have nothing in Prospect but poverty and want? Such an article seems calculated for the Latitude of Philadelphia, which has been exempt from all suffering, but I fancy will hardly suit the Climate of Boston, Charlestown, etc." *Hannah Winthrop to Mercy Warren*, April 2, 1776. MS.

[1] Written after an illness of three weeks, which kept him confined to his house.

several (at least trading) powers in Europe, forming alliances to support an independence declared many months past. But so it is. May God in his good Providence carry us safely through this difficulty, and I shall think we have gained the summit of the mountain. By the best intelligence we have the Commissioners are appointed. They are to consist of thirty-nine, three to each Colony; that they are instructed not to treat with Congress. Can they with all their negro policy be so stupid as to suppose that they will be able to avail themselves of the advantage of getting different terms from different colonies, and by that means, without any trouble but a voyage from Britain, destroy a union so formidable to the existence of that nation?

Anxiety marks every countenance. People can't account for the hesitancy they observe. While some apprehend that you are startled at the measures already taken, others wonder why the principles and dictates of common sense have not the same influence upon the enlarged minds of their superiors that they feel on their own, and none can see safety or happiness in a future connection with B[ritain], void as they are of true policy, justice or humanity. All wish to see a brisk foreign trade, that will both make us rich and safe.

I am in a poor situation to give you intelligence. I have but a very imperfect account of the military operations. The bombardment and cannonade of Boston begun on Saturday last, and our army took possession of Dorchester Hill on Monday or Tuesday night, without any difficulty, and have strongly entrenched. What is to be next I know not. I presume you will have every particular from Head quarters. Whether Howe has a design to evacuate Boston or not is to me very uncertain, but some circumstances look like it. Where he will go if he does, is equally uncertain. Can Administration, with all their stupidity, view with indifference the French force in the West Indies, or is not that true? If true, it must be important to them or us. No prizes lately taken. A ship of 300 tons from Boston to New York, mounted with the carriage guns, thirty men, some coal, 7000 cannon ball, and a few other articles, lately run on shore on the back of the Cape, the ship bilged, and everything on board taken possession of and secured by our people. I can give you no particular account of the three regiments for Canada from those governments, but I dare say they are gone. Every thing was favourable when I last heard. I want to hear from your fleet, their destination, success, etc. I want to hear the character, the business, etc. of the Baron de Woedke, Knight of Malta, who passed through this town in his way to Congress, with letters to Dr. Franklin, etc. . . .[1]

The House have voted a bounty of £6 to those that shall inlist for two years into the two battalions to be raised here; of £3 for one year; and of thirty shillings to those who shall inlist into any of the five battalions left here. I have my doubts and fears about this measure. I fear that bounties will rise faster than money can depreciate or goods rise. I fear the displeasure of Congress, that they will be disgusted. The Board have prudently stopped it for the present. I don't know but the result will be to write to you before it goes further.

Samuel Adams to James Warren

PHILADA., *March* 8, 1776

MY DEAR SIR, — I now sit down just to acknowledge the rect of your favor of the 14th. of Feby., and to mention to you a Matter which considerd in itself may appear to be of small Moment but in its effects may possibly be mischievous. I believe I may safely appeal to all the Letters which I have written to my Friends since I have been in this City to vindicate myself in affirming that I have never mentioned Mr. C.,[2] nor referred to his Conduct in any of them excepting one to my worthy Colleague Mr. A., when he was at Watertown a few Weeks ago, in which I informd him of the side Mr. C. had taken in a very interesting Debate; and then I only observd that he had a Right to give his Opinion whenever he thought himself prepard to form one. Yet I have been told it has

---

[1] Frederick William de Woedtke. On March 16 Congress elected him to be a Brigadier General. He died, near Lake George, N.Y., in July, 1776. In the *Journals of the House of Representatives* (Mass.), April 2, 1776, he is described as "Chevalier del Ordre de St. Jean Jerusalem de Malta."

[2] Cushing.

been industriously reported that Mr. A. and myself have been secretly writing to his Prejudice, and that our Letters have operated to his being superceded.[1] So fully persuaded did some Gentlemen seem to be of the Truth of this Report, and Mr D[uer] of N.Y. in particular, whom I have heard express the warmest Affection for Mr. C., that he appeard to be surprizd to hear me contradict it. Whether this Report and a Beliefe of it inducd the Friends of Mr. C. to open a charitable Subscription in Support of his Character I am not able to say. If it was so, they ought in Justice to him to have made themselves certain of the Truth of it; for to offer Aid to the Reputation of a Gentleman without a real Necessity is surely no Advantage to it. A Letter was handed about addressd to Mr. C. The Contents I never saw. His Confidential Friends signd it; other Gentlemen at their Request also set their hands to it, perhaps with as much Indifference as a Man of Business would give a Shilling to get rid of the Importunity of a Beggar. I hear it is supposd in Watertown to be a Vote of Thanks of the Congress to Mr. C. for his eminent Services, in which his Recall is mentiond with Regrett; but this is most certainly a Mistake. The Gentlemen signd it in their private Capacity with Submission, should they not have addressd it to another person, or publishd it to the World after the Manner of other Addresses? For if they intended it to recommend Mr. C. to his own Constituents, was it not hard to oblige him to blow the Trumpet himself which they had prepard to sound his Praise. But Major Osgood is in haste; I must therefore drop *this* Subject *for the present* and conclude, affectionately yours.

[No signature.]

JOHN ADAMS TO JAMES WARREN

March 21, 1776

MY DEAR SIR, — I have not recd more than one Letter from you since I left you and that was a very Short one. I have written as often as I could. If you get a Sight of the New York and Phila-

---

[1] On January 18 Massachusetts had reelected its representatives in Congress, but chose Elbridge Gerry in the place of Cushing.

delphia News Papers you will see what a mighty Question is before the Tribunal of the Public. The Decision is yet in suspence, but a Guess may be formed what it will be.

The Day before Yesterday the Committee of Observation of this City, a virtuous brave and patriotic Body of Men 100 in Number, voted with only one dissentient Voice to petition their Assembly now sitting, to repeal their deadly Instructions to their Delegates in Congress. This Assembly a few days ago, upon a Petition from the Same Committee and some other Bodies, has voted seventeen additional Members in order to make the Representation of this Province more adequate.

You will soon see a sett of Resolutions, which will please you — the Continental Vessels the Provincial Vessels and Letters of Marque and Privateers will be let loose upon British Trade.[1]

I hope, and believe it will not be long before Trade will be open. Foreign Nations, all the World I hope, will be invited to come here, and our People permitted to go to all the World except the Dominions of him, who is adjudged to be *Nerone Neronior*.

I think the Utmost Encouragement must be given to Trade, and therefore We must lay no Duties at present upon Exports and Imports, nor attempt to confine our Trade to our own Bottoms or our own seamen. This for the present.

We have so much Work to do, by sea and Land, and so few Hands to do it, that We shall not be under any Necessity, nor will it be good Policy, I think, to attempt such Restrictions as yet.

The Act of Assembly here for seventeen additional Representatives will give a finishing Blow to the Quaker Interest in this City — at least to its Ascendency. It will strip it of all that unjust and unequal Power which it formerly had over the Ballance of the Province. The Tories here, attribute this Maneuvre to your Friends, to whom you are sometimes so partial. If the Charge is true, the Posterity of Pennsylvania will have cause to bless your Friends from Generation to Generation.

You can't think how much I am flattered with it. As I have the Pleasure of a particular Acquaintance and frequent friendly Conversations with several Gentlemen of this City belonging to

[1] *Journals of the Continental Congress*, IV. 229.

the Committee of Observation I am inclined to hope, that a small Portion of this Merit is due to me. But I would not be too vain and proud of it.

[*No signature.*]

JAMES BOWDOIN TO MERCY WARREN

MIDDLEBOROUGH, *March* 23, 1776

I perfectly agree with you, Dear Madam, that G. Britain is in a disgraceful situation, not only with regard to what you have with great Propriety instanced in, but also in her sending Commissioners to treat with those she calls Rebels. These Commissioners are probably by this time arrived at Philadelphia, but how they can introduce with a good grace, the errand they are come upon, is difficult to conjecture. We are told they will not have anything to do with the Congress, but will treat with the Colonies seperately. If this be their plan, it requires no great share of the prophetic spirit to foretell, they will not be able to execute it; for it is not likely that any of the united Colonies will enter into a seperate treaty with them, but will undoubtedly refer them to the Congress, which represents the whole, and which for many reasons is the only suitable body to negotiate with them. The ministry have hitherto refused to acknowledge that body as the Representative of the Colonies, and do not allow that the Colonies conjunctly can legally be represented at all; and from hence, and also from the hope of gaining advantages by seperate treaties, proceeds the disinclination to treat with the Congress. But it appears likely they must bring their stomachs to it, if they mean to do anything in a way of negotiation. The Commissioners have undoubtedly a discretional power to act according as they find things circumstanced; and when they are informed of the disgraceful precipitate flight of their troops from Boston, the firmness and entirety of the union of the Colonies, and their preparedness and capacity to defend themselves, and therefore that the british troops can make no great impression, they will condescend, I imagine, to treat with the Congress. But if you should ask, Madame, how will the Congress conduct on this occasion? My answer is, extremely well; for it is manifest by their proceedings hitherto, they are good politians, and have requisites for negotiation — good sense, historical knowledge, and integrity. The two former of these will secure them from imposition and circumvention, and the latter, I trust, from bribery and corruption. If they are not corruptible, we need not be distressed about the issue of the negotiation. But as M[inis]try are said to be complete Adepts in the practice and acts of bribery, it is highly probable those they employ on so interesting and important an occasion are not less so; and come amply provided from the national coffers with the means of it. They are therefore in an especial manner to be guarded against in that view. If a treaty should be entered upon, I apprehend it cannot be done with dignity and propriety on the part of America, before the whole british Armament both by sea and land depart from America; and this ought to be insisted on as an essential preliminary to the negotiation. In this idea some Europeans do, and all Americans should, concur.

As to the treaty itself, in order to be lasting, it must be founded on meer interest, the mutual interest of the parties; the free discussion and settlement of which imply mutual independance, without which it is in vain to expect they can take place. In order to such a discussion, settlement, does it not seem necessary on our part, there should be a declaration of independance on Great Britain? and without such a declaration, must not the Congress enter upon the treaty with great disadvantage? as their silence on that head will be construed to imply an acknowledgement, that the Interests of America are to be considered as subordinate to those of Great Britain, and to be regarded no farther than they have a tendency to promote her interests.

Divers objections may be made against such a declaration: but I would refer the objector to that excellent Pamphlet intitled *Common Sense;* which, if he is not influenced by private interest and attachment, will probably silence all his objections, and disciple him to the author's doctrine, that an Independance on Great Britain has now become absolutely necessary to the well being of the Colonies. Thus, Madame, in obedience to your Command, for such I esteem the most distant intimation of your pleasure, I have given you some crude thoughts on the subject of the expected negotiation. I wish they were intitled to the approbation of so good a judge in politics. Such as they are, I beg leave to submit them to your candour, and am with the greatest Esteem, Madame, your most obedt. and very hble. servt.,

JAMES BOWDOIN

We all present our best regards to you and your good Gentleman, who we hope is perfectly recovered. The report of my D[aughter]'s [1] arrival is a mistake.

JOHN ADAMS TO JAMES WARREN

March 29, 1776

Since the joyfull News of the Reduction of Boston by the Forces of the united Colonies, my Mind has been constantly engaged with Plans and Schemes for the Fortification of the Islands and Channells in Boston Harbour. I think that if Cannon and Ammunition, in the necessary Quantities can possibly be obtained, Fortifications ought to be erected upon Point Alderton, Lovells Island, George's Island, Castle Island and Governor's Island, Long Island and Moon Island, and Squantum, the Heights of Dorchester and Charlestown and Noddle's Island. The Expence of the Quantities of Cannon necessary to make this Harbour impregnable, will be very great, But this must not be regarded.

Cannot Vesseaux de Frize be placed in the Channell? Cannot Hulks be sunk? Cannot Booms be laid across? Nay, cannot the Channell be filled up or at least obstructed with Stone?

Cannot Fire be employed as a Defence? I mean Fire Ships and Fire Rafts? Cannot Gallies or floating Batteries be used to Advantage?

We suppose that the Fleet and Army, under General Howe are gone to Hallifax with Design to go up the River of Saint Lawrence, as early as possible in the Spring. They may go up the River early in May, if not the latter end of April.

---

[1] Elizabeth, who had married, in 1767, John Temple, then Surveyor-General of Customs, and later Sir John Temple.

We are taking Measures to give them such a Reception as they ought to have.

The Baron de Woedke is gone to Canada, a Brigadier. A Lady at Braintree can furnish you with his Credentials which are very good. He is a great officer.

Pray appoint a Committee to look for Sulphur in our Colony, and let me know what Progress Salt Petre makes.

[*No signature.*]

Favoured by Francis Dana, Esq.

JAMES WARREN TO JOHN ADAMS.   ADAMS MSS.

WATERTOWN, *March* 30, 1776

MY DEAR SIR, — When I wrote you last I was at Plymouth sick and confined. I did not return to this place till three days ago. On my way Mrs. Warren and I lodged at Braintree, and had the pleasure of finding Mrs. Adams and family well. Here I find the world turned topsy turvy to such a degree that I can scarcely realize the present appearances of things; the enemies army fled and our own marching into other colonies. The last division of the British fleet sailed on Wednesday last. I had a view of them without the lighthouse from Pens Hill, about sixty or seventy sail. They made a pretty appearance. What their destination is we are not able to ascertain. The general opinion is that they are gone to Halifax, and some circumstances seem to confirm it. I presume before this you have had a full account of their principle embarkation, their fright and their depredations, etc., etc. Two or three ships only, with one of their store ships ashore on George's Island, remain in the harbour. Four hundred of our men under the command of Colonel Tupper[1] were to have gone last evening on Petticks Island with some artillery, to render their station uneasy, and perhaps destroy the store ship. I suppose the storm may have prevented. What is to be the next movement of the British fleet and army, I can't devise. There is no reasoning on their conduct and I must leave abler heads than mine to conjecture. The General proposes to leave only four or five regiments here. This num-

[1] Benjamin Tupper (1738–1792).

ber we think very small, considering that we have been first and principally marked for vengeance and destruction, and the possibility and even probability that the attack may be renewed, as well as the necessity of fortifying the harbour of Boston.[1] But we must submit. We have a committee gone to view the harbour of Boston, and to report the best method of securing it. Whether that will be best done by fortifications or by obstructing the channels, or by both, I can't say, but surely it ought to be done effectually and speedily. Who is to command here I don't learn. General Ward perhaps, if his resignation (which I hear he has sent) don't prevent, by being accepted before a subsequent letter he is said to have wrote reaches you.[2]

Upon my arrival here I applyed to the General to know what he expected from me as paymaster on this occassion. His answer was that he expected I should go with the army, but was content, if it was more agreeable to me, that I should send somebody I could rely on. I could not see the necessity of this, as there must be and undoubtedly is a paymaster at [New] York; but he thought it regular the Paymaster General should be with the Commander in Chief. As my interest and connections here are such as would render it very disagreeable and scarcely honourable for me to leave this Colony, for the emoluments of that office, I desired him to accept my resignation. But as I was appointed by Congress, he declined it. I am therefore obliged to employ Mr. William Winthrop to accompany the army to [New] York. I can confide in him as well as any young gentleman, but I don't incline to trust such a risque in any hands. I shall therefore inclose to Congress, or rather to the President, a resignation, which you will please to see, seal and deliver, if I am not to be continued here.[3] How the troops that are left are to be paid and supported without a paymaster, I don't know. If a committee could be appointed this way to examine my accounts, I should be glad; if not, I suppose I must

[1] On March 25 the House of Representatives had asked Washington to leave six regiments of the continental troops and two companies of the artillery train, instead of the three or four he had said he intended to leave. *Journals.*

[2] On April 23 Congress accepted the resignations of Major General Ward and Brigadier General Frye. *Writings of George Washington* (Ford), IV. 1.

[3] It was laid before Congress April 18, referred to a committee composed of George Read, George Clinton and Carter Braxton, and accepted on the following day.

send to Philadelphia. The Council have appointed Colonel Foster and Sullivan judges of the Superiour Court, but some of the Council make difficulties about the last, and I can't tell how it will issue.[1] We have nothing material before the court.

I congratulate you on the success of our arms in North Carolina. We hear nothing from Quebec. As the seat of war is changing you will of course have shorter letters in future. All kinds of intelligence I am now to expect from you. When shall we hear that we are independent? Where are the Commissioners? What is become of our fleet, etc., etc. Remember you have not wrote me a long time. My compliments to all friends. Adieu, says your sincere friend, etc.

April 3, 1776. Yesterday Fessenden arrived. I thank you for a letter by him. It gives me fresh spirits. Thank Mr. Gerry for his last. I will write him as soon as I can. I am now much hurried, as the army is in such motion. I trust and believe there will be abundant reason for many generations yet to come to bless my particular friends. We are forming under the auspices and great influence of — a fee bill that will drive every man of interest and ability out of office. I dread the consequences of the leveling spirit, encouraged and drove to such lengths as it is. As to more general matters, people are as they should be, the harvest is mature. I can't describe the sighing after independence; it is universal. Nothing remains of that prudence, moderation or timidity with which we have so long been plagued and embarrassed. All are united in this question.

The letter I mentioned above to your President I have sent open to you, not only that you might see it, but that you might do with it as you please. If you would advise me yet to hold this place, you will keep it in your own hands. I shall be perfectly satisfied with whatever you do with it, knowing that friendship will direct your conduct in this matter. I can hardly determine what to do myself, not having such circumstances to judge from as you have. I have forwarded your letters, etc., to Mrs. Adams this day. No news since I wrote the above, only that the fleet have

[1] Jedidiah Foster and James Sullivan. They were both appointed.

steered eastward, and one of the Tory sloops is ashore on Cape Cod with a large quantity of English goods, and Black Jolly Allen and some other Tories.[1] We have had a false alarm from Newport. I recollect nothing else. This indeed is not a day of recollection with me, not having time even to overlook this scroll. Your ships I fear will, when done, wait for men. It will take time to inlist them.

Martha Washington to Mercy Warren

CAMBRIDGE, *April* the 2nd, 1776

MADAM, — You may be assured that nothing would give the General or me greater pleasure than to wait upon you at dinner this day, but his time is so totally engrossed by applications from one department and another, and [by the preparation of a R]eport, in which last I am also concerned and busy — as indeed all the Family are — that it is not in any of our powers to accept your polite and friendly Invitation, nor will it be in my power. I am persuaded, to thank you personally for the polite attention, you have shewn me since I came into this province. I must therefore beg your acceptance of them in this way and at this time, and that you will be assured that I shall hold them in gratefull remembrance. I am desired by the General to offer you his sincere thanks for your kind wishes and to present his compliments along with Mr. and Mrs. Custis's[2] and my own to you and Cols. Warren. With every sentiment of esteem I am and shall remane to be, your much obliged Friend and Hble. Servant.

[*Signature cut.*]

John Adams to James Warren

April 3, 1776

DEAR SIR, — As foreign Affairs become every day more interesting to Us no Pains should be spared to acquire a thorough Knowledge of them, and as the inclosed Extract contains some observa-

---

[1] Allen's account of his treatment and experiences is printed in 1 *Proceedings*, XVI. 69.
[2] John Parke Custis and Eleanor Calvert Custis.

tions which are new to me I thought it might not be uninteresting to you.

Howe has put 3000 Troops on board of Transports which lie, or at least lay last Saturday, at Staten Island. Whether this is a Feint or a serious Maneuvre, with Intention to go to the Eastern shore of Cheasapeak Bay, as they give out, I dont know or whether they aim at this City. I rather Suspect they mean another Course, i.e. up Hudsons River but Time will discover.

For God's sake and the Land's sake send along your Troops. They are wanted very much — I hope General Washington has informed you how much. Troops are now coming from North Carolina, Virginia and Maryland. If they come here We shall have scuffle for this City. The Languor of New England surprises me. If there had been half the Energy in those Governments that there was two years ago, Howe would now have been in Another World or the most miserable Man in this.

[*No signature.*]

JOHN ADAMS TO MERCY WARREN

April 16, 1776

MADAM, — Not untill yesterday's Post did your agreeable Favour of March the Tenth come to my Hands. It gave me great Pleasure, and altho in the distracted Kind of Life I am obliged to lead, I cannot promise to deserve a Continuance of so excellent a Correspondence, yet I am determined by Scribbling Something or other, be it what it may, to provoke it.

The Ladies I think are the greatest Politicians that I have the Honour to be acquainted with, not only because they act upon the Sublimest of all the Principles of Policy, viz., that Honesty is the best Policy, but because they consider Questions more coolly than those who are heated with Party Zeal and inflamed with the bitter Contentions of active public Life.

I know of no Researches in any of the sciences more ingenious than those which have been made after the best Forms of Government, nor can there be a more agreeable Employment to a benevolent Heart. The Time is now approaching when the Colonies will find themselves under a Necessity, of engaging in Earnest in this great and indispensible Work. I have ever Thought it the most difficult and dangerous Part of the Business Americans have to do in this mighty Contest, to contrive some Method for the Colonies to glide insensibly, from under the old Government, into a peaceable and contented submission to new ones. It is a long Time since this Opinion was conceived, and it has never been out of my Mind. My constant Endeavour has been to convince Gentlemen of the Necessity of turning their Thoughts to these subjects. At present, the sense of this Necessity seems to be general, and Measures are taking which must terminate in a compleat Revolution. There is Danger of Convulsions, but I hope, not great ones.

The Form of Government, which you admire, when its Principles are pure is admirable, indeed, it is productive of every Thing, which is great and excellent among Men. But its Principles are as easily destroyed, as human Nature is corrupted. Such a Government is only to be supported by pure Religion or Austere Morals. Public Virtue cannot exist in a Nation without private, and public Virtue is the only Foundation of Republics. There must be a positive Passion for the public good, the public Interest, Honour, Power and Glory, established in the Minds of the People, or there can be no Republican Government, nor any real Liberty: and this public Passion must be Superiour to all private Passions. Men must be ready, they must pride themselves, and be happy to sacrifice their private Pleasures, Passions and Interests, nay, their private Friendships and dearest Connections, when they stand in Competition with the Rights of Society.

Is there in the World a Nation, which deserves this Character? There have been several, but they are no more. Our dear Americans perhaps have as much of it as any Nation now existing, and New England perhaps has more than the rest of America. But I have seen all along my Life Such Selfishness and Littleness even in New England, that I sometimes tremble to think that, altho We are engaged in the best Cause that ever employed the Human Heart yet the Prospect of success is doubtful not for Want of Power or of Wisdom but of Virtue.

The Spirit of Commerce, Madam, which even insinuates itself

into Families, and influences holy Matrimony, and thereby corrupts the morals of families as well as destroys their Happiness, it is much to be feared is incompatible with that purity of Heart and Greatness of soul which is necessary for an happy Republic.

This Same Spirit of Commerce is as rampant in New England as in any Part of the World. Trade is as well understood and as passionately loved there as any where.

Even the Farmers and Tradesmen are addicted to Commerce; and it is too true that Property is generally the standard of Respect there as much as anywhere. While this is the Case there is great Danger that a Republican Government would be very factious and turbulent there. Divisions in Elections are much to be dreaded. Every man must seriously set himself to root out his Passions, Prejudices and Attachments, and to get the better of his private Interest. The only reputable Principle and Doctrine must be that all Things must give Way to the public.

This is very grave and solemn Discourse to a Lady. True, and I thank God, that his Providence has made me Acquainted with two Ladies at least who can bear it. I think Madam, that the Union of the Colonies, will continue and be more firmly cemented. But We must move slowly. Patience, Patience, Patience! I am obliged to invoke this every Morning of my Life, every Noon and every Evening.

It is surprising to me that any among you should flatter themselves with an Accommodation. Every appearance is against it, to an Attentive observer. The Story of Commissioners is a Bubble. Their real Errand is an Insult. But popular Passions and Fancies will have their Course, you may as well reason down a Gale of Wind.

You expect if a certain Bargain Should be complied with to be made acquainted with noble and Royal Characters. But in this you will be disappointed. Your Correspondent, has neither Principles, nor Address, nor Abilities for such Scenes, and others are as sensible of it, I assure you, as he is. They must be Persons of more Complaisance and Ductility of Temper as well as better Accomplishments for such great Things.

He wishes for nothing less, he wishes for nothing more than to retire from all public Stages and public Characters, great and small, to his Farm and his Attorney's Office and to both these he must return.

[*No signature.*]

SAMUEL ADAMS TO JAMES WARREN

PHILADELPHIA, *April* 16, 1776

MY DEAR SIR, — I have not yet congratulated you on the unexpected and happy Change of our Affairs in the removal of the Rebel Army from Boston. Our worthy Friend Major H[awley] in his Letter to me declines giving me Joy on this Occasion. He thinks it best to put off the Ceremony till the Congress shall proclaim Independency. In my Opinion, however, it becomes us to rejoyce and religiously to acknowledge the Goodness of the Supreme Being who in this Instance hath signally appeared for us. Our Countrymen are too wise to suffer this favorable Event to put them off their Guard. They will fortify the Harbour of Boston, still defend the Sea Coasts and keep the military Spirit universally alive. I perfectly agree with the Major in his Opinion of the Necessity of proclaiming Independency. The Salvation of this Country depends upon its being done speedily. I am anxious to have it done. Every Day's Delay trys my Patience. I can give you not the least Color of a Reason why it is not done. We are told that Commissioners are coming out to offer us such Terms of Reconciliation as we may with Safety accept of. Why then should we shut the Door? This is all Amusement. I am exceedingly disgusted when I hear it mentiond. Experience should teach us to pay no Regard to it. We know that it has been the constant Practice of the King and his Junto ever since this Struggle began to endeavor to make us believe their Designs were pacifick, while they have been meditating the most destructive Plans, and they insult our understandings by attempting thus to impose upon us even while they are putting these Plans into Execution. Can the King repeal or dispense with Acts of Parliament? Would he repeal the detestable Acts which we have complain of, if it was in his Power. Did he ever show a Disposition to do Acts of Justice and redress the Grievances of his Subjects? Why then do Gentlemen expect it? They do not scruple to own that he is a Tyrant; Are they then willing to be his Slaves and dependent upon a Nation so lost to all Sense of Liberty and Virtue as to enable and encourage him to act the Tyrant? This has been done by the British Nation against the Remonstrances of common Honesty and common Sense. They are now doing it and will continue to do it, until we break the Band of Connection and publickly avow an Independence. It is Folly for us to suffer ourselves any longer to be amusd. Reconciliation upon reasonable Terms is no Part of their Plan: The only Alternative is Independence or Slavery. Their Designs still are as they ever have been to subjugate us. Our unalterable Resolution should be to be free. They have attempted to subdue us by Force, but God be praisd! in vain. Their Arts may be more dangerous than their Arms. Let us then renounce all Treaty with them upon any score but that of total Seperation, and under God trust our Cause to our Swords. One of our moderate prudent Whigs would be startled at what I now write — I do not correspond with such kind of Men. You know I never overmuch admired them. *Their* Moderation has brought us to this Pass, and if they were to be regarded, they would continue the Conflict a Century. There are such moderate Men here, but their Principles are daily going out of Fashion. The Child Independence is now struggling for Birth. I trust that in a short time it will be brought forth and in Spite of Pharaoh all America shall hail the dignified Stranger.

[*No signature.*]

JOHN ADAMS TO JAMES WARREN

April 16, 1776

DEAR SIR, — I agree with you in yours of 30 March in opinion that five Regiments are too Small a Force to be left with you, considering the Necessity of fortifying the Harbour, and the Danger there is that the Enemy may renew their Designs upon our Province. Am happy to learn that you have sent a Committee to view the Harbour of Boston and report the best Method of Securing it.

When this Report is made I beg it may be transmitted to me. I wish you could transmit to me a good Plan of the Harbour at the same Time, for I want to convince this Congress that that Harbour may be made as strong and impregnable as Gibraltar, that they may be induced to contribute somewhat to the Fortification of it. I have a great opinion of the Efficacy of Fire, both in Rafts and Ships, for the Defence of that Harbour, among the numerous Shoals and Narrows and the Multitudes of Islands. Will not Row Gallies be very usefull? Would not they dodge about among those Islands and hide themselves at one Time, and make themselves dangerous to a ship at another?

Batteries must not be omitted upon the Heights on the Islands. Nor must We forget to obstruct the Channell. I am a miserable Engineer, I believe, but I will not Scruple to expose my own Ignorance in this Usefull science for the Sake of throwing out any broken Hints for refreshing the Memories of others who know more. If I was to write a Letter to my little Tom[1] I should say something to him about fortifying Boston Harbour.

Your Letter to the President I have shewn to My Friends Mr. Adams and Mr. Gerry. It has puzzled me a little what to do with it; but We are all of opinion upon the whole that it will be most for your Honour to deliver it, and indeed for your Interest, for there will be too much Risque in trusting this office to any one you can employ at a Distance from you.

You inform me that the Council have appointed [Foster] and [Sullivan] Judges. What, sir, do you think must be my Feelings upon this Occasion? I wish you would acquaint me whether Mr. Reed has accepted, and what the Court intends to do, about the Commissions and Salaries of the Judges. Whether they are to lie at the Mercy of Coll. Thompson, Coll. Bowers and Mr. Brown of Abington.

This is a great Constitutional Point in which the Lives, Liberties, Estates, and Reputations of the people are concerned, as well as the Order and Firmness of Government in all its Branches, and the Morals of the People besides. I may be suspected of sinister and interested Views in this, but I will give any Man a Pension

[1] Thomas Boylston Adams (1772–1805).

out of my own private Fortune to take my Place. It is upon Principle, and from this Principle, let Major Hawley think of it as he may, I cannot depart.

You will learn the Exploits of our Fleet, before you get this. They have behaved as all our Forces behave by Sea and Land. Every day convinces us that our People are equal to every Service of War or Peace by Sea or Land.

You say the Sigh's for Independence are universal. You say too what I can scarcely believe, that *Moderation* and Timidity are at an End. How is this possible? Is Cunning at an End too — and Reserve — and hinting against a Measure that a Man dare not oppose directly or disapprove openly? Is trimming at an End too? and Duplicity? and Hypocrisy? If they are, I give you Joy, sir, of a group of Tyrants gone. But I have not yet Faith in all this. You deal in the Marvellous like a Traveller. As to the Sighs, what are they after? Independence? Have We not been independent these twelve Months, wanting Three days?

Have you seen the Privateering Resolves? Are not these Independence enough for my beloved Constituents? Have you seen the Resolves for opening our Ports to all Nations?[1] Are these Independence enough? What more would you have? Why Methinks I hear you say, We want to compleat our Form and Plan of Government. Why don't you petition Congress then for Leave to establish such a Form as shall be most conducive to the Happiness of the People? But you say, Why don't the Southern Colonies Seize upon the Government? That I can't answer — but by all We can learn they are about it, every where. We want a Confederation, you will say. True. This must be obtained. But we are united now, they say, and the Difference between Union and Confederation is only the same with that between an express and an implied Contract.

But We ought to form Alliances. With Whom? What Alliances? You don't mean to exchange British for French tyranny. No, You don't mean to ask the Protection of French Armies. No, we had better depend upon our own. We only Want commercial Treaties.

[1] The resolutions on privateering were adopted March 23, and those on trade, April 6. *Journals of the Continental Congress*, IV. 231, 257.

Try the Experiment without them. But France and England will part the Continent between them. Perhaps so, but both will have good luck to get it.

But you will say what is your own opinion of these Things? I answer, I would not tell you all that I have said, and written, and done in this Business for a shilling, because Letters are now a days jumpd after. Why don't your Honours of the General Court, if you are so unanimous in this, give positive Instructions to your own Delegates, to promote Independency. Don't blame your Delegates untill they have disobeyed your Instructions in favour of Independency. The S[outhern] Colonies say you are afraid.

[*No signature.*]

MERCY WARREN TO ABIGAIL ADAMS   ADAMS MSS.

WATERTOWN, *April* 17, 1776

If my dear friend required only a very long Letter to make it agreeable, I could Easily Gratify her, but I know there Must be Many More Requisits to make it pleaseing to her taste. If you Measure by lines, I can at once comply; if by Sentiment, I fear I shall fall short. But as a Curiosity seems to be awake with Respect to the Company I keep and the Manner of Spending My time, I will Endeavor to Gratify you. I arrived at my lodgings before dinner the day I left you: found an obligeing family, Convenient Room and in the Main an Agreeable Set of Lodgers. Next Morning I took a ride to Cambridge and waited on Mrs. W[ashingto]n, at a 11 o'clock, where I was Received with that politeness and Respect shown in a first interview among the well bred, and with the Ease and Cordiality of friendship of a Much Earlier date. If you wish to hear more of this Lady's Character, I will tell you the Complacency of her Manners Speaks at once the Benevolence of her heart, and her affability, Cander, and Gentleness Qualify her to soften the hours of private Life, or to Sweeten the Cares of the Hero, and Smooth the Rugged pains of War. I did not dine with her, tho Much Urged. She desired me to Name an Early hour in the Morning when She would send her Chariot and accompany me to see the deserted Lines of the Enemy and the Ruins of

Charleston, a Melancholy Sight, the last which Evinces the Barbarity of the Foe and leaves a deep impression of the Sufferings of that unhappy Town. Mr. Custice is the only Son of the Lady above described — a Sensible, Modest, agreeable Young Man. His Lady, a daughter of Coll. Calverts of Mariland, appears to be as [of] an Engaging Disposition, but of so Extrem Delicate a Constitution that it Deprives her as well as her friends of part of the pleasure which I am persuaded would result from her Conversation did she Enjoy a greater Share of Health. She is pritty genteel, Easey and agreeable, but a kind of Langour about her prevents her being sociable as some Ladies. Yet it is evident it is not owing to that want of Vivacity which Renders Youth agreeable, but to a want of health which a Little Clouds her Spirits. This family which Consists of about 8 or 9 was prevented dining with us the Tuesday following by an Alarm from Newport, but calld and took leave of us the Next day, when I own I felt that kind of pain which arises from Affections when the Object of Esteem is Seperated perhaps forever. After this I kept House a Week amusing Myself with My Book, My work, and Sometimes a Letter to an absent friend. My Next Visit was to Mrs. Morgan, but as you are acquainted with her I shall Not be particular with regard to her person or Manners. The Dr. and she dined with us last Saturday in Company with General Putnam's Lady. She is what is Commonly called a very Good kind of Woman, and Commands Esteem without the Graces of politeness, the Briliancy of Wit, or the Merits of peculiar Understanding above the Rest of her Sex, yet to be Valued for an Honest, unornamented, plain hearted friendship Discovered in her Deportment at the first acquaintance. All other Characters or Occurrences I shall leave for another oppertunity — only shall Mention a Lady who has been a Lodger in our family for a week past and has been a great addition to the Chearfulness and Good Humour of the family. It is a Mrs. Orn of Marblehead,[1] a well disposed pleasant agreeable Woman.

The more regard you Express for a friend of Mine, the Greater My Obligation. I have sent forward My Letter to Mr. Adams, but Suppose I should have No answer unless Stimulated by you.

[1] Both Azor and Joshua Orne were members of the House at this time.

Therefore when you write again you will not forget your affectionate,

MARCIA

P.S. I am very Glad to hear Coll. Quincy's family are well to whom my regards.

JOHN ADAMS TO JAMES WARREN

April 20th, 1776

Last evening a Letter was received by a Friend of yours, from Mr. John Penn, one of the Delegates from North Carolina, lately returned home to attend the Convention of that Colony, in which he informs, that he heard nothing praised in the Course of his Journey, but Common Sense and Independence. That this was the Cry throughout Virginia. That North Carolina were making great Preparations for War, and were determined to die poor and to die hard if they must die in Defence of their Liberties. That they had repealed, or should repeal their Instructions to their Delegates against Independence. That South Carolina had assumed a Government, chosen a Council, and John Rutledge, Esqr., President of that Council, with all the Powers of a Governor; that they have appointed Judges, and that Drayton[1] is Chief Justice. "In short, sir," says this Letter, "the Vehemence of the Southern Colonies is such as will require the Coolness of the Northern Colonies, to restrain them from running to Excess."

Inclosed you have a little Pamphlet, the Rise and Progress of which you shall be told. Mr. Hooper and Mr. Penn of North Carolina received from their Friends in that Colony very pressing Instances to return home and attend the Convention, and at the Same Time to bring with them every Hint they could collect concerning Government.

Mr. Hooper applied to a certain Gentleman,[2] acquainted him with the Tenor of his Letters, and requested that Gentleman to give him his sentiments upon the subject. Soon afterwards Mr. Penn applied to the Same Gentleman and acquainted him with the Contents of his Letters, and requested the Same Favour.

[1] William Henry Drayton (1742–1779). [2] John Adams.

THOUGHTS

ON

GOVERNMENT:

APPLICABLE TO

The PRESENT STATE

OF THE

AMERICAN COLONIES.

In a LETTER from a GENTLEMAN
To his FRIEND.

PHILADELPHIA,
PRINTED BY JOHN DUNLAP.
M,DCC,LXXVI.

JOHN ADAMS' TRACT
From the Ford collection in the New York Public Library

THOUGHTS

ON

GOVERNMENT

APPLICABLE TO

THE PRESENT STATE

OF THE

AMERICAN COLONIES.

In a LETTER from a GENTLEMAN
To his FRIEND.

By J. A. Esqr.

PHILADELPHIA, PRINTED;

BOSTON:
RE-PRINTED BY JOHN GILL, IN QUEEN-STREET.
M,DCC,LXXVI.

JOHN ADAMS' TRACT
From the Ford collection in the New York Public Library

The Time was very short. However the Gentleman thinking it an opportunity providentially thrown in his Way, of communicating Some Hints upon a subject which seems not to have been sufficiently considered in the Southern Colonies, and so of turning the Thoughts of Gentlemen that Way, concluded to borrow a little Time from his Sleep and accordingly wrote with his own Hand, a Sketch, which he copied, giving the original to Mr. Hooper and the Copy to Mr. Penn, which they carried with them to Carolina. Mr. Wythe getting a sight of it, desired a Copy which the Gentleman made out from his Memory as nearly as he could. Afterwards Mr. Serjeant of New Jersey requested another, which the Gentleman made out again from Memory, and in this he enlarged and amplified a good deal, and sent it to Princetown. After this Coll. Lee, requested the same Favour, but the Gentleman having written amidst all his Engagements five Copies, or rather five sketches, for no one of them was a Copy of the other, which amounted to Ten Sheets of Paper, pretty full and in a fine Hand, was quite weary of the office. To avoid the Trouble of writing any more he borrowed Mr. Wythe's Copy and lent it to Coll. Lee, who has put it under Types and thrown it into the shape you see.[1] It is a Pity it had not been Mr. Serjeant's Copy, for that is larger and more compleat, perhaps more correct. This is very incorrect, and not truly printed. The Design however is to mark out a Path, and putt Men upon thinking. I would not have this Matter communicated.

I think by all the Intelligence We have that North Carolina Virginia, Maryland, and New Jersey will erect Governments, before the Month of June expires. And, if New York should do so too, Pennsylvania, will not neglect it — at least I think so.

There is a particular Circumstance relative to Maryland, which you will learn e'er long, but am not at Liberty to mention at present, but will produce important Consequences in our favour, I think.

But, after Governments shall be assumed, and a confederation formed, We shall have a long obstinate and bloody War to go

---

[1] *Thoughts on Government: applicable to the present State of the American Colonies.* Phila., 1776, and reprinted in Boston.

through and all the Arts, and Intrigues of our Enemies as well as the Weakness and Credulity of our Friends to guard against.

A Mind as vast as the Ocean or Atmosphere is necessary to penetrate and comprehend all the intricate and complicated Interests which compose the Machine of the Confederate Colonies. It requires all the Philosophy I am Master of, and more than all, at Times to preserve that Serenity of Mind and Steadiness of Heart which is necessary to watch the Motions of Friends and Enemies, of the Violent and the Timid, the Credulous and the dull, as well as the Wicked.

But if I can contribute ever so little towards preserving the Principles of Virtue and Freedom in the World my Time and Life will be not ill spent.

A Man must have a wider Expansion of Genius than has fallen to my share to see to the End of these great Commotions. But on such a full Sea are We now afloat that We must be content to trust to Winds and Currents with the best Skill We have under a kind Providence to land us in a Port of Peace, Liberty and Safety.

[*No signature.*]

JOHN ADAMS TO JAMES WARREN

April 22, 1776

The Management of so complicated and mighty a Machine, as the United Colonies, requires the Meekness of Moses, the Patience of Job and the Wisdom of Solomon, added to the Valour of David.

They are advancing by slow but sure Steps, to that mighty Revolution, which You and I have expected for Some Time. Forced Attempts to accellerate their Motions, would have been attended with Discontent and perhaps Convulsions.

The News from South Carolina has aroused and animated all the Continent. It has Spread a visible Joy, and if North Carolina and Virginia should follow the Example, it will spread through all the rest of the Colonies like Electric Fire.

The Royal Proclamation, and the late Act of Parliament have convinced the doubting and confirmed the timorous and wavering.

The two Proprietary Colonies only are still cool, But I hope a few Weeks will alter their Temper.

I think, it is now the precise Point of Time for our Council and House of Representatives either to proceed to make such Alterations in our Constitution as they may judge proper, or to Send a Petition to Philadelphia for the Consent of Congress to do it. It will be considered as fresh Evidence of our Spirit and Vigour, and will give Life and Activity and Energy to all the other Colonies. Four Months ago, or indeed at any Time since you assumed a Government, it might have been disagreeable and perhaps dangerous; but it is quite otherwise now. Another Thing, if you are so unanimous in the Measure of Independency and wish for a Declaration of it, now is the proper Time for you to instruct your Delegates to that Effect. It would have been productive of Jealousies, perhaps, and Animosities a few Months ago, but would have a contrary Tendency now. The Colonies are all at this Moment turning their Eyes that Way. Vast Majorities in all the Colonies now see the Propriety and Necessity of taking the decisive Steps, and those who are averse to it are afraid to Say much against it, and therefore Such an Instruction at this Time would comfort and cheer the Spirits of your Friends, and would discourage and dishearten your Enemies.

Coll. Whipple's Letters from New Hampshire are nearly in the Same Strain with yours to me, vizt. that all are now united in the great Question. His Letters inform him that even of the Protesters there is now but one left, who is not zealous for Independency.

I lament the Loss of Governor Ward exceedingly, because he had many Correspondents in Rhode Island, whose Letters were of service to Us, an Advantage which is now entirely lost.[1]

After all, my Friend, I do not att all Wonder, that so much Reluctance has been shewn to the Measure of Independency. All great Changes are irksome to the human Mind, especially those which are attended with great Dangers and uncertain Effects. No Man living can foresee the Consequences of such a Measure, and therefore I think it ought not to have been undertaken untill

---

[1] Samuel Ward, a delegate from Rhode Island, died March 25, 1776. *Journals of the Continental Congress*, IV. 236.

the Design of Providence by a Series of great Events had so plainly marked out the Necessity of it that he who runs might read.

We may feel a Sanguine Confidence of our Strength! Yet in a few Years it may be put to the Tryal.

We may please ourselves with the prospect of free and popular Governments, but there is great Danger that these Governments will not make Us happy. God grant they may. But I fear, that in every Assembly, Members will obtain an Influence, by Noise not Sense, by Meanness not Greatness, by Ignorance not Learning, by contracted Hearts not large Souls. I fear, too, that it will be impossible to convince and persuade People to establish wise Regulations.

There is one Thing, my dear Sir, that must be attempted and most Sacredly observed, or We are all undone. There must be a Decency, and Respect, and Veneration introduced for Persons in Authority, of every Rank, or We are undone. In a popular Government, this is the only Way of supporting order, and in our Circumstances, as our People have been so long without any Government att all, it is more necessary than in any other. The United Provinces were so sensible of this that they carried it to a burlesque Extream.

I hope your Election in May will be the most solemn and joyfull that ever took Place in the Province. I hope every Body will attend. Clergy and Laity should go to Boston, every Body should be gratefully pious and happy. It should be conducted with a solemnity that may make an Impression on the whole People.

[*No signature.*]

Abigail Adams to Mercy Warren

Braintree, *April* 27, 1776

I set myself down to comply with my Friend's request who I think seems rather low spiritted.

I did write last week, but not meeting with an early conveyance I thought the Letter of but little importance and tossed it away. I acknowledg my Thanks due to my Friend for the entertainment she so kindly afforded me in the Characters drawn in her Last Letter, and if coveting my Neighbour's Goods was not prohibited by the Sacred Law, I should be most certainly tempted to envy her the happy talent she possesses above the rest of her Sex, by adorning with her pen even trivial occurances, as well as Dignifying the most important. Cannot you communicate some of those Graces to your Friend and suffer her to pass them upon the World for her own, that she may feel a Little more upon an Equality with you? Tis true I often receive large packages from P[hiladelphi]a. They contain, as I said before, more Newspapers than Letters. Tho they are not forgotten, it would be hard indeed if absence had not some alleviations.

I dare say he writes to no one unless to Portia oftener than to your Friend, because I know there is no one besides in whom he has an equal confidence. His Letters to me have been generally short; but he pleads in Excuse the critical State of Affairs and the Multiplicity of avocations and says further that he has been very Busy, and writ near ten sheets of paper about some affairs which he does not chuse to Mention for fear of accident. He is very saucy to me in return for a List of Female Grievances which I transmitted to him.[1] I think I will get you to join me in a petition to Congress. I thought it was very probable our wise Statesmen would erect a New Government and form a New Code of Laws. I ventured to speak a Word in behalf of our Sex who are rather hardly Dealt with by the Laws of England, which gives such unlimited power to the Husband to use his Wife Ill. I requested that our Legislators would consider our case, and as all Men of Delicacy and Sentiment are averse to exercising the power they possess, yet as there is a Natural propensity in Humane Nature to domination, I thought the most Generous plan was to put it out of the power of the Arbitrary and tyrannick to injure us with impunity by establishing some Laws in our favour upon just and Liberal principals.

I believe I even threatned fomenting a Rebellion in case we were not considerd, and assured him we would not hold ourselves bound by any Laws in which we had neither a voice nor representation.

[1] Her letter of March 31, in *Familiar Letters*, 149.

In return he tells me he cannot but Laugh at my Extraordinary Code of Laws; that he had heard their Struggle had loosned the bonds of Government; that children and apprentices were disobedient; that Schools and Colledges were grown turbulent; that Indians slighted their Guardians, and Negroes grew insolent to their Masters. But my Letter was the first intimation that another Tribe more Numerous and powerfull than all the rest were grown discontented. This is rather too coarse a compliment, he adds, but that I am so sausy he won't blot it out.

So I have helpd the Sex abundantly; but I will tell him I have only been making trial of the disinterestedness of his Virtue and when weighd in the balance have found it wanting.

It would be bad policy to grant us greater power, say they, since under all the disadvantages we labour we have the assendancy over their Hearts.

And charm by accepting, by submitting sway.[1]

I wonder Apollo and the Muses could not have indulged me with a poetical Genious. I have always been a votary to her charms, but never could ascend Parnassus myself. I am very sorry to hear of the indisposition of your Friend. I am affraid it will hasten his return and I do not think he can be spaired.

> Though certain pains attend the cares of State
> A Good Man owes his Country to be great
> Should act abroad the high distinguishd part
> Or shew at least the purpose of his heart.

Good Night, my Friend, you will be so good as to remember me to our Worthy Friend, Mrs. W[inthrop]e when you see her, and write soon to your

PORTIA

JAMES WARREN TO JOHN ADAMS.   ADAMS MSS.

WATERTOWN, *April* 30, 1776.

MY DEAR SIR, — Were I as ceremonious as I suppose the ladies will be about their tea visits, after the late indulgence of Congress,

[1] The letter of Mrs. Adams did produce effect. See *John Adams to James Sullivan*, May 26, 1776. *Works of John Adams*, IX. 375.

I should hardly have taken up my pen at this time to disturb your repose, or interrupt your business. Are you sensible how seldom you write to me, or does it proceed from choice or necessity? My writing at this time is merely to discharge a duty of friendship. I have scarcely a single thing to say that you don't already know. No sort of intelligence is stirring here. We are still drudging on at the General Court, much in the old way. Several bills are gone and on their way through the Court. A confession bill, a fee bill,[1] a bill to alter the stile from King, etc., to Government and people of M. Bay,[2] Another for a test,[3] and some others of less importance. The attention of the Court has been fixed on fortifying the harbour and town of Boston.[4] We have in the beginning of the session chose a committee of both houses. All seem to be agreed in the importance of the measure, and to be very zealous in pursuing it. But if you was told how little is yet effected, you would certainly be astonished. The committee has from time to time represented to us that General Ward could spare no men to go on Noddle's Island, etc. We have therefore ordered one regiment of 728 men to be raised. This is not yet compleated, tho' we are about it, and some few have come in. We have some thoughts of another regiment to fortify below; but if you send us a spirited general to succeed General Ward upon his resignation, the troops here may do it without. I hope therefore you will send us one that is active, and will dare to go into his works when constructed, and fight upon occasion. I don't insist on his being a native of this Colony. Rhode Island or New Hampshire will suit me as well. Fort Hill is, however, at last got into a tolerable posture of defence, and the General has ordered some men to assist some we hire by the day at the Castle, and works are going on pretty well at Dorchester. No hulks are yet sunk: the people of Boston seem much against it; and whether it will be done or not I can't say.

---

1 *Mass. Acts and Laws*, 1776, 36.
2 *Journals*, April 18. *Mass. Acts and Laws*, 1776, 49. "I hear our jurors refuse to serve, because the writs are issued in the King's name." *Abigail Adams to John Adams*, April 11, 1776. *Familiar Letters*, 153. It is significant that the caption in the official volume of *Acts and Laws* changed abruptly on page 32 from "In the Sixteenth Year of the Reign of GEORGE the Third, King, &c." to "In the Year of our LORD, One Thousand seven Hundred and Seventy-six."
3 *Mass. Acts and Laws*, 1776, 36.   4 *Journals*, April 9, 22, 24.

We propose to rise this week. I hope we shall. I long to see my little farm, etc. I expect to hear from you before I leave this town on the subject of my last letter. Whoever is to command the army, or to pay them, I would call your attention to the good policy as well as justice of having some little money beforehand. When the payment of the militia that last reinforced the army is compleated, there will be little or nothing left; and the regiments here have been paid only for the month of February, though the General engaged to pay them monthly. This shortness of money has very much injured the service. The manufacture of salt petre continues to flourish abundantly; our powder makers find some difficulty in graining it. Some arrivals of powder and arms. A vessel belonging to Newbury is into Kennebeck with ten tons powder, ten tons sulphur, some cannon, etc. Mr. Gerry's brigantine at Bilboa, was there five weeks ago, the powder landed and safe. Her business was betrayed by a villain who was second mate. She was stopped by the Consul, and the merchant intends shipping the powder on other bottoms. My regards to all friends, especially Mr. Adams and Gerry. I am your sincere friend, etc.

We looked for a declaration of *independence*, and behold, an indulgence to drink *tea*.

Since writing the inclosed I have received a confirmation of the vessels being in to Kennebeck, and inclose an extract of a letter from the Master to Mr. Greenleaf, by which we may at least learn that they mean to exert all their power and malice this summer....

This minute we are advised that two ships have joined that one in Nantasket road; from them are re-landed a number of men on George's Island, who are fortifying it. From this I am convinced they have not taken their leave of Boston. We have not men enough left here, and we must have a good officer to command, or men will signify nothing. So many of ours are gone into the army, that we find the regiment we have ordered raises slowly. Mr. Read has resigned....

JAMES WARREN TO JOHN ADAMS. ADAMS MSS.

WATERTOWN, *May* 8, 1776

MY DEAR SIR, — Since my last we have the formidable accounts of the exertion of the powers and malice of Britain, which I suppose have reached you by this time, or will tomorrow. It is reported here that the Fleet and army are arrived at Halifax and are determined to attack this Colony again. This is confirmed by some deserters from the ship below, who say that they have heard the officers talk of their expectation of the fleet here. All serves only to confirm me in the sentiment I have ever had, that they would return here. Could it ever be supposed that any good policy would ever operate so strongly as revenge and the national pride, or rather the pride of the ministry, army, etc.? Would the loss of 10,000 men be of any consequence compared with a chance of repairing the disgrace suffered here? If I am right, and they come again, we are certainly in a miserable situation to receive them. Our men and arms gone to the southward, and our militia yet in a broken state. We should certainly have more of the Continental forces here and an officer of spirit to command them, or they will signify nothing. We are going on pretty well with the fortifications of Boston. The works at the Castle, Dorchester, Noddles Island, etc. are in good forwardness, and will soon be able to make a defence. We have ordered Hulks to be sunk, fire ships to be prepared, and two row gallies to be built. We do all we can with little or no assistance from the Continent. Is not Boston and this Colony of as much consequence as New York? Upon my word I think they are, and at least as much exposed. You must not be surprised if, after all our warning and care, you should hear some of the most considerable towns are destroyed, and the country ravaged before we shall be able to stop them. The continental army have got our tents, our arms, our men, our ammunition and cannon. We are in a worse situation than twelve months ago, but I will say no more on this subject, only that we have ordered another regiment to be raised of which Marshal [1] has the command,

[1] Thomas Marshall. See *Massachusetts Soldiers and Sailors in the Revolutionary War*, x. 265.

and a regiment consisting of seven companies of artillery to be commanded by T. Crafts, as lieutenant colonel, and Trott, as Major. I wish things had been more agreeable to you with regard to certain appointments in a certain Court, but they are going from bad to worse. So barren is our poor country that they have been obliged to appoint the most unsuitable man in the world.[1] He had no suspicion of it before hand. He reasonably supposed that many blockheads might be hit on before it came to his turn; he had therefore no opportunity to prevent it. He is therefore embarrassed beyond measure. He fears your displeasure; he is puzzled with the solicitations of friends, or those who would get clear of this matter; but his conscience tells him he will by accepting injure his country and expose himself. He must therefore decline, and you must excuse his conduct upon those principles. Nothing is yet done about the tenure of commissions, etc. You must therefore lie at the mercy of —— ——,[2] etc. But the major says things shall be set right. I thank you for the pamphlet. I like it very well in general. I am not certain I should agree with the author in three branches of the Legislature. I am at present inclined to think two properly formed may do as well.

I last Saturday evening received from the President your resolve accepting my resignation. This may be ranked among the minutiae, but it seems to me a little hurried and huddled, no determination what is to be done with the money in my hand. I have 40,000 dollars here which are wanted, but I have no authority to act till somebody supplies this place. Surely it must be supplied. I am glad to see the spirit in the southern governments. I am afraid they will all get the start of Congress in declarations of Independence. We are certainly unanimously ripe here for the grand revolution. I have tried to get instructions for you, but have been so sick for three weeks past, as not to be fit for executing anything, and the Major thinks we had better have the instructions of our towns for that, and the purpose of assuming government. We rise today or tomorrow, and are to have a full representation. As the law stood thirty freeholders and inhabitants were to send

[1] He is speaking of himself.
[2] It may be intended to represent three names, there being three broken lines.

one, and one hundred and twenty, two members. Being threatned to be overrun from the frontiers, the county of Essex stirred themselves and sent a petition well supported for a more equal representation. This produced a new act by which every two hundred and twenty may send three; three hundred and twenty, four, and so on.[1] So we are to have a house full.

I have just received yours of the 22d. The weather is so bad, that I keep house this afternoon. I sent it to the Major to read. I hope something will yet be done. I improve your letters to do a great deal of good. I have spoke for a copy of the report you mention and engaged, a plan of the harbour of Boston. If I am not disappointed, you will find them enclosed. Your letters hold up to view many important matters, and never fail to please me. I am entirely of your sentiments with regard to the advantages of some measures, and disadvantages of others; but time will only permit me to inform you that the only news we have is, that Captain Tucker, in the schooner Manly used to command, yesterday took two brigantines, one from Ireland with provisions and goods, and the other from Fial with wine, and got them safe into Lyn. One of them he took close by the light house, while the man-of-war fired at him. While I am writing, there is a firing of cannon below. What that is I know not. Perhaps I may give you more news in the morning. . . .

I am not fond of English or French tyranny, tho' if I must have one, I should prefer the last. I don't want a French army here, but I want to have one employed against Britain, and I doubt whether that will ever be done, till you make a more explicit declaration of independence than is in your privateering resolves, or those for opening the ports. You will never be thought in earnest, and fully determined yourselves, and to be depended on by others, till you go further.

Mr. Bowdoin has carried away some days ago the resolves and plan, and has disappointed you by not returning it.

[1] *Mass. Acts and Laws*, 1776, 57.

JOHN ADAMS TO JAMES WARREN

May 12, 1776

MY DEAR FRIEND,— Yours of April 30 was handed me yesterday. My Writing so seldom to you proceeds from Necessity not Choice, I assure you. I can sympathize with you in your ill Health, because I am always unwell myself— frail as I am, at best, I am feebler in this Climate than at home. The air here has no Spring, and My Mind is overborne with Burdens. Many Things are to be done here and many more to think upon by day and by night. Cares come from Boston, from Canada, from twelve other Colonies, from innumerable Indian Tribes, from all Parts of Europe and the West Indies. Cares arise in this City, and in the most illustrious Assembly; and Cares Spring from Colleagues— Cares enough! Don't you pity me? it would be some Comfort to be pitied; but I will scatter them all— Avaunt ye Demons!

An Address to the Convention of Virginia[1] has been published here as an Antidote to the popular Poison in *Thoughts on Government*. Read it and see the Difference of Sentiment. In New England, the *Thoughts on Government* will be disdained because they are not popular enough; in the Southern Colonies, they will be despised and desulted[2] because too popular.

But my Friend, between you and me, there is one Point, that I cannot give up. You must establish your Judges Salaries— as well as Commissions. otherwise Justice will be a Proteus. Your Liberties, Lives and Fortunes will be the Sport of Winds.

I don't expect, nor indeed desire that it should be attempted to give the Governor a Negative, in our Colony; make him President with a casting Voice. Let the Militia Act remain as it is.[3] But I hope you will make a Governor or President in May. Congress have passed a Vote with remarkable Unanimity for assuming Government in all the Colonies, which remains only for a Preamble;[4] you will see it in a few days. It is the Fate of Men and

1 By Carter Braxton, a delegate in the Congress from Virginia.
2 The word may have been intended for "dissected" or "distrusted."
3 *Mass. Acts and Laws*, 1776, 15.
4 The resolution was adopted May 12; the preamble, which was prepared by John Adams, was passed May 15. *Journals of the Continental Congress*, IV. 342, 357. It is given in Adams' letter of May 15, p. 245, *infra*.

Things which do great good that they always do great Evil too. "Common sense," by his crude ignorant Notion of a Government by one Assembly, will do more Mischief, in dividing the Friends of Liberty, than all the Tory Writings together. He is a keen Writer but very ignorant of the Science of Government. I see a Writer in one of your Papers, who proposes to make an Hotch Potch of the Council and House. If this is attempted, farewell. Who will be your Governor or President — Bowdoin or Winthrop or Warren? Don't divide. Let the Choice be unanimous, I beg. If you divide you will Split the Province with Factions. For God's Sake Caucass it, before Hand, and agree unanimously to push for the same Man. Bowdoin's splendid fortune would be a great Advantage at the Beginning. How are his Nerves and his Heart? If they will do, his Head and Fortune ought to decide in his favour.

The Office of Governor of the Massachusetts Bay Surrounded as it will be with Difficulties, Perplexities and Dangers of every Kind, and on every Side, will require the clearest and coolest Head and the firmest Steadyest Heart, the most immoveable Temper and the profoundest Judgment, which you can find any where in the Province. He ought to have a Fortune too, and extensive Connections. I hope that Mr. Bowdoins Health is such, that he will do. If not you must dispense with Fortune, and fix upon Winthrop, I think. I know not where to go, for a better — unless the Major General for the old Colony[1] can be agreed on with equal Unanimity, whom I should prefer to both of the other, provided an equal Number would agree to it. For I confess, my Rule should be to vote for the Man upon whom the Majority run, that the Choice might be as unanimous and respectable as possible. I dread the Consequences of Electing Governors, and would avoid every Appearance of and Tendency towards Party and Division, as the greatest Evil.

I have sent down a Resignation of my Seat at the Board, because this is not a Time if ever there was or can be one for Sinecures. Fill up every Place — they ought to be full. I believe I

[1] Warren himself. On May 8 the House of Representatives had chosen three Major Generals of militia, John Hancock, James Warren and Benjamin Lincoln. Warren declined, and Azor Orne was named in his place.

must resign the office, which the Board have assigned me for the same Reason, but I shall think a little more about that and take Advice.

[No signature.]

Samuel Adams to James Warren

PHILADA., *May* 12, 1776

MY DEAR SIR, — I had the pleasure of receiving your very friendly Letter of the 2d Instant by a Mr. Park. I can readily excuse your not writing to me so often as I wish to receive your Letters, when I consider how much you are engaged in the publick Affairs; and so you must be, while your Life is spared to your Country.

I am exceedingly concernd to find by your Letter, as well as those of my other Friends, that so little Attention has been given to an Affair of such weight, as the fortifying the Harbour of Boston. To what can this be attributed? Is it not wise to prevent the Enemies making Use of every Avenue, especially those which lead into the Capital of our Country? I hope that no little party Animosities can ever exist much less prevail in our Councils to obstruct so necessary a Measure. Such Contentions you well remember, that Fiend Hutchinson and his Confederates made it their constant Study to stir up between the Friends of the Colony in different parts of it in order to prevent their joynt Exertions for the Common Good. Let us with great Care avoid such Snares as our Enemies have heretofore laid for our Ruin, and which we have found by former Experience have proved too successful to their wicked purposes. This will, I think, be an important Summer. I confide therefore in the Wisdom of our Colony; and that they will lay aside the Consideration of smaller Matters for the present, and bend their whole Attention to the necessary Means for the Common Safety. I hope the late Scituation of Boston since the Enemy left it is by this time very much altered for the better. If not, it must needs be a strong Inducement to them to re-enter it, and whether we ought not by all means in our power to endeavor to prevent this, I will leave to you and others to judge.

.Yesterday the Congress resolvd into a Committee of the whole, to take under Consideration the Report of a former Committee, appointed to consider the state of the Eastern District, which comprehends New England. It was then agreed that the Troops in Boston should be augmented to 6000. The Question now lies before Congress and will be considered tomorrow. I am inclind to think the Vote will obtain.[1] But what will avail the ordering additional Battalions if men will not inlist? Do our Countrymen want Animation at a Time when all is at Stake! Your Presses have too long been silent. What are your Committees of Correspondence about? I hear Nothing of *Circular Letters*, of *joynt Committees*, etc., etc.

Such Methods have in times passd raisd the Spirits of the People, drawn off their Attention from *picking up pins*, and directed their Views to great objects. But not having had timely Notice of the Return of this Express, I must conclude, (earnestly praying for the Recovery of your Health). Very affectionately your

S. A.

Congress have orderd 400,000 Dollars to be sent to the Paymaster General at N.Y., for the Use of the Troops there and in Massachusetts Bay.

JOHN ADAMS TO JAMES WARREN

May 15, 1776

This Day the Congress has passed the most important Resolution that ever was taken in America.

It is as nearly as I can repeat it from Memory, in these Words.

Whereas his Britannic Majesty, in Conjunction with the Lords and Commons of Great Britain, has, by a late Act of Parliament, excluded the Inhabitants of these united Colonies from the Protection of his Crown; and Whereas No answer whatever has been given or is likely to be given, to the humble Petitions of the Colonies for Redress of their Grievances and Reconciliation with Great Britain; but on the Contrary, the whole Force of the Kingdom, aided by foreign Mercenaries, is to be exerted for our Destruction and Whereas it is irreconcileable to Reason

[1] The resolution as adopted, May 14, is in *Journals of the Continental Congress*, IV. 355.

and good Conscience, for the People of these Colonies to take the Oaths and Affirmations necessary for the Support of any Government under the Crown of Great Britain and it is necessary that the Exercise of every Kind of Authority under the said Crown should be totally Suppressed, and all the Powers of Government under the Authority of the People of the Colonies exerted for the Preservation of internal Peace, Virtue and good order, as well as to defend our Lives, Liberties and Properties, from the hostile Invasions and cruel Depredations of our Enemies, therefore

Resolved — that it be recommended to the several Assemblies and Conventions to institute such Forms of Government as to them shall appear necessary, to promote the Happiness of the People.[1]

This Preamble and Resolution are ordered to be printed and you will see them immediately in all the News Papers upon the Continent.

I shall make no Comments, upon this important and decisive Resolution.

There remains, however, a great deal of Work to be done besides the Defence of the Country. A Confederation must be now pursued with all the Address, Assiduity Prudence, Caution, and yet Fortitude and Perseverance, which those who think it necessary are possessed of. It is the most intricate, the most important, the most dangerous and delicate Business of all. It will require Time, We must be patient. Two or three days We have spent in Considering the state of the Massachusetts Bay. Congress have at last voted that the Five Battallions now in that Province be recruited to their full Complements and that three Battallions more be forthwith raised.[2] The Province has raised one, lately as I am informed. You will have nothing to do, but return the Names of the Field Officers to Congress and have continental Commissions for them. The other two Battallions may be raised in Mass. Bay, Connecticutt and New Hampshire, in what Proportions is not determined. Congress have voted that a Major General and a Brigadier General be sent to Boston.[3] Who they will be I know not — Gates and Mifflin, I hope, but cant promise.[4]

1 Some verbal differences from the version in the *Journals* may indicate that Adams used the preamble as originally written, before being amended in the Congress.
2 *Journals of the Continental Congress*, IV. 355.
3 *Ib.*, 356. The choice was to rest with Washington.
4 On May 16 Congress elected them Major General and Brigadier General respectively.

This Letter you may communicate if you think it necessary. I am, sir, your Affectionate Friend

[*No signature.*]

JOHN ADAMS TO JAMES WARREN

May 18, 1776

MY DEAR SIR,—Yours of 8 May received this Morning, and am, as I ever have been, much of your Opinion that the Enemy would return to the Massachusetts if possible. They will probably land at Hingham or Braintree, or somewhere to the Northward of Boston, not make a direct Attempt upon Boston itself, the next Time. I hope no Pains, no Labour or expense will be neglected to fortify the Harbour of Boston however.

Your Militia you say is in a broken state, but don't explain what you mean. I was in hopes that the late Militia Law had put them in a good Condition. You must depend upon them chiefly. We have been labouring here to procure you Some Assistance, and have obtained a Vote, that the 5 Battallions now with you be filled up, and three Additional ones raised, two in Mass. one in Connecticutt.[1] A Major General and Brigadier are to go to Boston. You must not hesitate at any Thing for your own Defence. New York and Canada will take an infinite Expense. We did our best, but could procure no more at present. If an Impression should be made on you, the Continent will interpose; but they never will believe it untill it takes Place.

This Day has brought us the Dismals from Canada — Defeated most ignominiously.[2] Where shall we lay the blame? America, duped and bubbled with the Phantom of Commissioners, has been fast asleep, and left that important Post undefended, unsupported.

The Ministry have caught the Colonies, as I have often caught a Horse, by holding out an empty Hat, as if it was full of Corn, or as many a Sportsman has shot Woodcocks, by making an old Horse Stalk before him, and hide him from the Sight of the Bird.

---

[1] *Journals of the Continental Congress*, IV. 360.
[2] The *Journals* record the receipt of three letters from the commissioners to Canada.

Nothing has ever put my Patience to the Tryal so much as to see Knaves imposing upon Fools, by such Artifices. I wash my Hands of this Guilt. I have reasoned, I have ridiculed, I have fretted and declaimed against this fatal Delusion, from the Beginning.

But a Torrent is not to be impeded by Reasoning, nor a Storm allayed by Ridicule. In my situation, altho I have not and will not be restrained from a Freedom of Speech yet a Decorum must be observed, and ever has been by me. But I have often wished that all America knew as much as I do of the Springs of Action and the Motions of the Machine. I do not think it prudent, nor Safe, to write freely upon these Subjects even to my most faithfull Friends.

Providence has hitherto preserved us, and I firmly believe will continue to do so. But it gives me inexpressible Grief that by our own Folly and Wickedness We should deserve it so very ill as We do.

What shall We say of this scandalous Flight from Quebec? It seems to be fated that New England officers should not support a Character. Wooster is the Object now of Contempt and Detestation of those who ought to be the Contempt and Detestation of all America for their indefatigable Obstruction to every Measure which has been meditated for the Support of our Power in Canada. Our Province must find some Way of making better Officers and of engaging abler Men in her Councils as well as her Arms, or I know not what will be the Consequence. Instead of which she Seems to me to be contriving Means to drive every Man of real Abilities out of her service.

I hope you will not decline the Appointment you mention, however. Nothing would make me so happy as your Acceptance of that Place. I am extreamly unhappy to hear of your ill Health; hope that will mend. There is certainly no Man in the Province who would be so agreable to me. I cant bear the Thought of your refusing.

Rejoice to hear that my Friends, Crafts and Trott, are in the service. Will it do to promote my Pupil Austin?[1] His Genius is

---

[1] Jonathan Williams Austin, now a major. He was "dishonorably discharged" from the service November 13, 1776, and had not been promoted.

equal to any Thing. Would not promotion mend him of his Faults? Can nothing be done for Ward,[1] Aid de Camp and Secretary to General Ward? He is an honest, faithfull daring Man, I think, and sensible enough. He really deserves Promotion.

Is it possible to get in Boston Silver and Gold for the service in Canada? Our Affairs have been ruined there for Want of it and can never be retrieved without it. Pray let me know if any sum can be had in our Province.

I shall inclose you a News Paper, which when you have read send along to Braintree.

I am, and have been these twelve Months, fully of your Opinion that we have nothing to depend upon for our Preservation from Destruction, but the kind Assistance of Heaven to our own Union and vigorous Exertions. I was ripe therefore for as explicit Declarations as Language could express Twelve Months ago; but the Colonies seperately have neglected their Duty as much as the Congress, and We cannot march faster than our Constituents will follow Us. We dont always go quick enough to keep out of their Way.

JOHN ADAMS TO JAMES WARREN

May 20, 1776

MY DEAR SIR, — Every Post and every Day rolls in upon Us. Independence like a Torrent. The Delegates from Georgia made their Appearance this Day in Congress with unlimited Powers and these Gentlemen themselves are very firm.[2] South Carolina, has erected her Government and given her Delegates ample Powers, and they are firm enough. North Carolina have given theirs full Powers, after repealing an Instruction given last August against Confederation and Independence. This Days Post, has brought a Multitude of Letters from Virginia, all of which breath the same Spirit. They agree they shall institute a Government — all are agreed in this they say. Here are four Colonies to the

[1] Joseph Ward. He became Commissary General of Musters in 1777.
[2] Lyman Hall (1725-1790) and Button Gwinnett (*c.* 1732-1777). Their "powers" are printed in *Journals of Continental Congress*, IV. 367.

Southward who are perfectly agreed now with the four to the Northward. Five in the Middle are not yet quite so ripe; but they are very near it. I expect that New York will come to a fresh Election of Delegates in the Course of this Week, give them full Powers, and determine to institute a Government.

The Convention of New Jersey, is about Meeting and will assume a Government.

Pennsylvania Assembly meets this Day and it is said will repeal their Instruction to their Delegates which has made them so exceedingly obnoxious to America in General, and their own Constituents in particular.

We have had an entertaining Maneuvre this Morning in the State House Yard. The Committee of the City summoned a Meeting at Nine O'Clock in the State House Yard to consider of the Resolve of Congress of the fifteenth instant. The Weather was very rainy, and the Meeting was in the open air like the Comitia of the Romans, a Stage was erected, *extempore* for the Moderator, and the few orators to ascend — Coll. Roberdeau [1] was the Moderator; Coll. McKean,[2] Coll. Cadwallader [3] and Coll. Matlack [4] the principal orators. It was the very first Town Meeting I ever saw in Philadelphia and it was conducted with great order, Decency and Propriety.

The first step taken was this: the Moderator produced the Resolve of Congress of the 15th inst. and read it with a loud stentorian Voice that might be heard a Quarter of a Mile. "Whereas his Britannic Majesty, etc." As soon as this was read, the Multitude, several Thousands, some say, tho so wett rended the Welkin with three Cheers, Hatts flying as usual, etc.

Then a Number of Resolutions were produced, and moved, and determined with great Unanimity. These Resolutions I will send you as soon as published. The Drift of the whole was that the Assembly was not a Body properly constituted, authorized, and qualified to carry the Resolve for instituting a new Government into Execution and therefore that a Convention should be called. And at last they voted to support and defend

---

1 Daniel Roberdeau (1727–1795).
3 John Cadwalader (1742–1786).

2 Thomas McKean (1734–1817).
4 Timothy Matlack (1730–1829).

the Measure of a Convention, at the Utmost Hazard and at all Events, etc.

The Delaware Government, generally, is of the same Opinion with the best Americans, very orthodox in their Faith and very exemplary in their Practice. Maryland remains to be mentioned. That is so eccentric a Colony — sometimes so hot, sometimes so cold; now so high, then so low — that I know not what to say about it or to expect from it. I have often wished it could exchange Places with Hallifax. When they get agoing I expect some wild extravagant Flight or other from it. To be sure they must go beyond every body else when they begin to go.

Thus I have rambled through the Continent, and you will perceive by this state of it, that We can't be very remote from the most decisive Measures and the most critical events. What do you think must be my Sensations when I see the Congress now daily passing Resolutions, which I most earnestly pressed for against Wind and Tide Twelve Months ago? and which I have not omitted to labour for a Month together from that Time to this? What do you think must be my Reflections, when I see the Farmer [1] himself now confessing the Falsehood of all his Prophecies, and the Truth of mine, and confessing himself, now for instituting Governments, forming a Continental Constitution, making Alliances, with foreigners, opening Ports and all that — and confessing that the defence of the Colonies, and Preparations for defence have been neglected, in Consequence of fond delusive hopes and deceitfull Expectations?

I assure you this is no Gratification of my Vanity.

The gloomy Prospect of Carnage and Devastation that now presents itself in every Part of the Continent, and which has been in the most express and decisive nay dogmatical Terms foretold by me a thousand Times, is too affecting to give me Pleasure. It moves my keenest Indignation. Yet I dare not hint at these Things for I hate to give Pain to Gentlemen whom I believe sufficiently punished by their own Reflections.

[*No signature.*]

[1] Dickinson.

JAMES WARREN TO JOHN ADAMS.   ADAMS MSS.

WATERTOWN, *June* 2, 1776

My DEAR SIR, — I received yours of the 20th of May with the pamphlets inclosed. I am much obliged to you for them. I am quite satisfied that you have wrote to me as often as your situation would admit of, that your cares are great and press on you from many quarters. I never suspected your friendship. I pity you as much as you can wish a friend to do, and admire your spirit and resolute perseverance in the publick cause. I have read and see the difference of sentiment in the two pamphlets. The *Thoughts on Government* are far from being disdained in New England. They were admired here. Very few exceptions are made by any body; the only one of any consequence that I have heard is that the author seems rather inclined to a negative in the third branch, which is hardly popular enough for our climate, poor and sterile as it is. I believe the author never expected it would comport with the Monarchick and aristocratic spirit of the South. Whether it is best there should be a perfect similarity in the form and spirit of the several governments in the colonies, provided they are all independant of Britain, is a question I am not determined on. For some reasons it may be best for us there should be a difference. I therefore consider the address to the Convention of Virginia with the more indifference, as it may (if successful) neither injure the publick or us.

I regretted my not being able to write by Mr. Winthrop, who left this place two days ago. You will have by him a list of our new House, and I suppose a list of the Council chosen, as he promised me not to go without it. Colonel Orne and Danielson [1] refused. We chose Eldad Taylor and Colonel Thayer [2] in their room. You will find in the House more abilities, tho' perhaps not more zeal for the present system of politicks than in the last, and you will see in the list of councillors some that I did not vote for. We have had yet nothing before us to determine what we are to expect from the conduct of this new House. The election took us two entire days, and controverted elections filled up the rest of the

[1] Azor Orne and Timothy Danielson.   [2] Ebenezer Thayer, junior.

last week. We yesterday sent home the Salem members for the irregularity of the proceedings of the town in their choice.[1] Colonel Palmer is again in the House, I dare say you are informed how.

I presume as we are now at liberty to establish a form of government, we shall soon take up that matter. I shall do everything in my power to promote unanimity in the choice of a Governor or President, let the general voice be as it may. I thank you for your partiality. I could pitch on a much more suitable person than either of the three you mention, by going as far as Philadelphia, tho' what we should do without him there I can't tell. Tis our misfortune that the same men can't be in two places at the same time. I shall write you as soon as any thing on this subject takes place. The piece you mention published in our papers is in total oblivion; so desire you not to take your leave of us. I shall do everything in my power to have the salaries and commissions of the judges established. I have long been convinced of the necessity of it, and I am sure we can do nothing more advantageous to our internal police. The nerves of one of the gentlemen you mention are weak, owing perhaps to his state of health. His heart, I believe, is good, tho' not so decisively zealous as I could wish, perhaps owing to his splendid fortune. His head is undoubtedly good.

We have no news, frequent rumours of battles and victories in Canada since our late misfortune there, but nothing to be depended on. I am mortified by the little zeal and readiness shewn by our country men to enter into the service. Neither Marshal's, Whitney's or Craft's regiments are yet half full. What hopes can we entertain that the five old battalions left here will be filled up, or the two new ones raised. Can you advise as to give them a bounty by way of encouragement, or should you disapprove of it? It certainly would be very advantageous to us to have them, and our delegates deserve our thanks for their exertions on this occasion. But how to get them is the question. I suppose it would not do to have the two regiments we are now raising converted

---

[1] "It being represented to the House, that at the election of the gentlemen returned from *Salem*, the electors voted by kernels of corn and pease. It was moved that the sense of the House be taken, whether their election was made agreeable to law, and the question being put, it passed in the negative." *Journals of the House of Representatives* (Mass.), 1776, 10.

into Continental regiments. I can't account for the difficulties we have in raising men. Great numbers are indeed gone from us, and the southern governments have agents here inlisting seamen for their particular services, with full wages and large bounties. I fear therefore you will find it difficult to man your ships. You should attend to it without delay.

We have a promising season, fine showers, the crops look flourishing, tho' the weather has been cooler than usual. Mr. Winthrop has with him my accounts. I expect there will be some small deficiency, owing to the multiplicity of business in that office, and the hurry and crowd we have been obliged to do it in. I have directed him to charge for a clerk, as it was impossible to execute it without one, and to charge the expences of going to Philadelphia to settle account, as I am out of pay. I hope all these will be allowed me. The army here are in distress for want of money. I have run the venture at the solicitations of General Ward to pay several sums since I had notice that my resignation was accepted. I hope the publick advantage and the General's solicitations will justify my conduct. I have desired Mr. Winthrop to call on you for any assistance he may have occasion for. I know you will give it to him, and I tho't I need make no apology for the freedom....

I never yet congratulated you on the almost miraculous interposition of Providence in sending us the prize ship carried into Boston. I do it now. The gallant defence made by our small vessels against the men of war boats is perhaps as noble a one as any this war. I can't give you an exact account of the loss on their side, but I believe in killed and wounded little short of a hundred. ... You must not think of a resignation; we shall be ruined if you do.

JAMES WARREN TO JOHN ADAMS. ADAMS MSS.

WATERTOWN, *June* 5th, 1776

MY DEAR SIR, — The inclosed letter was sealed to go by the last Post, but I unluckily missed it I have now an opportunity to inclose one from Braintree. Doctor Church is arrived here. Is not your resolve relative to him somewhat extraordinary? I fear the People will kill him if at large. The night before last he went to lodge at Waltham, was saved by the interposition of the selectmen but by jumping out of a chamber window and flying. His life is of no great consequence, but such a step has a tendency to lessen the confidence of the people in the doings of Congress.

A large Sugar Ship from Jamaica with 300 hhds. sugar, 80 puncheons rum, some Madeira wine, etc., etc., is taken and got into the vineyard in her way to Bedford. It is said that four or five others are taken by two Privateers who took this. What Privateers they are I cant learn.

Must not something be done to prevent British Property being covered by the West Indians? We shall loose our Labour, and discourage our Seamen. Why should not all English property going to Britain be liable to capture? this matter must be considered. We should fight them on equal terms. We have a number of Seamen here supported at your expence. If your Generosity and Civilized Sentiments prevent, won't good policy dictate recourse to the *Lex talionis?* They are wanted. you will find the want of them when you man your ships.

[*No signature.*]

SAMUEL ADAMS TO JAMES WARREN

PHILADA., *June* 6, 1776

MY DEAR SIR, — I have for some time past been expecting to visit my Friends in New England which has made me the less sollicitous of writing to them, but Business of the most interesting Importance has hitherto detaind me here. Our Affairs in Canada have of late worn a displeasing Aspect, but Measures have been adopted which I trust will repair Misfortunes and set Matters right in that Quarter. This will, in my Opinion, be an important Summer, productive of great Events which we *must* be prepard to meet. If America is virtuous She will vanquish her Enemies and establish her Liberty. You know my Temper. Perhaps I may be too impatient. I have long wishd for the Determination of some momentous Questions. If Delay shall prove mischeivous I shall have no Reason to reflect upon myself; Every one here knows what my Sentiments have been. However, tomorrow a Motion will be made,[1] and a Question I hope decided, the most important that was ever agitated in America. I have no doubt but it will be decided to *your* satisfaction. This being done, Things will go on in the right Channel and our Country will be saved. The Bearer waits. Adieu.

S. A.

Let me intreat you, my Friend, to exert your Influence to prevent unnecessary Questions in the Assembly which may cause Contention.[2] Now if ever Union is necessary — Innovations may well enough be put off, till publick Safety is secured.

John Adams to James Warren

June 9, 1776

I shall address this to you as Speaker, but you may be Councillor, or Governor, or Judge, or any other Thing, or nothing but a good Man, for what I know. Such is the Mutability of this World.

Upon my Word I think you use the World very ill to publish and send abroad a Newspaper since the 29 May without telling Us one Word about the Election, where it was held, who preached the sermon,[3] or etc., etc. I write this in haste only to inclose to you a little Treatise upon Fire Ships. It may be sending Coals to New Castle, but it appears to me of such Importance that I thought myself bound to procure and send it, least this Art should not be understood among you. This Art carries Terror and Dismay along with it, and the very Rumour of Preparations in this Kind may do you more service than many Battalions.[4]

---

1 "Certain resolutions respecting independency being moved and seconded," etc. The resolutions are in *Journals of the Continental Congress*, v. 425. They are in the writing of Richard Henry Lee, and were seconded by John Adams. The endorsement on the original, printed in the *Journals*, gives an interesting glimpse of the proceedings of Congress upon the motion.

2 Warren had been re-elected Speaker of the House.

3 The sermon was preached by Rev. Samuel West, of Dartmouth, May 29, 1776. His text was Titus, III. 1.

4 This may refer to a MS. The only printed work of the kind was a translation by Major Lewis Nicola of Chevalier de Clairac's *L'Engenieur de Campagne*, to which was added "A short Treatise on Sea Batteries." It was issued by Robert Aitken, of Philadelphia, in 1776.

I am not easy about Boston and have taken all the Pains in my Power with G. Washington, to engage him to send G[ates] and M[ifflin] there; but he is so sanguine and confident that no attempt will be made there, that I am afraid his security will occasion one.

The News Papers inclosed when you have read them please to send them to the Foot of Penn's Hill.

JOHN ADAMS TO JAMES WARREN

PHILADELPHIA, *June* 16, 1776

DEAR SIR, — Your Favours of June 2d and 5th are now before me. The address to the Convention of Virginia makes but a small Fortune in the World. Coll. Henry in a Letter to me expresses an infinite Contempt of it, and assures me that the Constitution of Virginia will be more like the *Thoughts on Government*.[1] I believe, however, they will make the Election of their Council, Septennial. Those of Representatives to Governor annual. But I am amazed to find an Inclination so prevalent throughout all the southern and middle Colonies to adopt Plans, so nearly resembling, that in the *Thoughts on Government*. I assure you, untill the Experiment was made I had no adequate Conception of it. But the Pride of the haughty must I see come down, a little in the South.

You suppose "it would not do to have the two Regiments you are now raising converted into continental Battallions." But why? Would the officers or Men have any objection? If they would not, Congress would have none. Indeed this was what I expected and intended when the Measure was in Agitation. Indeed I thought, that as our Battalions with their arms were carried to N. York and Canada in the Service of the United Colonies, the Town of Boston, and the Province ought to be guarded against Danger by the united Colonies.

You have been since called upon for Six Thousand Militia for Canada and New York. How you will get the Men I know not. The Small Pox, I suppose will be a great Discouragement.[2] But

[1] Henry's letter, dated May 20, is in *Life, Correspondence and Speeches of Patrick Henry*, II. 412.
[2] "The reigning Subject is the Small Pox. Boston has given up its Fears of an invasion and is busily employed in communicating the Infection. Straw beds and Cribs are daily

We must maintain our Ground in Canada. The Regulars, if they get full Possession of that Province, and the Navigation of St. Lawrence River above Dechambeault at least above Mouth of the Sorrell, will have nothing to interrupt their Communication with Niagara, Detroit, Michilimachinac; they will have the Navigation of the five great Lakes quite as far as the Mississippi River; they will have a free Communication with all the numerous Tribes of Indians, extending along the Frontiers of all the Colonies, and by their Trinketts and Bribes will induce them to take up the Hatchett, and spread Blood and Fire among the Inhabitants by which Means, all the Frontier Inhabitants will be driven in upon the middle Settlements, at a Time when the Inhabitants of the Seaports and Coasts, will be driven back by the British Navy. Is this Picture too high coloured? Perhaps it is; but surely We must maintain our Power, in Canada.

You may depend upon my rendering Mr. Winthrop all the service in my Power.

I believe it will not be long before all Property belonging to British Subjects, Whether in Europe, the W. Indies, or elsewhere will be made liable to Capture. A few Weeks may possibly produce great Things. I am, etc.

[*No signature.*]

JAMES WARREN TO JOHN ADAMS.   ADAMS MSS.

PLYMOUTH, *July* 10th, 1776

MY DEAR SIR, — I have for some time past been at Home in daily expectation of the Court's riseing. It has however continued setting till this time. What they have lately been employed about I am not able to say — I believe nothing very important. A very large Committee are out to raise the men, I mean the 5000 requested by Congress for Canada and York. I hope they will by the large Encouragement of £7. for Canada, and £3. for York, with some additional Bounty from Individuals in the several

carted into the Town. That ever prevailing Passion of following the Fashion is as Predominant at this time as ever. Men, Women and Children eagerly crowding to innoculate is, I think, as modish as running away from the Troops of a barbarous George was the last year." *Hannah Winthrop to Mercy Warren*, July 8, 1776. MS.

towns, be soon raised, and sent forward. The Court have spent much more time about this business than was consistent with the exigency of the service. There was no objection to a compliance with the Requisition; but the manner of doing it, or rather the places from whence they should be taken have occasioned the delay. Indeed the Levies on particular Towns fall very heavy. A much greater proportion of our men are in service than Congress seems to be aware off. How we are to get the 1500 now called for I can't tell, nor do I know how Congress will like the Bounties given already; but it was thought impossible to raise them without a large encouragement, especially at this season of the year.

I had a few days ago the pleasure of your favour of the 9th June. I presume the Papers before this have informed you that I am in the same station you left me in, and I can inform you that I am in that only; and if it be my *ne plus ultra*, perhaps it can't be said of me as it may of some others that I have not my deserts. Calls for men and other matters of the same kind have hitherto prevented our doing any thing about the matter of Government. Our Recess will be short, and if we are not pressed with such matters when we meet next I presume we shall go upon it. I congratulate you on the discovery of the plot at New York. I hope it will do great service.[1] I expect soon to hear of some great events from that quarter. If they should be favourable to us, what will they do next? We have but little news here. Now and then a prize from the West Indies is sent in. Last Saturday got into Cape Ann two prizes taken by a small Sloop belonging to four or five persons in and about Boston; one from Jamaica, a three decker, with 400 hhds. sugar, 200 hhds. rum, 30 bales cotton, etc., etc.; the other from Antegua with 400 hhds. rum. This sloop could have taken another ship but had not men to bring her off, and so let her go. When are we to hear of your proceedings on the first Instant what Alliances, and Confederations have you agreed on? I want to see some French Men of War on the coast. Our borders seem to be in a state of peace and tranquility; how long they will continue so I

[1] See *Minutes of the Trial and Examination of Certain Persons, in the Province of New York, charged with being engaged in a conspiracy against the Authority of the Congress, and the Liberties of America.* London, 1776.

know not. The Small Pox prevails, and is scattered about the country. In Boston they have given up all thoughts of stopping it, and everybody is inoculating. I wrote to Mr. Gerry a few days ago, and among other things about some of my private affairs, in the paymaster's office. I desired him to communicate to you, so shan't trouble you with a repetition. I will thank you for your assistance. If I can't help myself I must loose this money, but it will be a hard case. I did great services to the Army in and out of this office, which I executed with diligence, oeconomy, and integrity, and you will see this loss was sustained in Winthrop's hands. I have no reason to question his integrity. My regards to all friends. I am yours, etc.

[*No signature.*]

P.S. I see advertised in one of the Philadelphia papers a piece on Husbandry.[1] If it is well executed and of any consequence, shall be obliged to you to purchase and send me one.

JOHN ADAMS TO JAMES WARREN

July 15, 1776

DEAR SIR, — I have Time only to tell you that I am yet alive and in better Spirits than Health.

The News you will learn from my very worthy Friend Gerry. He is obliged to take a Ride for his Health, as I shall be very soon, or have none. God grant he may recover it, for he is a Man of immense Worth. If every Man here was a Gerry, the Liberties of America would be safe against the Gates of Earth and Hell.

We are in hourly Expectation of Sober Work at New York. May Heaven grant Us Victory, if We deserve it; if not Patience, Humility, and Pennitence under Defeat. However I feel pretty confident and Sanguine that We shall give as good an Account of them this Year as we did last.

[*No signature.*]

[1] Arthur Young's *Rural Oeconomy: or Essays on the Practical Parts of Husbandry*, printed at Philadelphia in 1776, by James Humphreys, Jr.

JAMES WARREN TO JOHN ADAMS. ADAMS MSS.

BOSTON, *July* 17th, 1776

MY DEAR SIR, — When you are informed that in the variety of changes that have taken place in this town, it is now become a Great Hospital for Inoculation, you will wonder to see a letter from me dated here; but so it is that the rage for inoculation prevailing here has whirled me into its vortex, and brought me with my *other self* into the croud of patients with which this town is now filled. Here is a collection of good, bad, and indifferent of all orders, sexes, ages and conditions, your good Lady and Family among the first. She will give you (I presume) such an account of herself, etc., as makes it unnecessary for me to say more on that head. She will perhaps tell you that this is the reigning subject of conversation, and that even politics might have been suspended for a time, if your Declaration of Independence, and some other political movements of yours had not reached us. The Declaration came on Saturday, and diffused a general Joy. Every one of us feels more important than ever; we now congratulate each other as Freemen. It has really raised our spirits to a tone beneficial to mitigate the malignity of the small pox, and what is of more consequence seems to animate and inspire every one to support and defend the Independency he feels. I shall congratulate you on the occasion and so leave this subject and go to one not quite so agreable. Congress have acted a part with regard to this Colony, shall I say cunning, or politic, or only curious, or is it the effect of agitation. Has the approach of Lord Howe had such an effect on the southern Colonies, that they have forgot the very Extensive Sea Coast we have to defend, the Armed Vessels we have to man from South Carolina to the northern limits of the United Colonies, that a large part of the Continental Army is made up from this Colony, that the General has not only got our men but our arms, and that they within two months ordered a reinforcement of three Battalions to the five already here. Lucky for us you did not give time to raise these before your other requisitions reached us, or we should have been stripped indeed. Don't the Southern Colonies think this worth defending, or do they think with half our men gone the remainder can defend it, with spears and darts, or with slings (as David slew Goliah). I was surprised to find the whole five Battalions called away. No determination as yet taken how their places shall be supplyed. The General Court are not setting, they were prorogued on Saturday; the Council have this matter under consideration. What can they do but call in the militia, or perhaps stop the last 1500 men called for to go to Canada if in their power. The works for the defence of this Town must not be abandoned; they must be defended with or without Continental assistance. Don't suppose that I am a preacher of sedition, or intend to be factious, or that the eruptive fever is now upon me. Neither of these is true. I shall suppress all sentiments of uneasiness but to you and some few who I have reason to suppose think of these matters in the same way, and determine to do and suffer any and every thing for the good of the whole; but I think, tho' the Grand Object will be York and Canada, and their principal Force there, we are not so safe as we ought to be.

I can give you little or no news. Two of our vessels have been brought too by a Man of War at sea, and the masters taken as they were told before Lord Howe, who told them he was bound directly to Philadelphia to settle with the Congress the unhappy dispute. He dismissed both the vessels and gave them paper to protect them against any or all cruizers, haveing first reprimanded one of them for the violation of Acts of Parliament in the illicit trade at St. Petres, from which place he then came with French commodities. Our coast is clear. I hear of no Cruisers at present to interrupt the passage of vessels. Last Saturday was the first time I have been in this Town since the flight of the Invincible British Troops. I can't describe the alteration and the gloomy appearance of this Town. No Business, no Busy Faces but those of the Physicians. Ruins of buildings, wharfs, etc., etc., wherever you go, and the streets covered with grass. I have just heard that an honest man from St. Petres in twenty-five days says they had there intelligence of a declaration of War between Spain and Portugal. This is neither impossible or improbable, and may account for Lord Howe's being in a single ship, as we are told he had arrived at the

Hook. I wish you all happiness and am with regards to Mrs. Adams and Gerry, Yours etc.,

[*No signature.*]

JOHN ADAMS TO JAMES WARREN

PHILADELPHIA, *July* 24, 1776

MY DEAR SIR, — Yours of the 10th instant came by Yesterday's Post. This I suppose will find you, at Boston, growing well of the Small Pox. This Distemper is the King of Terrors to America this year. We shall Suffer as much by it as We did last Year by the Scarcity of Powder. And therefore I could wish, that the whole People was innoculated. It gives me great Pleasure to learn that such Numbers have removed to Boston, for the sake of going through it, and that Innoculation is permitted in every Town. The plentifull Use of Mercury is a Discouragement to Many; But you will see by a Letter from Dr. Rush which I lately inclosed to my Partner that Mercury is by him wholly laid aside. He practices with as much Success and Reputation as any Man.[1]

I am much grieved and a little vexed at your Refusal of a Seat on a certain Bench. Is another appointed? Who is it?

Before now you have the Result of our Proceedings the Beginning of this Month. A Confederation will follow very soon and other mighty Matters.

Our force is not Sufficient at New York. Have suffered much Pain, in looking over the Returns, to see no Massachusetts Militia at N. York. Send them along, for the Land's sake. Let Us drubb Howe, and then We shall do very well. Much depends upon that. I am not much concerned about Burgoine. He will not get over the Lakes this Year. If he does he will be worse off.

I rejoice at the spread of the Small Pox, on another Account. Having had the Small Pox, was the Merit, which originally, recommended me to this lofty Station. This Merit is now likely to be

[1] In April, 1776, Dr. John Morgan wrote *A Recommendation of Inoculation according to Baron Dimsdale's Method* (Boston, J. Gill, 1776), intended to serve as an introduction to an issue of Dimsdale's *Present Method of Inoculation for the Small Pox*. The *Recommendation* only was printed. Thomas Dimsdale (1712–1800) had inoculated, in 1768, the Empress Catherine of Russia and her son Paul, and his title of "Baron" was of Russian origin, still borne by a descendant.

common enough, and I shall stand a Chance to be relieved. Let some others come here and see the Beauties and Sublimities of a Continental Congress. I will stay no longer. A Ride to Philadelphia, after the Small Pox, will contribute prodigiously to the Restoration of your Health. I am, etc. [*No signature.*]

JOHN ADAMS TO JAMES WARREN
PHILADELPHIA, *July* 26, 1776

DEAR SIR, — My Health has lasted much longer than I expected, but at last it fails. The Increasing Heat of the Weather, added to incessant Application to Business without any Intermissions of Exercise, has relaxed me to such a degree that a few Weeks more would totally incapacitate me for any Thing. I must therefore return Home.

There will be no difficulty in finding Men suitable to send here. for my own Part as General Ward has resigned his Command in the Army I sincerely wish you would send him here. The Journey would contribute much to the Restoration of his Health, after the Small Pox, and his Knowledge in the Army and of military Matters is very much wanted here at present.

Send Dana along for another, and come yourself by all Means. I should have mentioned you in the first Place. Will Lowell do? or Sewall? You will want four or five new ones. Major Hawley must be excused no longer. He may have the Small Pox here without keeping House an Hour and without Absence from Congress four days. It would be vastly for his Health to have it.

Send Palmer, or Lincoln, or Cushing if you will. Somebody you must send. Why will not Mr. Bowdoin or Dr. Winthrop take a Ride? [*No signature.*]

JOHN ADAMS TO JAMES WARREN
PHILADELPHIA, *July* 27, 1776

DEAR SIR, — I have directed a Packett to you, by this days Post, and shall only add a few Words by Fessenden. I assure you the Necessity of your sending along fresh delegates here is not chimerical. Paine has been very ill for this whole Week, and remains in a bad Way. He has not been able to attend Congress, for several days, and if I was to judge by his Eye, his Skin, and his Cough, I should conclude he never would be fit to do duty there again, without a long Intermission, and a Course of Air, Exercise, Diet, and Medecine. In this I may be mistaken. The Secretary,[1] between you and me is compleatly worn out. I wish he had gone home six months ago, and rested himself. Then, he might have done it without any Disadvantage. But in plain English he has been so long here, and his Strength, Spirit and Abilities so exhausted, that an hundred such delegates, here would not be worth a Shilling. My Case is worse. My Face has grown pale, my Eyes weak and inflamed, my Nerves tremulous, and my Mind weak as Water—fevourous Heats by Day and Sweats by Night are returned upon me, which is an infallible Symptom with me that it is Time to throw off all Care, for a Time and take a little Rest. I have several Times with the Blessing of God, saved my Life in this Way, and am now determined to attempt it once more.

You must be very Speedy in appointing other Delegates, or you will not be represented here. Go home I will, if I leave the Massachusetts without a Member here. You know my Resolutions in these Matters are not easily altered.

I know better than any Body what my Constitution will bear, and what it will not, and you may depend upon it, I have already tempted it beyond Prudence and Safety. A few Months Rest and Relaxation will recruit me. But this is absolutely necessary for that End.

I have sent a Resignation to the General Court and am determined to take six Months rest at least—I wish to be released from Philadelphia forever. But in Case the General Court should wish otherwise, which I hope they will not, I don't mean Surlily to refuse them. If you appoint Such a Number, that we can have a Respit, once in Six Months at furthest, or once in three if that is more convenient, I should be willing to take another Trick or two. But I will never again undertake upon any other Terms

[1] In the *Works of John Adams* (IX. 428) the sentence reads "Mr. S. Adams, between you" etc.

unless I should undertake for a Year and bring my Wife and four Children with me, as many other Gentlemen here have done; which as I know it would be infinitely more agreeable, and more for the Benefit of my Children, so in my Sincere opinion, it would be cheaper for the Province, because I am sure I could bring my whole Family here and maintain it as cheap as I can live here Single at Board with a servant and two Horses. I am, etc.

[*No signature.*]

JAMES WARREN TO JOHN ADAMS.   ADAMS MSS.

BOSTON, *August* 7th, 1776

MY DEAR SIR, — Reading and writeing have for some time past been interdicted on account of the small pox affecting my eyes, which is the reason that you have heard from me so seldom of late. I generally scribble to you when opportunity presents, whether I have much or indeed any thing of consequence to say, or not. I received yours of the 24th, 25th, and 27th July, with the inclosed, which I have delivered as directed. I can't express the uneasiness they have given me. I have all along feared that the continual application to business, in a place and season so unfavourable to health would be too much for you; but had begun to flatter myself that either from being more used to the climate, or from a firmer state of nerves you would be able to go through this season. I hope a ride will recover you and my good friend the Secretary. This I hope for sincerely both for my own sake and that of the publick, for I know not how to fill your places. Sure I am that whoever succeeds must go on the great theatre under great disadvantages. However I am willing to give you all the relief in my power. You should have rest and relaxation. I would therefore make an addition to the delegation which might serve till you are recruited. I have mentioned it to Dana, who I think I should like for one. I suppose we shall not be able to persuade Major Hawley. I wish we could. The others you mention I fear, either for want of abilities or determined resolution, will not do. I am sorry to hear that Pain is also sick. Why do you fix yourselves down in a place so unhealthy? Is there no other on the Continent to which you might adjourn at least for the summer months? I shall expect you very soon. Our friend Mr. Gerry intends to return next week. I have no kind of news. Our attention is turned to New York, from which place we expect something important very soon. The spirit of privateering prevails here, and I think great numbers will soon be out. The General Court is prorogued to the last of this month. I hope our recruits are in the Army at York before now. I have done every thing I can to hurry them. I presume Mrs. Adams will give you a state of your family by this post and tell you they are well, and most of them through the small pox. This distemper has been generally more severe than usual, and attended with one circumstance unusual and very disagreable, the failure of Inoculation in many instances, and the uncertainty of it in many others, by which means many take it in the natural way. I wish you better health and every happiness, and am yours Sincerely.

[No signature.]

JAMES WARREN TO JOHN ADAMS.   ADAMS MSS.

BOSTON, *August* 11, 1776

MY DEAR SIR, — The singular situation and great sufferings of Mrs. Temple have induced me to advise her to write to you, and hope from an application to your justice and benevolence for all the aid and compensation that can with propriety be given. I have encouraged her to expect at least an answer to her letter, which is more than the President with all his politeness gave to one of which the inclosed is a copy. Had I known your state of health, or determination to return home, I should not have been the occasion of this trouble. I wish I could entertain you with any important intelligence. We have nothing going forward here but fixing out privateers, and condemnation and sale of prizes sent in by them, so many that I am quite lost in my estimate of them, and West India Goods are falling at a great rate. Yesterday arrived a prize taken by a York Privateer with several hundred bags of cotton (a capital article), etc., etc. While all this is going forward, and whole fleets have been here, and might have been taken by your ships if at sea, I can't sufficiently lament the languor, and seeming inattention to so important a matter. A very fine ship lies at Portsmouth waiting only for guns, and I am told there are not yet orders issued for manning those at Newbury Port. This delay disgusts the officers, and occasions them to repent entering the service. I informed you in my last that we were calling in every twenty-fifth man of the Train Band and Alarm List to supply the places of your Battalions called away, and already marched. These men are comeing into the place of Rendezvous, Dorchester Heights; but you have appointed no General Officer to command them, and unless General Ward can be prevailed on to continue, I know not how they can be furnished with pay, subsistence, barracks, utensils, or ordinance stores. Would it not be well to appoint a Major General to command in the Eastern department only? I am not aware of any disadvantages in such an appointment. I hope before this the Confederation, and matter of foreign Alliances are determined. As I suppose matters will go more glibly after the Declaration of Independence, which by the way was read this Afternoon by Doctor Cooper, and attended to by the Auditory with great solemnity and satisfaction.

Matters of great importance must after all remain to be settled. Among which I Conceive Coin and Commerce are not to be reckoned among the smallest. These are indeed such intricate subjects that I dont pretend to comprehend them in their full extent. Your currency still retains its credit, but how long that will last if you continue large emissions, is difficult for me to guess. Commerce is a subject of amazeing extent. While such matters are on the carpet how can we spare you. I suppose Mrs. Adams will inform you by this Post that she and the children are well, tho' Charles[1] has not yet had the small pox, which is the case with many others after being inoculated two, three, and even six or seven times. The Physicians can't account for this. Several persons that supposed they had it lightly last winter, and some before, now have it in the natural way. Mrs. Warren and myself have been fortunate enough to have it very cleverly and propose going home this week. She joins me in the sincerest regards, for you and Mrs. Adams, and wishes for your health and happiness. I am etc.,

[*No signature.*]

1 Charles Adams (1770–1800).

If the news you have from France be true, the ball must wind up soon. God grant a confirmation. I long to be a Farmer again.

JOHN ADAMS TO JAMES WARREN [1]

PHILADELPHIA, *August* 17, 1776

DEAR SIR, — I had a letter from you by the Post yesterday, congratulate you, and your other self, on your happy Passage, through the Small Pox.

I must intreat you to embrace the earliest opportunity, after the General Court shall assemble, to elect some new Members to attend here, at least one, instead of me. As to others they will follow, their own Inclinations. If it had not been for the critical State of Things, I should have been at Boston, e'er now. But a Battle, being expected at New York, as it is every day, and has been for some Time, I thought it would not be well to leave my Station here. Indeed if the Decision Should be unfortunate, it will be absolutely necessary, for a Congress to be sitting and perhaps, I may be as well calculated to sustain Such a Shock, as Some others, it will be necessary to have Some Persons here, who will not be Seized with an Ague fit upon the Occasion. So much for froth! now for Something of Importance. Our Province has neglected Some particular Measures, apparently of Small Moment, which are really important. One in particular let me mention at present. You should have numbered your Regiments; and arranged all your officers, according to their Rank, and transmitted them to Congress, at least to your Delegates here. I assure you, I have suffered much for Want of this Information. Besides this has a great Effect upon the Public. The five and Twentyeth Regiment from the Republic of Massachusetts Bay, would make a Sound. New York, New Jersey, Pensilvania, Virginia, etc., are very Sensible of this. They have taken this political precaution, and have found its advantage. It has a good Effect too upon officers. It makes them think themselves Men of Consequence, it excites their Ambition, and makes them stand upon their Honour.

Another Subject of great Importance, We ought to have been

[1] Printed in part in *Works of John Adams*, I. 253.

informed of, I mean your Navy. We ought to have known the Number of your armed Vessells, their Tonnage, Number of Guns, Weight of Metal, Number of Men, Officers Names, Ranks, Characters; in short, you should have given Us your compleat Army and Navy Lists. Besides this one would have thought We should have been informed by some Means or other, of the Privateers fitted out in your State — their Size, Tonnage, Guns, Men, Officers' Names and Characters. But in all these Respects I declare myself as ignorant, as the Duke de Choiseul, and I Suspect much more so.

Our People have a curious Way of telling a Story. "The Continental Cruizers *Hancock* and *Franklin*, took a noble Prize" Ay! but who knows any Thing about the Said Cruisers? How large are they? how many Guns? 6, 9, 12, 18 or 24-Pounders? how many Men? Who was the Commander? These Questions are asked me so often, that I am ashamed to repeat my Answer, I dont know, I can't tell, I have not heard, our province have never informed me. The Reputation of the Province, the Character of your officers, and the real Interests of both Suffer inexpressibly by this Inaccuracy and Negligence. Look into Coll. Campbell's Letter. With what Precision he states every particular of his own Force, of the Force of his Adversary, and how exact is his Narration of Facts and Circumstances, Step by Step? When shall We acquire equal Wisdom? We must take more Pains to get Men of thorough Education and Accomplishments into every Department, civil, military, and naval. I am as usual.

[*No signature.*]

My Horse upon which I depended is ruined. How and where to get another to carry me home, I know not. I wrote to my Partner to Speak to some Members of the G. Court, to see if they could furnish me with a Couple of good Saddle Horses. If not she will be put to some Trouble I fear.

JOHN ADAMS TO JAMES WARREN

PHILADELPHIA, *August* 21, 1776

DEAR SIR, — Yours of Aug. 11 reached me Yesterday. Mrs. Temple shall have all the assistance which I can give her, but I fear it will be without success. It will be a Precedent for So many others, that there is no seeing the End of it. I shall answer her Letter by the next Post, and if I cannot promise her any Relief, I can assure her of Mr. Temple's Arrival, and of his having Leave to go home, which I presume will be more welcome News.

The success of your Privateers is incouraging. I lament with you the Languor and Inattention to the Fleet. I wish I could explain to you my Sentiments upon this Subject, but I will not. I am determined you shall come here, and see, and hear, and feel for yourself, and that Major Hawley and Some others shall do the same. I must not write Strictures upon Characters. I set all Mankind a Swearing if I do. I must not point out to you, not even to you, the Causes of the Losses, Disgraces, and Misfortunes, that befall you. I make the Faces of my best Friends a mile long if I do. What then shall I do? Just what I have long Since determined, go home, and let two or three of you come here and fret yourselves, as long as I have done, untill you shall acknowledge that I had Reason.

There is a Marine Committee, who have the Care of every Thing relating to the Navy. Hopkins and his Captains, Saltonstall, and Whipple, have been summoned here, and here they have lingered and their ships laid idle. I cannot, I will not explain this Business to you; because if I should, it would get into a News Paper, I suppose. You must come and see.

We suffer inexpressibly for Want of Men of Business.—Men acquainted with War by Sea and Land, Men who have no Pleasure but in Business. You have them, send them along.

Have you got Boston Harbour sufficiently fortified? If not take no Rest untill it is done. Howe must have Winter Quarters, somewhere. If he can't obtain them at New York, he must attempt them at the Southward or Northward, it will be your Fault, if you are not prepared for him in the North. I took a Hint from your Letter and this day obtained a Resolution authorising and desiring General Ward to continue in the Command in the Eastern Department, untill further orders.[1] I hope he will comply. He has some good Officers about him, and he does very well. We give

1 *Journals of the Continental Congress*, v. 694.

him the Credit in the War Office of making the best Returns that We receive from any Department. The Scene brightens at Ticonderoga, and We have a very numerous Army at N. York. By the last Return We have more than Eight and twenty thousand Men including Officers, at New York, exclusive of all in the Jerseys. Since which Men have been pouring in from Connecticutt. Massachusetts I think is rather lazy this Campaign. Remember me with all possible Respect to your good Lady, and believe me to be as usual.

[*No signature.*]

Since the foregoing was written I have procured Mrs. Temple's Letter to be committed.[1] I must depend upon the Gen. Court to send me a Couple of good Saddle Horses.

JOHN ADAMS TO JAMES WARREN

PHILADELPHIA, *Septr.* 4, 1776

DEAR SIR,—It is in vain for me to think of telling you News; because you have direct Intelligence from Ticonderoga much sooner than I have, and from N. York sooner than I can transmit it to you.

Before this Time the Secretary has arrived, and will give you all the Information you can wish, concerning the State of Things here. Mr. G[erry] got in the day before yesterday, very well.

There has been a Change in our Affairs at New York. What Effects it will produce I cant pretend to foretell, I confess, I do not clearly foresee. Lord Howe is surrounded with disaffected American Machiavellians, Exiles from Boston and elsewhere, who are instigating him to mingle Art with Force. He has sent Sullivan here, upon his Parol, with the most insidious, 'tho ridiculous Message which you can conceive.[2] It has put Us rather in a delicate Situation, and gives Us much Trouble. Before this day no doubt you have appointed some other Persons to come here, and I shall embrace the first Opportunity, after our Affairs shall get into a more settled Train to return.

1 This was not done until August 23. The report of the Committee was adopted August 28. *Journals of the Continental Congress*, v. 699, 713.
2 *Ib.*, 730.

It is high Time, for me, I assure you; yet I will not go, while the present Fermentation lasts, but stay and watch the Crisis, and like a good Phisician assist Nature in throwing off the morbific Matter. The Bearer, Mr. Hare, is a Brother of the Gentleman of the same Name in this City, who has made himself so famous by introducing the Brewery of Porter into America. He wants to see our Country, Harvard Colledge, the Town of Boston, etc. If you can help him to such a Sight I should be glad. Can't you agree with him to erect a Brewery of Porter in Mass.?[1] Your Barley and Water too, are preferable to any here.

Upon the Receipt of yours and Mrs. Temple's Letters I communicated the Contents of them to Congress, who appointed a Committee to consider them, who reported that the Trees should be paid for as Wood. The President I suppose has communicated the Resolution upon it, which agrees with the Report. I should be glad to write Mrs. Temple an Account of this, but have not Time. You will be so good as to let her know it. I answered her Letter before her affair was determined.[2]

[No signature.]

JAMES WARREN TO JOHN ADAMS.   ADAMS MSS.

WATERTOWN, *Sep.* 19th, 1776

MY DEAR SIR, — I wrote you in my last that we were about raising every fifth man of our Alarm and Train Band List to go to the aid of the Army at New York. Except from some remote Counties and Seaport Towns, we have now concluded that business.[3] The orders are gone out and they are now executing. Only one Regiment of them are to be taken to go to Rhode Island.[4] That there should be no failure in this business we were last night

---

[1] Bishop (*History of American Manufactures*, I. 265) states that "pale ale and porter were first made in this country about the year 1774." Robert Hare and Son (the chemist), with whom was associated J. Warren, of London, were the original makers of Hare and Twells' porter. The brew-house, in 1785, was in Callowhill Street, between Front and Second, Philadelphia. Robert Hare died in 1810.

[2] A letter from Adams to Warren, dated September 8, 1776, is in *Works of John Adams*, IX. 440.

[3] *Resolves of the Mass. General Assembly*, September 10, 1776.

[4] The men drafted from Plymouth and Barnstable were to be sent to Rhode Island. *Ib.*, September 13, 1776.

adjourned to the 9th of October, that every member might go into his town, and give his assistance to spirit and encourage the men. The House chose me as a Major General to lead this detachment but I thought I could not at this time support the fatigue. They excused me and chose Lincoln.[1] We have in the course of this Session, which has been unusually short,[2] attended as much as we could to the capital articles of manufacturing cannon, small arms, saltpetre, lead, etc., and laid an embargo on the exportation of Lumber, even from one port to another till the first of November, least it should fall into the enemy's hands, and furnish them materials for winter quarters.[3]

I rec'd yours of the 4th Instant by Mr. Hare, but have not had an opportunity of seeing him, and am now just setting out for home. If he tarrys till I return shall take care to see him. We have not yet made an addition to our Delegates, no body seems to be against it, many are indifferent about it, and those that wish to have it done, are at a loss where to find the men; so it is procrastinated and left to the next setting. I can easily conceive this is such a juncture as you would not like to leave Philadelphia. I hope such physicians as we most depend on wont leave us at this time. Tho' I am anxiously concerned for your health, I could wish to have you stay a little longer. I have a great curiosity to know what the message carried by Sullivan was. We have had reports that Congress had chose a Committee to treat with Lord and General Howe and tho' we liked the Committee, you being one of them, we did not approve the measure, and it has made more sober faces than the advantages gained by our enemies at Long Island, etc. My company are ready to set out and I must conclude. Your Friend, etc.

[No signature.]

I shall call on Mrs. Adams this day.

1 *Journals of the House of Representatives* (Mass.), September 14, 1777.
2 From August 28.
3 *Mass. Prov. Laws*, v. 558.

JOHN ADAMS TO JAMES WARREN

Sept. 25, 1776

DR. SIR, — This Express carries a new Plan of an Army[1] I hope the Gen. Court without one Moments delay will Send Commissions to whole Corps of their officers, either by Expresses or Committees to New York, and Ticonderoga, that as many Men may be inlisted without delay as possible. It may be best to send a Committee with full Powers to each Place. There is no Time to be lost. I inclose you a sett of Articles as lately amended. Discipline I hope will be introduced at last. I am,

JOHN ADAMS

SAMUEL ADAMS TO JAMES WARREN

PHILADA., *Nov.* 6, 1776

MY DEAR SIR, — I just now receivd your obliging Letter of the 24th of October by the Post. I am exceedingly pleasd with the patriotick Spirit which prevails in our Genl. Assembly. Indeed it does them great Honor. I hope the Increase of Pay will be confind to the Militia to induce them to continue in the Army till a full Inlistment of our Quota for a new Army shall be compleated on the Encouragement offerd by Congress, which I have found since I left you is increasd by a suit of Cloaths annually. Congress could not account for the Delay of the Assemblies to send Committees to the Camp agreeable to their Recommendation, but by your Letter I am led to believe that the answer of our Assembly was among those Letters which were lately stolen from an Express on the Road. The Necessity of immediate Application to the important Business of inlisting a new Army inducd Congress to direct the Commander in Chief to give orders for that Purpose even though the Committees should not have arrivd. I am glad however that your Committee is gone to Head Quarters, for I am persuaded they will be very usefull. I hear with Pleasure that you have appointed a Committee of War.[2] It has ever appeared

[1] *Journals of the Continental Congress*, v. 762.
[2] The House of Representatives passed a resolve for appointing a Board of War, October 24, and on October 30 named the following members: James Bowdoin, George Whitcomb,

to me to be necessary and it must be attended with happy Effects. While we are taking such Measures as I trust will be effectual to put a Stop to and totally defeat the Designs of the open Invaders of our Rights, are we not too inattentive to the Machinations of our secret and perhaps more inveterate Enemies? Believe me, it is my Opinion that of the two, the latter are by far the more dangerous. I hope you have not many of these among you, Some I know you have. Measures are taking here to suppress them.

Nov. 9th. Mr. Partridge [1] arrivd in this City the last Evening, having been dispatchd by your Committee at Genl. Washington's Head Quarters, who have consulted with the General concerning the Augmentation made by our Assembly of the Pay of the Troops to be raisd by our State. The General advisd them to lay the Matter before Congress. We intend to bring it on this day.[2] I have strong Doubts whether it will succeed here. Men must be prevaild upon to inlist at some Rate or other, and I think it must be confessd that our State have shewn a laudable Zeal for the publick Service. But if the other States which are to have Troops in the Army should not consent to give the same Encouragement, it may cause great Uneasiness among them. I am the more ready to believe it will not be well receivd in Congress because a proposal made not long ago by the Maryland Convention for them to offer to their Men Ten Dollars in Lieu of the 100 Acres of Land was rejected.

Nov. 11. On Saturday last Congress considerd the Business on which Mr. Partridge is here. A Comte. was appointed who have this day reported against your Resolution and the Report is agreed to, but as the Resolution must be known to the Soldiers, it has greatly embarrassd us. A Motion was made to limit the Duration of the Inlistments, which after Debate was postpond and is to be determind tomorrow. If the present Encouragement offerd by Congress is continued only for a limited Time of three

---

Joseph Palmer, Henry Bromfield, Samuel Philips Savage, James Prescott, Samuel Alleyne Otis, Jonathan Jackson and Jonathan Glover.

1 George Partridge (1740–1828). He brought a letter from Timothy Danielson, chairman of the Massachusetts Committee sent to headquarters.

2 It was referred to a committee composed of James Wilson, Edward Rutledge and George Wythe, and their report is in *Journals of the Continental Congress*, VI. 944.

or four years, it certainly would be very great. I will inform you further of this Affair tomorrow.

Nov. 12th. The Motion I yesterday mentiond has been this Day considered and Congress have resolvd upon an Alternative; that is, so far to reconsider their former Resolution as to admit of Inlistments for three years with the Bounty of 20 Dollars and the Suit of Cloaths annually, or during the War, with the Addition of the 100 Acres of Land; and our Committee is desired not to offer the further Encouragement of 20/ You will have a Copy of this Resolution sent to you by the President. Would it not be proper to send immediate Instructions to your Committees at the several Camps to settle the Affair of Officers, and exert themselves in the most important Business of procuring a new Army? I am affectionately yours,

S. A.

SAMUEL ADAMS TO JAMES WARREN

PHILADA., *Novr.* 16th, 1776

MY DEAR SIR, — I have already wrote to you by this Conveyance. The Express having been delayed till this Time affords me an Opportunity of congratulating you and my other Friends on the Retreat of General Carleton with his whole Force from Crown Point into Canada, an Account of which we had the day before yesterday in a Letter from General Gates.[1] Yesterday we had a Letter from a Gentleman[2] living on the Sea Coasts of New Jersey, acquainting us that near 100 Sail of the Enemies Transports, with a 50- or 60-Gun Ship and two Frigates, were seen coming from Sandy Hook and steering Eastward [southward].

We had also a Letter from Genl. Greene,[3] who informs that he had Intelligence by a Gentleman of good Credit who came from Staten Island, that Ten Thousand of the Enemies Troops were embarqued, and it was given out that they were destind to South Carolina. It is said that Lord Dunmore is to take the Command, from whence one would suppose they are bound to Virginia. Some

---
[1] Dated November 5. Printed in Force, *American Archives*, 5th ser., III. 526.
[2] James Searle, of Long Branch, New Jersey. *Ib.*, 669.
[3] Dated November 12. *Ib.*, 652. Justice Mesereau was his informant.

think they are coming to this City, which I confess as an American I would chuse. The People here are preparing to give them a proper Reception. Wherever they may make the Attack, I flatter myself a good Account will be given of them. If so great a Part of the Enemies Army is withdrawn from New York may we not reasonably expect that the Remainder will be easily conquered this Winter. I am earnestly sollicitous that they may have a handsome Drubbing. We must not, however, suffer any flattering Prospect to abate our Zeal in procuring a sufficient Army. We know not what Game our Enemies may play. There is no Reason to believe they will quit their darling Plan of subduing, if possible, the New England States. We ought therefore to be very vigilant and active. An Army we must keep up. A Plan is now in Agitation to prevent the Soldiers being abusd by the Extortion of Sutlers.

Nov. 17th. I know not what detains this Express, but he is still here, which affords me an Opportunity of informing you that we have this day recd a Letter from Genl. Gates.[1] Your advancd Pay to the Soldiers is as disagreeable to him as it is to Genl. Washington and for the same Reason.

Pray write to me by every opportunity and believe me to be your Friend.[2]

[*No signature.*]

Samuel Adams to James Warren

Philadelpa., *Dec.* 6, 1776

My dear Sir, — I wrote to you two days ago by a Captn. Potes. This will be deliverd to you by Mr. Livingston who is employed by a Committee of Congress to repair to the Eastern States to purchase cloathing for the Army. I inclosd to you not long ago a Resolve of Congress relating to Shoes and Stockings which it is supposd can be procured in very considerable Quantities in those States.[3] I then mentiond to you my hopes that your

---

1 Dated at Ticonderoga, November 6. *Ib.*, 549.
2 A letter from Samuel Adams to James Warren, December 4, 1776, is in Wells' *Life of Samuel Adams*, II. 452.
3 *Journals of the Continental Congress*, VI. 984.

Committee had collected a good Stock of Cloaths. I had venturd almost to assure Congress that this had been done. There is a fatality attends the Post notwithstanding all that has been done to regulate it, so that we can seldom get Intelligence from our Constituents, while the Gentlemen of other States have Advice from theirs either by Post or Express at least every Week. Would you believe it, we had but one Post from the Eastward since my last Arrival here on the 24th of October. I wish we could hear often from you. Much is to be done this Winter to prepare for the ensuing Spring. The Enemy it is now said, are in retreating order from Brunswick.

By the last Accounts from the Northward we are informd that the Ice begins to make on the Lakes. A few choice Friends have conceivd it very practicable when the Enemies Vessels are closd in the Ice to destroy them by burning. Could this be done it would exceedingly distress the Enemy and confound them. I confess I am enthusiastical in this Matter. I wish you would consult *a few* concerning it. If it is a Proposal worth your Notice. and I hardly doubt you will think it so, it must be communicated to a very few. I should think it would be best set on foot and executed by the New England People and I dare say there are trusty Men in our State who thoroughly understand such kind of Business. *Sat Verbum Sapienti.* Think seriously of it. Adieu.

[*No signature.*]

SAMUEL ADAMS TO JAMES WARREN

PHILADELPHIA, *Decr.* 12, 1776

MY DEAR SIR, — As I keep no Copies of my Letters, you must excuse me if I sometimes make Repetitions. I recollect that in my last I gave you some Account of the Movements of the two Armies. The Enemy have advanced as far as Trenton, thirty Miles from this City, and this Evening we are informd that a body of about 400 Hessians are got to Burlington, about 17 miles distance on the opposite Side of the Delaware. Nothing can exceed the Lethargy that has seizd the People of this State and the Jerseys. Our Friends who belong to those States are unwilling to have it imputed to Disaffection and indeed I am unwilling myself to attribute it to so shameful a Cause. Non-Resistance is the professed Principle of Quakers, but the Religion of many of them is to get money and sleep, as the vulgar Phrase is, in a whole Skin. The Interest of the Proprietor is at Antipodes with that of America. At least I suppose he thinks so, and though he is apparently inactive, there are many Engines which he can secretly set to Work. These are no doubt partly the Causes of the Evil. Besides there are many Tories here who have been for Months past exciting a violent Contest among the well affected about their new form of Government, on purpose to imbitter their Spirits and divert their Attention from the great Cause. But the foundation of all was laid Months ago through the Folly, I will not say a harsher Word, of that excellent superlatively wise and great Patriot D[ickinson], who from the 10th of Septr. 1774, to the 4th of July, 1776, has been urging upon every Individual and Body of Men over whom he had any Influence, the Necessity of making Terms of Accommodation with Great Britain. With this he has poisend the Minds of the People, the Effect of which is a total Stagnation of the Power of Resentment, the utter Loss of every manly Sentiment of Liberty and Virtue. I give up this City and State for lost until recovered by other Americans. Our cause however will be supported. It is the Cause of God and Men, and virtuous Men by the Smiles of Heaven will bring it to a happy Issue. Our Army is reducd to an handful and I suppose by the last of this Month will be reduced to Nothing; and Some of the *Friends* think the Congress will soon be taken napping. There are I am well assured, Materials in this great Continent to make as good an Army, if not a better Congress. There are indeed some Members of that respectable body whose Understanding and true Patriotism I revere. May God prosper them and increase the Number! Where are your new Members? I greatly applaud your Choice of them. Mr. J. A. I hope is on the Road. We never wanted him more. Mr. P[aine] has this day left the Congress having leave after laboring in the service Sixteen Months without Cessation. I wish him safe with his Family. We seldom hear from N. England. One Post perhaps in a Month! I am told that Soldiers inlist there very briskly. I wish I could have an Assurance of it from you. Have you provided a good Stock of Cloathing? I have ventured almost positively to assert that you have. It would be a Satisfaction to me to be authorized by you to assert it. Britain will strain every Nerve to subjugate America the next year. She will call wicked Men and Devils to her Aid. Remember that New England is the Object of her Fury. She hates her for the very Reason for which virtuous Men even adore her. Are you enough on your Guard? Is Boston sufficiently fortified? For your Comfort I will tell you that in my Opinion our Affairs abroad wear a promising Aspect. I wish I could be more explicit, but I conjure you not to depend too much upon foreign Aid. Let America exert her own Strength. Let her depend upon Gods Blessing, and He who cannot be indifferent to her righteous Cause will even work Miracles if necessary to carry her thro this glorious Conflict, and establish her feet upon a Rock. Adieu my Friend, the Clock strikes — Twelve.

[No signature.]

SAMUEL ADAMS TO JAMES WARREN

BALTIMORE, *Jany.* 1, 1777.

MY DEAR SIR, — I am determined to omit no opportunity of writing to you although I have very seldom of late receivd a Letter from you. Your second Favor came to my hands a few days ago, inclosing Copies of Papers from Spain. I am much obliged to you for them. Our Affairs in Europe look well, and additional Measures have been taken here, to establish them in that Part of the World on a solid Foundation. I assure you Business has been done since we came to this place, more to my Satisfaction than any or every thing done before, excepting the Declaration of Independence, which should have been made immediately after the 19th of April, '75.

Our Ministers abroad are directed to assure *foreign Courts*, that notwithstanding the artful and insidious Representations of the Emissaries of Britain to the Contrary, the Congress and People of the United States are determin to maintain their Independence at all Events.[1] This was done before the Success of our Arms in Jersey of which you will doubtless have receivd Intelligence before this Letter will reach you. Generals Sullivan and Green commanded the two Divisions. The Enemy had before made Lee a Prisoner; but we have convincd them that great as his Abilities are, we can beat them without him. I now think that Britain will make a contemptible Figure in America and Europe, but we must still make our utmost Exertions. Pray let the levies required of our State be raisd with all possible Expedition. By this Conveyance you will have a Resolution vesting large Powers in General Washington, for a *limitted* time.[2] It became in my Opinion necessary. The Hint I gave you some time ago I still think very important. Genl. Gates arrivd here the day before yesterday. I have conversd with him upon it. He told me he had conceivd it before and wishes the Measure may be tryed. It requires Secrecy and Dispatch. Lt. Colo. Stuart[3] will set off tomorrow with Directions to proceed as far as Boston to purchase Ordnance and other Stores, if they cannot be procured elsewhere. He is General Gates' Aid de Camp and is very clever. I wish you would take Notice of him.

But I am now called off. Adieu my Friend.

[*No signature.*]

HANNAH WINTHROP TO MERCY WARREN

Jan. 14, 1777

I feel myself much obliged to my dear Friend every time I peruse her kind favors which I often do over and over again in the room of a fresh supply. It would give me additional pleasure to bring you often in arrears if it was not for trespassing on those important hours which from your extensive Correspondence and the happy arrangement of your domestic Concerns can admit — but of little vacancy. I must confess to you the inauspicious appearances of the last year together with the clouded brow of a great and good Patriot, the unfavourable Imagery you thot recent

---

[1] *Journals of the Continental Congress*, VI. 1054. It was passed December 30.
[2] *Ib.*, 1045.   [3] Walter Stewart?

in his mind encreasd the anxiety of my too often desponding imagination but I think a New Year presents a brighter View. I congratulate you on our late Success, let us my friend enjoy this Victory, and tho a Skillful General has been meanly kidnapped let us not think the Fate of America hangs on the Prowess of a single person. My son William receivd a letter last night from an officer of distinguished rank in the army who writes — The Scale is turnd greatly in our Favor. The enemy are intimidated and fleeing before them and says if we had but 5000 Continental Troops he makes no doubt they would be able to cut them all off. However he hopes to diminish them greatly. What a pity it is to want men at so important a Crisis. He gives the N. Englanders great merit in the Late glorious Action. He mentions a brisk Cannonade supposed to be at Princetown Jany the 3d from whence we expect some important news. The description you give of the meeting of our Ambassadors on Long Island is romantically pleasing. The Sage the Venerable Mentor who is gone beyond Sea I think gives a dignity to all his Negotiations. I wish to Heaven he may succeed in what ever he undertakes. He wrote a short leave to the small Circle of His Favorites intimating that His encreasing Years forbid him thinking of a return to his Native Clime; 'but he left them with the most invigorating Sentiments of Affection for His dear Country.' How happy would it be if such Valuable lives might be protracted beyond the four score Limits. I hear the other gentleman is now blest with returning Spirits. I long to know your Sentiments of present Appearances. I hear Plimouth has producd lately a Prophetical Egg that bodes no good to America for the year '77, but as it is said to be laid by a Tory hen I interpret it to be what is wishd rather than what will happen. The inscription on it is said to be Howe will Conquer America, but I believe the Prophecy will prove as Brittle as the Tablet on which it is engravd.

If I tho't you would not charge me with an Affectation of dabbling in Astronomy I would tell you I was lately an Humble Attendant on my observer of the grand movements of the Celestial Orbs in His observation of Cynthia in Eclipsing that glorious Luminary that rules the day. However enwrapt in incertainty the events in which we of this Terrestrial ball are interested a perfect regularity reigns there. No intervening accident can prevent the Completion of their appointed route. The Sky at the begining of the Eclipse was unkindly overspread with Clouds but soon Cleard off, and gave so good a View as to be able to judge with Precision the Quantity and duration of the Moon's path over the Sun. He has also this fall taken a trip with little Mercury across the Sun similar to the Transit of Venus. I think a beautifull Sight. I assure you these are great Points to an astronomer, tho the greater part of Mankind are so inattentive to these Glorious works of an Almighty Creator that they rise and shine and perform their amazing Circuits without any other observation than its being sometimes a fine sunshine day, or a fine Starlight Evening. Now I have incurrd your Censure pray pass Sentence; however I hope the inhabitants of those States are better employd than in spreading devastation and death among their Loyal Subjects and brethren. My Sister has been obligd to make another move, they reside in Coll. Phips's House. Her pearly drops are often flowing at her unhappy Situation — five removes since the Cruel burning of Charlestown. I endeavor to bring to her View the Scenes of ravage and bloodshed which mark the progress of British and Hessian Troops thro the Jerseys, enough to thaw the most frozen heart, but it is much easier to Preach Fortitude and Patience under Sufferings than to Practice them. You and I are enjoying our homes, but I dare not indulge the thought how it will be with us in the Spring — the only Consolating Consideration is an alwise Superintendant at Helm with Universal Nature at Command.

I give you joy on the recovery of Your Sons from the Small Pox. A great easment to the mind of anxious parents when they enter on the Theatre of business. General Warren, I hear, is closely engagd in matters of great moment. Mr. Winthrop joyns me in wishing him health and happiness and in kind regards to you. Allow me to Subscribe Your Ever Attentive Friend,

HANNAH WINTHROP

Miss Chrisy presents her most respectfull regards to Mrs. Warren.

SAMUEL ADAMS TO JAMES WARREN

BALTIMORE, *Jany.* 16, 1777

I [have] receivd a Letter a few days ago from the Council of Massachusetts Bay, requesting a Sum of Money for [paying the] Bounty to the Troops to be raisd in that State. Accordingly three hundred thousand Dollars are orderd for that Purpose,[1] which will be forwarded to the Paymaster in Boston[2] as soon as it can conveniently be done. In the Mean Time I hope our Assembly will advance if necessary, for the Levies must be made at all Events. I observe that our Assembly have made it necessary that three of their Delegates should be present and concurring in Opinion, before the Voice of our State can be taken on any Question in Congress.[3] I could wish it had been otherwise. Three only of your Delegates are now present. It may so happen at other Times. One of them may be sick. He may be on a Committee or necessarily absent on publick Business, in which Case our State will not be effectually represented. While I am writing at the Table in Congress a worthy Colleague is unavoidably employd on Business of the Publick at home, and the two present cannot give the Voice of the State upon a Matter now in Question. Were all the three present, one of them might controul the other two so far as to oblige them to be silent when the Question is called for. But I only mention the Matter, and submit, as it becomes me, to the Judgment of my Superiors.

Major Hawley and my other patriotic Fellow Labourers, Are they alive and in Health? I have not receivd a Line from any of them excepting my worthy Friend, Mr. Nath. Appleton, whose Letter I will acknowledge to him by the first Opportunity. My Friends surely cannot think I can go thro' the arduous Business assignd to me here, without their Advice and Assistance. I do not know whether you ever intend to write to me again. Assure the Major from me that a few more of his "*broken Hints*" would be of eminent Service to me. You cannot imagine how much I am

[1] *Journals of the Continental Congress*, VII. 28. [2] Ebenezer Hancock.
[3] *Journals of the Continental Congress*, VII. 25. It was altered by the Massachusetts General Court, February 4, so that any two of the delegation could act. *Ib.*, 169.

pleasd [with the Spir]it which our Assembly discovers. They seem [to arouse] every County into Motion. This forebodes in [*torn*] that something great will be done. I [never have] since this Contest began had so happy Feelings as I now have. I begin to anticipate [the coming] of Peace on such Terms as independence [seems] to demand, and I am even now con[sidering] by what Means the Virtue of my Country[men can] be secured for Ages yet to come — Virtue which is the Soul of a Republican Government. Future Events I have learnd by Experience, are uncertain and some unlucky Circumstance may before long take place, which may prove sadly mortifying to me. But no such Circumstance can deprive me of the Pleasure I now enjoy of seeing at a Distance (not I believe very long) the rising Glories of this new World. Adieu my Friend and Believe me to be unfeignedly Yours,

S. ADAMS

The Bearer, Mr. Allen,[1] I think, is a good Man. Congress have appointed him Agent to the Indians of Nova Scotia.

SAMUEL ADAMS TO JAMES WARREN

BALTIMORE, *Feb.* 1, 1777

MY DEAR SIR, — The Proceedings of the Committee of the four New England States have been read in Congress and are now under the Consideration of a Committee of the whole.[2] They are much applauded as being wise and salutary. I had heard that one of your Delegates at that Convention[3] had written a long Letter to his Friend and *Confident* here; and hearing it whisperd that the Massachusetts State had disapprovd of those Proceedings I was led to ask the Gentleman who had receivd the Letter concerning it. He confirmd it, and said that not only the Trade, but the landed Gentlemen in the House of Representatives were sanguine against

---

[1] John Allan. His instructions are in *Journals of the Continental Congress*, VII. 38.

[2] Transmitted to Congress by Governor Trumbull, January 12, and received by that body the 28th. The convention met at Providence December 25, 1776, and separated January 2. The proceedings are printed in Hoadley, *Records of the State of Connecticut*, I. 585. The approval of the Continental Congress is in the *Journals*, VII. 124.

[3] The delegates from Massachusetts were Thomas Cushing, Azor Orne and Tristram Dalton. Cushing was probably the writer of the letter.

it. I beggd him to let me see his Letter; but he refusd in a kind of Pet, telling me it was a *private* Letter. I was left to conjecture, whether I had been really impertinent in asking a Sight of his Letter, or whether the Contents of it were such as it was not proper for me to see. You will easily conceive what a Scituation one must be in here, who having receivd no Intelligence himself, of the Sentiments of his Constituents, is obligd in vain to ask of another, upon what Principles they have disapprovd of a Measure (if indeed they did disapprove of it) upon which he is called to give his own Opinion. But it is difficult to account for men's peevish Humors, and it is generally not worth ones while to attempt it. You see, my Friend, from this Instance, the Necessity of your writing to me oftener. When I was told upon the forementiond Occasion, that I would be intitled to see the Letters of Another, whenever I should be disposd to communicate those which I receive myself, I could have said truly that I had scarcely receivd any.

Two only *from you* in the Space of near four Months. But I have no Claim to your Favors, however much I value them, unless perhaps upon the Score of my having not neglected to write to you by any Opportunity. Your omitting of late even to acknowledge the Receipt of my Letters, I might indeed construe as a Silent Hint that they were displeasing to you.

But I will not believe this till I have it under your own Hand.

While I am writing, your very acceptable Letter is brought to me by Mr. Lovell. You therein speak, as you ever have done, the Language of my Soul. Mr. Adams tells me you are President of the Board of War; I am therefore inducd to recall what I have just now said, which you may construe as an implied Censure for your not having written to me oftener. I am sure you must have a great Deal of Business. I am not sorry for it, for a Reason which I need not mention. I pray God to preserve the Health of your Body and the Vigor of your Mind. We must chearfully deny ourselves domestick Happiness and the Tranquility of private Life, when our Country demands our Services.

Give me leave to hint to you my Opinion that it would be a Saving to our State in the Way of Supplys, if the Board of War would consign the Cargoes which they order here to a Merchant of good Character rather than to the Master of the Vessel. Possibly there may be some Exceptions; But I have Reason to think that a Cargo which arrivd about a Fortnight ago, consisting as I am told, chiefly of Rum and Sugars which were scarce Articles, was sold at least 30 pCt under what it would have fetchd, if it had been under the Direction of a Person acquaintd in the Place; and Flour is purchasing by the Person who bo't the Cargo, and I suppose expects an Allowance therefor, at an unlimitted Price. I am perswaded, if you had by a previous Letter directed a Cargo to be procurd, you might have had it 20 pCt cheaper. If the Board should be of my Mind, I know of no Gentlemen whom I would more freely recommend than Messrs Samuel and Robert Purvyance. They are Merchants of Character, honest and discrete Men, and warmly attached to our all-important Cause.

But I get out of my Line when I touch upon Commerce. It is a Subject which I never understood. Adieu my dear Friend. Believe me to be yours,

S. A.

P.S. I forgot to tell you that, a fair Occasion offering, I movd in Congress that the Eldest son of our deceasd Friend Genl. Warren might be adopted by the Continent and educated at the publick expense. The Motion was pleasing to all and a Committee is appointed to prepare a Resolve. A Monument is also proposd in Memory of him and Genl. Mercer whose youngest Son is also to be adopted and educated. But these things I would not have yet made publick.[1]

JOHN ADAMS TO JAMES WARREN

BALTIMORE, *Feby.* 3, 1777

DEAR SIR — After a very tedious Journey through the severest Weather, and over very bad Mountains in one Part of it, and perfect Mortar in the other Part, I am arrived in good Health and Spirits at Baltimore.

Congress is Sitting, and by the best Information I can obtain

[1] *Journals of the Continental Congress*, VII. 243.

from our Friends, are very well united and much more Spirited than ever.

The Recruiting Service goes on as every Body tells me from Boston to Baltimore, very well, and it is here said, in Virginia. I cannot sufficiently express the Sense I have of the indispensible Importance that our State should be the earliest and most exemplary in compleating our Quota. It may be depended upon, that our State is the Barometer at which every other Looks. If the Mercury rises there, it will rise in every other Part of the Continent, if it falls there, it will fall everywhere.

By all that I can gather, the British Ministry have sollicited for Cossacks. The Success is doubtfull. But it is the opinion of a Man in England whose Intelligence has heretofore proved extreamly exact that the Ministry will be able to obtain near Twenty thousand Recruits in England, Scotland, and Ireland, and Germany. If this Conjecture is right, there is great Reason to Suppose that they will not Venture upon So dangerous a Step as that of procuring Siberians. Their late great Successes will in their Opinion render them unnecessary.

But in all Events, it is our Wisdom, our Prudence, our Policy, our Cunning, our Duty, our every Thing, to destroy those who are now in America. They are compleatly in our Power and if We do not embrace the Opportunity, We shall not only in dust and ashes repent of our Sloth, but it will be but Justice that We should Suffer the wretched Consequences of it. I am Sure our brave New Englandmen can break the Force at Newport, and even the main Body at Brunswick may be imprisoned. But an Army is wanting. Don't let it be wanting long.

Congress will do and have done what they can, but if the States will not execute the plans and Resolutions of Congress, what is to be expected?

New England I find is now in higher Estimation than it has been. Our Troops have behaved nobly, and turned the Fortune of the War. Pray let us keep up our Credit as I am sure We can. Adieu, my dear Friend.[1]

[*No signature.*]

---

[1] Another letter, of the same date, is in *Works of John Adams*, IX. 450.

SAMUEL ADAMS TO JAMES WARREN

BALTIMORE, *Feb.* 11, 1777

MY DEAR SIR, — I beg Leave to inclose my Account of Expences from the 26th of April, 1775, to the 27th of August, 1776, amounting to [*blank*]. I intended to have laid it before the House of Representatives when I was last in New England; but the sudden Adjournment of the General Assembly in September and my Hurry in preparing for my Journey hither, after its sitting again in October, prevented my attending to it.

When I set off from Lexington after the memorable Battle there I had with me only the Cloaths upon my Back, which were very much worn, those which I had provided for myself being in Boston, and it was out of my Power then to recover them. I was therefore laid under a Necessity, in order to appear in any kind of Decency of being at an extraordinary Expence for Cloathing and Linnen after my Arrival in Philadelphia, which I think makes a reasonable Charge of Barrils, Leonards, and Stilles Bills in my Account.

It may perhaps be necessary to say something of the Charge of Horsehire in the last Article. When I left Watertown in September, '75, two Horses were deliverd to me out of the publick Stable by Order of the Honble. Council, for my Self and my Servant. They were very poor when I took them, and both tired on the Road as you will observe by my Account. One of them afterwards died in Philadelphia, which obligd me to purchase another in that City; and with this Horse I returnd to Boston the last Fall. His being my own Property, having purchasd him without Charge to my Constituents I think gives me a Right to make a Charge of horse hire, which is left to be carried out in a Sum which shall be thought just and reasonable. Mr. A[dams] tells me he is obligd to pay seven pounds 10/ for the Hire of each of his horses to Philadelphia. The other horse I left at Boston (being worn out) to be disposd of as should be judgd proper.

I shall take it as a Favor if you will present the Account to the Honble House and acquaint the Committee to whom it may be referrd with the Reasons of the Charges above mentiond: and make any other Explanations which you may judge necessary.

Mrs. A. has the Vouchers, to whom I beg of you to apply for them in Person before you present the Account. I wish it may be settled as soon as the House can conveniently attend to it. If an Allowance for my Services is considerd at the same Time, which I have a particular Reason to wish may be done, you will please to be informd, that I sat off from Lexington to Worcester, on the 26th of April, '75, and returnd to Watertown on the 14th of August following. And again I sat off from Watertown on the first of September, '75, and returnd to Boston on the 27th of August, '76. I have troubled you with this Epistle of Horse hire and Shop Goods at a Time when, no doubt, your Attention is called to Affairs of the greatest Concern to our Country. Excuse me, my dear Friend, for once, and be assured that I am your affectionate,

S. A.

PHILADA., *March* 25, 1777

DR. SIR, — The foregoing Letter I have detained for want of such Conveyance as I wishd for. Your two Letters of the — and— of Feby I have receivd, and have Time at present only to acknowledge the Receipt of them, the Bearer being just now going. I cannot however omit sending you the agreeable Intelligence that a Vessel arrivd yesterday in this part with ten thousand Stands of Arms. This is indeed a very timely Supply.

Mrs. A. will give you her Reasons, if you will ask her, why an Allowance should be made as soon as it can be done with Convenience, for my Services. This I suppose may be done altho' any Circumstance should prevent the Adjustment of my account of Expense, which I do not foresee. Adieu.

S. A.[1]

SAMUEL ADAMS TO JAMES WARREN

BALTIMORE, *Feb.* 16, 1777

MY DEAR SIR, — A few days ago, a small Expedition was made by the Authority of this State aided by a Detachment of Conti-

---

[1] A letter from John Adams to Warren, February 12, 1777, is in *Works of John Adams*, IX. 452.

nental Regulars, to suppress the Tories in the Counties of Somerset and Worcester on the Eastern Shore of Chessepeak, where they are numerous and have arisen to a great Pitch of Insolence.[1] We this day have a Rumour that one of their Principals, a Doctor Cheyney,[2] is taken and we hope to hear of the Business being effectually done, very soon. In my Opinion, much more is to be apprehended from the secret Machinations of these rascally People, than from the open Violence of British and Hessian Soldiers, whose Success has been in a great Measure owing to the Aid they have receivd from them. You know that the Tories in America have always acted upon one System. Their Head Quarters used to be at Boston — more lately at Philadelphia. They have continually embarrassed the publick Councils there and afforded Intelligence, Advice, and Assistance to General Howe. Their Influence is extended throughout the united States. Boston has its full Share of them, and yet I do not hear that Measures have been taken to suppress them. On the Contrary, I am informd that the Citizens are grown so polite, as to treat them with Tokens of Civility and Respect. Can a man take Fire into his Bosom, and not be burnd? Your Massachusetts Tories communicate with the Enemy in Britain as well as New York. They give and receive Intelligence, from whence they early form a Judgment of their Measures. I am told they discoverd an Air of insolent Tryumph in their Countenances, and saucily enjoyd the Success of Howe's Forces in Jersey before it happend. Indeed, my Friend, if Measures are not soon taken, and the most vigorous ones, to root out these pernicious Weeds, it will be in vain for America to persevere in this generous Struggle for the publick Liberty.

General Howe has declared that he intends that General Lee shall be tried by the Laws of *his* Country. So he is considerd as a deserter from the British Army. You know the Resolution of Congress concerning this Matter.[3] It is my Opinion that Lt. Colo. Campbel[4] ought immediately to be secured. He is to be detained as one upon whom Retalliation is to be made. Would you believe

1 *Archives of Maryland*, XVI. 157, 175.
2 Andrew Francis Cheney.
3 *Journals of the Continental Congress*, VII. 16.
4 Archibald Campbell.

it, that after the shocking Inhumanities shown to our Countrymen in the Jerseys, plundering Houses, cruelly beating old Men, ravishing Maids, murdering Captives in cold Blood, and systematically starving Multitudes of Prisoners under his own Eye at New York, this humane General totally disavows his even winking at the Tragedy and allows that a few Instances may have happend which are rather to be lamented. Congress is now busy in considering on the Report of the joynt Committees of the Eastern States. A curious Debate arose on this Subject, which I have not time now to mention. I will explain it to you in my next.[1] Adieu my Friend.

S. A.

JOHN ADAMS TO JAMES WARREN

BALTIMORE, *Feb.* 17, 1777

MY DEAR SIR, — I have the melancholly Prospect before me of a Congress continually changing, untill very few Faces remain, that I saw in the first Congress. Not one from South Carolina, not one from North Carolina, only one from Virginia, only two from Maryland, not one from Pennsylvania, Not one from New Jersey, not one from New York, only one from Connecticutt, not one from Rhode Island, not one from New Hampshire, only one, at present, from the Massachusetts. Mr. S. Adams, Mr. Sherman, and Coll. Richard Henry Lee, Mr. Chase and Mr. Paca, are all that remain. The rest are dead, resigned, deserted or cutt up into Governors, etc. at home.

I have the Pleasure however to See every day, that the Governments of the States are acquiring fresh Vigour and that every Department is working itself clear of Toryism, Timidity, Duplicity, and Moderation. New Jersey was never so well represented as it is now.[2] Pensilvania whose Assembly will maintain its Ground have the last Week appointed a New Delegation, every Man of whom is as firm as a Rock.[3] Maryland also the last Week

1 See Burke's "Abstract of Debates," in *No. Ca. Colonial Records*, XI. 391.
2 The delegates chosen were Richard Stockton, Jonathan D. Sergeant, John Witherspoon, Abraham Clark and Jonathan Elmer. In the absence of recorded votes it is not possible to say who attended the sessions at this time.
3 On March 10 the General Assembly elected as delegates: Benjamin Franklin, Robert Morris, Daniel Roberdeau, Jonathan Bayard Smith, George Clymer and James Wilson.

compleated their new Government, chose Mr. Johnson[1] Governor, chose a new privy Council to the Governor, every Man of whom is an honest Whigg [2] and also chose a new Delegation in Congress, every Man of whom is equally Stanch, leaving out all who have been suspected of Trimming and hankering after the Leeks of Egypt.[3]

This evening too we have an ex[press *torn*] with an Account of the new Delegates [*torn*] who are said to be sound.[4]

Thus We see that our new Governments [are taking firm] root and Spreading their Branches [*torn*] ing Changes have We seen? [*torn*] done?

I write you no News from the Army. [You are so placed] as to hear from it, oftener than [I can *torn*] rumour that gaind Credit of [an engagement *torn*] Sennight, the Enemy leaving 327 dead on the Field.

Congress have this day voted to return to Philadelphia tomorrow Week. The new Army, my dear Sir, the new Army. I feel as much Pain at loosing the fine Opportunity We now have of destroying the Brunswickers, as I should if a surgeon was sawing off my Limbs.

[*No signature.*]

JAMES WARREN TO JOHN ADAMS ADAMS MSS.

PLYMOUTH, *Feb'y* 22d, 1777

MY DEAR SIR, — I had the pleasure yesterday of receiving your favours of the 3d and 5th Inst., the first that have come to hand since your departure. I am extreamly glad to hear of your safe arrival in health and good spirits at Baltimore. I have had some uneasiness about you, the weather has been very severe, and I supposed you must pursue a disagreeable if not a dangerous route;

---

1 Thomas Johnson, jr.   2 Josiah Polk, John Rogers and Edward Lloyd.

3 In November, 1776, Maryland had chosen the following representatives in Congress, to serve until March, 1777: Matthew Tilghman, Thomas Johnson, jr., William Paca, Thomas Stone, Samuel Chase, Benjamin Rumsey, and Charles Carroll. On February 15, Chase, Rumsey, Carroll, Stone, and Paca were re-elected, and William Smith added. This leaves Tilghman as the "trimmer." *Journals of the Continental Congress*, VI. 963; VII. 131.

4 This probably refers to the new delegation from South Carolina, chosen January 10 and 21: Arthur Middleton, Thomas Heyward, jr., Henry Laurens, Charles Pinckney and Paul Trapier, jr. *Ib.*, VII. 129.

My Dear Mercy   Concord Octr of 14th 1774

I had the pleasure of yours last
Night, & supposed you would at the same time
have recd. a Letter from me wrote Yesterday Morning
to go by Mr. Hunt, but have since heard that he is
still in this Town. we are still yet waiting for
Intelligence from the Grand Congress, & you may
presume some of us Impatient for it's arrival
we last Night reported from our Committee an
Address to the General relating to his Fortifications
the Bearer goes with Twenty others to deliver it
this is an Entertaining Wedge. we are a very large
Body suppose about 300. & are Indeed the most respectable Assembly I ever saw. many of them are distinguished by Fortune or Abilities or both. all determin'd
to take vigorous measures before they rise, & most of
them determined to save this Country, or perish in
the Attempt. we Voted to Last Night to Adjourn
to Cambridge when we adjourn over the Sabbath.
I presume that will be this Afternoon. I shall then
go off Tomorrow Morning in order to see you at
Boston. tho' many of my Judicious friends here
think it not safe for so Obnoxious a Person to put
himself in the power of the Army. Indeed I can't
but wonder that those who have Families in Town
can be easy to remain there. we have a curious
Extract of a Lett. from Br Edwards Person now in
Boston revealing their Plans. Lett refer you to the
Bearer for an Acct. of it. may neither Drums, or
any fearful Appreh. ensign disturb your Slumber,
or Repose. May you be happy here, & Infinitely so
hereafter is the Prayer of your Affee
                                        Husband. Jas. Warren

My Regards to Brother! & Sisters &c

but the climbing mountains and wadeing in difficulties of every kind has become so familiar to the politicians of this age, that I hoped one of the first of them would be able to go through it without any bad effect on his health and spirits. Every letter I receive from Baltimore gives me the most pleasing accounts of the union and spirit of Congress. I hope soon to see the effects of them, but I observe that while you mention the probability that England is applying for Cossacks, etc., and that she will be able to raise a large number of men in her own dominions, and Germany, you say nothing of any expectations we are to entertain from foreign aid. I long to see a fleet of French and Spanish Men of War on our Coast, and our harbours full of their Merchantmen. I am very sensible of the prudence, policy, duty, etc., of destroying the army our enemies have already here before the arrival of any reinforcement, and have no doubt it might be effected. I am anxiously concerned that the honour and reputation of this State should be supported by the wisest and most exemplary exertions. The mercury rises as high in our political barometer as I could wish, but the misfortune is there are no steady fixed laws or principles to regulate its motions. The laws of gravity and uniformity have given place to levity, versatility, and impatience, the zeal in some to give every thing to the soldier, the impatience in others in taking new measures before they could see the effects of what was already done, is such that no reason, argument, or influence, I am master of could carry through a resolve fixing upon something certain as an ultimatum beyond which in the way of encouragement we would not go; or prevent the sending out a resolve holding up to the soldiers a design of makeing a levy on the Towns which is in effect offering them a bounty of 50 or 60 dollars more,[1] and has as I expected and prophesyed stopped the inlistment of thousands, who now wait for the opportunity of filching as much money from their neighbours as they can. From hence has arisen all our difficulties in raising our quota. I hope however we shall get through them, but it will be at an amazeing expence, three-quarters of which will be absolutely hove away. General Schuyler just before the Court rose wrote us a letter full of apprehensions of an attack

[1] *Resolves of the Mass. General Assembly*, January 28, 1777.

on Ticonderoga. Four of the Battalions raising here, with what they have already got, have been under marching orders for that place sometime. Some of them are gone; the whole may amount to 1000 or 1200 men, and I left the Court considering what other measures should be taken. I can't tell you what, if anything, has been done. The Court rose the day I left it, a fortnight ago by adjournment to the 5th March.

I hope the British Troops now at Newport will not be able long to keep that place. What remains of them after 2000 gone to York, are a considerable part invalides. I believe there will soon be an attempt made in that quarter. I hope the service will not be injured, by any dissentions or want of subordination there or elsewhere. Congress have been very rapid in their promotions, and possibly in some instances have not had the necessary information; but I could wish to see the officers appointed to any service so disposed that the spirit and authority of the chief should be able to check and controul all the subordinates of every rank, however impatient of submission. I am glad to hear that the enlistments to the Southward go on well. I hope by this means the service will be supported till the New England quotas are compleat. I thank you for the account you give of the perticular situation of the other Colonies.[1] When we shall form our Constitution, or in what manner we shall do it I am unable to say. Our own delays have embarrassed us, and I am persuaded the longer we delay this business the greater will be the difficulty in executing it. I am therefore constantly urgeing the necessity of going about it. Various are the opinions both as to the manner of doing it, and as to the thing itself. Many are for haveing it done by a Convention, and many are for one Branch only. I hope both will be avoided. I don't see a better way as things are than by sending to the several Towns desireing them at their next elections to have it in view and vest their members with special powers for this purpose.[2]

I am extreamly pleased with the conduct of Virginia and Carolina with regard to religious establishments. The dissenters there you say by this means have compleat Liberty of Conscience. Do

[1] *Works of John Adams*, ix. 450.
[2] *Journals of the House of Representatives* (Mass.), September 17, 1776.

you mean that all distinctions in point of privileges and advantages are abolished? This is an evidence that Episcopacy and Liberty will not flourish in the same soil. I have intended to write to you before this but have been prevented by the multiplicity of business on my hands. The House have set generally to near nine and sometimes to ten o'clock in the evening, and my station you know requires constant attendance. If you enquire what we are about, I must tell you, many things which in my opinion we have nothing to do with, and which ought to be done by your G——l here, if you mean he should do any thing for his pay and perquesites; and many others which would be done with more ease and dispatch if the powers of such a *rara avis in terra* were once defined and known, and whether the publick stores here might be applied to publick uses and how. As to news we have none. A few prizes, some of them valuable, have been sent in. Your Navy here still remains in port. When any of them go to Sea I can't say. The conduct of this part of your operations will be a subject of curious enquiry. I hear we are going to have another frigate and a 74-gun ship built here. Will the conduct of this matter be put into hands of persons who scarcely know the difference between a ship and a wheelbarrow, and who seem to have no ideas of the importance of dispatch, or know not how to make it? I want to give you a few anecdotes and to say many things which I dare not commit to writeing. Adieu, my Friend.

[*No signature.*]

When will there be an end of requisitions to us? The Continent seem to consider us as the repository of manufactures and warlike stores. We shall not be able to supply their demands, and provide for our own defence.[1]

JOHN ADAMS TO JAMES WARREN

PHILADELPHIA, *March* 6, 1777

MY DEAR SIR, — Dr. Jackson,[2] by whom this will go, is a Manager of the State Lottery, and is bound to the New England States,

---
[1] Adams' reply to this letter, dated March 18, 1777, is in *Works of John Adams*, IX. 456.
[2] David Jackson. *Journals of the Continental Congress*, VI. 982.

to forward the Sale of the Ticketts. He wishes to be recommended to proper Persons for the Purpose. If you can assist him with your Advise you will do a public service.

I can give you no News — but the Skirmish at Spanktown.

This State of Pensilvania have at last compleated their Government. Wharton [1] is Governor and Bryan [2] Lt. Governor. Their Council too is at last filled.[3] Johnson [4] is Governor of Maryland. Govr. Livingston's [5] Speech you will see. I hope now the Loan Offices will supply us with Money, and preclude the Necessity of any further Emissions. If they don't, what shall We do? But they will.

I am at last got to think more about my own Expences than any Thing else: twenty dollars a Cord for Wood. Three Pounds a Week for Board, meaning Breakfast, Dinner, and bed, without one drop of Liquor or one Spark of light or fire. I am lost in an Ocean of Expence. Horse feed in Proportion. Five hundred Sterling will not pay my Expences for this Year, at this Rate. Pray make every Body who has Money lend it, that Things may not grow worse.

The loan Office in this Town is very successfull.

[*No signature.*]

GEORGE WASHINGTON TO JAMES WARREN

HEAD QRS., MORRISTOWN, *March* 15th, 1777

SIR, — I was sometime since honoured with your Letter of the 3d. Ulto. The polite manner in which you have been pleased to express your wishes for my happiness and congratulations upon the agreeable reverse of our Affairs, after a series of misfortunes, demand my gratefull acknowledgements; and assured that they are more than mere professions of Compliment, with equal sincerity I return you my thanks. The duties of my Office 't is true and the various business incident to it, allow me but little time for a

---

1 Thomas Wharton, jr.   2 George Bryan.
3 John Evans, Jonathan Hoge, George Taylor, John Lowdan, John Proctor, John Hubley.
4 Thomas Johnson, Jr.   5 William Livingston, of New Jersey.

friendly correspondence. However, Sir, I shall ever be obliged by your Favors, and a communication of such things as you may consider either agreeable or interesting.

The policy adopted for raising your Quota of Men, I could not but reprehend in some degree, having regard to the influence of the Precedent upon the States at large. At the same time I am willing to ascribe it to the motives you mention, and am well convinced that those and those only gave rise to it. I heartily wish the Batallions may be soon compleated and for that purpose beg leave to suggest, that none should be wanting in their exertions. The Enemy now have a formidable force in the Country and are only waiting the Season to be a little more advanced, to begin their Operations; and I am persuaded, they indulge a pleasing hope of effecting some Capital Stroke, before we have an Army to oppose 'em, it behoves every nerve to be strained to baffle their views, and I flatter myself it might be accomplished, if our Troops can be collected, 'ere they open the Campaign, but of this I am not without the most painfull apprehension. A few days more, and the Spring is upon us, and nothing prevents their movements now, but the badness of the Roads. No material event has occurred of late worthy of mention and of which you will not have heard before this reaches you. Now and then there has been a skirmish which in the issue have been generally favourable.

You will be pleased to inform Mrs. Warren that I transmitted her letter to Mrs. Washington by the earliest Opportunity after it came to hand, and requesting a tender of my respects to her, I have the Honor to be with great esteem, Sir, Your most Obedt Servant,

Go. Washington

John Adams to James Warren

Philadelphia, *March* 21, 1777

Dear Sir, — It is not easy to penetrate the Designs of the Enemy. What Object they have in View cannot certainly be determined. Philadelphia most probably, and Albany. They have near Ten Thousand Men in the Jersies, at Brunswick, Amboy,

Bordentown and Piscataqua;[1] the two last Posts are very near their main Body.

I think, but may be mistaken, that they will not hazard an Attempt upon this City or Albany, before they receive a Reinforcement. If they do, they must evacuate New Jersey, entirely, because they have not Men enough to leave sufficient Garrisons in Brunswick and Amboy, and march to Philadelphia, or to Albany with the Remainder.

It is the Opinion of our General Officers, however, that they will march, within a very few days from South Amboy, through the Pines towards the Delaware. They are building Boats in N. York which may serve either for the Delaware, or Hudsons River, or indeed they may serve to draw their Army off, from Brunswick, by Rarriton River, Brunswick being about twelve Miles from the Sound between N. Jersey and Staten Island.

What Reinforcements they will be able to obtain is uncertain. Is it not more probable that they will bring their Army round by Water, from Canada, and join General Howe, than that they will come over the Lakes? From England and Ireland, they can derive no great Reinforcement; it is not known how many they can obtain from Germany. The Russian Auxiliaries are uncertain, but if they come they will certainly bring a French War with them. But in all Events I think We need not fear any considerable Reinforcement from Europe before Midsummer. The British Troops here, are not more sickly than usual: But the Hessians are sickly with Pleurisies and other Fevers.

It is certain that if they should march to Philadelphia, and gain Possession of it, they have not Men enough to maintain a Line of Posts, by which a Communication can be kept open by Land, with New York. They must therefore evacuate New Jersey, which would leave their miserable Friends in that State in absolute Despair, and the Whiggs, already exasperated to a great degree, would assume new Vigour. Troops in the mean Time will be coming into N. Jersey from the Eastern States and into Pensilvania from the Southern; and the Militia of Philadelphia and Pensilvania will not be idle. So that they must expect to be cooped up in

[1] Piscataway, New Jersey.

the City and there perhaps destroyed, before a Reinforcement shall arrive. Besides this, they will be at such a Distance from New York and long Island that they may be under Apprehensions for those Places. Another Thing, I think they will not choose to divide their Fleet so much. They will not attempt Philadelphia, without a Force by Water, as well as by Land. They must keep a large Number of their Ships at New York, to protect that and the neighboring Islands, and many are at Newport. So that they cannot Spare so many Ships as will be necessary to come up the River Delaware.

These Reasons persuade me to differ from the Opinion of our General Officers, and to believe that no Attempt will be made upon Philadelphia, before a Reinforcement comes. I wish I may not be deceived, as this City by her central situation, Wealth, Artificers and several other Qualities, is of much Importance to us. But if they get it, they will not find so much Advantage from it, as they expect. It will cost them most or all of their Force to keep it, which will make it a Security to other Places. I am my Friend, Yours, etc.

[*No signature.*]

JAMES WARREN TO MERCY WARREN

BOSTON, *March* 21, 1777

MY DEAR MERCY, — I wrote you Yesterday by Major Wadsworth, which I hope will reach you this day. Since which the Brigt. *Independence* has Arrived here. I met Cotton in the State House yesterday who seems to have pretty well recovered of his wound. One Mr. Wentworth came to town from Portsmouth also since I wrote, He is gone to Congress with Letters. From him is obtained a general Invoice of the Ship's Cargo, Copy of which I enclose you.[1] We also learn that with the 50-Gun Ship Bound here are comeing 2 frigates of 30 odd Guns each and a number of small vessels all loaded. Doctor Franklin was recd in France with

[1] This was the cargo of the *Mercury* of Nantes, a ship of 317 tons, commanded by Captain John Herand, as is shown by the *Journals of the Continental Congress*, VII. 211. She had been dispatched by Beaumarchais. Wharton, *Diplomatic Correspondence of the Revolution*, II. 276.

every demonstration of Joy, with ringing of Bells, Bonfires, Illuminations, &c. and at Court like an Embassador, insomuch that Lord Stormont declared that he could not stay at Court under such Circumstances, and so retired. I have heard that he brings an account that the french Court have declared to the English Court that they consider America as an Independent State and therefore that they have, with the Consent of the Americans as good a right to trade there as any Nation, and that they shall Consider any interruption given by the English as a declaration of War. However that may be, which I am not able to ascertain, it is certain they have remonstrated against foreign troops comeing here. Dr. F. is in the Cabinet with the King almost every day, and I think we have a tolerable Earnest of his success. The Tories, poor Unhappy Creatures, had just fabricated and put into Circulation a Story that the Doctor was frowned on at the french Court and would be glad to get away. This is all the news I can give you at this time. No Letter from you yet. I hope for one before Night. If I could hear you was well and in good spirits I should be happy. I am better myself. Do attend to your Health, that we may have a Chance of Enjoying some of the pleasing prospects before us. Give love to my Boys and accept a large Share to yourself from your Afft Husband,

J. WARREN

If you have any wheat ground do let the Brann be saved for the Bacon.

SHIPS CARGO ARRIVED AT PORTSMOUTH ON CONTINENTAL ACCOUNT

364 Cases of Arms   or? 11.987 Fire Arms
1000 barrels powder
5 Bales Cloath
24 Ditto Coarse Woollens
8 Do Woolen Coverlids
10 Do Woolen Caps and Stockins
1 Do Small Cloaths
5 Do handkfs, th[rea]d and cotton
2 Do printed Linnens
1 Do Thread
2 Cases Shoes
5 Boxes Buttons and Buckles and fig[ure]d Lawns Needles, silk, Necloaths etc.
11000 flints.

34 sail had left and were leaving France for America with supplies.

A Brigadier Genl.[1] and a Conductor of Artillery came in this Vessel, were recd. with Ceremony at Portsmouth and are Expected here in a day or two.

JAMES WARREN TO JOHN ADAMS. ADAMS MSS.

BOSTON, *March* 23d, 1777.

MY DEAR SIR, — I wrote you last from Plymouth about three weeks ago after which I was detained at home longer than I expected and did not get here till last Tuesday. I understand that letter and one wrote at the same time to Mrs. Adams went by the Post. As I wrote with some freedom I should be glad to hear of the receipt of it. Since I have been here I have had the pleasure of yours of the 17th Feb'y, and am glad to find the New Governments in the Southern States so well established and things going so agreably to your mind.

Your reflections on the changes in Congress are very natural. I have the same feelings. I love to see the same faces, and lament the loss of my old acquaintance and connections; but changes and vicissitudes we must expect in the state we are now in, and perhaps it is in many instances best, if not all it should be so, and in political bodies more especially.

The New Army has been raised very slowly, and it is probable many advantages must be lost by it, but I hope we shall compleat it at last. If our Assembly could be kept from any new measures I believe we should soon get ours; but they have an unaccountable itch to be meddling every day, and by that means keep the minds of the people always afloat, make them mercenary, and uncertain when to engage if inclined. We have, however, under all the disadvantages ariseing from the instability of our own conduct got as near as I can collect about 7000 Non-Commissioned Officers and privates, and they are now inlisting fast. The idea of a levy on the several Towns, which we have I think injudiciously and without any necessity held up, has occasioned an immense expence

[1] Prudhomme de Borré.

to individuals in addition to the publick bounty. We have lately voted the same bounty to a Battalion of the Train as we gave before,[1] and are now sollicited to do the same for three new Battalions. I suppose we must comply and comfort ourselves with the hopes that it is but for once. We have had no news for some time till the arrival of a French Ship at Portsmouth, with a valuable cargo and agreable intelligence which you will have more perfectly than I can give you, gratified for a moment our curiosity, raised our spirits and gave us a subject of conversation. I shall therefore only congratulate you on this occasion, and inform you that we have three or four vessels out to furnish the other Ships expected here with pilots, and orders are given to receive them with ceremony, salutes, etc. No attempt has yet been made upon Rhode Island, which was expected and preparations made for it long ago, and now we are not in a condition for it; for tho British Troops are many of them gone, not more than 2500 remaining. Ours are reduced in a greater proportion. In short there are but about 500 men from this State in addition to the Troops of their own State. Applications are made to us for a reinforcement, and a Committee are now considering in what way it shall be done. Our sea coasts and perticularly this harbour is also in a defenceless state and must be provided for. All these things are difficulties that interfere with compleating our quota, and embarrass us much. New Hampshire have got their part of the Army some time ago, but Connecticut are more behind hand than we are.

General Ward resigned his Command last Thursday to Heath. What he is designed to command I know not. I neither see or hear of any men. About three hundred men only are here, besides Craft's Regiment, and their time expires in about ten days.

But no one thing gives me more uneasiness than the conduct of your Fleet. The *Hancock, Boston, Alfred* and *Cabot* are all yet in port. It is said the *Hancock* is ready to sail and was to have gone yesterday, but remains here yet. I fear the consequences of their going out single. But McNeil and Manly it is said like the Jews and Samaritans will have no connections or intercourse; they will not sail together. I believe McNeil is near ready for the sea. I am

[1] *Resolves of the Mass. General Assembly*, March 11, 1777.

told that he and the Agent, Mr. Cushing, have had a breeze; but I am not acquainted with the perticulars or how it terminated. I have still a worse account of the situation of your frigates at Providence. I don't know the officers, but understand to say no more of them that they are not agreable to the people and never can man their ships. You must fall on some new plan for conducting your Naval Affairs at a distance from you, or be content never to shine in that way. Perhaps to establish a Board in each district upon an honourable footing, and with extensive powers or something (I know not what) else. If you should have occasion for a new Commander for one of your Ships I would venture to recommend one I think equal to the business, and perhaps to any you have. Capt. Simeon Samson [1] who was lately taken in the service of this State I have a very good opinion of as a Seaman. A man of judgment, prudence, activity and courage, he behaved like a Hero in the action, but the force against him was so superiour to his that he had no chance. He is yet in captivity but his redemption is expected very soon as proper measures are taken for it. Our measures in General Court are so complicated and various that it would take a volume to give you an account of them.

The regulating Act [2] has been observed in some places, and disregarded in others, and perticularly here, where it is constantly violated in open daylight, and has yet produced no other consequences but bitterness and wrath between the Town and Country, the last of which is endeavouring to starve the Town in return for what they consider ill usage from them and have succeeded so well, that the market here is little superiour to what it was in the siege. I ever thought this Act impracticable in its nature, and prophesied that it would end in bringing the Authority of Government into contempt. My prophesies are likely to be compleated.

[1] Simeon Samson (son of Peleg), of Plymouth, commander of the brigantine *Independence*. He was taken by the British ship *Rainbow*, sent to Halifax, and was listed for exchange, June, 1777. He received a commission from Massachusetts to command an armed vessel then under construction, which may have been the *Hazard*, of which he was in command in August of that year. The following June he resigned on account of ill health, but appears to have sailed the *Mars* and *Mercury*. In the latter he carried Elkanah Watson to France in 1779. The *Hazard*, of 16 guns, was built by John Peck, of Plymouth, and was burned in the Penobscot expedition of 1779. Deborah Sampson was a cousin. *Mass. Prov. Laws*, v. 1317.

[2] *Mass. Prov. Laws*, v. 583.

Now I mention Government I will tell you that one day this week is assigned to determine in what way a new one shall be formed. I fear the determination will be in favour of a Convention.

This is designed to go by Major Ward,[1] who was Aid de Campe to the General of that name, by whom also I shall forward a packet received this day from your good lady. This gentleman I suppose is known to you; if not I beg leave to recommend him to your notice. He has had the misfortune to fall into a very inactive department, and now to be wholly excluded from any appointment in the Army. I take him however to be a sensible, worthy man, and one very capable of doing publick service in some way or other. I believe it is time to conclude this long scroll. I am therefore, with wishes for your happiness, your Friend, etc. [*No signature.*]

My regards to Mr. Adams and Gerry. I shall write to one or both of them by this opportunity, if I can.

JOHN ADAMS TO JAMES WARREN
PHILADELPHIA, *March* 24, 1777

DEAR SIR, — This Morning a Vessell has arrived in this City with 6800 stand of excellent Arms and 1500 Gun Locks, belonging to Congress, and 1500 more private Property. These last We have ordered to be bought.

This News you may depend on. The Letters were brought into Congress, in the Midst of a Debate concerning a Resolution to impower the General to procure Arms wherever he could find them.[2]

Thus it is. On how many Occasions when We have been unable to see any Way to help ourselves has Providence sent Us an unexpected Relief! Thus it has been, and thus it will be. I am, etc.,

JOHN ADAMS

JOHN ADAMS TO JAMES WARREN
PHILADELPHIA, *March* 26, 1777

There are two ingenious Artificers here who have made a beautifull Field Piece of Bar Iron. The Barrs were not bound together

---
1 Joseph Ward.   2 *Journals of the Continental Congress*, VII. 197.

with Hoops, like that which was made in Boston: But welderd together and afterwards bored out. It is very light. it is a Three Pounder and weighs no more than two hundred and twenty four Pounds. it has been tried every Way, and has stood the fullest Proof. It has been discharged Twenty times and upon discharging it three Times successively as fast as it could be loaded and fired, with several Ounces of Powder more than the usual Quantity, it was observed not to be heated so much as other Guns of the same calliber commonly are where of Brass or cast Iron.

It is so light, that it may be transported about with the Utmost Ease, by a few soldiers alone without Horses, and is therefore admirably adapted for a Regimental Field Piece. The Generals Gates, Green and Mifflin, have examined it, and admire it. We are about contracting for a Number of them. They are cheaper than Brass. They carry a Ball as far and as direct. The only objection is that they rebound too much. But this Inconvenience is easily remedied by strengthening the Carriage. The names of the Smiths who made it are Wheeler and Wiley.[1]

[*No signature.*]

JOHN ADAMS TO JAMES WARREN

PHILADELPHIA, *March* 31, 1777

DEAR SIR, — We have this day received Letters from Europe, of an interesting Nature.[2] We are under Injunctions of Silence concerning one very important Point: and indeed I don't know how far I am at Liberty concerning some others: but thus much I may venture to communicate: That We have an offer of three Millions of Livres in Specie, without Interest, and to be paid when We shall be settled in Peace and Independence; that all Europe wish Us well, excepting only Portugal and Russia; that all the Ports of France and Spain and Italy and all the Ports in the Mediterranean, excepting Portugal, are open to our Privateers and Merchant Ships. That there is no danger of our wanting Arms or

1 Samuel Wheeler was the inventor of the gun. A 3-pounder cost £60. 10*s*. or 161 30/90 dollars.
2 Probably among these letters was that from the American Commissioners in Paris, January 17, 1777, printed in Wharton, *Diplomatic Correspondence of the Revolution*, II. 248.

Ammunition for the future — between six and seven hundred Barrells of Powder having arrived in Maryland, and indeed, We had plenty of Powder before. In short, my Friend, altho We have many grievous Things to bear, and shall have more; yet there is nothing wanting but Patience. Patience and Perseverance, will carry Us through this mighty Enterprize — an Enterprize that is and will be an Astonishment to vulgar Minds all over the World, in this and in future Generations. An Enterprize however, which, Faithfullness to our Ancestors who have sett Us Examples of Resistance to Tyranny, Faithfullness to the present and future Generations, whose Freedom depend upon it laid us under every moral and religious obligation to undertake. Our Accounts from Europe are that great Preparations are making for War and that every Thing tends to that Object, but when or where, or how Hostilities will commence is yet unknown. France and Spain, will act in concert and with perfect Amity, neither will take any Step without the other.

The American Ministers abroad, advise Us to exert ourselves in every Respect, as if We were to receive no Assistance from abroad. This is certainly good Advice and if We have Wisdom enough to follow it, a Division by a War in Europe will be a more effectual Relief to us. I am, etc.

[*No signature.*]

John Adams to James Warren

Philadelphia, *April* 1, 1777

Having an Opportunity by so carefull an Hand as Captain Wentworth of Portsmouth, I have ventured to inclose you a copy of a Letter which appears to me to be of Consequence.[1] You will make use of it with Caution, among such Friends only as can be trusted to make a discreet Use of it.

Inclosed is also a state of the Stocks in Amsterdam on the seventh and twelfth of November, by which you will see that the British Funds were falling very fast notwithstanding the News

---

[1] This is the letter referred to in the note on p. 307.

from New York and the precipitate Efforts in England to equip a Fleet of Observation.

The Dutch dont appear so inimical to Us, or so indifferent to our Fate as We apprehended they would be. Letters from that Quarter, are fully of Opinion that the Opportunity for the House of Bourbon is too fair and inviting to be let slip.

[*No signature.*]

JAMES WARREN TO JOHN ADAMS. ADAMS MSS.

BOSTON, *April* 3d, 1777

MY DEAR SIR, — I had the pleasure yesterday of receiving your favours of the 15th and 18th of March. There are few things I wish for more than a war between Britain and France, etc. I am therefore greatly pleased with the accounts you have of the probability of it. Such has been the situation of matters for some time that I could not see how it could be avoided, and yet my impatience makes me uneasy at the delay, least something might intervene to prevent it. I have a right to pray for it as an event that may serve my Country, and the chastisement of Britain for their own good, or their destruction for the good of Mankind perhaps are not improper subjects of prayer.

I am glad you have raised your interest to six per Ct.[1] and am told that it has had a favourable influence here. Your Loan Office is successful. How much has been received I can't inform you. Your tickets that were sent here were all nearly sold in a few days, and perhaps double the number would have sold. Whether patriotism or the hopes of Gain has occasioned this rapid sale of 12. or 15.000 tickets in so short a time is a question that deserves the attention of the politician; but either of them will answer the present purpose.

I hope the late inconvenience you have seen in voting by States will stimulate you to form your Constitution.[2] That seems to be a matter as long in agitation with you as with us, and if something dont accelerate your motions we shall get the start of

[1] *Journals of the Continental Congress*, VII. 158.
[2] That is, the Articles of Confederation.

you. We have agreed, I mean the House, upon a recommendation to the people at their next election to choose their Representatives for that among other purposes. The form they shall agree on however to be subject to the approbation of their Constituents.[1]

We have no news; are straining our nerves to forward our men, but our motions are slow. The enemy continue at Rhode Island, and have lately been reinforced from whence we know not. They now consist of about 4000. We have not been so attentive of late to the defence of that State as I think we ought to be; but we have now a Committee, and I hope if the enemy make no attempt on Providence, etc., in a few days, they will be in a posture of defence. The enemy are fortifying the Island, which looks as if they intended to continue there. There seems to be a prospect of a small breeze between the present College Treasurer[2] and some of his friends, as I am informed he refuses to resign, and has wrote some letters threatening vengeance if left out. The Overseers have however recommended to the Corporation to choose a new one, and I suppose they intend it.[3] I wrote Mr. Adams yesterday about Mrs. Temple's affairs. I wish you would attend to it if any thing can be done. I am much hurried this morning and must conclude and am, as usual, your Sincere Friend, etc.

[*No signature.*]

[Memorandum,] Ans. Ap. 27.

JOHN ADAMS TO JAMES WARREN

PHILADELPHIA, *April* 6, 1777

DEAR SIR, — Yours of 23d March was handed to me this Evening by Major Ward. Your Letter from Plymouth by the Post I duly recd, and immediately wrote an Answer to it; but upon reviewing it afterwards I found so many bold Truths in it that I concluded not to send it, less Peradventure it should get into Hugh Gaine's Gazette; and I thought it a Pitty that so many Sacred

---

1 *Resolves of the Mass. General Assembly,* May 5, 1777.
2 John Hancock. The story is told in Quincy, *History of Harvard University,* II. 182.
3 Ebenezer Storer was chosen in his place.

Truths should appear in Company with so many infamous Lyes as that Paper ushers into the World whenever it appears.

I am much obliged to you for your Sentiments concerning the Navy. A Board I believe will be established at Boston, and a Commissioner in each considerable Port in New England. Complaints are frequently brought here from Boston and from Providence concerning the Continental Agents and other Officers. I am sorry for this, but cannot help it. At Providence I fear, by what I have lately heard, there has been a System of Selfishness, and at Boston of Incapacity. I had the Honour of belonging to the first Naval Committee, which set all our maritime Affairs agoing;[1] and they did it with a Vigour, Assiduity and Dispatch, which precluded all Censure and Complaint: But I went home last December was twelve Month, and Advantage was taken of that Opportunity, one or two other Members being absent at the same Time — Coll. Lee went home, and Gadsden and Langdon and Deane was left out — to choose a new Committee.[2] Since which there has been nothing but Languor, Censure and Complaint. Upon my Return they did me the Honour to put me upon the Board of War, which takes up my whole Time, every Morning and Evening, and renders it totally impossible for me to look into the marine Department, which if I had Leisure to do, ignorant as I am of every Rope in the Ship, I would perish if I did not put that Department in a respectable order. There is nothing wanting but some one Person whose Vigour, Punctuality, and Constancy, should draw the Committee together every Morning and Evening, direct their Attention to the Object, and keep it fixed there. There are Gentlemen enough of the Committee who understand the Business, and the Board of Assistants are pretty well qualified and every Man upon the Continent who knows any Thing of the Subject might easily be induced to contribute the Assistance of his Knowledge at least by Letter. The Fracas between [Manley] and McNeal had reached this Place before your Letter, hope it

[1] *Journals of the Continental Congress*, III. 277 n.
[2] Benjamin Harrison was elected in place of Lee, Edward Rutledge in place of Gadsden, and Samuel Huntington in place of Deane. Langdon was never on the Marine Committee, and Adams probably intended to mention Stephen Crane, whose place was taken by Jonathan Dickinson Sergeant. The new committee was elected March 6, 1776.

will do good. Am glad to hear that our Quota is likely to be raised at any Rate. Send them along and let Us beat the Scoundrels to Attoms, as I am Sure we can and shall. I am, etc.

[No signature.]

This Letter, so full of myself and so abusive to others, is intended barely to exculpate myself. I cannot bear any share of the Blame of the failures in the marine Department.

JOHN ADAMS TO JAMES WARREN

PHILADELPHIA, *April* 6, 1777

MY FRIEND, — The Business of the naval and marine Department will I hope be soon put in a better Train than it has been. A Board of Assistants has been appointed here consisting of three Gentlemen, not Members of Congress, whose whole Time is devoted to the Service, Mr. Hopkinson, Coll. Nixon and Mr. John Wharton are the Men.[1] The first is a Gentleman of Letters, the second an able Merchant, the third an eminent shipwright.

There is a Talk of appointing a similar Board at Boston[2] and a Commissioner at every considerable Port in N. England. Who would be proper Persons for those Places? They should be well acquainted with Navigation. They should be well informed in Trade. They should be Men of Character and Credit.

The Marine Committee have lately recd. Letters from Captns Thompson, McNeal[3] and several others, pointing out Defects, Abuses and Mismanagements, and proposing Plans of Improvement, Redress and Reformation. These will do good. This is the Way to have things go right; for Officers to correspond constantly with Congress and communicate their Sentiments freely.

McNeal, I suppose, by his Letter, before this, has sailed[4] and I hope your Embargo is off, before now, that the Privateers may have fair Play. Indeed I am sorry it was ever laid. I am against

---

1 *Journals of the Continental Congress*, VI. 929 — November 6, 1776.
2 It was established April 19, 1777, and the commissioners were James Warren, William Vernon, of Providence, and John Deshon, of New London.
3 Thomas Thompson and Hector McNeil.   4 He commanded the *Boston*.

all Shackles upon Trade. Let the Spirit of the People have its own Way, and it will do something. I doubt much whether you have got an hundred Soldiers the more for your Embargo, and perhaps you have missed Opportunities of taking many Prizes and several Hundreds of Seamen.

South Carolina seems to display a Spirit of Enterprize in Trade superior to any other State. They have Salt at half a Dollar a Bushell and dry Goods in great Plenty, tho dear. Many french Vessels have arrived there, some Bermudians, and some of their own. They have exported their Crop of Indigo and a great deal of Rice. They have some Privateers and have made several Prizes. Tobacco too begins to be exported in large Quantities from Maryland, Virginia and North Carolina. Vessels sell at very high Prices in all these States. In short in one more Year I fancy Trade will be brisk in every Part of the Continent, except with Us, the Destruction of whose Fishery has deprived Us of our Staple and left Us nothing to export. We must build Ships and cutt Masts and take Fish with our Privateers, etc. I am, etc.

[*No signature.*]

JOHN ADAMS TO JAMES WARREN

April 16, 1777

An unfortunate Vessell has arrived from France, the brave Fellow who commanded her is blown to Pieces in her. A French Nobleman who came in her got on Shore and brought the Letters.

We have Letters from our Commissioners of the Sixth of Feby., much in the same Strain with the former of Jany. 17, tho not quite so encouraging.[1] They say there is an universal Apprehension that We shall submit. They had not heard of the Turn of Affairs at Trenton. A Letter from London says so many Bankruptcies were never known. Two W[est] I[ndia] Houses have failed for one Million two hundred Thousands Pounds. "Stand firm, say our Friends in England, and nothing can hurt you."

The British Ministry are very angry with France for the Assistance she gives Us and threatens to declare War. A Quarrell be-

---
1 Wharton, *Diplomatic Correspondence of the Revolution*, II. 261.

tween the Ministry and the Court of Spain about the Musketo Shore — a fresh Quarrell between Turks and Russians.

[*No signature.*]

Samuel Adams to James Warren

Phila., *April* 17, 1777

My Dear Sir, — I should before this time have acknowledged your Favors of the 2d and 24th of Feb., had I not constantly been in the Situation which you represent to be yours in your last of the 2d of April. "Something or other has always taken Place to call me off." We have for some time past been threatened with an Invasion by Sea, and the last Accounts receivd from the Capes say, there are nine of the Enemies Ships of War within the River. I inclose this day's paper which gives an account of the Misfortune of the Ship *Morris* and other Intelligence.

By the last Letters from France dated in February we are informed that a War is inevitable and our Affairs there still wear a favorable Aspect. My worthy Friend Dr. L[ee] who you have heard is got to Paris writes to me in these Words. "The Politicks in Europe depend on too many Whims and Refinements for us to hazard the downright Defence of every thing dear to us upon them. It is well to cultivate Europe but not to depend upon it." He speaks my Sentiments, and, I believe, yours. I have been always of Opinion, that we must depend upon our own Efforts under God for the Establishment of our Liberties. When it suits the interest of foreign Powers they will aid us substantially. That some of them will find it their Interest to aid us I can hardly doubt but there seems not to be Virtue enough left in the World from generous and disinterested Motives to interpose in Support of the Common Rights of Mankind. We are told that fresh disputes have arisen between Russia and the Turks and a Quarrel is likely to ensue. France and Spain are preparing mighty Fleets to consist of thirty Sail of the Line each and to be ready for the Sea the first of March. The Merchants of Britain in a Memorial laid before Lord Sandwich reckon their Losses by the Captures our Privateers have made in their West India Trade to be £1,800,000.

Insurance had arisen to 28 pr. ct. and Bankruptcys had taken place. There is no kind of Relaxation here, says a London Correspondent, in Warlike Preparations, and yet the Ministry have so contrivd it that but few People believe there is any Danger of War. I am much puzzled, says he, about the real Intention in respect of these great and hasty Armaments; they are certainly too expensive to be mere scarecrows, and improbable as on one account it seems, there is Reason to believe they intend when their present Loan is compleated either to attack France, or at least to hold very high Language to her. Certain it is, that Lord Weymouth has of late seriously and warmly urgd an immediate Declaration of War with France, and tho' such Declaration has not been made it is perhaps only *suspended*. With regard to America we are informd that Transports were getting ready to bring out the additional British and Hessian Troops and it was intended they should all sail by the beginning of March. The Campaign is to be opend *unusually early* and the Operations directed *wholly and from all sides against New England*, that by early and vigorous Exertions they may crush the Northern Colonies.

I think I have given this to you and my other Friends as my opinion in my Letters the last Winter. If they can subdue those stubborn States, they flatter themselves the rest will submit. It is necessary that New England should sustain her Character and Firmness. Their Intention is to extirpate the People there and make Slaves of the rest of America. I wish the Nest of Hornets on Rhode Island had been before now destroyd. I expected it would have been done. I have been informd of the Reason why it was not done. The Congress have now recommended it to the States of M[assachusetts] B[ay], C[onnecticut] and R[hode] I[sland], to call forth their Militia for that Purpose and have directed Genl. Washington to send a suitable Officer to take the Command.[1] I hope it will now be done. It is certainly wise to conquer our Enemies in Detail before their Reinforcements can arrive. I fear N.E. will be chargd with the Loss of her former military Pride if it is not done. I have been sanguine in urging it here and have almost pawnd my Reputation on the Success of the Undertaking as well

---

[1] *Journals of the Continental Congress*, VII. 272.

as the Valor of my Countrymen. I wish for more of an enterprizing Spirit and shall feel myself happy in the Revival of such a Spirit in New England.

Capt. Collins who will deliver this Letter is now ready to set off and waits. Adieu, my Friend. I will speak to Genl. Mifflin again who is now here about Mr. Temple's affair. I am glad to hear of the brisk Sale of Lottery Ticketts in Boston and that the Loan office is successfull. I hope Boston will be made as strong as Gibraltar. Our 15 Battalions must be completed. I am pleasd with the Measures you are taking with the Tories. Don't let the Execution of the good Law be abated an Iota in a single Instance. If they take the Oath you must nevertheless keep a watchful Eye over them. They are a cursed Generation. We are plagued with them here beyond bearing.

[*No signature.*] [1]

JAMES WARREN TO JOHN ADAMS. ADAMS MSS.

BOSTON, *April* 23d, 1777

MY DEAR SIR, — I have been very unwell and absent for a fortnight. I returned here yesterday. While I was at home I had the great pleasure of receiving several of your favours, perticularly those of March 31, April 1st and 3d, with the inclosures, and since my return yours by Capt. Arnold of the 6th Instant. I think myself greatly obliged to you for the entertainment as well as intelligence and information derived from them. as these have all come safe I regret the loss of that that you say contained the bold truths.

I am pleased to see our affairs in so good a way. I think a war in Europe must soon take place. It is impossible that under all circumstances it should even by the meanness of Britain be prevented, and if our Army is obtained, with the powder and arms sent us by the kindness of Providence, I believe we shall be ready and able to fight Britain with or without a war in Europe, especially if their funds begin to fall. Almost every thing is done to fill up the

[1] Letters from John Adams to Warren, April 27 and 29, 1777, are in *Works of John Adams*, IX. 462, 464.

Army, and since the arrival of the arms here they are all on the march. On Sunday last arrived here a french ship loaded with goods, on account of private adventurers. Her cargo is very valuable and consists of some articles much wanted. Arms she has a few, and has 5000 blankets. She is armed with [ ] guns, has a Commission to make reprisals if disturbed, and the super cargo is ready to take Continental Bills. I begin to be very easy about their credit, and to conceive they will be as valuable as silver.

We had last Sunday a prize brought into Plymouth. She was bound to Antigua with a load of beef and butter, and last evening I heard of the arrival of another at Cape Ann, with 2000 bbs. beef and pork. I suppose she was bound to York. The amazing damage we should have done them, as well as the advantages derived to ourselves, make me execrate the policy of stopping our privateers. I always opposed it. We have now got a resolve passed to let them loose on conditions they will cruise with Manly under his command twenty-five days.[1] Perhaps we shall make a fleet of ten or twelve sail of them soon and some of them 20 Gun Ships. We hope by this to sweep one of their fleets, and to do great execution. We have for encouragement engaged an indemnification for losses which prizes are not sufficient for. I can easily conceive we might have had a fine fleet of our own by this time. Our frigates in concert might have taken several of theirs, that have for the most part cruised single. Your ships are however in harbour here, but it is said have consented to sail together. Last evening the Board of War received an express from Cape Ann, that the *Milford* and a tender were yesterday nigh there and took a Schooner. They are endeavouring to get out Manly and McNeal to take her.[2]

We are sending in a reinforcement of 2000 men to Rhode Island a draft from the Militia for two months.[3] What the state of the enemy is there I am not able to say. I believe their land force is inconsiderable. I was told yesterday not more than 1400. I wish

[1] *Resolves of the Mass. General Assembly*, April 20, 1777.   [2] *Ib.*, April 24, 1777.
[3] "Tuesday last, the Corps of Independents, commanded by HENRY JACKSON, Esq., marched off from this Town for Providence, in order to assist our Brethren in that Place, against all the Encroachments of the worst of Tyrants — the Hirelings of the British King; should they attempt a Landing on that Shore of FREEDOM." *Boston Gazette*, April 21, 1777.

your ships at Providence were out. there is no difficulty in effecting it, and I wish the troops on the Island whether 1400 or 4000 were driven of. I think there is no difficulty in effecting that. The Honour of New England is concerned in this matter and men enough for such an enterprize might be had at once. They must, however, be Militia, and the estimation of them runs very low with our Military Gentry who have forgot from whence they came, and of what materials they are now some of them half formed. This is to go by Capt. Ayres,[1] who informed me yesterday of his design to set out this morning. I dont know his business but I suppose to apply for some appointment in the Navy. I have not much acquaintance with him. He seems to be an active smart man, has been long at sea, and as he has commanded one of your Schooners with reputation, I could wish he might succeed. I am Yours, etc.

[*No signature.*]

I have this moment an account of an arrival at Portsmouth of great consequence. The perticulars of the cargo as they come to us are as below. There came in her a Coll. and a number of officers of the Train to the number of twenty-four.[2]

58 Brass Cannon and Carriages.
Tents for 10,000 men.
Cloathing for 12,000 men.
Stands of Arms 5.700.
Powder about 10 Tons.
Great Numbers Blankets.
Lead and Ball, uncertain how much.

3 Mo. passage arrived last Sunday.

JAMES WARREN TO JOHN ADAMS.   ADAMS MSS.

BOSTON, *April* 27th, 1777

MY DEAR SIR, — Since I wrote you by the post on last Thursday, nothing very material has taken place here. Two Frigates have for some time been infecting our coasts — a species of insult that has ever gauled me, and more especially since we had Ships sufficient either to take or drive them off, lying in our harbours for

1 John Ayres, commander of the Continental vessel, the *Lynch.*
2 Du Coudray and his party. Lists are in *Journals of the Continental Congress,* VIII. 606, 705; IX. 877.

months sufficient to build and equip a large fleet. The ships now on the coast have taken several vessels mostly small ones. One of them they gave their prisoners and sent them on shore with a message and challenge to Manly and McNeil and all the armed vessels in this harbour. This has roused the indignation of the officers and tarrs, united their wishes with ours, and given us an opportunity which many of us thought should not be neglected. We accordingly appointed a Committee [1] to confer with your Captain and Agents, and to treat and contract with the owners and commanders of private vessels to go to sea and meet the challengers. We have by lending money to Manley and McNeil satisfied them. We have contracted for two or three 20-Gun Ships, and six or seven smaller ones, to be ready to sail on the first day of May and to continue with, and be under the command of Manly for twenty-five days, we insuring the owners against loss and damages, giveing the men a month's pay, and puting them on your Establishment in case they loose life or limbs. With these a number of others will go, and agree to continue under the Commodore's command for the same time for the sake of getting out. If we don't meet the ships we shall get the Continental Ships, and the privateers to sea, instead of detaining them here by an Embargo against all good policy. It will be therefore a great point gained. I hope Congress will approve the measure, and refund the expences.

I have been several times in company with the Colonel [2] who came into Portsmouth in the ship lately arrived there, and am much pleased with him. He is sensible and polite, has a fine appearance, and every air and manner of a Soldier; he is an Irishman brought up in France from his youth, and talks pretty good English. He is modest, but if I have any skill in physiognomy will fight. He says he is determine[d] to deserve any thing you give him, will not serve under the Baron de Bore who arrived in the first ship, had rather be a drummer under an American officer.

I hope the Court will rise this week and give me a little respite

[1] Warren, Dalton, Cooper and Captain Gardner, from the House, and Thomas Cushing, Moses Gill and Benjamin Austin from the Council. *Resolves of the Mass. General Assembly*, April 25, 1777.
[2] Thomas Conway (1733-1800?).

and time to study Tull; but after all our study, I don't know but Mrs. Adams' native genius will excel us all in husbandry. She was much engaged when I came along, and the farm at Braintree appeared to be under excellent management. I tryed to persuade her to make a visit to her friend Mrs. Warren, but she can't leave home this *Busy Season.*

I could wish the Agents you may send here to purchase cloathing or other necessaries for the Army may be instructed not to violate our Laws, assume too great a superiority, or interfere with our Board of War, who are really agents for you without commissions or pay, and do business for you in the best manner. This wish is suggested to me by an altercation now subsisting between some of them and the Board, who shall purchase the cargo of the French-man lately arrived here, tho the Board of War had engaged what they chose to take and have offered the Agents every article they may want. Such things may give the French an ill opinion of us. My regards to all Friends. I am as usual yours, etc.

[No signature.]

I thank you for your two letters of the 6th of April which came safe to hand. I am glad to hear you have it in contemplation to put your Naval Affairs on a better footing. I have not the least difficulty in supposing that they would have made a very different figure in other hands. The selfishness and incapacity you mention are well placed, and have injured them much.

Livingston [1] and Turnbul,[2] two young gentlemen, are employed here by your secret Committee to purchase cloathing etc. they inform me they are going to return soon, and expect there will be a new appointment in their room. Would it not be better to appoint some person here. Mr. Otis [3] on the Committee of Cloathing, last fall, procured and sent forward great quantities of cloathing for the Army. If agreable to you I could wish you would mention him to that Committee. He has by his conduct on that Committee and the services he did the Army deserved the appointment.

1 Abraham Livingston.   2 William Turnbull.
3 Samuel Alleyne Otis (1740–1814), deputy under James Mease, Clothier General.

I intended this for a short letter, but I always fill the paper when I write to you. I want to see some resentment shown to the Portuguees. It wont perhaps do to declare war against them or to make captures of their Ships, for they do only what they cant help; but an interdiction of commerce with them made in the stile of the high and mighty States of America might, as Carmichael [1] hints, have an happy effect.

JOHN ADAMS TO JAMES WARREN

May 2, 1777

DEAR SIR, — Dr. Brownson [2] a Delegate from Georgia in Congress and a worthy spirited sensible Man, a Native of Connecticutt will deliver you this. He will be able to tell you much News, because he intends a circuitous Journey by Albany, and the New Hampshire Grants, who have lately made themselves a State, to Boston. The British Daemons have rec'd a little Chastisement in Connecticutt.

J. ADAMS

JOHN ADAMS TO JAMES WARREN

PHILADELPHIA, *April* [*May,*] 3, 1777

MY DEAR SIR, — Yours of April 3d I recd. I must confess, that I am at a Loss to determine whether it is good Policy in Us to wish for a War between France and Britain, unless We could be sure that no other Powers would engage in it: But if France engages Spain will, and then all Europe will arrange themselves on one side and the other and what Consequences to Us might be involved in it I don't know. If We could have a free Trade with Europe I should rather run the Risque of fighting it out with George and his present Allies, provided he should get no other. I don't love to be intangled in the Quarrels of Europe. I don't wish to be under

---

[1] William Carmichael (–1795). His suggestion was made in a letter from Amsterdam to the Committee of Foreign Correspondence, November 2, 1776. Wharton, *Diplomatic Correspondence of the Revolution*, II. 189.

[2] Nathan Brownson (1743-1796). See Dexter, *Yale Biographies*, II. 690.

Obligations to any of them, and I am very unwilling they should rob Us of the Glory of vindicating our own Liberties.

It is a Cowardly Spirit in our Countrymen, which makes them pant with so much longing Expectation, after a French War. I have very often been ashamed to hear so many Whiggs groaning and Sighing with Despondency and whining out their Fears that We must be subdued unless France should step in. Are We to be beholden to France for our Liberties? France has done so much already that the Honour and Dignity and Reputation of Great Britain is concerned to resent it, and if she does not, France will trifle with her forever hereafter. She has recd. our Ambassadors, protected our Merchant Men, Privateers, Men of War and Prizes, admitted Us freely to trade, lent Us Money, and supplied Us with Arms, Ammunition and Warlike Stores of every Kind. This is notorious all over Europe, and she will do more, presently, if our dastardly Despondency, in the midst of the finest Prospects imaginable, does not discourage her. The surest and the only Way to secure her Arms in this Cause is for Us to exert our own. For God's sake then don't fail of a single Man of your Quota. Get them at any Rate, and by any Means rather than not have them.

I am more concerned about our Revenue than the Aid of France. Pray let the Loan Offices do their Part, that We may not be compelled to make Paper Money as plenty and of Course as cheap as Oak Leaves. There is so much Injustice in carrying on a War with a depreciating Currency that We can hardly pray with Confidence for success.

The Confederation has been delayed because the States were not fully represented. Congress is now full, and We are in the Midst of it. It will soon be passed.

God prosper your new Constitution. But I am afraid you will meet the Disapprobation of your Constituents. It is a Pity you should be obliged to lay it before them; it will divide and distract them. However, their Will be done; if they suit themselves they will please me. Your Friend.

[*No signature.*]

JAMES WARREN TO JOHN ADAMS.   ADAMS MSS.

BOSTON, *May* 5, 1777

MY DEAR SIR,—We have no late arrivals, no foreign intelligence. the affair of Danbury has wholly engrossed the conversation here for a week past, and we were never able to determine whether what we heard was true or false, or even that there had been an expedition there till yesterday, when we were beyond a doubt ascertained of the loss of the stores there, and the indelible stigma fixed on the N. England Militia by the Cowardly conduct of the Connecticut men.[1] Had these men never the Lexington and Bunker Hill spirit, or have they been laughted out of it by our Continental regulars, and made to believe they can't fight? If they won't fight what have we to depend on here but Miracles, for we have nothing else, and here it is said is to be the campaign. My superiour officer in the Militia [2] you retain at the head of the Supreem Legislative; the next to me you have advanced to a more important station. I am therefore left alone, and find the misfortune of being ranked with important folks. The Militia is so despised, and I suppose is designed with all its officers to be directed by Continental Generals, that I intend to embrace the first opportunity to quit it, that shall offer without any imputation. The late intelligence alone has prevented. We have lately ordered 1,500 Militia from the County of Hampshire to Ticonderoga; one half of the County of Berkshire are gone to Albany at the desire of General Gates; two thousand men are ordered and most of them marched to reinforce the State of Rhode Island. We have voted the same bounty to the Regiments of Lee, Henley, and Jackson, before given to the 15 Battalions. We have ventured on a draft on such of our Towns as have not already inlisted a number aequal to 1/7th part of all their Male Inhabitants from sixteen and upwards, to be made on the 15th of this month, and now must raise some Regiments for the defence of this Harbour, or leave it defenceless. If we do all this, if our Board of War deals out the stores they collect as fast as they come in to the Army, if we strip our beds of blankets, and our backs of cloaths for them, if we suffer all our

[1] Bailey, *History of Danbury*, 60.   [2] John Hancock.

provisions to be purchased for them, in short, if for the good of the whole we are contented to be naked, cold, hungry, and defenceless, will the Southern Gentry give us credit, and call us good fellows? Or will they say we are selfish and provideing for a Seperate Interest, which I have it hinted to me is the case? Some people employed here have done more hurt than good.

I suppose the Court will rise tomorrow. You will next hear from me at Plymouth, where I long to be to set out a few trees, etc., to flourish in the age of peace and happiness. Since my last I am to thank you for yours of the 16th April. I have a great curiosity to know what operation the turn of our affairs last winter will have in Europe. I yesterday wrote to the General, and gave him a detail of the situation of things here, and the motives we have acted from. If he has any confidence in me he will entertain no prejudices against us.[1] If N England is to be the scene of action, are no troops to be sent here? I am called and must conclude. Please to give my regards to my Friends, and inform Mr. Adams that his account is past, and a grant for his services up to August last. Perhaps he should send an order to receive it, if his Lady has not one. I am as usual your Sincere Friend, etc.

[No signature.]

JOHN ADAMS TO JAMES WARREN [2]

PHILADELPHIA, *May* 6, 1777

DEAR SIR, — About Ten Days ago I had the Boldness to make a Motion that a Navy Board should be established at Boston. Certain Gentlemen looked struck and surprised; however, it passed.[3] I have moved I believe fifteen Times, that a Nomination should take Place; certain Gentlemen looked cold.

Two or three Days ago, the Nomination came on. Langdon, Vernon, Deshon, Dalton, Orne, Henley, Smith, Cushing and Warren, were nominated.

1 Washington's reply, May 23, 1777, is in *Writings of Washington* (Ford), v. 379. The original letter, written by Hamilton, but signed by Washington, is in the Warren Papers.
2 Although this letter is printed in the *Works of John Adams*, IX. 464, it is reprinted, as it gives the reasons for appointing Warren to the Navy Board.
3 *Journals of the Continental Congress*, VII. 281. The resolution was adopted April 19.

This Day the Choice came on. At last Vernon, Warren, and Deshon were chosen. The Board are to appoint their own Clerk who is to have 500 Dollars a year. I hope you will engage in this Business and conduct it with Spirit. You cannot be Speaker and do this Duty too I believe.

I think the Town of Boston will be offended. But I could not help it. This you will not mention. The Salary for the Commissioners is 1500 Dollars a Year. You will have the Building and fitting of all Ships, the appointment of Officers, the Establishment of Arsenals and Magazines, etc., which will take up your whole Time. But it will be honourable to be so capitally concerned in laying a Foundation of a great Navy. The profit to you will be nothing, But the Honour and the Virtue the greater. I almost envy you this Employment. I am weary of my own and almost with my Life. But I ought not to be weary in endeavoring to do well.

[No signature.]

JAMES WARREN TO JOHN ADAMS. ADAMS MSS.

BOSTON, May 8th, 1777

MY DEAR SIR, — I wrote to you a letter which will accompany this with a design it should have gone by last Monday's post, but he gave me the slip. Nothing very material has occured since. We had yesterday very agreeable accounts of a late Action in the Jersies. If it proves true, it is a good beginning. Our Fleet is still in the harbour. We have had easterly winds and thick weather almost constantly for a fortnight past. They were to sail this day, if possible, but there is no alteration in the weather. Three Cruisers chased a Vessel between the Capes yesterday. The intelligence from Halifax is that eight sail of their Ships and some small Vessels are between that place and this, that the topic of conversation among the officers is the attack on Boston, and the manner how, etc. The Court is still setting but will rise to night or tomorrow. We have voted the Bounty, etc., to two Battalions of Lee and Jackson, the same as the other fifteen. This makes the Bounty to be given to eighteen Battalions. We have established or voted a Regiment of the Train, and two others for the defence of

Boston, the first for three year twenty dollar Bounty, the others for one year with ten dollars. I won't tell you the present state of Boston till my next. The long experience of the people here, the intelligence they have from the Southward of the enmity and conspiracies of the Tories, and the expectation of an attack here have wrought them up to such a pitch that a seperation seems necessary. We have passed a Bill for that purpose. Each Town are to meet and in public meeting form a List of such as are Inimical, and supposed dangerous to choose thirteen of a Committee to Try them, and if that is the Judgment send them to the Board of War who are to provide Vessels and transport them Immediately. If they return they are to be hanged. This Bill is before the Council. If it passes there and the business is not done, it will not be the fault of the Court, the people must blame themselves. My regards to all friends. I am, Yours Assuredly.

[*No signature.*]

The Post in last evening and no letters from my friends.

JAMES WARREN TO JOHN ADAMS.   ADAMS MSS.

BOSTON, *June* 5th, 1777

MY DEAR SIR, — You will perhaps wonder that you have not heard from me for so long a time. I have had so little time at home of late, and found so much to do there, that I did not attend Election, and returned to this town not before yesterday. On my way I had the pleasure to find Mrs. Adams and family well. I left Mrs. Warren to spend this week with her friends at Braintree. I dare say every hour of it will be improved and enjoyed. While at home I had the pleasure of your several favours of April 29, May 2, 3, and 6. I have now the pleasure of informing you that the draft on the several towns to compleat our quota has succeeded beyond my expectations, and I hope soon to have our whole number in Camp, some of them however will not be for three years. When I came to Town it was with a full determination not to act as Speaker; but I was forced to accept for a few days, so that I have not had time to make such enquiry into the state of this matter as I could wish. I will inform you more perticularly in my next. In the mean time I hope the result of our exertions will rescue you from the pain of enduring more reflections on your Constituents. We always meant well, and if our policy had been equal to the goodness of our intentions, we should have done better than we have; but as it is have we not done better than those who abuse us for not doing more. I should be glad to know the state of the Quotas in the southern states. If I have a right notion of them, and don't flatter myself too much with the present state of our own, you may revenge yourself at pleasure. I am told now that General Washington's Army is in a good state. I think there can't be less than 7,000 of our men gone and most of them in Camp. We had however yesterday an extract of a letter from Poor at Ti., forwarded by Gov. Trumbull, letting us know that the Enemy were approaching and the Garrison weak, which is to me unaccountable. However the Hampshire Militia was in soon after, and with other Troops I hope will be an effectual relief. The letter is committed and perhaps something more will be done. I intended to have enlarged a little but have been interrupted. I can now only express my obligations for the late instance of your friendship. I have had yet no other notice of the appointment you mention but from common report. It appears to me to be a business of some magnitude, and I have taken such a lurch lately for a more private way of life that I am undetermined what I shall do. I am told here that an actual residence in Boston is required. If so I must of course excuse myself, as I should be loath to move from and loose my interest in my native Town and County. I am however very glad there is a Board established; never such a thing was wanted more. It gives universal Satisfaction; every body applauds the measure. If I undertake it, I shall exert myself to do as much honour to your Nomination as I am able. We have a House of one-half new Members: the upper Counties are largely represented, more than 60 already returned from the County of Worcester. They come high charged and yesterday moved for a repeal of the Act for a more equal representation. They did not however carry it. Some of them had patience to wait till a Constitution was formed. Adew.

[*No signature.*]

JOHN ADAMS TO JAMES WARREN

PHILADELPHIA, *June* 11, 1777

MY DEAR SIR, — The honourable Samuel [Joseph] Hewes, Esqr,[1] a Delegate in Congress from North Carolina from 1774 to 1777, being bound on a Journey, to Boston for the Recovery of his Health, I do myself the Honour to introduce him to you.

He has a large share in the Conduct of our naval and commercial affairs, having been a member of the naval and marine Committees, and of the Secret Committee from the first.

I wish you would be kind enough to introduce him to some of our best Company, and give him a line to Dr. Winthrop, that he may have an opportunity of seeing the curiosities of Harvard Colledge. I have not time to write the Doctor.

What Mr. Howe's present Plan is no Conjurer can discover. He is moving and maneuvring with his Fleet and Army, as if he had some Design, or other, but what it may be no Astrologer can divine. It is disputed among the Writers, upon military Science, whether a Faculty of penetrating the Intentions of an Enemy, or that of acquiring the Love of his Soldiers is the first Quality of a General. But whether this Penetration holds the first or second Place, it cannot discover Designs that are not, and Schemes that were never laid. Howe's behaviour Strongly indicates a Want of System.

Some conjecture he is bound to the West Indies, others to Europe; one Party to Hallifax, another to Rhode Island. This set sends him up the North River, that down the East River and the other up the Delaware. I am weary of Conjectures. Time will solve them.

One thing is certain, that in the Jersies his whole Army was seized with Terror and Amazement. The Jersey Militia, have done themselves, the highest Honour, by turning out in such great Numbers, and with such Determined Resolution. This was altogether unexpected to the British and Hessian Gentry. They were persuaded that the People, would be on their side, or at least inactive; but when they found Hundreds, who had taken their Protection, and their oaths of allegiance, in Arms, against them,

[1] Joseph Hewes (1730–1779).

and with terrible Imprecations, vowing Vengeance, their Hearts sank within them and they sneaked away in a Panic. This Militia, was dismissed too soon, and they took advantage of it, to come out, again with their whole Army upon a predatory Expedition, but soon returned, and evacuated New Jersey altogether.

I am most apprehensive they will go to Rhode Island. If not, I think, unless they have prepared Reinforcements with such Secrecy that no Intimations of them have reached us, they will give us but a languishing and inactive Campaign.

I hope you proceed, in the Formation of a Constitution without any hurtfull Divisions, or Altercations. Whatev[er] the Majority determine, I hope the Minority will cheerfully concur in. The fatal Experience of Pennsylvania, has made me dread nothing so much as Disunion, upon this Point. God grant you may lay the Foundations of a great, wise, free and honourable People.

[*No signature.*]

JAMES WARREN TO JOHN ADAMS. ADAMS MSS.

BOSTON, *June* 11th, 1777

MY DEAR SIR, — It is a long time since I have had the pleasure of a line from you. I looked for one last post, and was disappointed. I wrote to you by the Thursday post, since which nothing of consequence has taken place here. A number of Men of War are cruiseing on our Coast and three or four of them in our Bay. I suppose their design is [to] get our frigates, and to intercept the prizes taken by the Privateers lately sailed. I fear they will succeed too well in the last, if not in the first. Where Manly and McNeil are we don't hear, but I am in some pain for them. I am sorry to hear there is any difficulty in Gates haveing the command of the Northern Army. Will not this produce a resignation and some confusion in our affairs. Besides I have no notion of a General who is not on the spot, and to fight if there be occasion. Our Expedition some time ago recommended by Congress has fallen through in a strange manner. I can give you no account of this event, but from a want of spirit and activity. When I left Boston I supposed it was to be executed in a short time, but now I hear nothing of it.

The whole matter was left with our Council and they were vested with powers accordingly. They perhaps can give a reason. The Enemy at this time have but a small force, and I think might with the greatest ease be driven off in the course of ten days from this moment; but there is no General sent as mentioned, and nothing can be done without a Continental General. Their holding this Post at a time when they so much want reinforcements to their main Army is the only circumstance that looks like an invasion of N. England. What their movements will be, seems to us very uncertain here. It is generally believed their reinforcements will fall much short of their expectations, but we want some fresh intelligence from Europe. Every thing we do hear looks like a French War. I never wish to be beholden to any other Power but that of Heaven, and to our own virtue and valour for our Liberties; but it seems to me a war between France and England will make a diversion very favourable to us. At least it will Gratifie my resentment and curiosity. I wish to see Britain distressed and reduced to circumstances that shall make her appear ridiculous and contemptible to herself, and I have a curiosity to see the operation and the event.

Your Loan Office in this State I am informed succeeds well. I hope our money has got to its lowest ebb. I think our regulating Act has among other evils injured our Currency by introducing barter, etc.; but our House have after a long debate and a torrent of eloquence and wisdom (for we have eloquent and wise folks among us who affect great sublimity in both without decision), determined against a repeal 122 to 31. We seem generally agreed on a large Tax — not less than 150. perhaps 200,000£. If the other N.E. states would tax in the same proportion, our money would soon be on a better footing: pray let me hear from you. I want to have intelligence from Europe, to hear how your Confederation, etc., go on, and how your health is. I wish you happiness and am, Yours, etc.

[No signature.]

Mrs. Warren desires compliments and best wishes to Mr. Adams.

My regards to Mr. Adams. I will write him soon, tho he has almost dropped the correspondence.

My dear Sir   Philad'a June 10 1777

This Letter will be deliver'd to you by my worthy Friend Col Whipple a Delegate of the State of New Hampshire. He is a Gentleman of Candor, and I wish he may have an Opportunity of conversing freely with some one of Influence in the Massachusetts Bay upon Matters which concern that State particularly. I know of no one to whom I can recommend him on this Occasion with more Propriety than to your self. He will be able to give you such Information of Persons & Things as one would not chuse to trust on Paper in this precarious Time, when an Accident might turn the Intelligence into a wrong Channel.

I observe by the Boston Papers last brought to us, that you are again placed in the Chair of the House of Representatives, with which I am well pleased. Mr Sam Speaker pro Temp. Mr Hancock first Member of the Boston Seat and Mr S Cushing a Commoner at large. I have the Honor of knowing but few of your Members. I hope my Countrymen have been wise in their Elections, and I pray God to bless their Endeavors for the Establishment of publick Liberty Virtue and Happiness.

You will hear before this will reach you of the Movements of the Enemy. It has been the general Opinion for some Months past that Philadelphia is their Object. Should they gain this Point, what will it avail them, unless they beat our Army. This I think they will not do. My Wish is that our Army may beat them, because it would, in my opinion, put a glorious End to the Campaign, & very probably the War. I confess I have always been so very wrong headed as not to be over well pleased, with what is called the Fabian War in America. I conceive a great Difference between the Situations of the great Fabius and the British Generals. But I have no Judgment in Military Matters, and therefore will leave the Subject to be discussed, as it certainly will be, by those who are Masters of it.

I cannot conclude this Letter without thanking you for your Care in carrying on a Matter in which I was interested through the General Assembly, of which I have been informed by our Friend Mr J A. I wish to hear from you.
                                        Adieu my Friend
                                                     S A

James Warren Esq

SAMUEL ADAMS TO JAMES WARREN

PHILADA., *June* 18, 1777

MY DEAR SIR, — This Letter will be delivered to you by my worthy Friend, Colo. Whipple,[1] a Delegate of the State of New Hampshire. He is a Gentleman of Candor, and I wish he may have an opportunity of conversing freely with some one of Influence in the Massachusetts Bay upon Matters which concern that State particularly. I know of no one to whom I can recommend him on this Occasion with more Propriety than to yourself. He will be able to give you such Information of *Persons* and Things as one would not chuse to throw on Paper in this precarious Time, when an Accident might turn the Intelligence into a wrong Channel.

I observe by the Boston Papers last brought to us, that you are again plac'd in the Chair of the House of Representatives, with which I am well pleased — Mr. Pain Speaker *pro Temp.*, Mr. Hancock *first* Member of the Boston Seat, and Mr. T. Cushing a Councellor *at large*. I have the Honor of knowing but few of your Members. I hope my Countrymen have been wise in their Elections, and I pray God to bless their Endeavors for the Establishment of publick Liberty, Virtue and Happiness.

You will hear before this will reach you of the Movements of the Enemy. It has been the general Opinion for some Months past that Philadelphia is their Object. Should they gain this Point, what will it avail them, unless they beat our Army? This I think they will not do. My Wish is that our Army may beat them, because it would, in my opinion, put a glorious End to the Campaign, and very probably the War. I confess I have always been so very wrong headed as not to be over well pleased, with what is called the Fabian War in America. I conceive a great difference between the situations of the Carthaginian and the British Generals. But I have no Judgment in Military Matters, and therefore will leave the Subject to be discussed, as it certainly will be, by those who are Masters of it.

I cannot conclude this Letter without thanking you for your

[1] William Whipple (1730–1785).

Care in carrying a Matter in which I was interested through the General Assembly, of which I have been informed by our Friend Mr. J. A. I wish to hear from you. Adieu, my Friend.

S. A.

JOHN ADAMS TO JAMES WARREN

PHILADELPHIA, *June* 19, 1777

DEAR SIR, — Yours of the 5th inst. is before me. It may be very true, that your Regiments are as full, as those of any other State; but none of yours were so early in the Field, and we must, not flatter ourselves with the Reflection that ours are as full as others. When many Daughters do virtuously, we must excell them all. We are the most powerfull State. We are so situated as to obtain the best Intelligence. We were first in this Warfare: and therefore We must take the Lead, and set the Example the others will follow.

The Armies at Ti and in the Jersies begin to be very respectable: but not one half so numerous as they ought to be. We must not remit our Exertions.

You must not decline your Appointment to the Navy Board. If you should, I know not who will succeed. Congress have passed no order for a constant Residence at Boston. No doubt the most of your Time will be taken up at Boston, but you need not renounce your Native Town and County. It is a Board of very great Importance. I hope your Commissions and Instructions will be soon forwarded. The Cause of their Delay so long is the same, I suppose, that has retarded all other marine affairs — Causes, which it would be thought inexpedient to explain.

I am very sorry to see in the Papers, the Appearance of Dissensions between the General Court and the Town of Boston, and to learn from private Letters, that there are Divisions between the Eastern and Western Part of our Commonwealth. I wish to know, the Run of the Instructions from the Towns, on the Subject of a Constitution, and whether you are in a way to frame one. Surely the longer this Measure is delayed, the more difficult it will be to accomplish. The Rage of Speculation, Improvement and Refinement is unbounded, and the longer it is suffered to indulge itself the wilder it will grow.

I am much mortified that our State have neglected so long, to Number their Regiments, and to send us a List of them and of all their officers. We loose one half the Reputation, that is due to us, for want of a little Method and Regularity, in Business.

We are much embarrassed here, with foreign officers.[1] We have three capital Characters here, Monsr. de Coudray, General Conway, and Monsr De la Balme. These are great and learned Men. Coudray is the most promising officer in France. Coudray is an officer of Artillery, Balme of Cavalry, and Conway of Infantry. Coudray has cost us dear, his Terms are very high, but he has done us such essential service in France, and his Interest is so great and so near the Throne, that it would be impolitick, not to avail ourselves of him.

I live here at an Expence, that will astonish my Constituents, and expose me, I fear to Reflections. I spend nothing myself, I keep no Company, and I live as simply, as any Member of your Houses, without Exception. But my Horses are eating their Heads off, and my own and servants Board are beyond any Thing you can concieve. I would have sold my Horses and sent home my servant, but we have been every Moment in Expectation of the Enemy to this Town, which would oblige me to move and in that Case such Confution would take Place, and such a Demand for Horses to remove Families and Effects into the Country, that I should not be able to obtain one to ride fifty Miles for Love nor Money.

I have not made, and I can't make an exact Computation; but I don't believe, my bare Expences, here, if I should stay with my servant and Horses the whole year will amount to less than two Thousand Dollars. If my Constituents are startled at this, I can not help it, they must recall me.

We are in hourly Expec[ta]tion of momentous Intelligence, from every Quarter. Heaven grant it may be prosperous and pleasing.

[*No signature.*]

[1] Washington had complained of the demands made by these officers. See *Writings of Washington* (Ford), v. 369, 403; Ballagh, *Letters of Richard Henry Lee*, I. 293.

JAMES WARREN TO JOHN ADAMS.   ADAMS MSS.

BOSTON, *June* 22d, 1777

MY DEAR SIR, — If any conjecture may be formed from the intelligence or rather reports prevailing here you may leave Philadelphia before this letter will get there. It is said the Britons are determined at all events to attempt that City, and I presume the discretion and wisdom of your Body will induce you to decamp and retire, before the Siege commences, if our Army is in the situation we are told it is. I wish one side or the other would open the Campaign. I long to hear of enterprizes, of battles fought and victories gained on our side; but our intelligence about the Army and every thing else to the Southward is of late miserably deficient and uncertain. Do you recollect that you, on whom I principally depend (because you used to write me often and give me much intelligence), have missed four or five posts and that in that time I have wrote you several letters? I intended home tomorrow or next day, but believe I shall wait till Thursday in hopes of letters from you and my other friends. If I fail I shall be disappointed. All things remain here pretty much in the same situation as when I last wrote you. The regulateing Act has been the subject of frequent and tedious debates, and it yet remains undetermined by the House whether to repeal, inforce, or suspend it for a time. While the people abroad pay very little or no regard to it, the only notice taken of it is the continual disputes and execrations that meet us in every company. The prevailing sentiment in the opposition seems to be for a suspension and let it die in some sort by the authority of Government a lingering death. We have now a Committee for reporting a Constitution. They have met several times, and are well agreed as to the main points in the Connecticut Form. I conceive the matter of Representation will be our greatest difficulty. They have agreed on the qualification of Electors, that they should be Freemen of 21 years of age, resident for a certain time in each Town, and such as have paid publick Taxes. I could wish that a certain degree of property had been another; but as it is to have the sanction of the people at large I question whether that would not render the whole abortive, and from that principle have conceded to it as it is. What number of Electors is to intitle a Town to one Representative or more is the next question not yet settled. Tho we have the advantage of a Member of Congress on this Committee, I am never with them but I wish you was one of us. We want you much. This is a subject of such a magnitude and extent that I feel myself very unequal to, and in want of the judgment and wisdom of those who I have the greatest confidence in and opinion of, instead of the narrow sentiments, trite trifling, and sometimes ludicrous observations of those whose abilities and judgments I despise. I guess at your curiosity with regard to a Certain Member and wish to gratify it; but letters have been intercepted and may be again you will therefore excuse me. I hope your next will contain some observations on a form of Government for this State. They would be seasonable at this time.

We have had a Bill before us for freeing the Negroes, which is ordered to lie, least if passed into an Act it should have a bad effect on the Union of the Colonies. A letter to Congress on that subject was proposed and reported, but I endeavoured to divert that, supposeing it would embarrass and perhaps be attended with worse consequences than passing the Act. All our other business I can now mention is of smaller consequence and in the common course.

As to news we have very little of late. There are a number of Cruisers on our Coast who have taken divers vessels, and two days ago drove ashore on the back of the Cape a Brigantine belonging to this State from the West Indies with 80 bbl. powder, 500 Arms, some duck and salt, etc., which they took possession of; when the inhabitants mustered and marched down to the shore with a piece of cannon, upon which they left her and cargo which was all except a few trifles saved. We hear nothing lately from Manly and McNeil. It is said eight frigates are in quest of them. I expect they will have a brush before they return. The *Alfred* remains in port, not quite man'd, otherways ready to go to sea. Our fleet at Providence still shut up. It is said Hopkins is determined to attempt to get out, and it is generally believed he will fail if he does. Some prizes are sent in. A vessel arrived here yesterday in eighteen days from St. Eustatia and brings an account that the *Oliver*

Cromwell Privateer of Philadelphia of 24 guns was lately taken by a Sloop of War of fourteen. This is an indignity that Oliver never suffered.

I suppose you have reconsidered your Resolve for a Navy Board here. We hear nothing of it lately. I am with great Sincerity Your Friend, etc.

[No signature.]

My best Friend gives her regards to you. Please to inform Mr. Gerry that the Ship expected from Bilboa is not yet arrived.

SAMUEL ADAMS TO JAMES WARREN

PHILADA., June 23d, 1777

MY DEAR SIR, — I wrote to you a few days ago by Colo. Whipple, with whom I hope you have had free Conversation. As he must have been not far from the Spot, he can give you a more particular Account than has yet been handed to us, of the late Scituation and Movements of the two Armies. The main Body of our Army were encampd at Middlebrook and a considerable Force consisting of Continental Troops and Militia lay at a place called Sourland Hills within Six Miles of the Enemy, who were posted at Somerset Court House, Nine Miles on this side of Brunswick. The Right of the Enemy was at Brunswick and their Left at Somerset. They were well fortified on the Right, and had the Rariton River in Front and Millstone River on the left. In this Scituation General Washington thought an Attack upon them would not be warranted by a sufficient Prospect of Success and might be attended with bad Consequences. His Design was to collect all the Forces that could possibly be drawn from other Quarters so as to reduce the Security of his Army to the greatest Certainty, and to be in a Condition to embrace any fair opportunity that might offer to make an Attack on advantageous Terms. In the mean time by light Bodies of Militia seconded and encouraged by a few Continental Troops to harrass and diminish their Numbers by continual Skirmishes. But the Enemy made a sudden Retreat to Brunswick, and from thence with great Precipitation to Amboy. All the Continental Troops at Peeks Kill except the Number necessary for the Security of the Post were ordered to hasten on to the Army in Jersey, and a Part of them had joynd. I am not disposd to ascribe great military Skill to General Howe; but if he designd to draw the whole of our Forces from the East to the West Side of Hudson's River, in order to gain Advantage by suddenly crossing the River with his own Army, I cannot but hope they will be cut off and his Design frustrated. Great Credit is due to the Jersey Militia who have turnd out with Spirit and Alacrity. I congratulate you on the Success of our State Vessels of War.

Will you be so kind as to call on Mrs. A. and let her know that you have receivd this letter, for she charges me with not writing to my Friend so often as she thinks I ought.

The Watchman tells me it is past twelve o'Clock. Adieu, my dear Friend.

S. A.

SAMUEL ADAMS TO JAMES WARREN

PHILADA., *June* 30, 1777

DEAR SIR, — I have the pleasure of receiving your friendly Letter of the 16th Instant, and have little more than time enough barely to acknowledge it. There is an unaccountable uncertainty in the conducting the Post office. About a month ago I remonstrated to the Post Master General that the Time allowd the Eastern Delegates to answer the Letters they received (being on the Monday between the Hours of 9 and 2) was altogether spent in Congress, and requested that we might have one Evening for the purpose. He granted it, and the Post has been since detaind till tuesday Morning. But I am now informd that the former Regulation is revivd, for what Reason I know not, and our Letters must be ready at two o'Clock. I do assure you I should hardly forgive my self, if I could reflect upon my having once neglected to write to so valuable a Friend as you.

You wish to hear "how our Confederation goes on." I do not wonder at your Anxiety to have it completed, for it appears to me to be a Matter of very great Importance. We every now and then take it into Consideration, but such a Variety of Affairs have demanded the Attention of Congress, that it has been impracticable hitherto to get it through. There are but two or three things which in my Opinion will be the Subjects of further Debate, and upon these I believe most if not all the Members have already made up their Minds. One is, what share of Votes each of the States which differ so much in Wealth and Numbers shall have in determining all Questions. Much has been said upon this weighty Subject, upon the Decision of which the Union of the States and the Security of the Liberty of the whole [depend]. Perhaps it would be more easy for a disinterested Foreigner to see, than for the united States to fix upon the Principles on which this Question ought in Equity to be decided. The Sentiments in Congress are not various, but, as you will easily conceive, opposite. The Question was very largely debated a few days ago, and I am apt to think it will be tomorrow determind, that each State shall have one Vote, but that certain great and very interesting Questions shall have the concurrent Votes of Nine States for a Decision. Whether this Composition will go near towards the Preservation of a due Ballance, I wish you to consider. For if your Life and Health is spared to your Country *you* will have a great Share in the Determination of it hereafter.

You have Advices from abroad later than ours. Our last Intelligence I gave you pretty minutely in a Letter which I sent and suppose was deliverd to you by Capt. Collins.

I find by the Newspapers that the General Assembly under the Denomination of a Convention are forming a new Constitution. This is a momentous Business; I pray God to direct you! Shall I be favord with your own and others Sentiments upon it. I am greatly afflicted to find that angry Disputes have arisen among my dear Countrymen, at a time especially when perfect good Humour should subsist and every Heart and Tongue and Hand should unite in promoting the Establishment of publick Liberty and securing the future Safety and Happiness of our Country. I am sure you will cultivate Harmony among those who love the Country in Sincerity. With Regard to *others*, I will say in the Apostolick Language "I would they were all cut off" (banishd at least) "who trouble you."

Will it too much infringe upon your precious Time, to acquaint Mrs. A. that I am in good Health and Spirits; and have not opportunity to write to her by this Post. I am with the most friendly Regards to your Lady and Family, very affectionately, your Friend,

S. A.

JOHN ADAMS TO JAMES WARREN

PHILADELPHIA, *July* 7, 1777

MY DEAR SIR, — Yours of June 22d recd. only today. We have no Thoughts of leaving Philadelphia. I believe Howe has no Thoughts of attempting it, but if he has We are determined to keep it. Our Army, with the assistance of the Militia, will be sufficient to defend it.

Why our Army fills up no faster I can't conceive. The Massachusetts Regiments at Ti are not one Third full, and We cannot learn from Peeks Kill, that Putnam ever had above Six Thousand Men, in all, from Mass., Rhode Island, Connecticutt, and New York. You must have been deceived in the Numbers inlisted.

There is a loud Complaint here, about Arms. Eighteen Thousand Arms have arrived at Portsmouth [1] and We know not what becomes of them. Other Arms have arrived in Mass., but We know not where they are, and it is said the *Game Cock* carried Six Thousand into Dartmouth. Where are they?

I wish you Joy of your Employment in making a Constitution, hope you will make a good one. I hope to sit quietly under it, altho I shall have no hand in forming it. Do you intend to make every Man of 21 a Voter for the Council? I have nothing to say, but I fear you will find a Fountain of Corruption, in making so many Voters.

The Bill for freeing the Negroes, I hope will sleep for a Time. We have Causes enough of Jealousy Discord and Division, and this Bill will certainly add to the Number.

I am weary enough of Complaints, concerning Navy Matters.

[1] By the *Amphitrite*.

I do all I can in public and private to stimulate, but all in vain. The Commissions were never sent untill 4 or 5 days ago by Mr. Sherman.[1] The Instructions are not sent yet.[2] Who is in Fault, I dont say. It is enough for me to answer for my own Faults.

Is a certain elevated Citizen [3] to put his Hand upon the Pummell of one Chair, and leap into another, at 370 Miles Distance?

For my own Part I wish to see Gravity, Wisdom, Constancy and Fortitude in every Chair upon the Continent. My Hopes were placed upon Mr. B.,[4] but his Retirement, has damped if not extinguished them. My next Expectations were from the Philosopher.[5] But I doubt whether the popular Breath, will blow that Way. My Wishes, and Judgment are entirely for another.[6] But I know not the Chance.

I should be more anxious about the Chair, if I were to be near it. But — I pant, and sigh for private Life and rural Felicity. Here all my Wishes terminate, and the sooner I reach it, with an eternal Renunciation of all Concerns with the public, the better for me. An Idol in the Chair that I cannot and will not worship, will only facilitate my Progress, to that Condition in human Life, where alone I can be happy or even comfortable.

[*No signature.*]

JAMES WARREN TO JOHN ADAMS   ADAMS MSS.

BOSTON, *July* 10th, 1777

MY DEAR SIR, — I returned to this Town on Tuesday and found the Court had just adjourned to September. Last evening I had the pleasure of yours of the 19th June. Am much obliged to you for it. It is a rarity being the only one for a month. I hope the laudable ambition you so frequently discover for your Country's excelling in her exertions for carrying on this war will be gratified. I believe we have 8000 already marched, and some more to go. If the other States had done as well, we should certainly have had a

---

[1] Roger Sherman, who had been placed on the Navy Committee June 5, 1777, and superseded on June 30 by Richard Law.
[2] The letters and orders for continental ships were printed for the Navy Board in February, 1777.
[3] John Hancock?   [4] James Bowdoin.   [5] Prof. John Winthrop.   [6] James Warren.

more numerous Army in the field. We shall not remit our exertions till our Quota is compleat.

In my last I informed you that we were proceeding on a Constitution of Government, and what kind of a one we were likely to have. Very little has been since done as I am told. You must know that the Council (of whom several are on the Committee) are almost to a man against a new Constitution, and are forced to come to it with the greatest reluctance; some of us are lukewarm and others consider it as a business by the bye. So the Committee is, instead of improveing this interval and going on that business, immediately adjourned to the week before the Court meets, so that I have a prospect of a little leisure. I shall go home tomorrow, and hope to get more than one ramble among the herds at Ealriver. The season here is uncommonly fine, there is a profusion of grass round this Town — the finest crops of hay I have ever seen.

You need give yourself no concern about any appearance there was of disunion between the Town and the Court. It was a sudden movement of the Town, from the sudden caprice of a few individuals, and seemed to be done without any fixed principles against assuming a Constitution, and like most other sudden and violent things, very quickly subsided, without leaving so much as an appearance of opposition. Nor do I apprehend any danger from the other division you mention. Some gentlemen came down with a few prejudices against the Tradeing Interest, others with very self important notions, and when the first had examined a little, and the others had vented themselves, the cloud dispersed without much lightning, and no bad effects.

I will again try to have our Regiments numbered, and to furnish you with a list of them and their Officers. I can easily conceive it is somewhat embarrassing to have so many foreign officers on your lists. It must increase the number of your General officers faster than perhaps you inclined.

Give your self no trouble about the expences of your liveing. Your Constituents must be reconciled to it, without recalling you. For my own part I wish you to live genteely and in character, cost what it will. I am sure I would if I was in your place. Keep your servant and your horses. I am sure we should not begrutch you any thing you incline to eat, drink, or spend. If it should be necessary to make you another grant of money, let me know it, and I will endeavour to have it done as soon as we meet. We are not unacquainted with extravagancies here. We give five dollars for board, etc., which gives us feelings we were not used to. Since my last nothing material has turned up in the General Court, nor have we any news but from the Jersies and Ti., which you know more about than I do. I hope Ti. will be saved. Schuyler must certainly exert himself now. He will strain every nerve. Many here are very anxious for the fate of that place, but I am not much concerned if the Army there do their duty. Where will Howe next bend his course? After his late curious expedition and retreat, I think New England as probable an object as any. If he comes I hope we shant mortifie the pride you have for the reputation of your Country. A few prizes drop in and we have another valuable arrival of Arms, powder, etc. I suppose Mrs. Adams will herself inform you she is well. My regards to Mr. Adams and Gerry and to other friends. I shall write them as soon as I have opportunity. With my best wishes I am Your Friend, etc.

[*No signature.*]

Let Mr. Gerry know the Ship *Lidia* is not yet arrived. She left Bilboa and was chased into another port by a small English privateer. Two of ours were gone after her. I hope she will be taken and the Ship releived.

JAMES WARREN TO JOHN ADAMS   ADAMS MSS.

BOSTON, *July* 11, 1777

DEAR SIR, — We have this moment an account of the Evacuation of Ticonderoga in consequence of a Council of General Officers, who determined it to be absolutely necessary to save the small Army there.[1] This intelligence is by a letter from St. Clair to the president of the Convention at Vermont. This letter was dated the 7th. He was then on his way to Bennington, and he intended to throw himself on the North River, which as it appears to

[1] See *Proceedings of a General Court Martial . . . for the Trial of Major General St. Clair* (N. Y. Hist. Soc. Collections, 1880), and Smith, *Life of St. Clair.*

me will lay open our Country to the Enemy who were in possession of Shrewsbury. The letter does not inform us of the number of either Army, nor of the loss we sustained; only that he was not able to make his retreat with the Stores so perfectly as he could have wished, and that there had been a severe Action in the rear, the event of which he did not exactly know. I am your Friend,

J. W.

SAMUEL ADAMS TO JAMES WARREN

PHILADA, *July* 22, 1777

MY DEAR SIR, — I now sit down to write to you in great Haste. We have still further but I think confusd Accounts from the Northward. Schuyler lays the blame of the Disaster upon Sinclare and the General officers. "What could induce them," says he, "to a Step that has ruind our Affairs in this Quarter God only knows." They impute it to the Want of Men. They say there were but about 2000 effective Rank and file; but by the Quartermasters Return of the 25 of June, which was ten days before the Evacuation of the Garrison, I assure you there were fit for Duty of the 9 Continental Regiments

Commissd. and non Comd. and Staff officers included	2738
Wells [1] and Leonards [2] Massachusts. Regimts. of Militia	637
Long's [3] Regmt. of N. H. Militia	199
Stevens' [4] Corps of Artillery	151
5 Companies Artificers [5]	178
Three Companies of Rangers, viz. Whitcomb's,[6] Aldrich's [7] and Lee's	70
	3973
At out posts not included	218
besides sick in Camps and barracks	342
	4533

Schuyler in his Letter of 9th July says, "I am informed from *undoubted* Authority that the Garrison was reinforcd with 1200 Men at least two days before the Evacuation." Let us set them down only 967 to 967

make an even Number of the whole 5500

1 Agrippa Wells, of Greenfield.   2 David Leonard, of West Springfield.
3 Pierce Long.   4 Ebenezer Stevens.   5 Commanded by Jeduthan Baldwin.
6 John Whitcomb.   7 Not mentioned in the return made by St. Clair at his trial.

If half of these were officers, will anyone *presume* that they are preferable to Privates. You may make what use you please of this Scroll. I will write you further particulars very soon. I hope our Massachusetts friends will put it in our power to vindicate that State from Aspersion. Adieu. S. A——

Sinclair in a Letter of June 30 says "My People are in the best Disposition possible and I have no Doubt about giving a good Accot. of the Enemy should they think proper to attack us." [1]

SAMUEL ADAMS TO JAMES WARREN

PHILADA., *July* 31, 1777

MY DEAR SIR,— It is a long time since I had the Pleasure of a Letter from you. I have not heard your opinion of the Evacuation of T[i]conderoga. You are doubtless as much chagrind as I am. It is ascribd to different Causes. Congress is determind that the true Reasons shall be enquired into, and the Conduct of the General officers. Schuyler's Friends are endeavoring to clear him from all Blame, because, say they, *he was not there.* This is true. And as it was well known he had never been used to keep his own Person near his Army, perhaps it may be pertinently asked, Why *he* was pitched upon to take the Command.[2] *Your* Delegates, I can assure you, were utterly against it. And, notwithstanding it was publishd in one of the Boston News papers, said to be warranted by *a Letter from this City*, that General Schuyler had the entire Confidence of Congress, there were five only of eleven States present, in favor of it. The Paper I think was of the 5th of June.[3] I wish I could know who gave the Letter to the Printer. In order, I suppose, to give Credit to that Letter, there was another Publication in the Papers here, informing the World, that when he set off for the Northern Department, he was accompanied

[1] See the letter from Samuel Adams to Richard Henry Lee, July 12, 1777, in Wells, *Life of Samuel Adams*, II. 484.
[2] The Board of War reported in favor of Schuyler, May 15, 1777, but the report was not acted upon until May 22.
[3] The extract appeared in the *Independent Chronicle*, June 12, 1777, and read: "General Schuyler will return to the Northern Department, possessed of the full Confidence of Congress, his Conduct has been fully enquired into, and the Congress have given very honorable Proofs of their good opinion of him." The extract was dated May 27.

by the President and other Members of Congress, which I take for granted is true. These are trifling political Manuvres similar to those which we have formerly seen practicd in the Massachusetts Bay, when a Prop was wanted for a sinking Character. You may think them not worth your Notice; Excuse my troubling you with them. Cunning Politicians often make use of the Names of *Persons*, and sometimes of the *Persons themselves*, who have not the least Suspicion of it, to serve their own designs. When I mentiond five out of Eleven I should have explaind my self. There were five States for the Measure, four against it and two divided. Had not the State of Rhode Island been at that Juncture accidentally unrepresented, there would have been an equal Division, and the Measure would have been prevented. The most important Events may sometimes depend upon small Circumstances. Some Gentlemen of the State of N.Y. are exceedingly attachd to G. Schuyler. They represent him as *Instar Omnium* in the Northern Department. After all that has been said, I conceive of him, as I have for a long time, excellently well qualified for a Commissary or Quartermaster. The N.E. Delegates were (perhaps one excepted) to a Man against his having the Command of that Army. But of this I will write particularly in another Letter.

I am not willing to prejudge, but I must say, it is difficult to reconcile the sudden Evacuation of Ty. with the previous flattering Letters of General St. Clare. In one of his Letters written but a few days before he says "My People are in the best Disposition possible and I have no Doubt about giving a good Account of the Enemy if they shall think proper to attack us." He has been esteemed here a good officer and in his Letter he bespeaks the Candor of the Publick till he can be heard. Pains will be taken to lay the Blame upon the N.E. States, for not furnishing their Quota of Men. I wish therefore you would procure for me an authentick Account of the Number of Men, both regular and Militia sent to the Northward from our State, and how they were cloathd and armd. You may remember that Congress recommended to the Eastern States, some time I think in December last,[1] to send a

[1] *Journals of the Continental Congress*, VI. 1038. The recommendation was passed December 24, 1776.

Reinforcement of Militia to Ticonderoga, to remain there till they could be replacd by Continental Troops then raising. I have never been informd of the Effect of that Recommendation — or if I have I do not recollect it. Pray put it in our Power to state Facts precisely as far as they regard our State. It is agreed on all Sides that a Fault lies some where. I hope the Truth will be thoroughly investigated, and to use the homely Proverb, the Saddle laid on the right Horse.

We are looking every Moment for the Arrival of the Enemy in this River. Two hundred and 55 Sail were seen on Wednesday last steering from the Hook South East. Seventy Sail were seen from the Shore near Egg Harbour, about 20 Leagues from these Capes, on Saturday last steering the same Course. The Wind against them. They could not come here at a better time. Genl. W[ashington] is drawing his Troops into this Neighborhood. Some of them are arrivd. But as the Enemy has the Advantage of us by Sea, it is too easy for them to oblige us to harass our Troops by long and fruitless Marches; and I should not wonder to hear that they have tackd about and gone Eastward. I hope my Countrymen are prepared. *Let brotherly Love continue.* Adieu. Pay my friendly Respects to your Lady and family.[1]

[*No signature.*]

Samuel Adams to James Warren

DEAR SIR, — I wrote to you on the 30 Ulto. by Mr. Bruce, who did not leave the City on that day as I expected. His stay gives me the oppty. of acquainting you that, an Express who left the Capes yesterday informs us that the Enemies Ships all went out to Sea in the morning steering E.N.E., supposd to be going to Hudson's River, Rh. Island, or Boston. Mr. Bruce will give you as particular an Acct. as I can; I therefore refer you to him. This is what I expected. I trust you are upon your Guard.

Congress have orderd that an Enquiry be made into the Reasons of the Evacuation of Tyconderoga and Mount Independence and into the Conduct of the General officers who were in the Northn.

---

1 Endorsed: favord by Mr. Bruce.

Departmt. at the time of the Evacuation. That Schuyler, St. Clair, Poor,[1] Patterson [2] and Roche de Fermoy repair to Head Quarters, and that Genl. Washington order such Genl. officers as he shall think proper immediately to repair to the Northern Department to relieve Schuyler in his Command there.[3] A Comt. is appointed to digest and report the Mode of conducting the Enquiry.

It appears to me difficult to account for the Evacuation of those Posts even upon the Principle of Cowardice. The whole Conduct seems to carry the evident Marks of Deliberation and Design. My utmost Endeavors shall not be wanting to have the Matter searched to the Bottom.

If we are vigilant active spirited and decisive, I yet flatter my self, notwithstanding the present vexatious Situation of our Affairs at the Northwd., we shall humble our Enemies this Campaign. I am truly mortified at their leaving this place, because I think we were fully prepared for them, and I believe the cowardly rascals knew it. May Heaven prosper our righteous Cause. Adieu.

S. A——

PHILADA., *Augt.* 1, '77

JAMES WARREN TO JOHN ADAMS   ADAMS MSS.

BOSTON, *August* 10th, 1777

MY DEAR SIR,— I received your favours by Mr. Hewes and by the post since writing which you must have heard of the important event of the Evacuation of Ti. What will be the consequences of it time will discover. What will be the reflections upon it in the South you are able before now to say. I suppose many aspertions on these States. That languor, supineness, and want of public virtue, and spirit prevail here is too true, but do they not prevail in the Southern States? It is true we have not furnished our quota of the Army, have they furnished theirs? If they have where are

[1] Enoch Poor.   [2] John Paterson.
[3] On August 2 the New England delegates asked Washington to send Gates. Sparks, *Writings of Washington*, v. 14.

they? The General Court here have done all in their power, and more than the Southern States approved of. It is rather their misfortune than fault that our men are not all in the field; but will Congress impute the loss of Ti. to the negligence of these States? I see St. Clair's letter published by their order. You will hear that the General Court are now met on a special call of the Council. I presume we are able, and I hope before we rise we shall demonstrate that near 3500 of our Continental Troops must at that time have been at the places of their destination in that department: and N: Hampshire say more than 2000 of theirs, and at least 4000 of them perhaps more, equipt with the New Arms out of the French Ship at Portsmouth, as good as any on the Continent, and more Militia than they had would have been furnished if requested. If you ask how this is to be reconciled to St. Clair's letter, I answer that is for him and the other officers to do, upon a severe scrutiny which I hope will be made into this matter. The indignation and distrust that prevails here are extreem, and the want of confidence in your Commanders that way such that if it be not removed by Lincoln's [1] being sent there to command the Militia will very much impede our Reinforcements. We have ordered a sixth part of the Militia of Suffolk, Essex, Middlesex, Worcester, York, Hampshire and Berkshire, a small part of two of them excepted to be drafted, and marched directly,[2] these I think must make at least 4000 men. What Connecticut, or Hampshire have done I know not. We have also come to some severe resolutions for compleating our quota of the Army. We have just received an account that our Army have retreated from Saratoga to Stillwater, and that the British Fleet and Army had returned to the Hook, and General Washington to Morris Town. We have expected them here, which occasioned some confusion in this Town for a day or two. We now generally suppose they are going up the North River. Had they come I believe our Militia would have turned out with a spirit

[1] Benjamin Lincoln. He was at Worcester, and had written, August 7, to General Ward, "communicating his Sentiments with respect to a Disobedience to the Order of Court for raising this State's Quota of the Army, and the prevalent Suspicions of the People with respect to the Evacuation of Ticonderoga." *Journal of the House of Representatives* (Mass.), August 8, 1777.
[2] *Ib.*

equal to any of their Neighbours. Upon the alarm from Rhode Island, they marched from the Regiments that had orders with uncommon readiness and alacrity considering the business of the Season. Three or four days would have carried 10,000 of them there. No body on that occasion was more embarrassed than I was. I don't feel afraid to fight, and I believe you are sensible nobody has more zeal for the Cause than I have; but I have too much pride to submit to circumstances humiliateing and degradeing. Our Council ordered me to repair there, and take the command of them, and receive from General Spencer, *or such other officer as should be appointed to command there* from time to time, such directions as they should give me. The last part of the order was very extraordinary, and tho' the first may be conformable to a resolve of Congress you will suffer me to tell you I think that so. I know of nothing to determine an officer's rank but his Commission and the date of it. If we have no right to appoint Major Generals we should not have done it. If we have they ought to have their rank, with whatever troops they are called to serve, or at least the depreciation should have been settled prior to their appointment, and they should have known what proportion of one they were to be, when they came within the splendid orb of a Continental Officer. As you have Generals in every State sometimes without a man, even an Orderly Sargeant, to attend them, I suppose to command the Militia, I foresee the Militia are to be considered in the same light of inferiority with regard to the Continental Troops that I have been used with indignation to see them with regard to the British. This by depressing that spirit of military pride which alone can make them important to themselves and others, will soon render them of little consequence and make a standing Army necessary. As I am somewhat advanced in life, and have by the partiality of my countrymen been honoured with many civil and military distinctions, and acted a considerable part in the present great controversy, I have determined no longer to submit to such circumstances, and have therefore embraced this interval of security to resign my Commission. You are now to excuse being detained so long with a matter of so little consequence, I mean so far as relates to me.

Mr. Cushing and Mr. Paine have been to Springfield to meet the Committees from the other N. England States, and New York. they returned last evening.[1] Coll. Orne in his humorous way says he could not go without *Paine* and therefore did not go. I am told they have unanimously agreed to report a repeal of all regulateing Acts, and Land Embargos, and to call in all the money of those States by the first of December next, and to have no currency but Continental. How long we shall set I cant say.[2] Nothing will detain us more than two days longer but that matter, unless we issue a Tax this Session which should have been done before. Our Naval Affairs have had a sad reverse; instead of the triumph of a man-of-war prize, we have lost the *Hancock* a fine frigate.

The Commissions of the Navy Board or rather the instructions of the Marine Board arrived about a week ago. By them it appears we should be all three present in order to transact business. Mr. Deshon (tho' we have expected him ten days) is not yet arrived. I see the business is very large and extensive, must engross our whole time, and we are allowed but one clerk, which I think quite insufficient.[3] While I remain at this Board I shall do every thing I can to answer the design of our appointment, and the expectation of my friends; but with you I sigh for private life and domestic felicity, and incline to resign. I only delay it from respect to your sollicitations. Tomson,[4] Hinman,[5] and Jones[6] are at Portsmouth — have not yet been to sea; McNeil[7] at Casco Bay. A number of cruisers on our coast, who have taken and destroyed many vessels, and among them several privateers. Had we the ships now shut up in Providence, with those mentioned above, I think we should soon have a clear coast.

The Committee on a Constitution have done nothing lately. I hope when we meet again, we shall get along with it, and form a tolerable one, but I tremble with diffidence every step I take. Better heads than mine should be employed in this business. I lament the absence of some one or two. When this is com-

---

1 The proceedings are in Hoadley, *Records State of Connecticut*, 1. 599.
2 The General Court adjourned August 16.
3 October 23, Congress raised the pay of the clerk, and empowered the Board to appoint a second clerk, if found necessary.
4 Thomas Thompson.   5 Elisha Hinman.   6 John Paul Jones.   7 Hector McNeill.

pleated I believe in spite of my sentiments or yours the Citizen you mention will make the leap. I am in great Sincerity Yours, etc.

[*No signature.*]

You enquire what is become of Arms. Four thousand have been received from Mr. Langdon by this State and all but about 100 delivered to Continental Regiments; the remainder must be accounted for by your Agents. There is a mystery about all these matters. I hope time will perfect such arrangements as will prevent all uncertainty in future.

I have several letters from Mr. Adams and Gerry lately; not a word about this Navy Board. Do unravel that mystery. Don't they like the thing or the men.[1]

Samuel Adams to James Warren

PHILADELPHIA, *Augt.* 12, 1777

MY DEAR SIR, — The inclosed is an attested Copy of General Schuyler's Letter to the President of the Congress. It needs no Comment. How far the Massachusetts State deserves the strictures therein made, you can tell. I send it to you for the Perusal of the Members of your Honbl. House. If they have sent into the Army, Boys, Negroes and Men too aged to be fit for any Service, they will lay their Hands on their Mouths. If not, I hope some decent but *keen* Pen will vindicate them from that and other Aspersions. This, like all his other Letters, is written in such a despondent Stile, that it is no wonder that Soldiers decline fighting under him, though they may be under no Apprehension of Treachery. But he has by this time receivd his Quietus, at least till he can give a good Account of his Conduct. Gates is gone to take the Command, and Our Affairs in that Quarter, I dare say, will soon wear another Face.

The Enemies fleet have been again seen, 200 Sail, off Sinipuxin about 15 Leagues South of the Capes of Delaware. I think I have

---

[1] What remains of the papers of the continental Marine Committee and Board of Admiralty has been printed by the Naval History Society, New York.

now a just Demand upon you for a Letter. I shall be disappointed if I do not receive one by the next Post. Adieu my Friend.

S. A——

[Enclosure.]

STILWATER, *August* 4th, 1777

SIR, — By the unanimous advice of all the general officers, I have moved the army to this place; here we propose to fortify a camp in expectation that reinforcements will enable us to keep the ground, and prevent the enemy penetrating further. I wish I could say that we had any prospect of such reinforcements. None of the Militia from the State of Massachusetts or this, will remain with me above five or six days longer. The time of service for which colonel Long's regiment is engaged, expires on the 7th inst. This diminution with what we sustain by desertion, sickness, and in skirmishes with the enemy will reduce us to an alarming weakness.

What effect my repeated application to the State of Massachusetts will have, I cannot determine, as I have not yet been honor'd with an answer. Governor Trumbull informs me that he has requested General Washington to send troops, which he would replace; that he waits his excellency's answer, and in the mean time has ordered the militia brigadiers to draft and equip the men; but in what numbers, or when I may expect them he does not advise me of. I am equally uncertain whether I may expect any from this State.

It is a melancholly consideration that whilst our force is daily diminishing the enemy increase theirs, by a continued acquisition of tories in very considerable numbers.

It is impossible at present to procure a return, but I am very certain that we have not above four thousand continental troops; if men, one third of which are negroes, boys, and men too aged for field, or indeed any other service, can, with propriety be called troops. If it should be asked how boys, negroes, and such aged men come to be sent; I can only answer that the States from whence these troops are come, may possibly determine it. The fact is as I have stated it, literally so, and I may add, that a very great part of the army took the field, in a manner, naked; without blankets, ill armed, and very deficient in accoutrements, and still continue so to be, without a prospect of relief, and to add to our misfortunes, many, too many of our officers would be a disgrace to the most contemptible troops that were ever collected, and have so little sense of honor, that cashiering seems no punishment. They have stood by, and suffered the most scandalous depredations to be committed on the poor distressed, ruined, and flying inhabitants. I must not however, omit saying that we have many officers that would do honor to the best army that ever took the field; but their exertions being counteracted by the worthless; it is impossible for them to do what they wish. Perhaps Congress may think it necessary to invest me with a power in council of general officers to suspend officers for mal-conduct, until the pleasure of Congress is known. Should that power be conferred, and I receive it whilst we are still an army, it is possible that we may continue so, and get into some order.

General Burgoyne is at fort Edward. He has withdrawn his troops from Castletown, and is bending his whole force this way. He will probably be here in eight days, and unless we are well reinforced, as much farther as he pleases to go. I am Sir very respectfully, Your most obedt. Humble Servant,
(Signed) PH. SCHUYLER

The Honble John Hancock esquire, etc., etc.
Secretary's Office of Congress;
Copy of original, compared.
WILLIAM CH. HOUSTON, D. Secry.[1]

JOHN GLOVER TO JAMES WARREN

STILLWATER, 6th *Augt.*, 1777 (24 Miles above Albany)

DEAR SIR, — This will inform you we left Saratoga the 3rd, bringing off all our stores of every kind, with large Droves of Cattle, Sheep and Hoggs.

We arriv'd here 3 OClock in the morning of the 4th. During the three days at Saratoga, we were Constantly (Night and day) in an Alarm, Our scouting parties, a great part of them frequently cut off, killd, Scalp'd and taken Prisoners. The day we left it our Scouts were all drove in by the Indians — two Men brot. to my Quarters, one of them Scalp'd. It appeard they had not been dead more than half an hour.

I immediately detach'd 400 Men from my Brigade, to scour the Woods, where they remaind till 4 OClock. Saw nothing of the Enemy, save three Blanketts, suppos'd to be left by them. We have had 25 or 30 Men kill'd and scalp'd, and as many more taken

---

[1] "Schuyler has written a series of weak and contemptible *things* in a stile of Despondency which alone, I think, is sufficient for the Removal of him from that Command; for if his Pen expresses the true Feelings of his Heart, it cannot be expected that the bravest Veterans would fight under such a General, admitting they had no Suspicion of Treachery. In a letter dated the 4th Instant at Still Water, he writes in a Tone of perfect Despair. He seems to have no Confidence in his Troops, nor the States from whence Reinforcements are to be drawn. A third Part of his Continental Troops, he tells us, consists 'of Boys, Negroes and aged men not fit for the Field or any other Service.' 'A very great Part of the Army naked, without Blanketts, ill armed and very deficient in Accoutrements, without a Prospect of Relief.' 'Many, too many of the Officers would be a Disgrace to the most contemptible Troops that ever was collected.' The Exertions of others of them of a different character 'counteracted by the worthless.' 'Gen'l Burgoyne is bending his Course this Way. He will probably be here in eight Days, and unless we are well reinforced' (which he does not expect,) 'as much farther as he pleases to go.' Was ever any poor General more mortified? But he has by this Time received his Quietus. Gates takes the Command there, agreeably to what you tell me is the wish of the People, and I trust our Affairs in that Quarter will soon wear a more promising Aspect." *Samuel Adams to Roger Sherman*, August 11, 1777. MS.

prisoners, within four Days. This strikes a Panic on our Men, which is not to be wonderd at, when we Consider the Hazard they Run, when out on Scouts, by being fired on, from all Quarters (and the woods so thick, they can't see three yards before them), and then to hear the Cursed War hoop, which makes the Woods ring for Miles.

Our Army at this Post, is weak and shatter'd, much Confus'd, and the Number by no means equal to the Enemy; nor is there the Least probability of a Reinforcement.

Our Artillery, 4 pounders. The Enemys 6, 12, 18 and 24 pounders. Their flying Camp (as they call it) is now at Fort Edward, 24 Miles from this, which Consists of 3000 British Troops, 600 Indians, 1000 Tories and 200 Canadians, with 8 Field pieces, and 4 Howitzers, 200 Waggons for their Baggage. Their main body 5000 Men are at Fort Ann, 14 miles from Fort Edward, with their heavy Artillery. This moment brought in by our Scouts, two Tories in the Enemy's service. They left Fort Edward, Sunday Last, who say some Hessians, with some heavy Artillery, from Fort Ann, got in that Day, and that the flying Camp were to begin their march for Saratoga in three Days.

This day Colo. Long from N. Hampshire, leaves us with his Regt. which Consist of 200 Men, their time being out; nothing will induce them to stay one day Longer.

The 10th goes off 500 Men from Genl. Poor's Brigade, (Militia,) from the County of Hampshire. The 12th goes off from Genl. Nixon's Brigade, 600 Men, (Militia) from the County of Berkshire. We then shall have left 14 Regts. from the State of Massts. Bay — (Bigelow's is not yet got in) which Consist of about 150 Rank and File, fit for duty, Each; three Regts. from New Hampshr. 560 Men; One from New York 150 Ditto. Thus you see the whole strength of the Army at this Post will be but about 3000 Men (that will be on the Ground the 12th inst. unless some Reinforcemt. comes in) to Oppose the Enemy, who, from the best Accounts we can Collect, are at least 8000. and every day growing Stronger by the disaffected Inhabitants joining them, and ours growing Weaker.

If we are not Reinforc'd speedily, we may as well give up the Matter and come home. We cannot make a stand at this place with that handfull of Men we have, Compar'd with the Enemy. We must retire to Albany immediately, on the Enemy's Advancing from Fort Edward, which we expect will be tomorrow.

I'm extremely unhappy in this Departmt. as I know the Popular Clamour runs high, and the People at Large charge every Misfortune or Accident that happens, to either the Cowardice, Negligence or Treachery of the Officers. The Clamour of the People [torn] Schuyler and St. Clair [torn] Hill to Albany, which [torn] n them myself, but when [torn] true state of Facts, I must Confess [torn] was so much Alterd, I have not the least [complaint] against either of them. On the Contrary must say [I think] them to be exceeding good Officers, and that they have [don]e every thing in their power, or that could be done by any Officer in Like Circumstances.

I have Endeavourd to give you the true State of our Army at this Place. A Reinforcemt. lyes with you, and not with us. If we flee before the Enemy, it will be for want of Men. You may rely on it we shall not turn our Backs on equal Numbers.

Genl. Schuyler tells me he has wrote to the Assembly of our State repeatedly, but has Recd. no Answer.

We have an Account of Genl. Howe's 1st Division being Landed at New Castle. If this is true, your fear of an Attack in your Quarter must subside. That being the Case, I hope you will send on a Reinforcemt. immediately. Pray let no time be Lost. A Day's delay may be fatal to America. Let the Body be as Large as possibly can be Collected, furnish'd with Arms and Accoutremts. There is none to be had here. Let some Vigilant persons come on before them to provide Provisions, Waggons, etca. The marching of the Troops have been much Retarded for want of such a Regulation. I am, with Respect, Sir, Yr. most Obedt. hume Sert.

JOHN GLOVER *B. General*

JOHN GLOVER TO JAMES WARREN

STILLWATER, 11th *Augt.*, 1777. 24 Miles above Albany

DEAR SIR, — I wrote you the 6th inst. since which nothing Extraordinary has happen'd at this Post.

Yesterday an Express from Fort Schuyler, (upon the Mohawk

River) 120 Miles from Albany, which informs of an Action between a Body of Militia of 900 Men (from Tryon County) Commanded by B Genl. Harkermon,[1] (on their March to Reinforce that Post) who met with) and 1000 Indians and Tories, 6 miles this side the Fort, Commanded by Sir John Johnson; when an Obstinate Battle ensued,[2] in which were kill'd a Capt Watts of New York, and 50 or 60 Indians, on the side of the Enemy, which were found Dead on the ground our People beat them from. It's probable a great Number were Wounded, which they carried off.

Genl. Harkermon was shot thro' both his legs, broke the Bone of one, and much wounded the other. Notwithstanding this, he kept with his Men till he could procure Waggons to carry off his Wounded, (which were Considerable,) at 24 Miles Distance from the place of Action. The Number of Officers kill'd on our side are many; a Colo. Knox, 3 majors, and several more Subordinate Officers, with 22 Privates. The party that Remain'd pushd on to Fort Schuyler, which was attack'd at the same time, by about 800 of the Enemy. Colo. Gonsewert[3] who Commanded the Fort, sallied out upon them, beat them back, took 6 Field pieces and two Roiads. The number kill'd not ascertain'd.

Genls. Schuyler and St. Clair is order'd down to Hd. Quarters (by Congress,) to give an Accot. of the Evacuation of Ticonderoga and Fort Independence. This I fear will be of fatal Consequences to this Post, as the People in this Quarter are much Attach'd to them. I am, Sir, with Respect and Esteem Yr. most Obedt. Sert.

JOHN GLOVER

P. S. One of our Scouting parties just got in from Fort Edward, which informs the Enemy's Flying Army is at Fort Miller, and are to be at Saratoga to morrow, which is [on]ly 12 Miles from this. Yesterday 300 Militia Left us. This day and to morrow the whole goes off. We shall then be reduc'd to about 3000 Continental Troops, one tenth part of which is taken off for Artillery, and Waggon Drivers, including Boatmen.

If we are not to be Reinforc'd, you will not be surpris'd if the Enemy penetrate to New England.

1 Nicholas Herkimer.   2 At Oriskany, August 6.   3 Peter Gansevoort.

A part of Colo Bigelow's Regt. got in this day after being 30 days from Worcester.

J. G.

JOHN ADAMS TO JAMES WARREN

PHILA., *Aug.* 12, 1777

DEAR SIR, — I see by the Papers, our Assembly is called, and conclude it is now sitting.[1]

The Letters we receive from G. Schuyler, are enough to frighten any Body who does not know him. G. W[ashington] says that all the Regiments from N. H. and M. B. are at the Northward and yet, Schuyler tells us he has not above 5000 Men. I hope this matter will be investigated. I believe Gates will find greater Numbers; if not, I hope they will be sent him.

Burgoine is treading dangerous Ground, and proper Exertions will ruin him. These I hope will not be wanting.

I rejoice to see such a Spirit arise upon the Loss of Ti. and such determined Calls for Inquiry. The Facts must be stated from the Returns and other Evidence, and the innocent will be I hope acquitted, the guilty meet their Deserts. I see no Medium, I confess, between an honourable Acquittal and capital Punishment.

What is become of Howe? The Jersies are very happy, relieved from an heavy Burthen. What Fears were propagated in Boston last January, that the Jersies were lost. Not a single Village, has revolted. We have still Accounts of part of Howe's Fleet, coasting between the Capes of Delaware and those of Cheasapeak. What this Man's design is can not be conjectured; it is very deep or very shallow.

Washington has been here with a noble Army, very obedient, and orderly.

Our News from France, is agreable — Trade, Friendship, Assistance under hand, and Loans of Money, for the present — other Things by and by. I am, etc.

[*No signature.*]

[1] It began its session August 5, one month earlier than intended.

ABIGAIL ADAMS TO MERCY WARREN

August 14, 1777. BRAINTREE.

This is the memorable fourteenth of August. This day 12 years the stamp office was distroyd. Since that time what have we endured? What have we suffer'd? Many very many memorable events which ought to be handed down to posterity will be buried in oblivion, merely for want of a proper Hand to record them; whilst upon the opposite Side many venal pens will be imployd to misrepresent facts and render all our actions odious in the eyes of future generations. I have always been sorry that a certain person who once put their Hand to the pen, should be discouraged, and give up so important a service. Many things would have been recorded by the penetrating genious of that person which, thro the multiplicity of events and the avocations of the times, will wholly escape the notice of any future Historian.

The History and the Events of the present day must fill every Human Breast with Horrour. Every week produces some Horrid Scene perpetrated by our Barbarous foes. Not content with a uniform Series of cruelties practised by their own Hands, but they must let loose the infernal savages, those 'dogs of warr,' and cry Havock to them. Cruelty, impiety, and an utter oblivion of the natural Sentiments of probity and Honour, with the violation of all Laws Humane and Divine, rise at one view and characterise a George, a How, and a Burgoine.

O my dear Friend, when I bring Home to my own Dwelling these tragical Scenes which are every week, presented in the publick papers to us, and only in Idea realize them, my whole soul is distressd. Were I a man, I must be in the Field. I could not live to endure the Thought of my Habitation desolated, my children butcherd, and I an inactive Spectator.

August 15

I enclose to you a Coppy of mr Lee's Letter. It came to me with some restrictions to be shewn only to those whom I could confide in. I think by that our affairs abroad look'd as favorable as we

My Dear Mrs Hawen   Braintree Sep'r 28 1775 —

I cannot work, I cannot read, I cannot talk — let me write to my friend and beg her sympathetick tears to prove faith by her pen. Jane healing Nature to ease & to console the wounded heart of her friend. I have just returned from the sick and almost dying bed of one of the best of parents, to my own habitation, where the same scene is only varied by a nearer connection. —

"Woes cluster; rare are solitary woes;"
"they love a train, they tread each others heel:"
                                    So frequent death,
"Sorrow he more than causes, he confounds;"
"for humane sighs his rival strokes contend,"
"And make distress distraction:"

In my late sickness the tenderness of my mother led her to hazard her health by being with me every day, and there I fear she took the distemper which is now likely to prove fatal to her. She has been 13 days and no alleviation or abatement of her disorder has yet taken place.   She is of so tender a constitution that a small illness soon reduces her strength; and this has seized her, and continues upon her with so much violence that she must soon quit her clay tabernacle for an house not made with hands.

But o my dear friend how shall I sustain the stroke? I know the will of Heaven must be done, and to that I desire to submit with christian resignation.

I know I have not been properly thankful for the many mercies of Heaven towards me, and I must acknowledge the justice of the hand that chastises me, and ought to bless the name of him who hath to this day lengthened out the lives of my parents. and that I have not been earlier in life & oftner made to drink of the bitter cup of affliction —

You my dear friend have often passed thro these heart rending scenes. you can feel for & pitty your friend. How severely do I feel the absence of that friend whose tenderness & sympathy would alleviate my affliction and into whose bosom I could pour my sorrows —   But there is still a higher consolater who is always present, and who has promised to be near to those who call upon him in the day of trouble. upon him I will cast all my cares, and unto him commit my dear parent, who knoweth what is best for us. I subscribe your afflicted both a

could expect; but we have a great many hardships to endure yet I fear, ere we shall receive any assistance from others.

Letters from my Friend to the 20 of july mentions the loss of Ticonderoga with much regreat, but says tis an event which he has feard would take place for some time; people that way were much disposed to censure, but that they had not received any perticular accounts by which a true judgment could be formd.

August 16

We are bless'd my Friend with a fine Season and hope the charming rains this afternoon have reachd Plimouth and refreshd the Fields of Eal river.

You mention some French cotton. I am much obliged to you, but I have since I saw you been accommodated in that way. The Mussel I should be very glad of, either one or two yards, just as you can spair it, and shoe binding, if it is to be had. Garlick Thread I am in great want of, do if you should know of any be so good as to let me know.

I am really ashamed to tell my Friend that I have not yet been able to get Home the cloth. All that was in my power to do to it, has been done 3 months ago and I have been sending and going almost every week since. I saw the Man yesterday and he has promised me that I shall have it next week; but if his word prove no better than it has done I can not say you may depend upon it. All I can say is that my endeavours have not been wanting. As soon as I can get it it shall be forwarded by your affectionate Friend,

PORTIA

JOHN ADAMS TO JAMES WARREN

Aug. 18, 1777

MY DEAR SIR, — The inclosed Copies, you will see must not be made public. You will communicate them in Confidence to such Friends as have Discretion. When you have made such use of them as you shall judge proper, be pleased to send them to the Foot of Pens Hill, because I have no other Copies and should be glad to preserve them.

It is in vain for me to write any Thing of the Northern Department, because you have all the Intelligence from thence, sooner than We have. The G. W[ashington] has orderd Morgan's Riflemen and two or three more Regiments there. There has been a smart Action near Fort Schuyler, in which, our People were successfull, but with a severe Loss.

I hope the Mass. will exert itself now, for the support of Gates and the Humiliation of the blustering Burgoine. It is of vast importance to our Cause that the Mass. should be exemplary upon this occasion.

Howe's Fleet and Army, are still incognito. When or where We shall hear of them, know not.

We are in deep Contemplation upon the state of our Currency. We shall promise Payment in the Loan offices of the Interest in Bills of Exchange on our Ministers in France. But Taxation, My dear Sir, Taxation, and Oeconomy, are our only effectual Resources. The People this way are convinced of it and are setting about it with spirit.

[*No signature.*]

COPIES OF LETTERS OF ARTHUR LEE.

LONDON, *Jan.* 31, 1777

DR. SIR, — I flatter myself with the pleasure of hearing from you soon, and in the mean Time, I wish to convey to you a Piece of important Secret Intelligence, relative to the Situation of this Court with Spain and which I procured in such a Way, as I gave my Honour I would not repeat it to any one, on this Side of the Water.[1] During the latter part of the Administration of Lord Dartmouth a Scheme was formed, for establishing a Colony on the Lands of the Musquito Indians, and Seven or Eight of that Tribe came hither, and gave Assurance that they would sell a Part of their Territory to the English. Dr. Ervin and Captn. Blair, were the Persons, who undertook to carry the Project into Execution, and accordingly loaded a Vessell and sailed with a Cargo of Goods, Implements of Husbandry, Servants, etc. to the Musquito shore. A legislative Council, and Justices of Peace were appointed from hence, for the Government of the Colony. The Spaniards were alarmed at the Settlement, and in consequence seized the Vessell and Cargo: and about Ten Weeks ago Captn. Blair came home to seek Redress. Lord Weymouth, immediately sent orders to the British Ambassadors at Madrid to demand the Restoration of the Vessell and Cargo. That Court peremptorily refused it, unless it was declared that Captn. Blair did not act by

1 Lee was at this time associated with Franklin and Deane.

Authority of the British Court. Lord Weymouth refused to say so, and has told the Cabinet, he dare not do it (which will account for his threatened Resignation, as was mentioned in one of my former Letters) altho it was a Plan adopted and carried into Execution before he came into office, and therefore he alledges he is bound to protect and support the Colony, and more especially as the Mosquito Indians disclaim all Subordination to the Court of Spain; and on the contrary upon the Arrival of each new Governor at Jamaica their King or Sachem, has for many years made it an invariable Custom to go to that Island and pay a Sort of Homage to its Governor, as the Representative of the Crown of England. The Substance of the last answer from Spain was, that if the British Court made it a Serious Matter, the Court of Madrid was determined to do the same. I shall not trouble you with any Observations upon this Intelligence. You will make your own use of it. Lord Weymouth, I am assured will not flinch from it, as he considers himself in a very delicate Situation.

The Indians in the above Letter returned in the Ship with Dr. Ervin and Capt. Blair to the Musquito shore. One of them was a Prince.

If I had two or three Aid de Camps and a Secretary, as the great Men of the Age have, I would present you with a fairer Copy. But we small Folks are obliged to do our own Drudgery, and we have so much of it to do, that we must do it in Haste.[1]

Extract

LONDON, 3 *Feb.*, [1777]

There is no kind of Relaxation here in warlike Preparations, and yet the Ministry have so contrived that few People believe there is any danger of war; this indeed is necessary to them for the present and untill the subscription to the ensuing Loan of Six Millions be compleated, as the Money would otherwise be necessarily borrowed at 10 or 12 greater loss. Transports are getting ready to carry out the additional British and German Troops to America and it is intended they shall all sail by the Beginning of March.

Administration intend the Campaign shall be opened unusually early in the Spring in America, and the Operations directed wholly and on all sides against N. England; and they expect by early and vigorous Exertions, to crush the Northern Colonies before they can be assisted from the Southward, and before any foreign Relief can be given, and thus end the War. It is of importance that this Plan of operations shd be known as early as possible in America that N. England may in due Season procure necessary Supplies of Flour, Troops, etc. from the other Colonies.

I am much puzzled about the real Intentions of the present Ministry in Respect of their great and hasty Armaments. They certainly are too expensive to be mere Scarecrows, and, improbable as it may seem on one Account, there is Reason to think they intend, when their present Loan is compleated, either to attack

---

1 Added by John Adams.

France, or, at least to hold a very high Language to her. Certain it is, that Lord Weymouth has of late seriously and warmly urged an immediate Declaration of War against France, and tho such Declaration has not been made, it is perhaps only suspended.

At any Rate France seems to have done enough to incur the utmost Resentment of our K. and Ministry, and if she should do no more, she will have Reason to think, she has done too much, as some of the Friends of Administration already insinuate, that as soon as an Accommodation with America can be affected the whole of the British Force now there will be turned against St Domingo, etc. It is said that the better to hasten an accommodation, offers of a more specific Nature will be sent out to America than former ones, perhaps in the dress of an Act of Parliament, as it is supposed that the Sword will soon have produced a Disposition in the Colonies to listen to them. Wedderburn I understand has been some time pressing something of this Nature.[1]

NANTES, *Feb.* 11, 1777

By the Information I have from London, which I think may be depended upon, the Plan of Operations is, for Howe and his recruited Army, to act against New England; while Carlton makes his way upon the Lakes to keep the middle Colonies, in Awe; and Burgoine with an Armament from England, of 10,000, if it can be procured, invades the South, probably Virginia, and Maryland. The Intelligence from England is, that 10,000 Germans, are actually engaged, while the French Minister, and the Spanish Ambassador both assure us, that it is with very great Difficulty, the Enemy can procure the Recruits, necessary to keep up the Number formerly stipulated. That the Force of their different Armaments, will fall greatly short of what they intend, I believe; but it seems to me almost certain, that the three Attacks will be made. That their utmost Efforts will be exerted this Campaign is infallible; because nothing is more certain than that the present State of Europe forbids every Expectation of their being long unemployed nearer home. If, therefore, they do not succeed this Year against us there is an End of their Prospects of Ravage and Revenge. Even at this Moment they have put every Thing in Hazard. England, Ireland, and Hanover are left almost defenceless by their Efforts against us. I should submit whether it is not fit, that it should be made known to the Army, that the Forces to be sent this year, both from England and Germany, are new raised, and therefore totally undisciplin'd because the attacking such Troops on their first Arrival, would be taking them in their weakest State, and they ought not to carry with them the Terror of disciplined Troops, which in Fact they are not, and of which it would encourage their opponents to be apprised. The French Minister told me, that the King of Great Britain had endeavoured in vain to get Troops in Germany to supply the Place in Hanover of those which he sent to garrison Gibralter. All these things concur to shew, that they are pressed on every Side to make this last Effort against our Liberties, which I trust will be met with Proportionable Exertions on our Part,

1 On February 7 Lee set out for the Spanish court, to see what could be done there in favor of the colonies.

and under the Providence of Heaven, defeated. The Losses, which the Enemies West India Trade has suffered by Captures the last Year, has determined the Government to make Provision against it, in future, by sending a Number of armed Cutters, which will take the small Cruisers, that have hitherto been so successful against their West Indiamen. These too are to be armed as in Time of War. I therefore submit to your Consideration the propriety of marking out another Line of cruising for the small Privateers, and sending such only into the Gulph, as are of Force to drive off the Cutters, and make Prize of the armed West Indiamen.[1]

Feb. 14. Our latest Intelligence from England informs us, that a Bill is now passing for granting Letters of Mark, against you, or rather for repealing so much of the former Act, as confined it to the Navy. The Press there still continues very violent but not equally productive. That, together with the great Preparations of France and Spain, seems to render the Continuance of Peace for many Months impossible. From every Thing I can learn, their Armaments against you will be very late, if the Situation of Europe will suffer them at all. But it is best to prepare for their Plan, as if it would be executed in its fullest Extent. For it is impossible to have such Relyance upon the Politicks of Europe, as would justify the hazarding much upon their Issue.

I believe you have not yet been apprised, of what it may be material for you to know, which is, that the British Government offered to deliver the Prisoners taken on long Island, to the East India Company, to be sent to their Settlements, if the Company would send for them to Gibralter. This Proposition is upon Record in the Company's Books, a General Court having been expressly held upon it. Compared with other Things, it may possibly shew their good Faith; and it is itself a sufficient Evidence of their merciless and tyrannical Disposition towards us.

This Letter is from A. Lee.

JAMES WARREN TO JOHN ADAMS. ADAMS MSS.

BOSTON, *September* 4, 1777

MY DEAR SIR, — I thank you for yours of the 12th and 18th August which came safe to hand. I am much gratified by seeing some account of your plans, and operations abroad. Your good Lady obliged me with a sight of a letter of a similar kind she received from you some time since. I think on the whole they are as well as we could expect, and perhaps in a better way than our enemies ever had an idea of. I shall soon forward the inclosed to the Foot of the Hill directed.

[1] To this point the letter is the same as that sent on February 11, to the Committee of Secret Correspondence. Wharton, *Diplomatic Correspondence of the Revolution*, II. 266.

Schuyler's letters, at the same time they discover marks of timidity unworthy a General, exhibit a spirit of rancour, partiality and malevolence to this state unworthy a Commissary or quarter Master, which station he is said to be qualified for. His representations are extreemly injurious, and I hope we are not to suffer for his negligence, etc. The change in that department has given great satisfaction here and, with the enquiry ordered to be made, has again engaged the confidence of the people. I hope every one will have his deserts. It is at least time to check the insolence of any officer that shall dare to make any State the object of his malice and indecent reflections. Burgoin is indeed treading dangerous ground. I expect to hear of his makeing a sudden retreat to save him and his Army. We have exerted ourselves and sent a fine reinforcement who I hope are all up before this time. A very pretty body of Militia had as I am informed marched to Connecticut River in their way to the Army, and were turned back by some General's Aid de Camp, because they would not engage to stay three months. These were volunteers and consisted of about 1200, but I will know more of the history of this matter.

I congratulate you on the success of our Arms at the Northward and Westward, very pretty affairs indeed, and to be done by the poor despised Militia too will give singular pleasure to some people. We have just heard of Sullivan's bringing a number of prisoners from Staten Island tho' not without some loss. We also hear that you have found Howe. I congratulate you also in being freed from conjecture on that head. I hope our Army will give a good account of him. He seems to have a great fancy for a trip to Philadelphia. Is it to shew his respects to Congress, or does Administration suppose that the possession of that City will be the Conquest of America? It is certainly a favourite plan. Our Committee sets on a Constitution of Goverment this day: the Court meets next week, our Navy Board are met. How shall I attend these several departments? We have no news. Some valuable prizes have arrived, particularly a ship with 1600 hogheads salt, etc., from Liverpool. It appears by all her letters that they expect the British Troops were in possession of Philadelphia at that time (June). This shews to me Howe's destination if we had no other evidence. I shall trouble you again soon. In the mean time bid you Adieu and am Yours Sincerely,

[*No signature.*]

The state of our Currency is in a wretched situation and requires the most capital attention. Taxation grows more popular here, and I believe the Assembly will risque a Tax of three, if not 400,000£. I shall write you hereafter on the subject of oeconomy, and how difficult it is to practice it.

The disposition of the vacant lands, I have no doubt may be made to furnish ample resources; but I have some apprehensions of the distant consequences if foreigners gain large and extensive grants and make settlements. However I dare say you will consider this matter and its consequences.

JAMES WARREN TO JOHN ADAMS.   ADAMS MSS.

BOSTON, *September* 7th, 1777

MY DEAR SIR, — I wrote you by the last post. I wonder whether all the letters I write you get to hand, and if they do whether you are not tired with the number and length of them, to say nothing of the composition, etc., which from the confidence I have in your candour I pay no regard to. I am now applying myself with all diligence to the business of the Navy Board in order to answer as far as I am able your expectations and those of the publick. I am greatly embarrassed with the forming a Constitution, the General Court setting this week, and the Naval Affairs, even if every thing in the last was as I could wish; but I think it peculiarly unhappy that we enter on this business when the circumstances of the Fleet are far from being such as promises any hopes that we can gratify the expectations of the people by our utmost exertions, especially as they are well pleased with the Appointment of such a Board, and consequently their expectations run high. The *Raleigh* and *Alfred* are gone to sea from Portsmouth; the *Ranger*, just ready to sail, will go in a few days under the immediate orders of the Marine Committee. Three Ships shut up in Providence in a manner without men, one in Connecticut River,[1]

[1] The *Trumbull.*

never to be got out without the greatest difficulty and risque, even if there was no enemy to prevent it, and a ship constantly watching her. The *Boston* in this Harbour, the only remaining Ship in our department, and she in a condition far from being agreable. And great misunderstanding between the Captain and his officers, who it is said will not again go to sea with him, and who say he never will again man his ship. Capt. McNeil's reputation on his first appointment was extreemly good; it seems to be now reversed. The last cruise was at first very successful, but did not end so. There was certainly great blame somewhere. I won't pretend to say where. He lays it on Manley, as you may see by his letters to the Marine Committee; while his officers dont scruple to say that if he had followed Manley's orders we might have had not only the *Fox*, but the *Flora*, and *Rainbow*.[1] We are not invested with powers to appoint or even suspend officers but this matter should be enquired into. We have ordered him to equip his ship for the sea, and man her immediately, and if it can be done shall send her to sea. We shall next enquire into the state of the Providence ships and the practicability of getting them out. We have wrote to the Marine Committee for money and the resolves and regulations of Congress relative to the Navy, both of which we are destitute of, and can do very little without. Large sums of money are now wanted. Do exert yourself to accelerate their motions in forwarding them to us. We have very agreable intelligence from the Westward this afternoon, that Arnold had cut of the whole Army on their retreat from fort Stanwix. I wish it may be true. I hope you will soon give me a pleasing account of the operations in the South. Nothing of late from the Northwest. Two valuable prizes lately arrived at Newbury port, one of them maned with Frenchmen and pretends to be French property, tho' the Captors say it is only a cover and they can prove the property English. All the papers were hove overboard. We have by the other late papers, and a passenger in nine weeks from London. I dont hear they are yet in Town, but I am told the papers mention that Howe was to go up to Maryland and from thence to Philadelphia. This passenger was sent for by Hutchinson and very perticularly enquired of about

---

1 Allen, *Naval History of the Revolution*, 1. 216.

the depreciation of our paper currency, with a malignity of heart that shewed he had great reliance on it. This is perfectly in character, and very probable. The rest of refugees or rather the most of them discovered an inclination to get cash. Do write me a few of your sentiments on Government. That is a great object with me. I wish you happiness. Adieu.

[*No signature.*]

All ideas of oeconomy seem to be lost, or at least in some measure rendered impracticable by the extravagance of the times. I thought the allowance you made for a clerk was handsome. We have tryed more than a week to get one even with the addition of £50. L. M. more, but can't yet effect it. If we give this additional sum, it will be from necessity. We must have a clerk and can't get one without. If Congress wont allow it we must pay it ourselves. Had you not had ample experience to the Southward I would attempt a description of it. Whoever begun it here at first, the Town or Country, is a dispute not settled, but I think the Countryman exceeds the merchant now. 3/ for butter 1/6 for mutton, etc., they have the effrontery to ask at a time when Providence has given them the finest season and crops you ever see, fruit in the same or still greater excess. 3*d.* for a single peach. If our Board are not to have a power of dismissing, or at least of suspending officers, I foresee our authority will be contemptible. I will stand in no contemptible station long. The good news from the westward I fear wants confirmation.

JAMES WARREN TO JOHN ADAMS. ADAMS MSS.

BOSTON, *September* 17th, 1777

MY DEAR SIR, — Yours with the inclosed came safe to hand last week, and have given me great pleasure. I wish I could in return give you any thing that would equally amuse, entertain, or gratify your curiosity, but there is not so much as a single piece of news here to hand you. We are all agreed that Burgoine is "treading dangerous Ground." You are doubtless better informed of the motions and intended movements on both sides than I am. Gates with our Main Army advancing in front, and Lincoln and Arnold in the rear of his Army, seems to me a situation not very eligible for a fine gentleman or a soldier. We expected to have heard of a general action in that quarter before this, as we were informed that the two Armys were advancing to each other; but we last evening heard that Burgoin had retreated to Fort Edward, and Gates advanced to Stillwater. I hope they will fight before they part. We have various rumours about skirmishes between the Southern Armies, which prevail, and as they are generally favourable to us, please for a while and then dye. I hope to have this evening from you the true situation of them. If you ask what we are about at Court, I answer we are provideing for our Soldiers, calling in our money, laying taxes, forming a Constitution, neither of which is yet done. We have been provideing for the defence of Machias and those parts. They are gallant fellows, a late instance of which you will see in our papers. They form a frontier, are connected with the Indians, and the Enemy have marked them for vengeance. We have also been forming an expedition which I can only say will be agreable to you. Are you tired of hearing of the forming a Constitution, so am I. It is a long time in hand, and I fear will not be marked with the wisdom of Ages. I hope you will see it before this Session ends. The spirit of enterprize in manufactures flourishes here. Great quantitys of salt are made here; in and about Sandwich there is or will very soon be made 200 bushels a day. The whole coast is lined with saltworks, but it is altogether performed by boiling, a few small works excepted. Molasses from corn stalks is also made in large quantities and is very good. It was begun too late or would have furnished a full supply and some for distillation. I h[e]ard of one little town, the Town of Manchester, that had made 90 barrels. An acre of tops but at the common season will make from thirty to forty gallons, and perhaps planted or sowed on purpose, and cut earlier might afford much larger quantities. The process is simple — three cilinders turned as cider cogs, at once grind and express the juice.

Extravagance, oppression, avarice, etc., are in their zenith I hope, and will never rise higher. What will be the consequence of them, or what will stop their progress I am unable to say. This

Town was in a tumult all day yesterday carting out Rascals and Villains — small ones. This seems to be irregular and affords a subject for Moderate Folks and Tories to descant largely and wisely against mobs, but the patience of the people has been wonderful, and if they had taken more of them, and some of more importance their vengeance, or rather resentment, would have been well directed. It therefore seemed wrong to wish to stop them. My regards to all friends. I am Yours, etc.

[*No signature.*]

I am informed by the Clothier General he shall next appoint such an Agent here as the delegates of this State shall recommend. If you will think proper to recommend Mr. Samuel Allyne Otis you will oblige me, and I believe he will execute the business extreemly well. Please to mention this to Mr. Gerry.

SAMUEL ADAMS TO JAMES WARREN

PHILADA., *Sept.* 17, 1777

MY DEAR SIR, — I receivd your favor of the 1st Instant. I have not Time at present to give you a particular Account of our Military Movements in this Quarter. I suppose you will have it from our Friend Mr. J. A. There was an obstinate Engagement last Thursday.[1] The Enemy were left Masters of the Field, but by all Accounts the Advantage was on our side. Howe and his Army remain near the Field of Battle. They have had much to do in dressing their wounded and burying their dead. General Washington retreated over the Schuilkil to Germantown a few Miles above this City, where he recruited his Soldiers. He has since recrossed the River and is posted on the Lancaster Road about 12 Miles distant from the Enemy. His Troops are in high Spirits and eager for Action. We soon expect another Battle. May Heaven favor our righteous Cause and grant us compleat Victory! Both the Armies are about 26 Miles from this Place. A Wish for the *New England* Militia would be fruitless. I hope we shall do the Business without them.

[1] At Brandywine.

I have a favor to ask of you in behalf of my very worthy Friend R. H. Lee. He supposes that Mr. Gardoque [1] of Bilboa has sent him some Jesuits Bark. I wish you would inquire of the Captains from Bilboa and forward it to him, if any is arrived, by the first safe opportunity. I have requested the same thing of Capt. John Bradford, not knowing but the Multiplicity of publick Affairs might render it impossible for you to attend to it, although I am sure you will oblige so good a Patriot as Mr. Lee if it may be in your Power.

We are told that the Enemy have landed in the Jerseys, 4000 strong. You can tell whether they have left Rhode Island. I have Reason to hope that an equal Number of spirited Jersey Militia are musterd under the Command of General Dickinson,[2] Brother of the late Patriot. These were designd for a Reinforcement to the Army here. If the Report be true, these Militia joynd with 1500 Troops from Peeks Kill (undoubtedly now in Jersey) under the Command of Brigr. General McDougal,[3] will be sufficient to give a good Account of them.

I think our Affairs were never in a better Scituation. Our troops are victorious in the North. The Enemies Troops are divided and scattered over a Country several Hundred Miles. Our Country is populous and fertile. If we do not beat them this Fall will not the faithful Historian record it as our own Fault? But let us depend, not upon the Arm of Flesh, but on the God of Armies. We shall be free if we deserve it. We must succeed in a Cause so manifestly just, if we are virtuous. Adieu my Friend.

S. A.

JAMES WARREN TO JOHN ADAMS. ADAMS MSS.

BOSTON, *October* 10th, 1777

MY DEAR SIR, — You will recollect that a long time has elapsed since I had a line from you. Our hopes and fears with regard to the operations of war in your quarter have alternately risen and fallen perticularly with regard to the fate of Philadelphia, till yesterday

---

1 Joseph Gardoqui and Sons.   2 Philemon Dickinson (1739-1809).
3 Alexander McDougall (1731-1786).

the post informs us that Howe is in peaceable and quiet possession of it, without a battle. Has General Washington after all not men enough to meet him, or does the high opinion of regulars yet remain among his troops so that he dare not oppose them to him? This acquisition will have no effect that I know of here, but it will be improved, and operate much against our interest in Europe. I hope it will not affect your new Funds.

Nothing decisive has yet taken place in the North. They all seem to agree that Burgoyne must retire, fight or starve. I should be content with either of the two last, but shall be mortified if the first takes place, and he gets off with his Army. No want of men in fine spirits, or of arms, provisions, or any thing else. I suppose you know as much about them as I can tell you. No descent is yet made on Rhode Island. The plan was to have gone on as soon as the men got together. They have all but the Connecticut troops, who were to have been there as soon as the rest, been on the spot ten days, in which time the Enemy have been fortifying. I hope however this want of vigour will be supplied by sound judgment in the execution, and that I shall be able to give you some agreable account from that quarter. We shall have near 10,000 men there. We have no other intelligence but the success of the *Randolph* of which I have wrote the Marine Board. Many prizes and valuable ones are frequently arriveing. If Howe is in Philadelphia I presume you are not. Where is your place of refuge?[1] I bid you Adieu and am sincerely yours, etc.

[*No signature.*]

JAMES WARREN TO JOHN ADAMS. ADAMS MSS.

BOSTON, *October* 12, 1777

MY DEAR SIR, — I want extreamly to hear from you to know what situation you are in, and what is the true situation of our public affairs. It is impossible to describe the confused, uncertáin accounts we have here of the military operations to the southward. We are at a loss who possesses Philadelphia. We hear that

[1] On September 27 Congress adjourned, to meet at Yorktown, Pennsylvania, on the 30th.

Congress have left it, but we know not what place they have retired to, and consequently I can't tell how to direct this but to the old place. We have a fine Army in high spirits and well supplied in the Northern department, but no decisive action has yet taken place there. I believe they will prevent Burgoyne advanceing, but I think that will be the ultimatum. He will for any thing I can see retire when he pleases. Our Troops have not yet landed on Rhode Island. There appears in that quarter a want of vigour, and I think of judgment. Things were not provided for the descent as soon as the Militia arrived and their spirit and genius you know does not admit of delays. When the expedition was formed General Spencer informed us every thing was prepared; he had occasion for nothing but two Howitzers which he desired us to supply — a very moderate demand. You can't suppose we did not comply. From the very circumstance of this delay my sanguine expectations are much abated. My next will tell you more of this matter which is important to us, and I dare say occasions anxiety to you. We have men enough there, I believe not less than 10,000.

We have no news. This will be handed you by Capt. Palmes,[1] who was Captain of Marines on board the *Boston*. I am not acquainted with his perticular business. I suppose he intends some application to Congress relative to that Ship. Her affairs are indeed in a curious situation. The quarrels between the Captain and his officers have already occasioned great delays, and when we shall be able to get her to sea or if ever under her present circumstances I am unable to say. You will be able to learn something of the matter from him. I dont wish to be vested with more powers, if the good of the service dont require it, but I plainly foresee that we never can answer your expectations unless we have at least a power of suspending, if we are not to be intrusted with a power of appointing.[2] As the matter now stands we are little better than a Board of Agency or factorage and tho' we are ordered to do many expensive things are not supplyed with a shilling to do it with. This is as bad as makeing bricks without straw. We have

[1] Richard Palmes.
[2] *Journals of the Continental Congress*, IX. 833; *Out-Letters of the Continental Marine Committee*, I. 165.

wrote repeatedly to the Marine Committee and have tryed to borrow of the Loan Office. He dont like to supply without orders. We lost many advantages, and indeed the business in all its parts laggs in such a manner as mortifies me, and will affect our reputation. The Marine Committee have given Capt. McNeil their own orders for his next cruise.[1] Dont you intend there shall be an enquiry into the conduct of the last? There is indeed a contrast between bringing in the *Fox* and *Flora* if not the *Rainbow*, and the looseing the *Hancock* and the *Fox*. I don't pretend to say who was to blame, but I think Congress should know, if they intend officers should do their duty in future. I love to see officers regard discipline and keep a proper command; but overbearing haughtiness and unlimited conceit, especially if joined with unbounded expence, will never promote the good of your service at sea or ashore. It is our business to correct the last in the Navy of this department as much as possible, and I think we should be impowered to controul the first. I wish you every happiness and am Yours, etc.

[*No signature.*]

Monday the 13th. We have just received the agreable news of a victory in the Northern department. I am not able to give you the perticulars but the action was general, and the defeat compleat. Our Army was still in the pursuit when the account came away. Arnold and Lincoln are wounded, on our side, and Frazier[2] killed on theirs. Our day however is a little damaged by hearing that fort Montgomery[3] is taken.

JOHN ADAMS TO JAMES WARREN

YORK TOWN, *Octr.* 24, 1777

MY DEAR SIR, — We have got to a Part of the World, where We are scarcely able to procure any Intelligence.

We have as yet no certain Information, concerning the events at the Northward, on the 14. and 15th. of this Month, the whole of which I dare say before this Time are familiar to you. We have had Rumours, which lifted us up to the Stars.

[1] He was ordered to sail to France. [2] Simon Fraser (1729-1777). [3] October 6.

We are now upon Confederation, and have nearly compleated it. I really expect it will be finished by the Middle of next Week.

We dispatched some Affairs, last Evening for your Board which Dr. Linn [1] I suppose will convey to you.

We shall consider immediately a Plan of Taxes for all the States. This is our Resource. I rejoice with Joy unspeakable that your Assembly, have adopted a Plan of such consummate Wisdom. I am,

JOHN ADAMS

SAMUEL ADAMS TO JAMES WARREN

YORK TOWN IN PENNSYLVA., *Oct.* 26, 1777

MY DEAR SIR, — We have just now receivd a satisfactory Account of the great Success of our Arms on the 14th Inst. under General Gates. The Express is expected every Hour. I have Time only to congratulate you on this and also on a successful Engagment on the Delaware, an account of which is contain in a Letter, Copy of which I inclose.

I hope our Countrymen will render the just Tribute of Praise to the Supreme Ruler for these signal Instances of his Interposition in favor of a People struggling for their Liberties. Congress will, I suppose recommend the setting apart *one* Day of publick Thanksgiving to be observd throughout the united States. If Burgoin is allowd to reside in Boston, will he not by his Arts, confound if not seduce the Minds of inconsiderate Persons? *Sat. Verbum Sapienti.* Adieu my Friend.

S. A——

[ENCLOSURE.]

Copy of a Letter from Colo. Jona. Mifflin, D. Q. M. G., dated Head Quarters, Oct. 25, 1777, to Genl. Mifflin.

The day before yesterday at 4 o'Clock P M Count Donop with 1200 Hessian Grenadiers made their Appearance before the Garrison at Red Bank and by a Flag demanded a Surrender; which being refused, they made an immediate Attack, forcd over the Abbatis, crossd the Ditch, and some few had mounted the Picketts. They were so warmly receivd, that they retired with great Precipita-

---

[1] Dr. John Linn, appointed by General Wooster a director of the hospital in the district of Quebec. The resolution of Congress gave to the Navy Board of the Eastern Department power to suspend officers of the continental navy within its district. Dr. Linn also brought 100,000 dollars for the Board.

tion, leaving the Count and his Brigade Major, who are wounded and in the Fort. The killed and wounded, agreeable to the Letter are five hundred. Lt. Colo. Green, who commanded, played upon them a very good Deception. When the Flag came in, he concealed all his Men but 50, saying "With these brave Fellows this Fort shall be my Tomb." He had five killed and fifteen wounded.

Yesterday an Attack was made upon Fort Mifflin by Six Ships which were warpd thro the Chevaux de Frize at Billingsport in the Night. They began the Cannonade at Daybreak, which continued very hot till 10 o'Clock, when the Gallies forced them to give way. In retiring a 64 Gun Ship (said to be the *Augusta*) and a Frigate, the *Liverpool*, ran aground, and were set on Fire by their own People. Two Men were wounded in the Fort.

Colo. Green[1] is one of the Rhode Island Batallions. Genl. Washington upon his Arrival at Camp honord him with the Command of the Fort at Red Bank.

Howe it is said has publishd a Hand bill in Philadelphia setting forth that Burgoyne has gaind a complete Victory having taken Gates and all his Army Prisoners, and that he is in full March with a victorious Army for Albany and New York.[2]

It needs no comment.

SAMUEL ADAMS TO JAMES WARREN

YORK TOWN, PENNSYLVA., *Oct.* 29, 1777

MY DEAR SIR, — I sent you a few days ago an Account of the Success we have had on the Delaware. The Honor of recovering Philadelphia seems to be intended for the brave Men who command there; for if the Enemy cannot get up with their Ships of War, Howe cannot long remain in the City. May Honor be given to whom Honor may be due.

Congress have applyd with Diligence to Confederation. Most of the important Articles are agreed to. Each State retains its Sovereignty and Independence with every Power, Jurisdiction, and Right, which is not by the Confederation expressly delegated to the United States in Congress assembled.

Each State is to have one Vote in Congress; but there must be a Concurrence of Nine States in all Matters of Importance.

---

1 John Green.
2 Evans (No. 15313) gives a folio of two pages, "Glorious authentic Intelligence," issued October 21, 1777, at Lancaster, Pennsylvania, by Francis Bailey, on the surrender of Burgoyne; but no issue such as is described in the text is known.

The Proportion of the publick Expence to be paid by Each State to be ascertaind by the Value of all the Lands granted to or surveyd for any Person, to be estimated according to such Mode as Congress shall from time to time direct.

All Disputes about Boundaries are to be decided by Judges appointed in the following Mode: The Representatives of Each State in Congress to be nominated, the contending States to strike off 13 each, and out of the remaining 13 not more than 9 nor less than 7 shall be drawn out by Lot, any five of them to hear and determine the Matter.

I hope we shall finish the Confederation in a few days when I intend to renew my Request for the Leave of Absence, and return home. I am determined by God's Assistance never to forsake the great Cause in which my Country is virtuously struggling; but there are others who have greater abilities and more adequate to *this* important Service, than I have. I hope therefore another will be appointed in my Room. It is the greatest Honor of my Life to have enjoyd the Confidence of my Country thus long; and I have the clear and full Testimony of my own Mind that I have at all Times endeavord to fill the Station they have thought fit to place me in to their Advantage.

This will be deliverd to you by Mr. Hancock, who has Leave of Absence till the first of January next.

I hope the Person to be elected in my Room will have understanding enough to know when the Arts of Flattery are played upon him, and Fortitude of mind sufficient to resist and dispise them. This I mention *inter Nos nostipsos*. In this evil World there are oftentimes large Doses prepared for those whose Stomachs will bear them. And it would be a Disgrace to human Nature to affirm there are some who can take the fullest Cup without nauseating.

I suppose you have by this time finished a form of Government. I hope the greatest Care will be taken in the Choice of a Governor. He, whether a wise Man or a Fool, will in a great Measure form the Morals and Manners of the People. I beg Pardon for hinting the Possibility of one of the last Character being chosen: But alas! Is there not such a Possibility! But I assure my self of better things. I believe my Country will fix their Eyes and their Choice on a Man of Religion and Piety; who will understand human Nature and the Nature and End of political Society; who will not by Corruption or Flattery be seducd to the betraying, even without being sensible of it himself, the sacred Rights of his Country.

We are told that the Prisoners taken at the Northward are sent into Massachusetts Bay. I hope Burgoyne will not be permitted to reside in Boston; for if he is, I fear that inconsiderate Persons of Fashion and some significance will be induced, under that Idea of Politeness, to form Connexions with him, dangerous to the Publick. There are other Reasons which I should think would make his or any other officers being fixed in a populous Town uneligible. There are Prison Ships, I suppose, provided for the Privates.

The Success of the present Campaign hitherto has been great beyond our most sanguine Expectation. Let us ascribe Glory to God who has graciously vouchsafd to favor the Cause of America and of Mankind. We are impatiently waiting to hear from Rhode Island. Should we succeed in every Quarter, yet we must not slack our Hands. Every Nerve must be exerted in preparing for another Campaign; for we may be attackd the next Spring with redoubled Vigor.

There is Nothing in my opinion so threatning to us as our depreciating Currency. Among the Train of Evils it is likely to bring upon us, is the Destruction of Morals; for many will be ready to think Extortion and Injustice necessary and justifiable for their own Security. I am much pleasd to hear that the People of our State are loudly calling for and the Assembly is about to lay on a heavy Tax. This, if punctually collected, will be an effectual Remedy. I hope the Payment of the Interest on Money borrowd, in Bills on France, will bring large Sums into our Loan offices. But I am come to a Necessity of concluding. Adieu, my dear Friend.

S. A.

SAMUEL ADAMS TO JAMES WARREN

YORK TOWN, *Octob.* 30, 1777

MY DEAR SIR, — I have just receivd your agreeable Letter of the 8th by the Post, for which please to accept my hearty thanks.

I had written and seald the inclosd Letter, before yours came to my Hand. Yesterday Morning Mr. H[ancock], who had several times before given Notice to Congress of his Intention to return to Boston agreeable to Leave he had obtaind at Philadelphia, made a formal Speech to Congress in which he reminded them of his having served them as President more than two years; whether he had conducted to their Approbation or not, was left to them; but he had the Testimony of his own Mind that he had done it to the best of his Ability. He thanked them for the Civility they had shown him, and if in the Course of Business he had faild in due Respect to any Member, as it was not intentional, he hoped it would be overlooked. It is likely as I have taken it from Memory upon hearing it once read, that I have not done it Justice in point of Expression. But it is not improbable that you may have a Copy of it; for a Motion was made in the Afternoon by Mr. D——of N.Y.[1] that a Copy should be requested, and Thanks returnd for his great Services, and a Request that he would return and take the Chair. This Motion was opposd by several Members, but it obtaind so far as to request the Copy, and this Day the latter Part of the Motion will be considerd.[2]

I have given you this merely as a Peice of News, leaving you to judge of the Tendency and probable Effect of the Speech and Motion. We have had two Presidents before, Neither of whom made a parting Speech or receivd the Thanks of Congress.

[*No signature.*]

SAMUEL ADAMS TO JAMES WARREN

YORK TOWN, PENNSILVA., *Novr.* 4, 77

MY DEAR SIR, — I wrote to you last Week by Mr. Hancock and gave you a curious Anecdote. The affair was brought on — it labord a whole Afternoon. The Principle was objected to, it was urged to be unprecedented, impolitick, dangerous. The Question was then put of the Propriety of the Measure in any Instance. Passd in the Affirmative 6 to 4. The original Question was then

---

[1] Both Duane and Duer were present.
[2] The speech is printed in *Journals of the Continental Congress*, IX. 852.

put. Passd in the Affve., the same Division. The Yeas and Nays were called for: yeas, C, N.Y., J, V, N.C., S.C. Nays, N.H., M, R., P.[1] Adieu.

ARTHUR LEE TO —— [2]

PARIS, *Novr.* 29, 1777

DEAR SIR, — I wish to represent to you a true State of Management of your Affairs here, which if not alterd must end in total Confusion and Disgrace. You have a Commercial Agent [3] against whom there are continual Complaints that every hour of his Life he is doing every thing to disgrace Congress and disgust others. At the same time you have given your Commissioners orders as Merchants and Factors. One Commissioner [4] was a Merchant and came over here with a View and Stipulation of trading for himself as well as for you. Under the Pretence of these orders and that no Reliance can be had on the Commercial Agent, the Commissioners appoint an Agent [5] and by that Means a mutual Interest is formd between two of them to disburse all the Monies receivd for the Publick, in merchantile Schemes, through the Hands of that Agent and others upon the same jobbing Principles.

In this Manner three Millions of Livres have been expended and near another Million of Debt incurrd, without, I believe, your having receivd a Livres worth; and I may venture to say you never will receive one half the Value.

The Time within which these Supplies were expected and ought to have been sent, is long ago expired.

It has not been in the Power of the Third [6] to prevent or correct this, from his having been absent a great Part of the Time, from the Mercantile Commissioner having assumd the Management to himself, and secured the Concurrence of the other thro the Medium of Advantages thrown into the Nephew's hands, from their having peremptorily told him (the Nephew) that two form the Commissioners and acting accordingly. This has put him to the alterna-

1 See the *Journals* for October 31.
2 The copy is in the writing of Samuel Adams, to whom the letter was probably written.
3 Thomas Morris, a nephew of Robert Morris.   4 Silas Deane.
5 Jonathan Williams, a nephew of Franklin.   6 Arthur Lee.

tive of approving what has been done without his knowledge, or openly quarreling with them, which I conceive would only add to the Confusion and Distress of the publick Affairs. He has desired from the beginning that regular hours for doing publick Business might be settled, and has been constantly refusd. He has repeatedly asked for an Account of the Expenditure of the three Millions. That too is denied. Whatever is gracious in the Commission, that is the Patronage, has been divided amongst the other two, without the smallest Participation on his part.

[Here he proposes a Remedy and then proceeds:] This will remove all pretence for their interposing and misapplying the publick Money. I say pretence, because they have continued the same Conduct since Mr. Alderman Lee's[1] being here, which they pursued when Mr. Morris was alone; and Mr. D[eane] has done every thing in his Power to render his coming needless. He will continue to do so let who will be Agent, unless that Agent submits to his Direction and acts to his Purposes, or unless you draw a clear Line between the Commercial and political Characters and forbid any Interposition with each other.

From their first Arrival here Mr. D[eane] seems to have considered Mr. L[ee] as a dangerous Check upon him; and therefore it has been a continued Course of Intrigue by Means of his Agents Mr. C.[2] and Dr. B.[3] to traduce Mr. L. and assume to himself all the Powers of the Commission, so as even to endeavor to have it generally believd that Mr. L. was either not a Commissioner or totally insignificant. From this Conduct in private they advancd into the publick Papers, until at last they have contrivd to have F[ranklin] and D[eane] constantly mentiond both in Print and in Conversation as the Commissioners. During Mr. L.'s Absence in Germany they contrivd to get over Dr. F. by affecting great Partiality for his Nephew, throwing considerable commercial Transactions into his hands and attempting to set him up as commercial Agent under the Appointment of the Comrs. to inspect the Arms and other things which they were to send out. They at the same time circulated a Report both here and in England that a Quarrel subsisted between Dr. F. and Dr. Lee, but that the other two

[1] William Lee.   [2] William Carmichael.   [3] Edward Bancroft.

(viz. F. and D.) acted in perfect Harmony. To confirm this in its full Extent, as soon as Mr. L. had apprizd the other Commisioners of his Intention and Time of returning, Mr. D. gives up a House which had been hired and furnishd at publick Expence in Paris, and took Possession of the Apartments he had before refusd which were fitted up for Mr. L. at Passie, in the same House with Dr. F. This Stroke was to hold out at once the Appearance of Union between them and Difference with Mr. L., and concentrate the publick Attention upon them alone. And the better to secure these Effects, it was whisperd that this was done by the particular Desire of Dr. F. . . . Mr. L. conceives that Nothing can be more detrimental to the publick Interest than an open Quarrel, he has determind to bear every thing rather than commence a Dispute. He proposd that one of the Millions they receivd should be funded to pay the Interest of your Loans and give Credit to your Paper, but every Livre is spent. He has urgd that this may be done with what they are to receive. That too is in vain.

[Mr. Dodd is going; more at another time.][1]

That too is in vain, for it is resolvd to spend the Money and trust to Fortune for the paying your Interest as the Commissioners promise. Yet it is adviseable to draw, because they may still be able to answer. But this expending Spirit will continue, till the disbursing of Money is taken entirely from them and placd where it ought to be.

Much ill humour is expressed by Mr. D. against the french Court, and he has endeavord to make others hold the same Language. But his Colleagues think very differently; and are of opinion that this Court has been compelled to every Step of Severity by gross Misconduct in others. The principal was Cunningham's Business at Dunkirk.[2] With the particulars of this Affair Mr. Lee is to this Moment unacquainted. Mr. D. is unwise enough to declare that he did it to excite a War. Such an Attempt, without the Advice and Concurrence of the others in the Propriety of it

[1] An expression of Samuel Adams. William Dodd was one of the express riders between Boston and the Congress.
[2] Gustavus Conyngham, arrested at Dunkirk for a breach of neutrality. See Neeser, *Gustavus Conyngham*.

and in the Means, was highly criminal. He is conscious of it and therefore seems to be searching for Shelter under a general Discontent and Disagreement, than which, if it operates on our Friends here, nothing can be more injurious. For tho' they do not all we wish, they certainly do more than any others. It would be both Ingratitude and Folly to repay it with ill humour and ill Will. They told the Commissioners from the Beginning the Line they meant to pursue, and repeatedly entreated them not to transgress it and involve them. It has been transgressd under this Gentleman's Advice and by his Agents, with strong Circumstances of ill Faith and with the ridiculous Idea of forcing them into a War. The Consequences of this have fallen upon our Heads, and we have not the least Pretence for Complaint.

I am not so little read in Men and Books as not to know that such Men and such Actions are found in all political Circles. But I lament that they are fallen upon in this important Moment and that they have been so detrimental to the publick Service. The Fear of increasing that Injury has made Mr. L. concur in Measures of which he disapprovd, prevented him from resenting most atrocious Injuries and determind him to stifle his Complaints to any but his confidential Friends. I hope the proposed Plan will remedy all.

[Our Success at the Northward last fall, I am inclind to think prevented those Differences and this Misconduct from having the most mischievous Effects.] [1]

1 By Samuel Adams.

END OF VOLUME I

/973.2M414W>C1>V1/